尾田栄一郎

When a new product is selling like hotcakes, they'll say, "It's a huge hit!" "A mega-hit!" "Smash hit!" "Colossal hit!!" Which makes me wonder... *Why can't we just call it a home run already?!* Volume 71 is off with the *crack* of the bat!!

-Eiichiro Oda, 2013

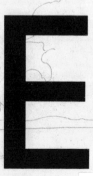

Eiichiro Oda began his manga career at the age of 17, when his one-shot cowboy manga **Wanted!** won second place in the coveted Tezuka manga awards. Oda went on to work as an assistant to some of the biggest manga artists in the industry, including Nobuhiro Watsuki, before winning the Hop Step Award for new artists. His pirate adventure **One Piece**, which debuted in **Weekly Shonen Jump** in 1997, quickly became one of the most popular manga in Japan.

ONE PIECE VOL. 71
NEW WORLD PART 11

SHONEN JUMP Manga Edition

STORY AND ART BY EIICHIRO ODA

Translation/Stephen Paul
Touch-up Art & Lettering/Vanessa Satone
Design/Fawn Lau
Editor/Alexis Kirsch

Printed in the U.S.A.

Published by VIZ Media, LLC
P.O. Box 77010
San Francisco, CA 94107

10 9 8 7
First printing, June 2014
Seventh printing, April 2021

viz.com

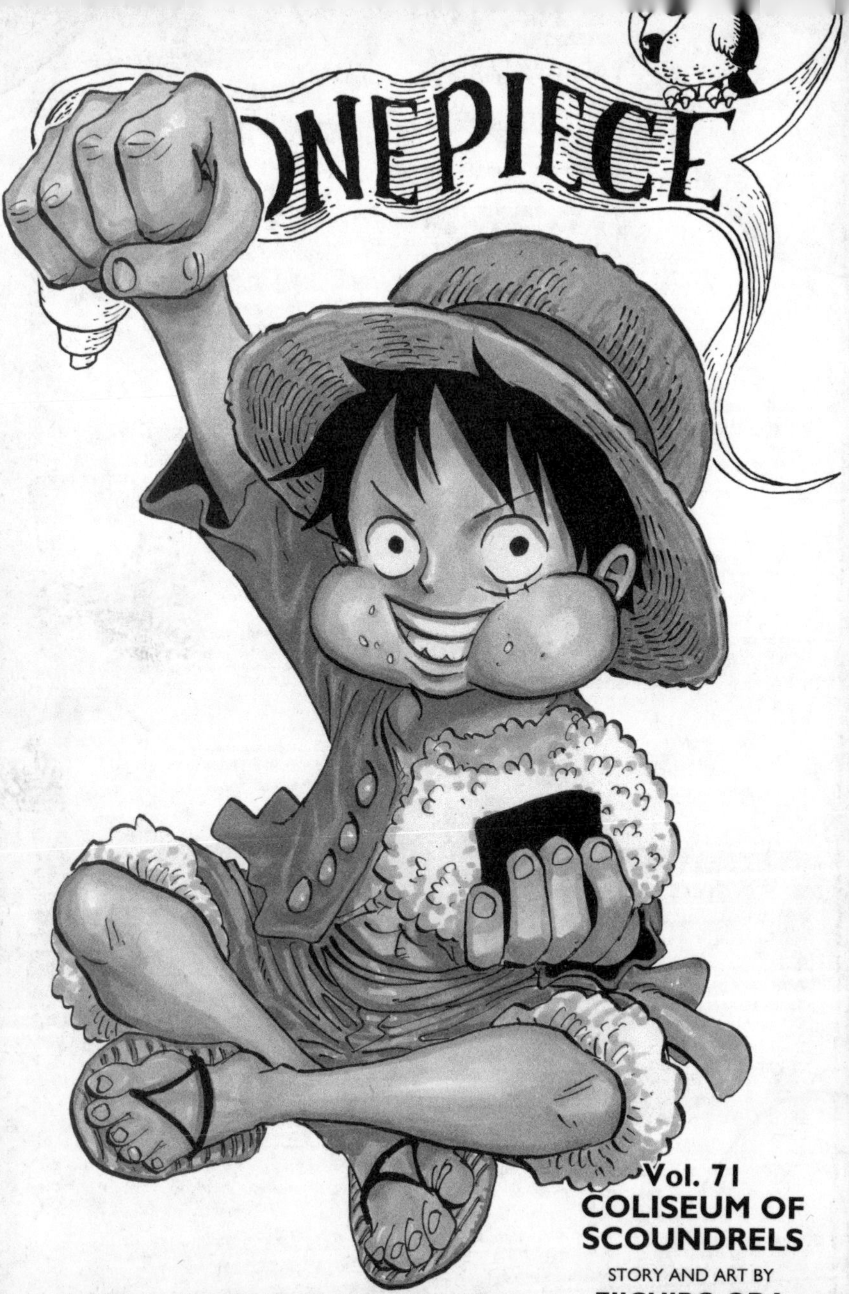
ONE PIECE

Vol. 71
COLISEUM OF SCOUNDRELS

STORY AND ART BY

EIICHIRO ODA

The Straw Hat Crew

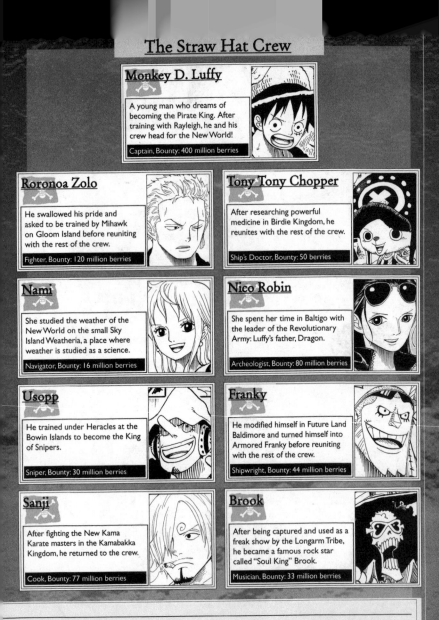

Monkey D. Luffy

A young man who dreams of becoming the Pirate King. After training with Rayleigh, he and his crew head for the New World!

Captain, Bounty: 400 million berries

Roronoa Zolo

He swallowed his pride and asked to be trained by Mihawk on Gloom Island before reuniting with the rest of the crew.

Fighter, Bounty: 120 million berries

Tony Tony Chopper

After researching powerful medicine in Birdie Kingdom, he reunites with the rest of the crew.

Ship's Doctor, Bounty: 50 berries

Nami

She studied the weather of the New World on the small Sky Island Weatheria, a place where weather is studied as a science.

Navigator, Bounty: 16 million berries

Nico Robin

She spent her time in Baltigo with the leader of the Revolutionary Army: Luffy's father, Dragon.

Archeologist, Bounty: 80 million berries

Usopp

He trained under Heracles at the Bowin Islands to become the King of Snipers.

Sniper, Bounty: 30 million berries

Franky

He modified himself in Future Land Baldimore and turned himself into Armored Franky before reuniting with the rest of the crew.

Shipwright, Bounty: 44 million berries

Sanji

After fighting the New Kama Karate masters in the Kamabakka Kingdom, he returned to the crew.

Cook, Bounty: 77 million berries

Brook

After being captured and used as a freak show by the Longarm Tribe, he became a famous rock star called "Soul King" Brook.

Musician, Bounty: 33 million berries

Devil Fruit that Doflamingo sells to Kaido, a member of the Four Emperors. After a fierce battle, the alliance kidnaps Caesar, then demands that Doflamingo leave the Seven Warlords in return for the scientist. When Doflamingo complies, Law tells him he will hand over Caesar at a small island north of Dressrosa. But somehow, Doflamingo has Ace's Devil Fruit in his possession...

Shanks

One of the Four Emperors. He continues to wait for Luffy in the second half of the Grand Line, called the New World.

Captain of the Red-Haired Pirates

Momonosuke

Kin'emon's Son

Foxfire Kin'emon

Samurai of Wano

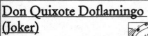

Don Quixote Pirates

Don Quixote Doflamingo (Joker)

One of the Seven Warlords of the sea and a weapons broker. He works under the alias of "Joker."

Pirate, Warlord (former)

Baby 5

Servant/ Assassin

Buffalo

Fighter

Trebol

?

Diamante

?

Trafalgar Law

The Surgeon of Death, wielder of the Op-Op Fruit's powers. Currently allied with Luffy.

Pirate, Warlord

Master Caesar Clown

An authority on weapons of mass-murder. Kidnapped by Law in an attempt to goad Doflamingo out of hiding.

Former government scientist

Story

After two years of hard training, the Straw Hat pirates are back together, first at the Sabaody Archipelago and then through Fish-Man Island to their next stage: the New World!!

The crew happens across Trafalgar Law on the island of Punk Hazard, run by Caesar Clown. At his suggestion, they form a new pirate alliance that seeks to take down one of the Four Emperors. In order to draw Doflamingo's attention, they must first capture Caesar, who is producing the artificial

NEW WORLD ONE PIECE

Vol. 71
Coliseum of Scoundrels

CONTENTS

Chapter 701: Adventure in the Land of Love, Passion and Toys 007

Chapter 702: Corrida Coliseum 027

Chapter 703: Waiting Room 042

Chapter 704: Lucy and the Statue of Kyros 063

Chapter 705: Maynard the Pursuer 083

Chapter 706: I Ain't Gonna Laugh at Ya 103

Chapter 707: Block B 118

Chapter 708: Coliseum of Scoundrels 137

Chapter 709: King Punch!! 153

Chapter 710: To Greenbit 172

Chapter 711: Adventure in the Land of the Little People 193

Chapter 701:
ADVENTURE IN THE LAND OF LOVE, PASSION AND TOYS

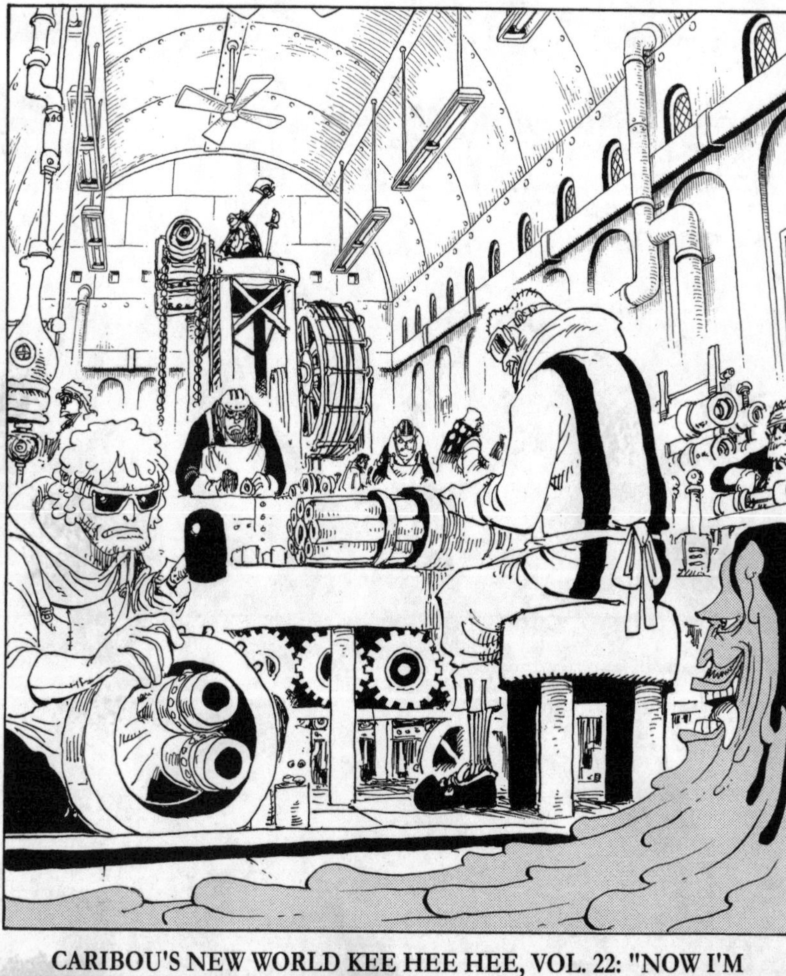

CARIBOU'S NEW WORLD KEE HEE HEE, VOL. 22: "NOW I'M CURIOUS—WHAT'S UP WITH THIS ISLAND'S WEAPON FACTORY?"

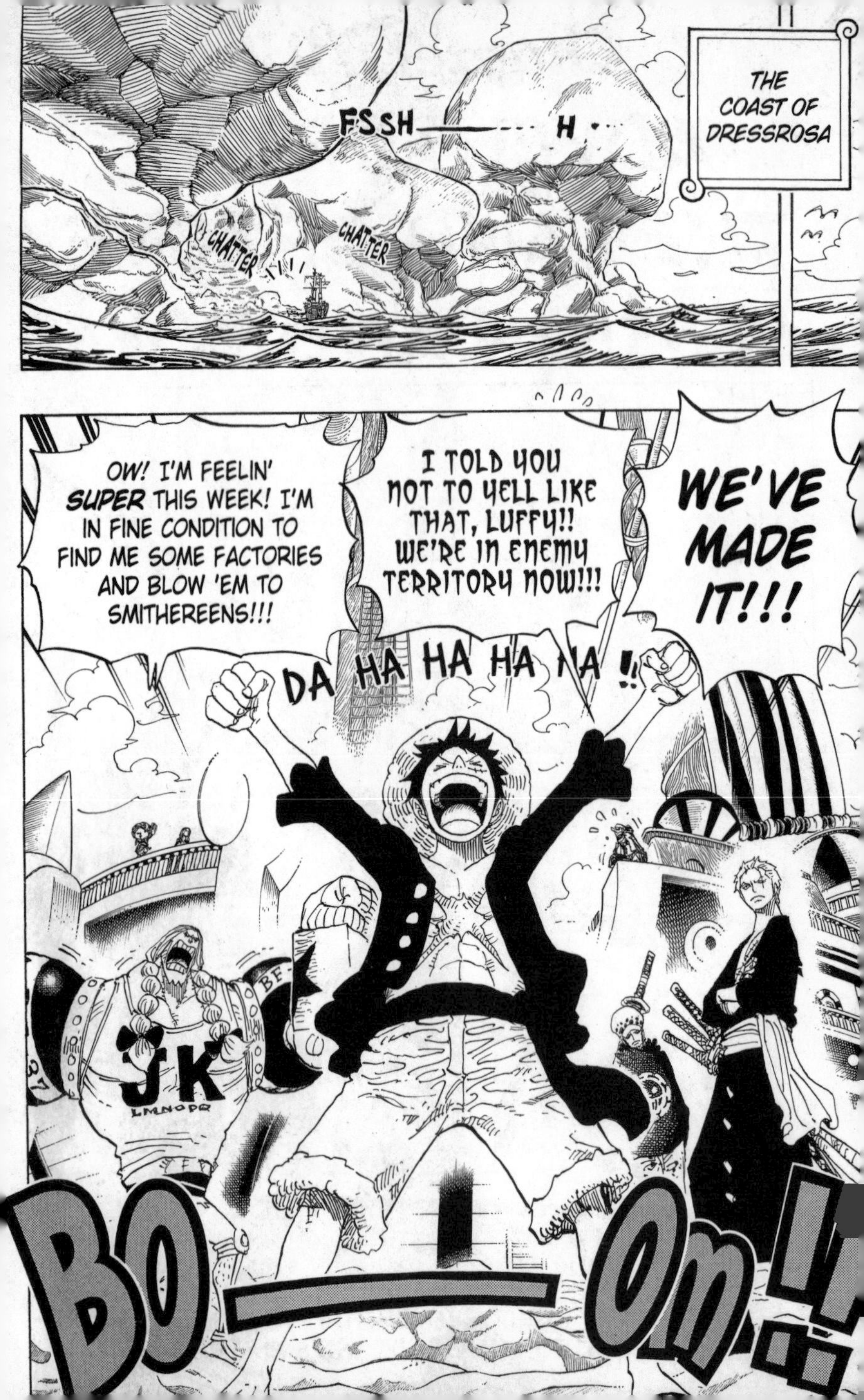
THE COAST OF DRESSROSA
FSSH— H
CHATTER
CHATTER
WE'VE MADE IT!!!
I TOLD YOU NOT TO YELL LIKE THAT, LUFFY!! WE'RE IN ENEMY TERRITORY NOW!!!
OW! I'M FEELIN' SUPER THIS WEEK! I'M IN FINE CONDITION TO FIND ME SOME FACTORIES AND BLOW 'EM TO SMITHEREENS!!!
DA HA HA HA HA!!
BO—om!!

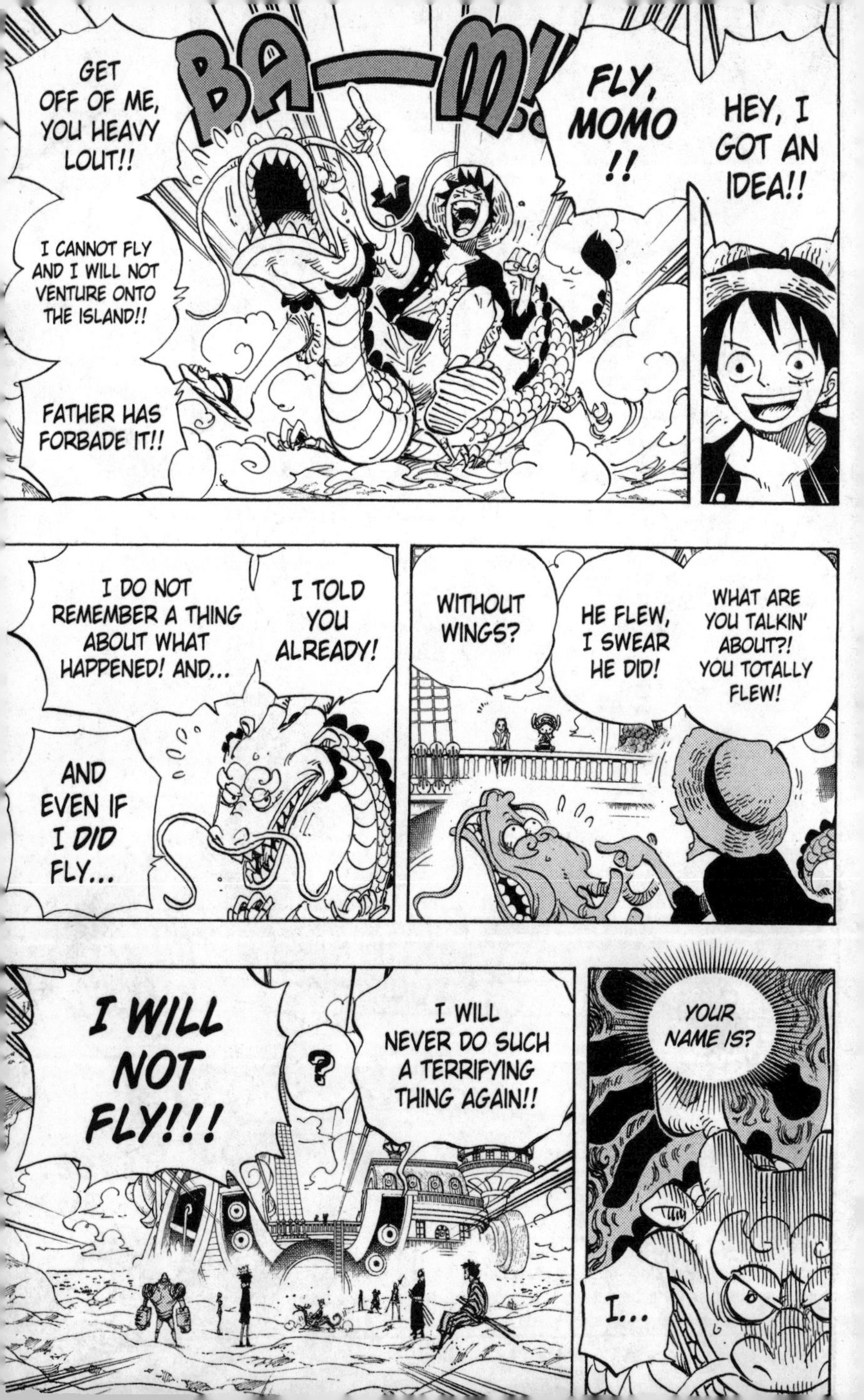
HEY, I GOT AN IDEA!!
FLY, MOMO!!
BA—M!
GET OFF OF ME, YOU HEAVY LOUT!!
I CANNOT FLY AND I WILL NOT VENTURE ONTO THE ISLAND!!
FATHER HAS FORBADE IT!!
WHAT ARE YOU TALKIN' ABOUT?! YOU TOTALLY FLEW!
HE FLEW, I SWEAR HE DID!
WITHOUT WINGS?
I TOLD YOU ALREADY!
I DO NOT REMEMBER A THING ABOUT WHAT HAPPENED! AND...
AND EVEN IF I *DID* FLY...
YOUR NAME IS?
I...
I WILL NEVER DO SUCH A TERRIFYING THING AGAIN!!
?
I WILL NOT FLY!!!

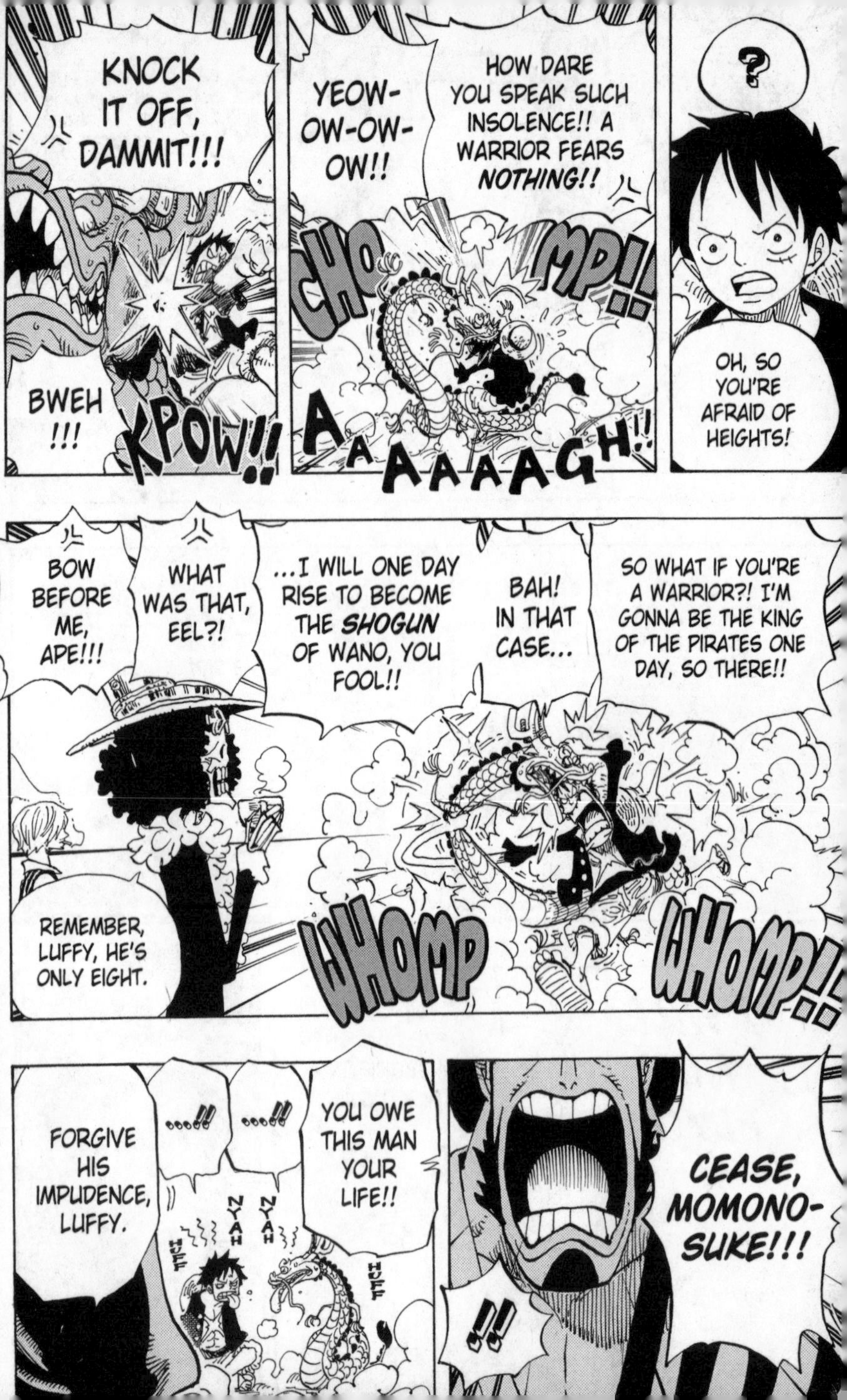
?
OH, SO YOU'RE AFRAID OF HEIGHTS!
HOW DARE YOU SPEAK SUCH INSOLENCE!! A WARRIOR FEARS NOTHING!!
YEOW-OW-OW-OW!!
CHOMP!!
AAAAAAGH!!
KNOCK IT OFF, DAMMIT!!!
KPOW!!
BWEH!!!
SO WHAT IF YOU'RE A WARRIOR?! I'M GONNA BE THE KING OF THE PIRATES ONE DAY, SO THERE!!
BAH! IN THAT CASE...
...I WILL ONE DAY RISE TO BECOME THE SHOGUN OF WANO, YOU FOOL!!
WHAT WAS THAT, EEL?!
BOW BEFORE ME, APE!!!
WHOMP!!
WHOMP
REMEMBER, LUFFY, HE'S ONLY EIGHT.
CEASE, MOMONOSUKE!!!
!!
YOU OWE THIS MAN YOUR LIFE!!
...!!
...!!
HUFF
NYAH
NYAH
HUFF
FORGIVE HIS IMPUDENCE, LUFFY.

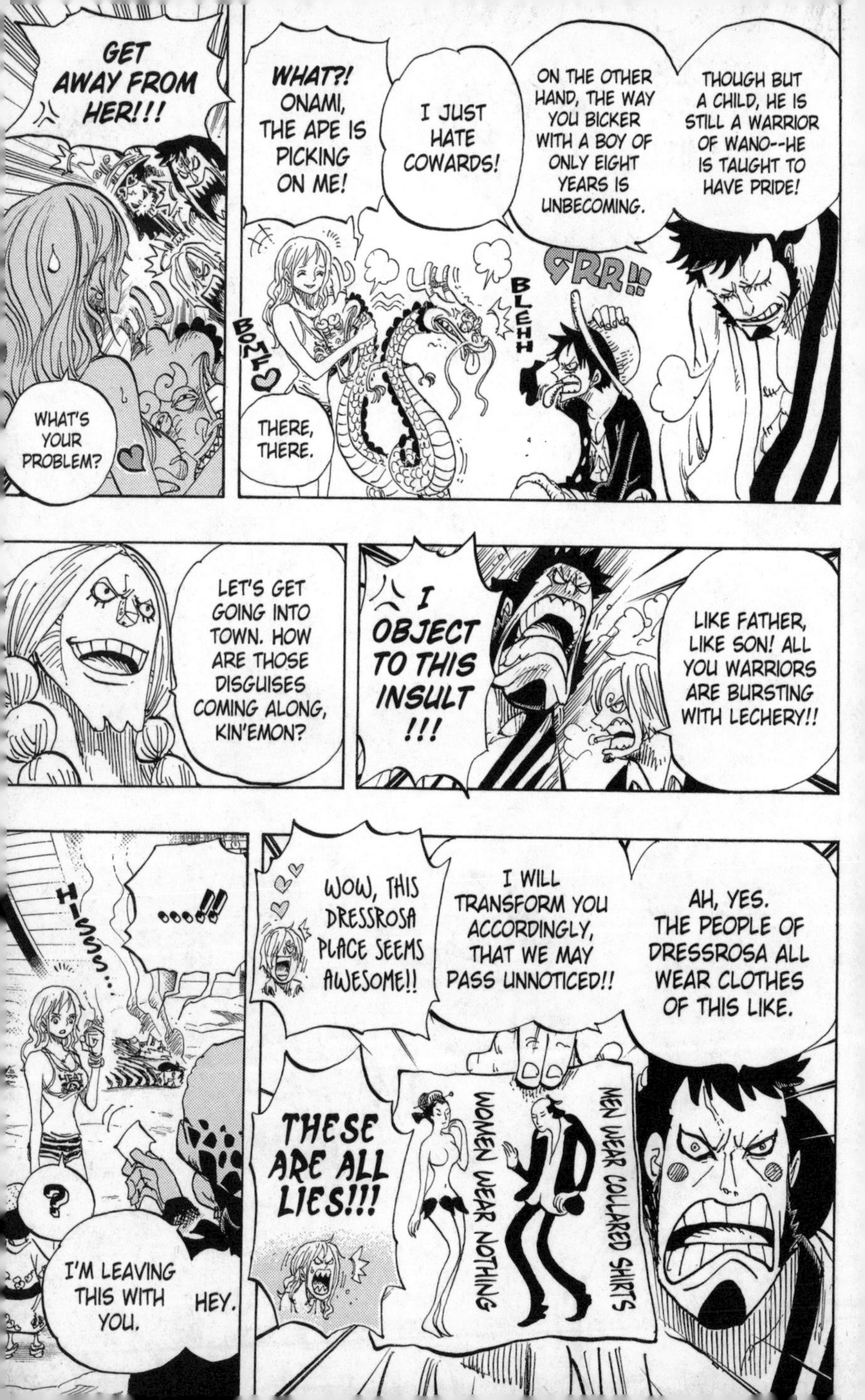
THOUGH BUT A CHILD, HE IS STILL A WARRIOR OF WANO--HE IS TAUGHT TO HAVE PRIDE!
ON THE OTHER HAND, THE WAY YOU BICKER WITH A BOY OF ONLY EIGHT YEARS IS UNBECOMING.
GRR!!
I JUST HATE COWARDS!
BLEHH
WHAT?! ONAMI, THE APE IS PICKING ON ME!
BOMF♡
THERE, THERE.
GET AWAY FROM HER!!!
WHAT'S YOUR PROBLEM?
LIKE FATHER, LIKE SON! ALL YOU WARRIORS ARE BURSTING WITH LECHERY!!
I OBJECT TO THIS INSULT!!!
LET'S GET GOING INTO TOWN. HOW ARE THOSE DISGUISES COMING ALONG, KIN'EMON?
AH, YES. THE PEOPLE OF DRESSROSA ALL WEAR CLOTHES OF THIS LIKE.
I WILL TRANSFORM YOU ACCORDINGLY, THAT WE MAY PASS UNNOTICED!!
WOW, THIS DRESSROSA PLACE SEEMS AWESOME!!
MEN WEAR COLLARED SHIRTS
WOMEN WEAR NOTHING
THESE ARE ALL LIES!!!
....!!
HISSS...
?
HEY.
I'M LEAVING THIS WITH YOU.

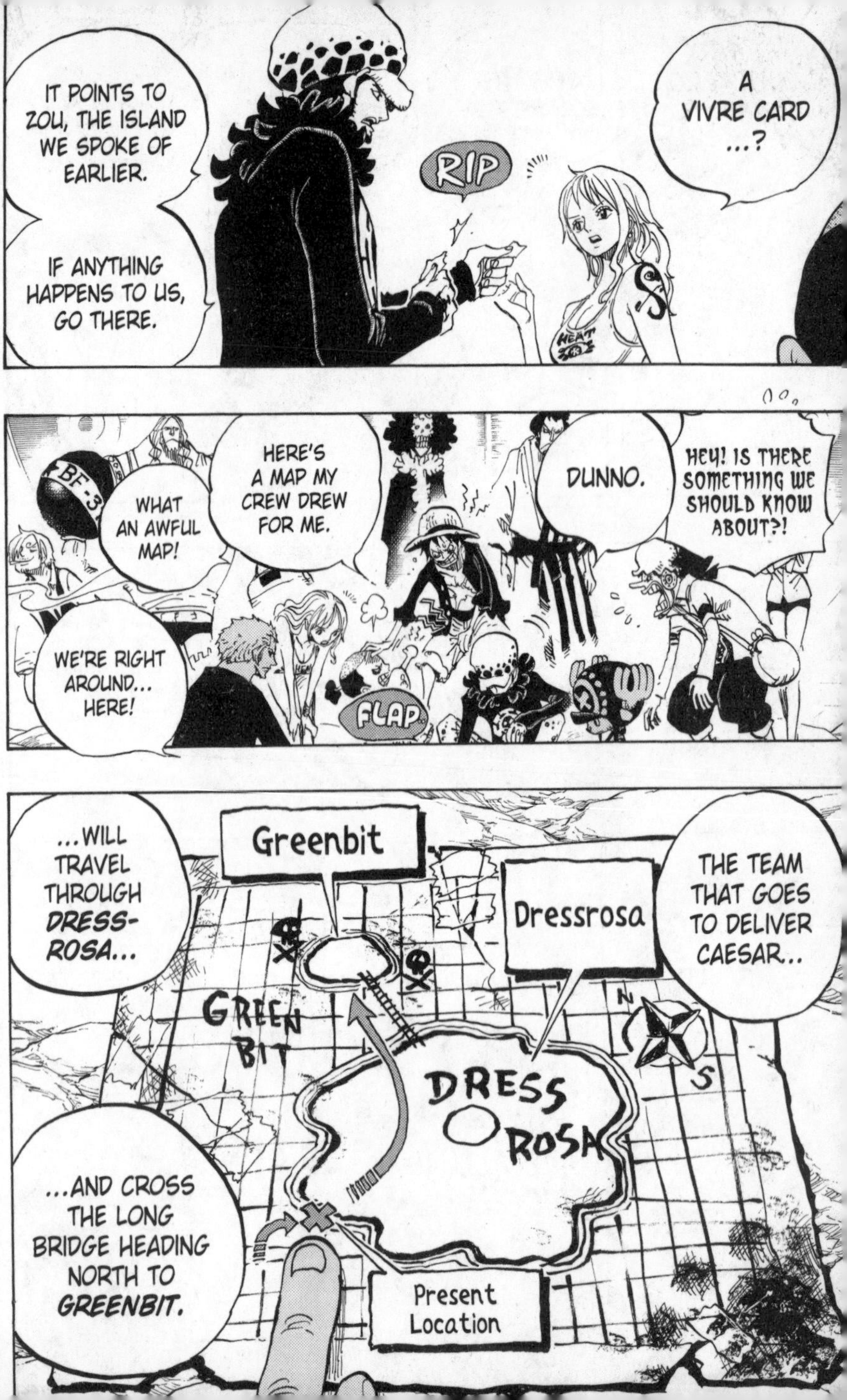
A VIVRE CARD ...?
RIP
IT POINTS TO ZOU, THE ISLAND WE SPOKE OF EARLIER.
IF ANYTHING HAPPENS TO US, GO THERE.
HEY! IS THERE SOMETHING WE SHOULD KNOW ABOUT?!
DUNNO.
HERE'S A MAP MY CREW DREW FOR ME.
WHAT AN AWFUL MAP!
WE'RE RIGHT AROUND... HERE!
FLAP
THE TEAM THAT GOES TO DELIVER CAESAR...
Dressrosa
Greenbit
...WILL TRAVEL THROUGH *DRESS-ROSA...*
GREEN BIT
N
S
DRESS ROSA
Present Location
...AND CROSS THE LONG BRIDGE HEADING NORTH TO *GREENBIT.*

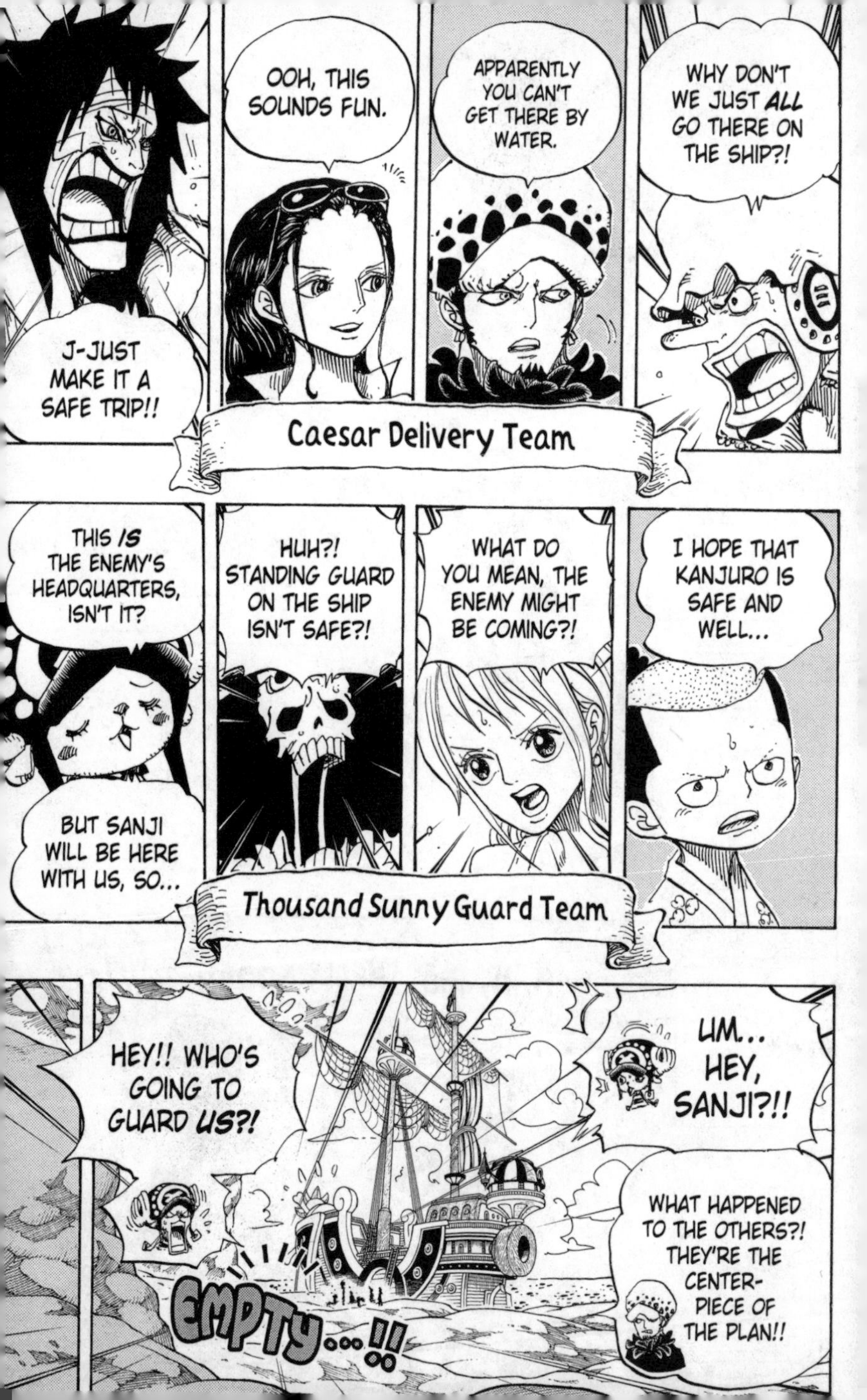
WHY DON'T WE JUST ALL GO THERE ON THE SHIP?!
APPARENTLY YOU CAN'T GET THERE BY WATER.
OOH, THIS SOUNDS FUN.
J-JUST MAKE IT A SAFE TRIP!!
Caesar Delivery Team
I HOPE THAT KANJURO IS SAFE AND WELL...
WHAT DO YOU MEAN, THE ENEMY MIGHT BE COMING?!
HUH?! STANDING GUARD ON THE SHIP ISN'T SAFE?!
THIS IS THE ENEMY'S HEADQUARTERS, ISN'T IT?
BUT SANJI WILL BE HERE WITH US, SO...
Thousand Sunny Guard Team
UM... HEY, SANJI?!!
HEY!! WHO'S GOING TO GUARD US?!
WHAT HAPPENED TO THE OTHERS?! THEY'RE THE CENTER-PIECE OF THE PLAN!!
EMPTY...!!

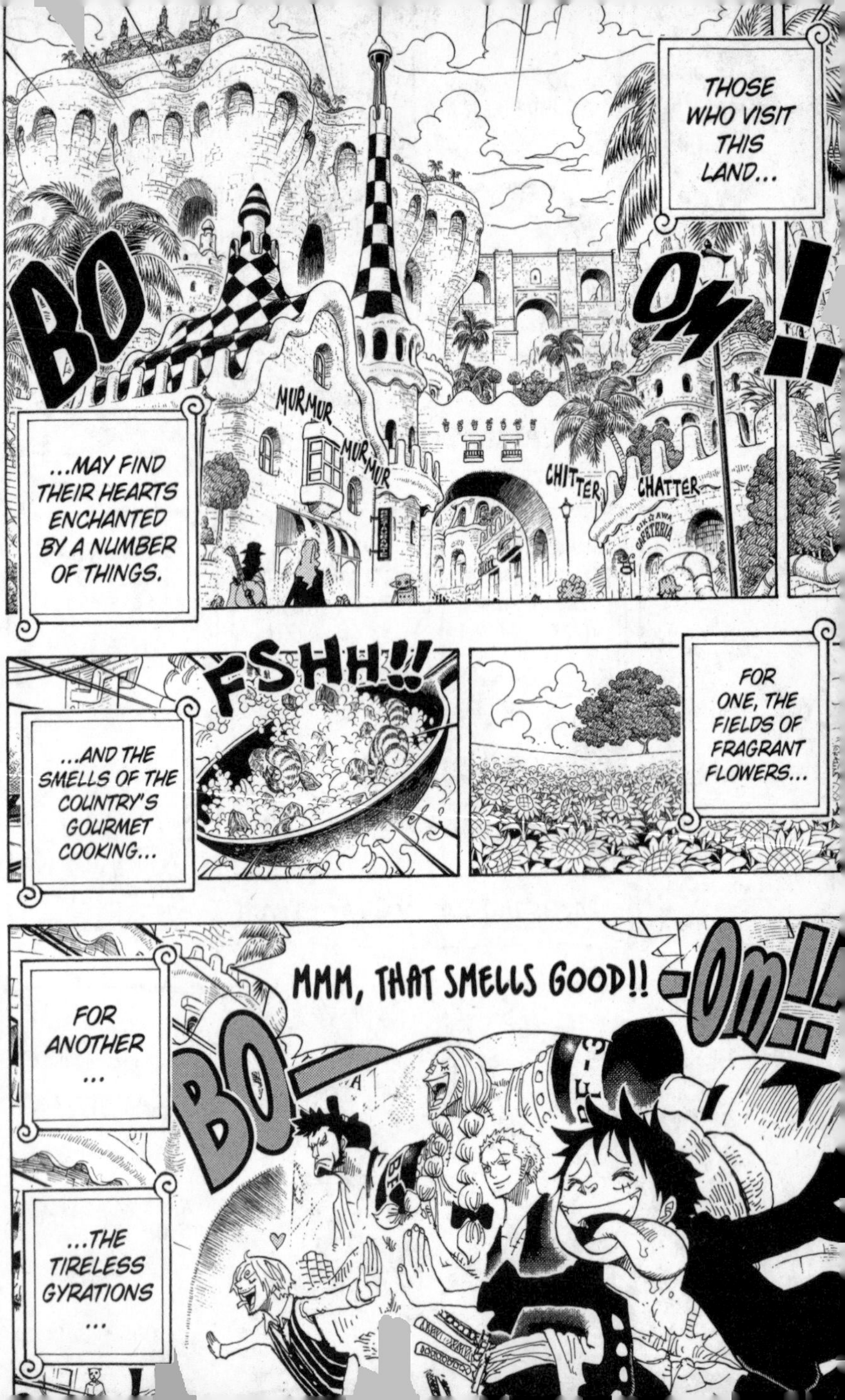
THOSE WHO VISIT THIS LAND...
BO
OM!!
MURMUR
MURMUR
CHITTER
CHATTER
...MAY FIND THEIR HEARTS ENCHANTED BY A NUMBER OF THINGS.
FOR ONE, THE FIELDS OF FRAGRANT FLOWERS...
FSHH!!
...AND THE SMELLS OF THE COUNTRY'S GOURMET COOKING...
-OM!!
MMM, THAT SMELLS GOOD!!
BO-
FOR ANOTHER ...
...THE TIRELESS GYRATIONS ...

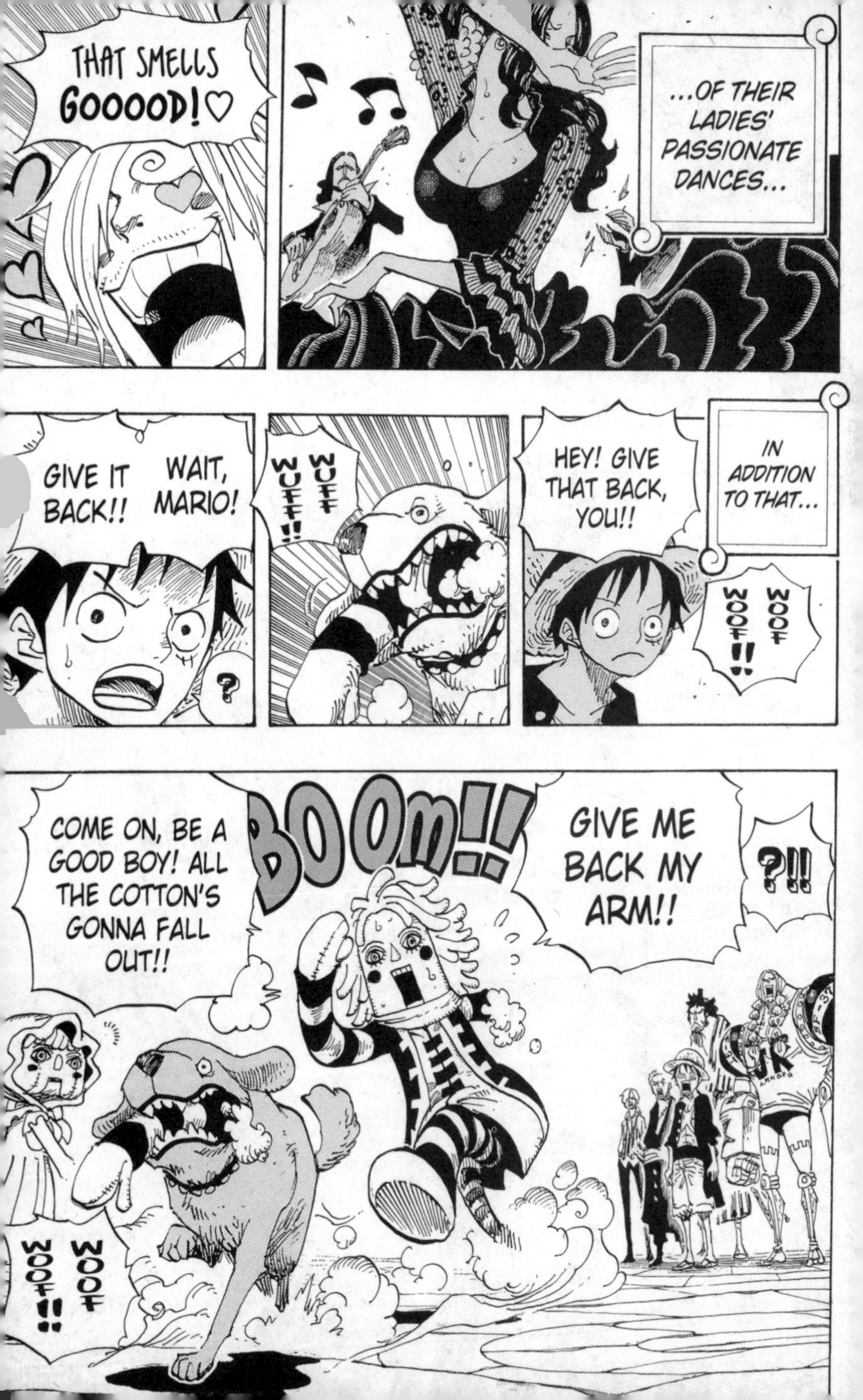
...OF THEIR LADIES' PASSIONATE DANCES...
THAT SMELLS GOOOOD!♡
IN ADDITION TO THAT...
WOOF WOOF!!
HEY! GIVE THAT BACK, YOU!!
WUFF WUFF!!
WAIT, MARIO!
GIVE IT BACK!!
?
?!!
GIVE ME BACK MY ARM!!
BOOM!!
COME ON, BE A GOOD BOY! ALL THE COTTON'S GONNA FALL OUT!!
WOOF WOOF!!

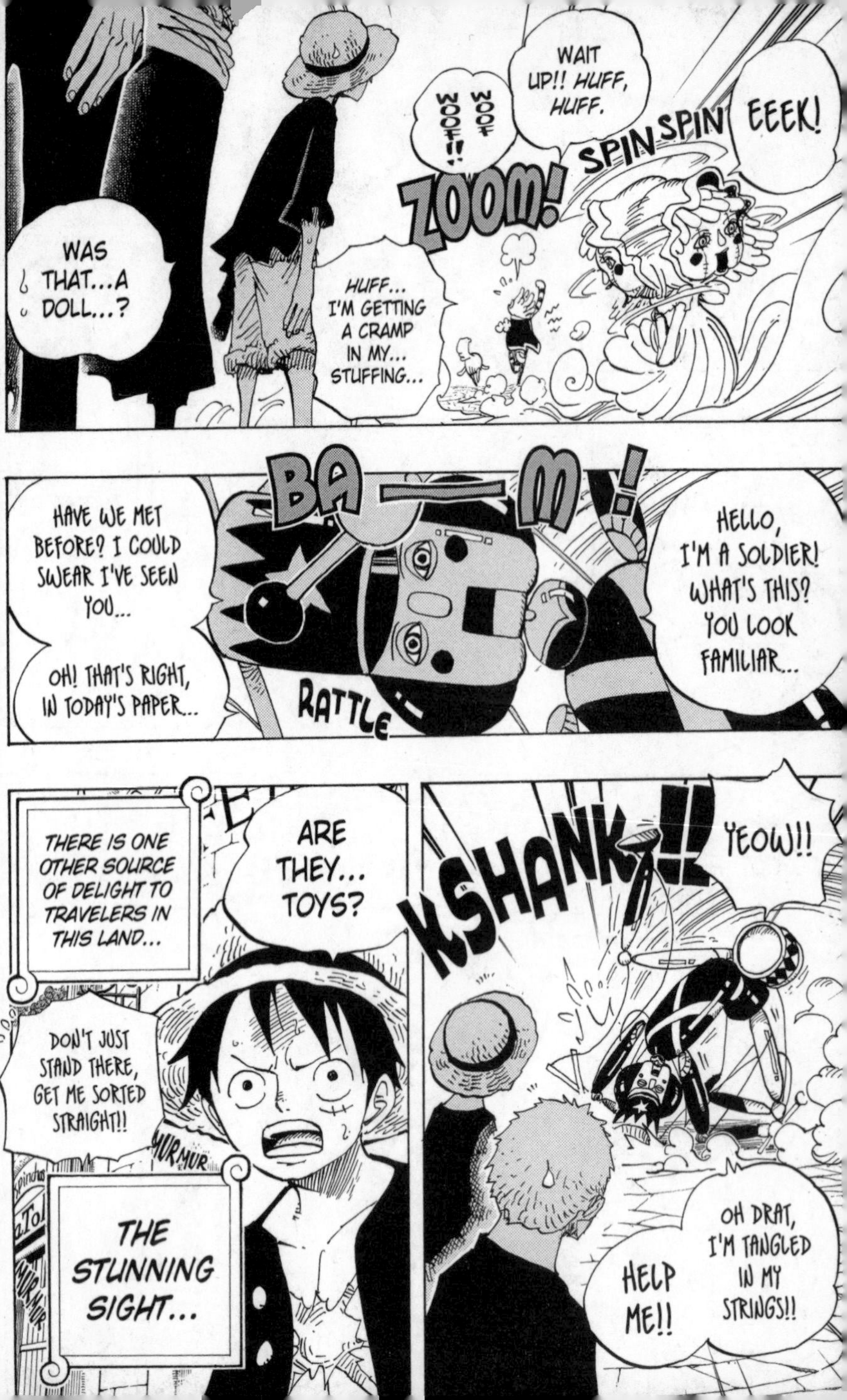
EEEK!
SPIN SPIN
WAIT UP!! HUFF, HUFF.
WOOF WOOF!!
ZOOM!
HUFF... I'M GETTING A CRAMP IN MY... STUFFING...
WAS THAT...A DOLL...?
HELLO, I'M A SOLDIER! WHAT'S THIS? YOU LOOK FAMILIAR...
BA—M!
RATTLE
HAVE WE MET BEFORE? I COULD SWEAR I'VE SEEN YOU...
OH! THAT'S RIGHT, IN TODAY'S PAPER...
YEOW!!
KSHANK!!
OH DRAT, I'M TANGLED IN MY STRINGS!!
HELP ME!!
ARE THEY... TOYS?
THERE IS ONE OTHER SOURCE OF DELIGHT TO TRAVELERS IN THIS LAND...
DON'T JUST STAND THERE, GET ME SORTED STRAIGHT!!
MUR MUR
THE STUNNING SIGHT...

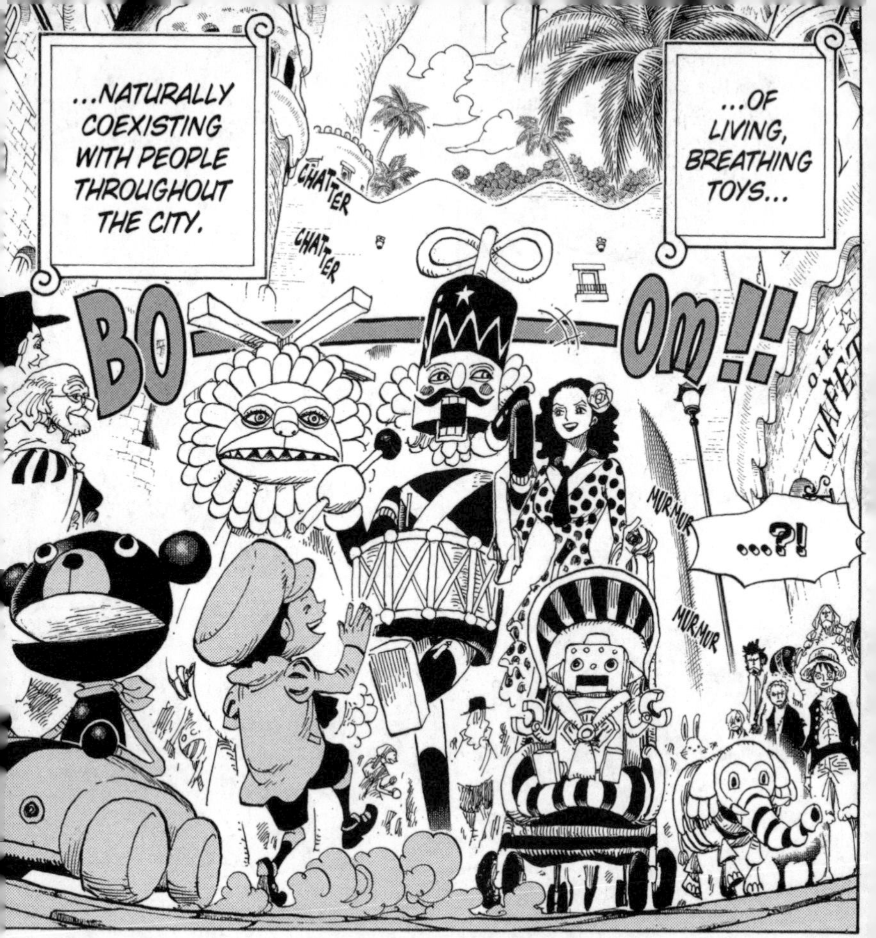
...OF LIVING, BREATHING TOYS...
...NATURALLY COEXISTING WITH PEOPLE THROUGHOUT THE CITY.
BO-OM!!
CHATTER CHATTER
MURMUR MURMUR
...?!

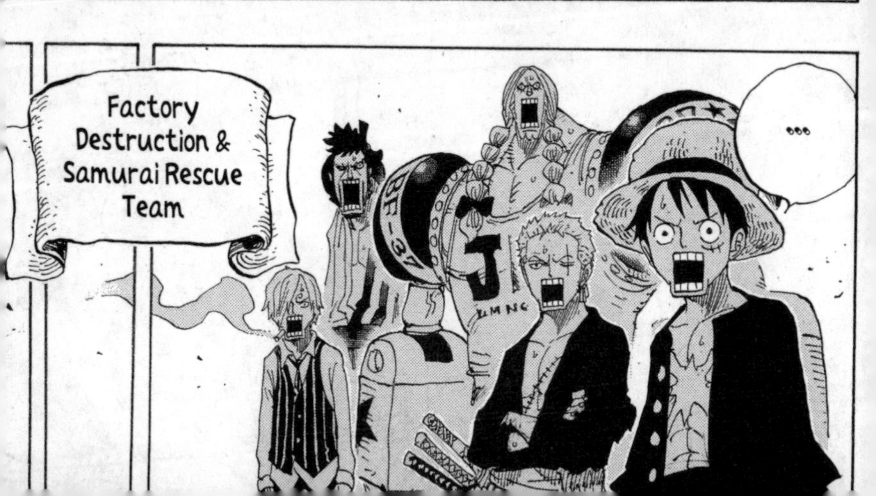
...
Factory Destruction & Samurai Rescue Team

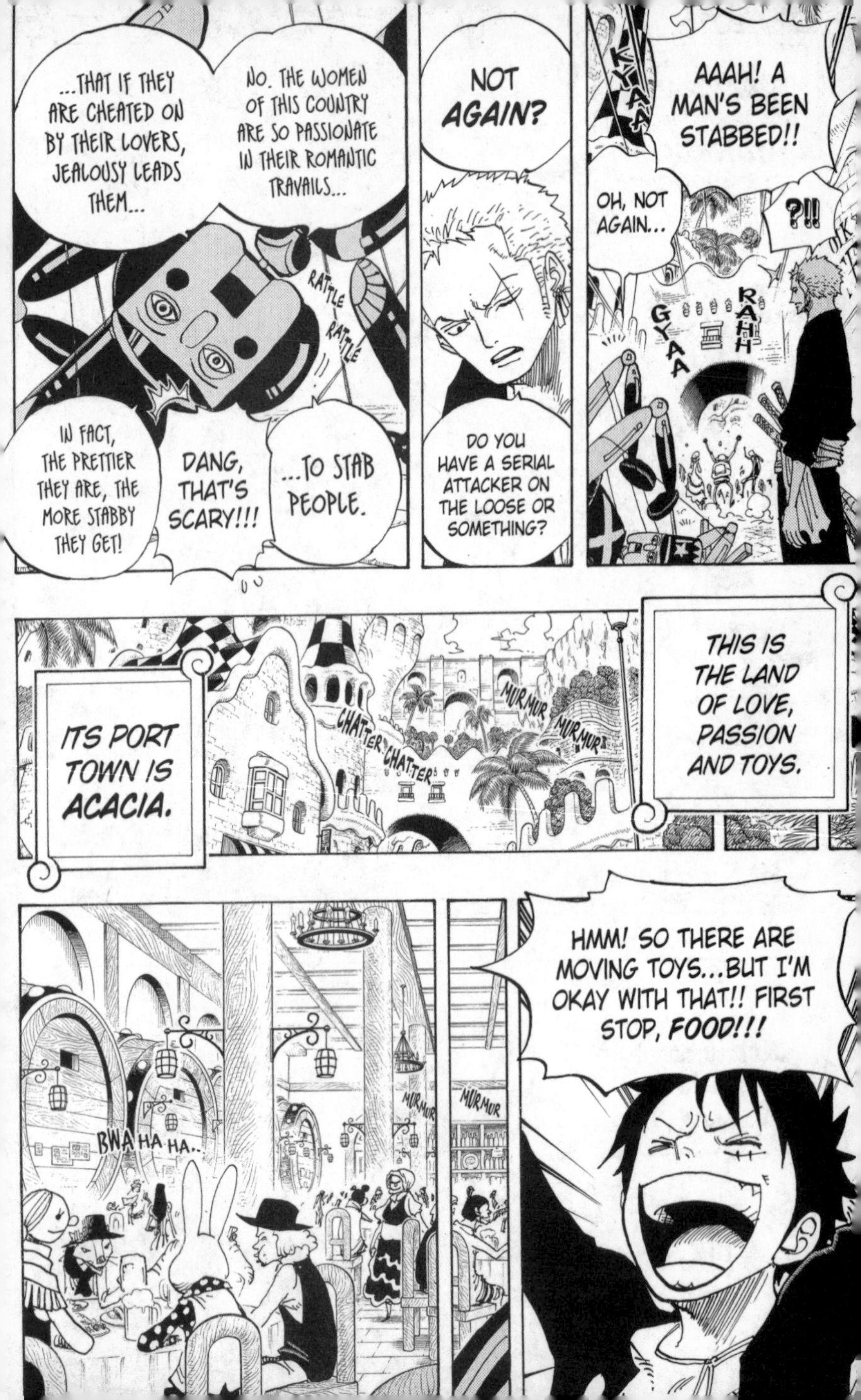
KYAAA
AAAH! A MAN'S BEEN STABBED!!
OH, NOT AGAIN...
?!!
GYAA
RAHH
NOT AGAIN?
DO YOU HAVE A SERIAL ATTACKER ON THE LOOSE OR SOMETHING?
NO. THE WOMEN OF THIS COUNTRY ARE SO PASSIONATE IN THEIR ROMANTIC TRAVAILS...
...THAT IF THEY ARE CHEATED ON BY THEIR LOVERS, JEALOUSY LEADS THEM...
RATTLE RATTLE
...TO STAB PEOPLE.
DANG, THAT'S SCARY!!!
IN FACT, THE PRETTIER THEY ARE, THE MORE STABBY THEY GET!
THIS IS THE LAND OF LOVE, PASSION AND TOYS.
MURMUR MURMUR
CHATTER CHATTER
ITS PORT TOWN IS ACACIA.
HMM! SO THERE ARE MOVING TOYS...BUT I'M OKAY WITH THAT!! FIRST STOP, FOOD!!!
MURMUR
MURMUR
BWA HA HA..

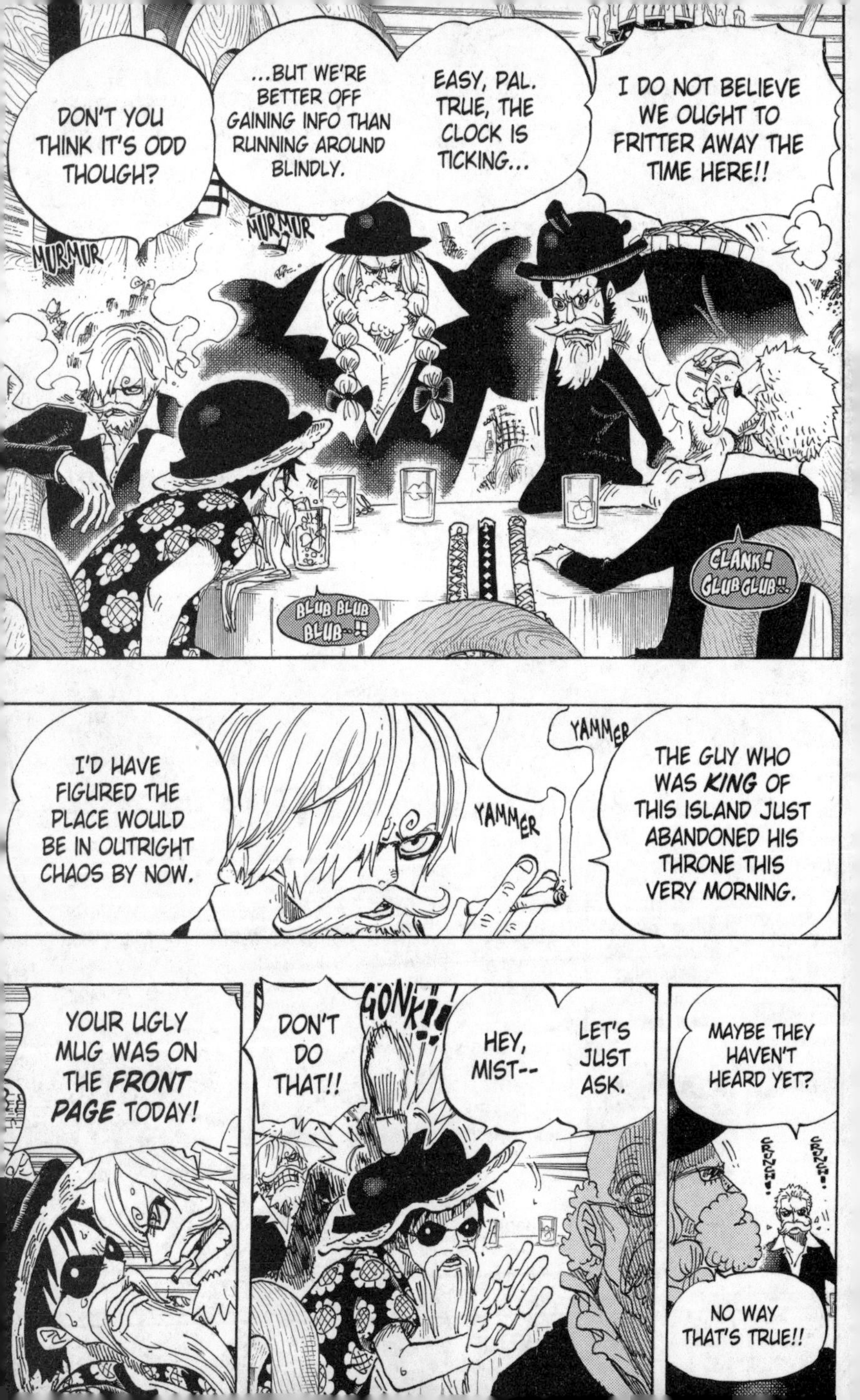
I DO NOT BELIEVE WE OUGHT TO FRITTER AWAY THE TIME HERE!!
EASY, PAL. TRUE, THE CLOCK IS TICKING...
...BUT WE'RE BETTER OFF GAINING INFO THAN RUNNING AROUND BLINDLY.
DON'T YOU THINK IT'S ODD THOUGH?
MURMUR
MURMUR
CLANK! GLUB GLUB!!
BLUB BLUB BLUB..!!
THE GUY WHO WAS KING OF THIS ISLAND JUST ABANDONED HIS THRONE THIS VERY MORNING.
YAMMER
YAMMER
I'D HAVE FIGURED THE PLACE WOULD BE IN OUTRIGHT CHAOS BY NOW.
MAYBE THEY HAVEN'T HEARD YET?
CRUNCH!
CRUNCH!
NO WAY THAT'S TRUE!!
LET'S JUST ASK.
HEY, MIST--
GONK!!
DON'T DO THAT!!
YOUR UGLY MUG WAS ON THE FRONT PAGE TODAY!

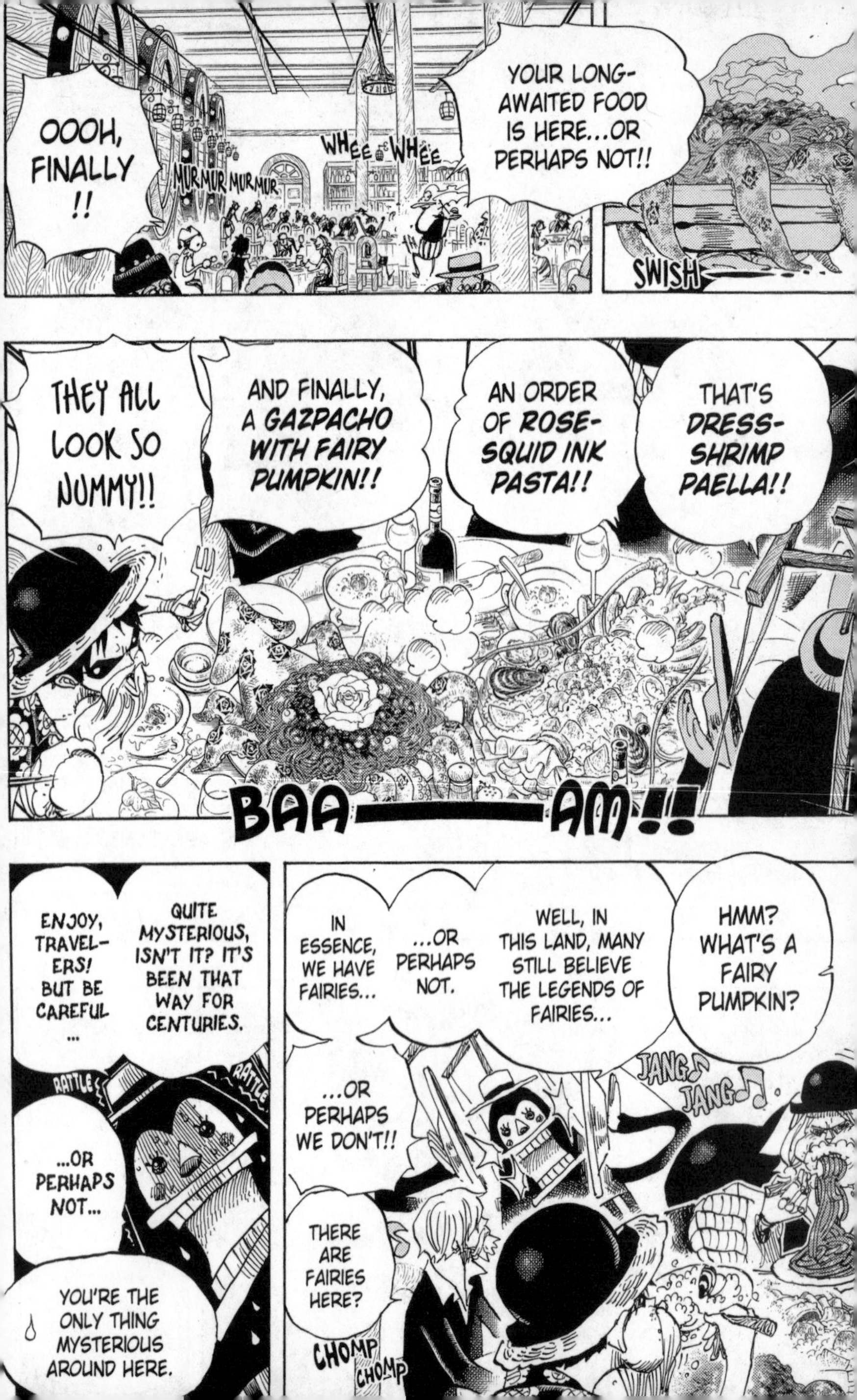
SWISH
YOUR LONG-AWAITED FOOD IS HERE...OR PERHAPS NOT!!
WHEE WHEE
MURMUR MURMUR
OOOH, FINALLY!!
THAT'S DRESS-SHRIMP PAELLA!!
AN ORDER OF ROSE-SQUID INK PASTA!!
AND FINALLY, A GAZPACHO WITH FAIRY PUMPKIN!!
THEY ALL LOOK SO NUMMY!!
BAA——AM!!
HMM? WHAT'S A FAIRY PUMPKIN?
WELL, IN THIS LAND, MANY STILL BELIEVE THE LEGENDS OF FAIRIES...
...OR PERHAPS NOT.
IN ESSENCE, WE HAVE FAIRIES...
JANG♪ JANG♪
...OR PERHAPS WE DON'T!!
THERE ARE FAIRIES HERE?
CHOMP CHOMP
QUITE MYSTERIOUS, ISN'T IT? IT'S BEEN THAT WAY FOR CENTURIES.
ENJOY, TRAVELERS! BUT BE CAREFUL...
RATTLE RATTLE
...OR PERHAPS NOT...
YOU'RE THE ONLY THING MYSTERIOUS AROUND HERE.

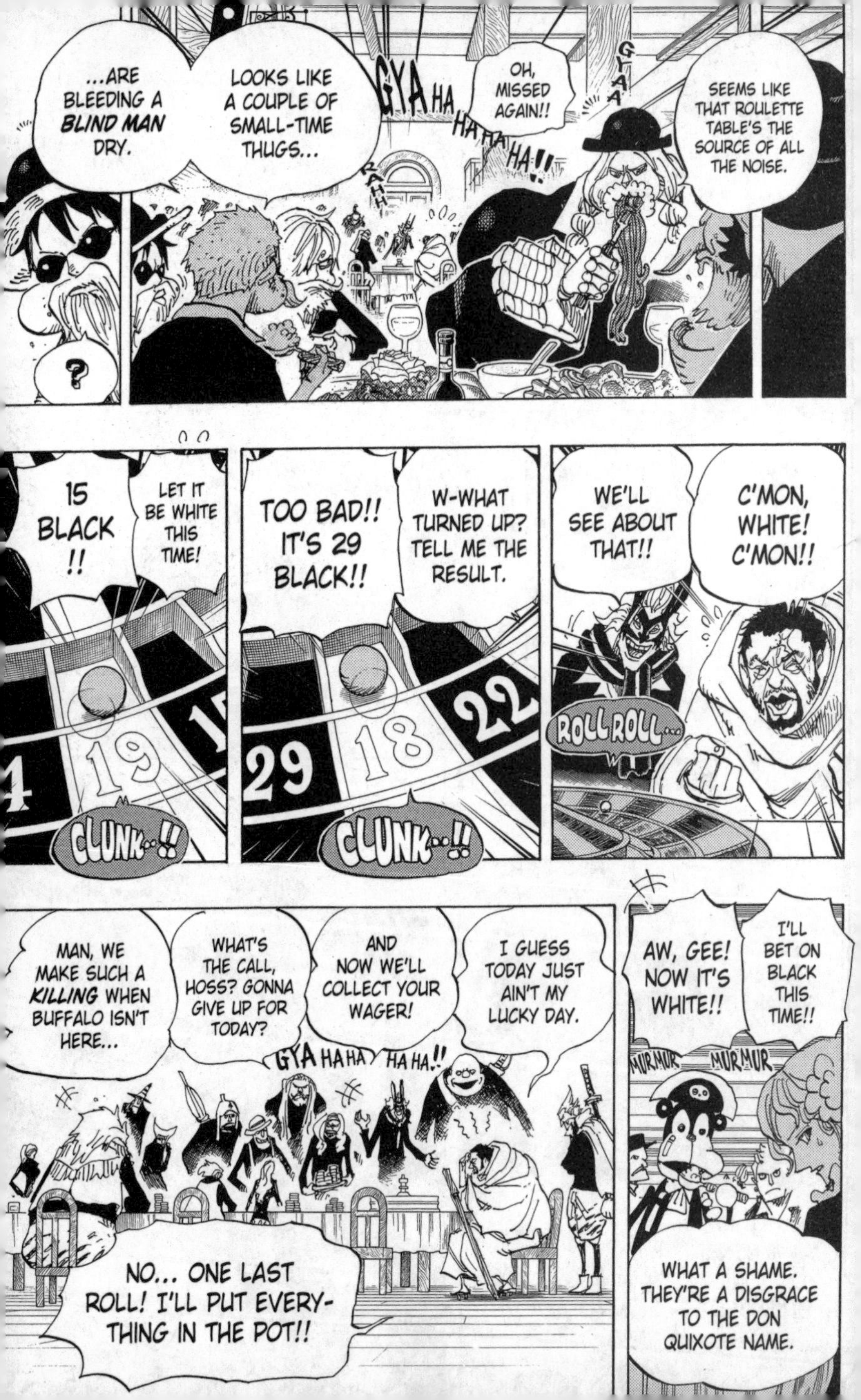
SEEMS LIKE THAT ROULETTE TABLE'S THE SOURCE OF ALL THE NOISE.
GYAA
OH, MISSED AGAIN!!
GYA HA HA HA HA HA!!
RAHH
LOOKS LIKE A COUPLE OF SMALL-TIME THUGS...
...ARE BLEEDING A BLIND MAN DRY.
?
C'MON, WHITE! C'MON!!
WE'LL SEE ABOUT THAT!!
ROLL ROLL...
W-WHAT TURNED UP? TELL ME THE RESULT.
TOO BAD!! IT'S 29 BLACK!!
22
18
29
CLUNK...!!
LET IT BE WHITE THIS TIME!
15 BLACK!!
19
CLUNK...!!
I'LL BET ON BLACK THIS TIME!!
AW, GEE! NOW IT'S WHITE!!
MURMUR MURMUR
WHAT A SHAME. THEY'RE A DISGRACE TO THE DON QUIXOTE NAME.
I GUESS TODAY JUST AIN'T MY LUCKY DAY.
AND NOW WE'LL COLLECT YOUR WAGER!
WHAT'S THE CALL, HOSS? GONNA GIVE UP FOR TODAY?
MAN, WE MAKE SUCH A KILLING WHEN BUFFALO ISN'T HERE...
GYA HA HA HA HA!!
NO... ONE LAST ROLL! I'LL PUT EVERYTHING IN THE POT!!

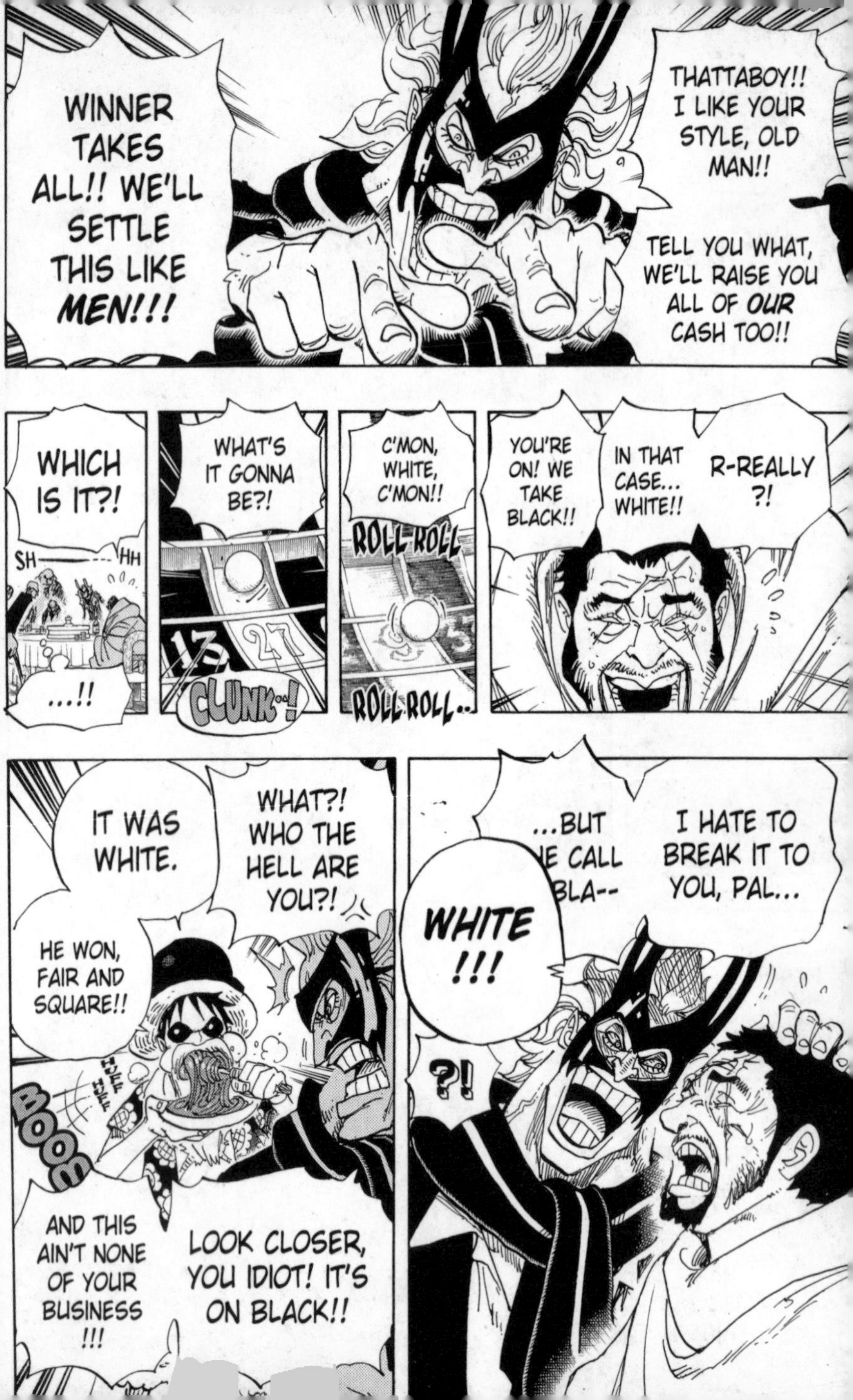
THATTABOY!! I LIKE YOUR STYLE, OLD MAN!!
WINNER TAKES ALL!! WE'LL SETTLE THIS LIKE *MEN!!!*
TELL YOU WHAT, WE'LL RAISE YOU ALL OF *OUR* CASH TOO!!
R-REALLY ?!
IN THAT CASE... WHITE!!
YOU'RE ON! WE TAKE BLACK!!
C'MON, WHITE, C'MON!!
ROLL ROLL
ROLL ROLL...
WHAT'S IT GONNA BE?!
13
27
CLUNK-!
WHICH IS IT?!
SH-----HH
...!!
I HATE TO BREAK IT TO YOU, PAL...
...BUT
E CALL
BLA--
WHITE !!!
?!
WHAT?! WHO THE HELL ARE YOU?!
IT WAS WHITE.
HE WON, FAIR AND SQUARE!!
HUFF HUFF
BOOM
LOOK CLOSER, YOU IDIOT! IT'S ON BLACK!!
AND THIS AIN'T NONE OF YOUR BUSINESS !!!

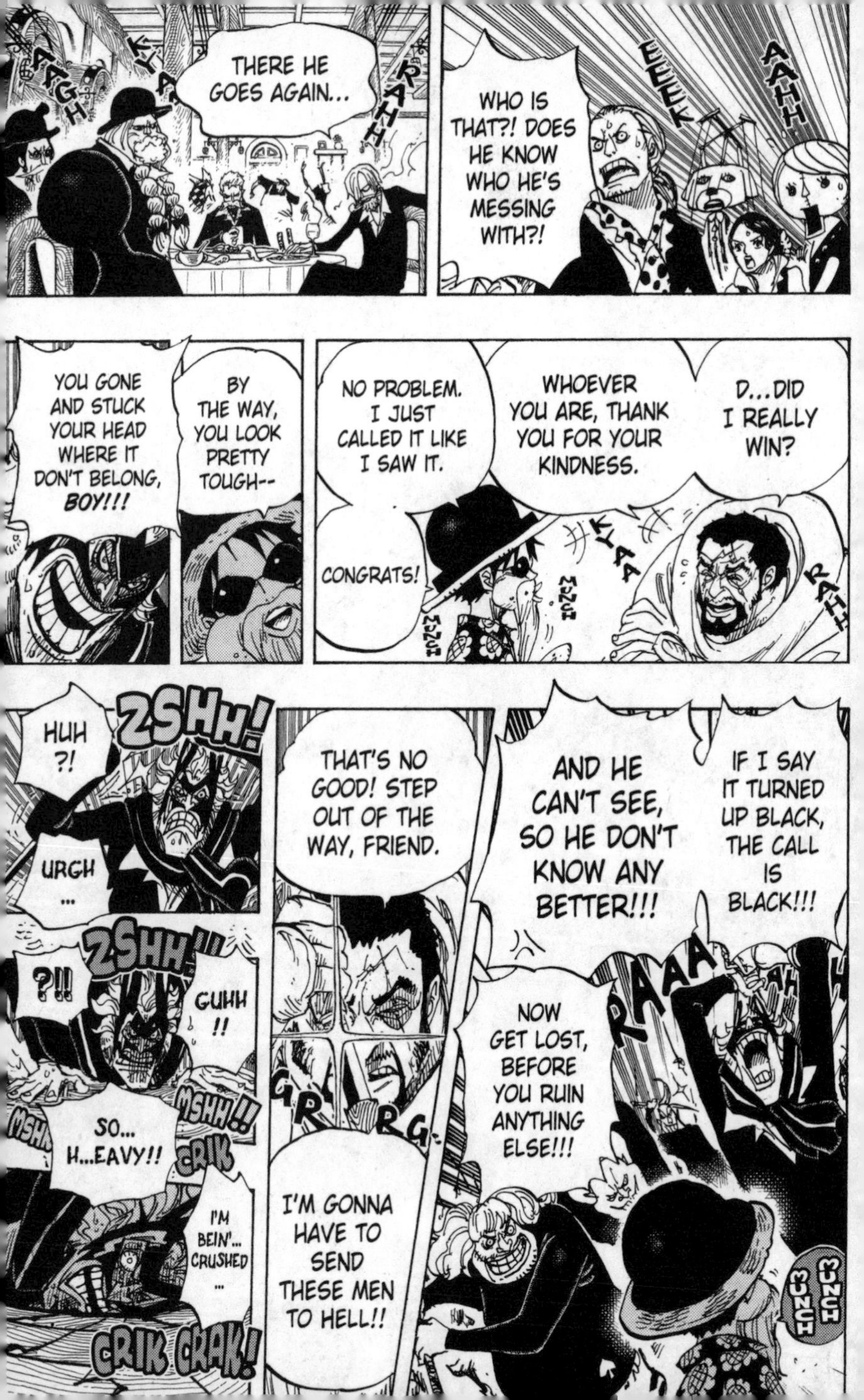
AAHH
EEEEK
WHO IS THAT?! DOES HE KNOW WHO HE'S MESSING WITH?!
RAHH
THERE HE GOES AGAIN...
KYAA
AAGH
D...DID I REALLY WIN?
WHOEVER YOU ARE, THANK YOU FOR YOUR KINDNESS.
RAHH
KYAA
NO PROBLEM. I JUST CALLED IT LIKE I SAW IT.
CONGRATS!
MUNCH
MUNCH
BY THE WAY, YOU LOOK PRETTY TOUGH--
YOU GONE AND STUCK YOUR HEAD WHERE IT DON'T BELONG, BOY!!!
IF I SAY IT TURNED UP BLACK, THE CALL IS BLACK!!!
AND HE CAN'T SEE, SO HE DON'T KNOW ANY BETTER!!!
RAAA
NOW GET LOST, BEFORE YOU RUIN ANYTHING ELSE!!!
MUNCH
MUNCH
THAT'S NO GOOD! STEP OUT OF THE WAY, FRIEND.
GRRG
I'M GONNA HAVE TO SEND THESE MEN TO HELL!!
ZSHH!
HUH ?!
URGH ...
ZSHH!!
?!!
GUHH !!
MSHH!!
SO... H...EAVY!!
CRIK
I'M BEIN'... CRUSHED ...
CRIK CRAK!

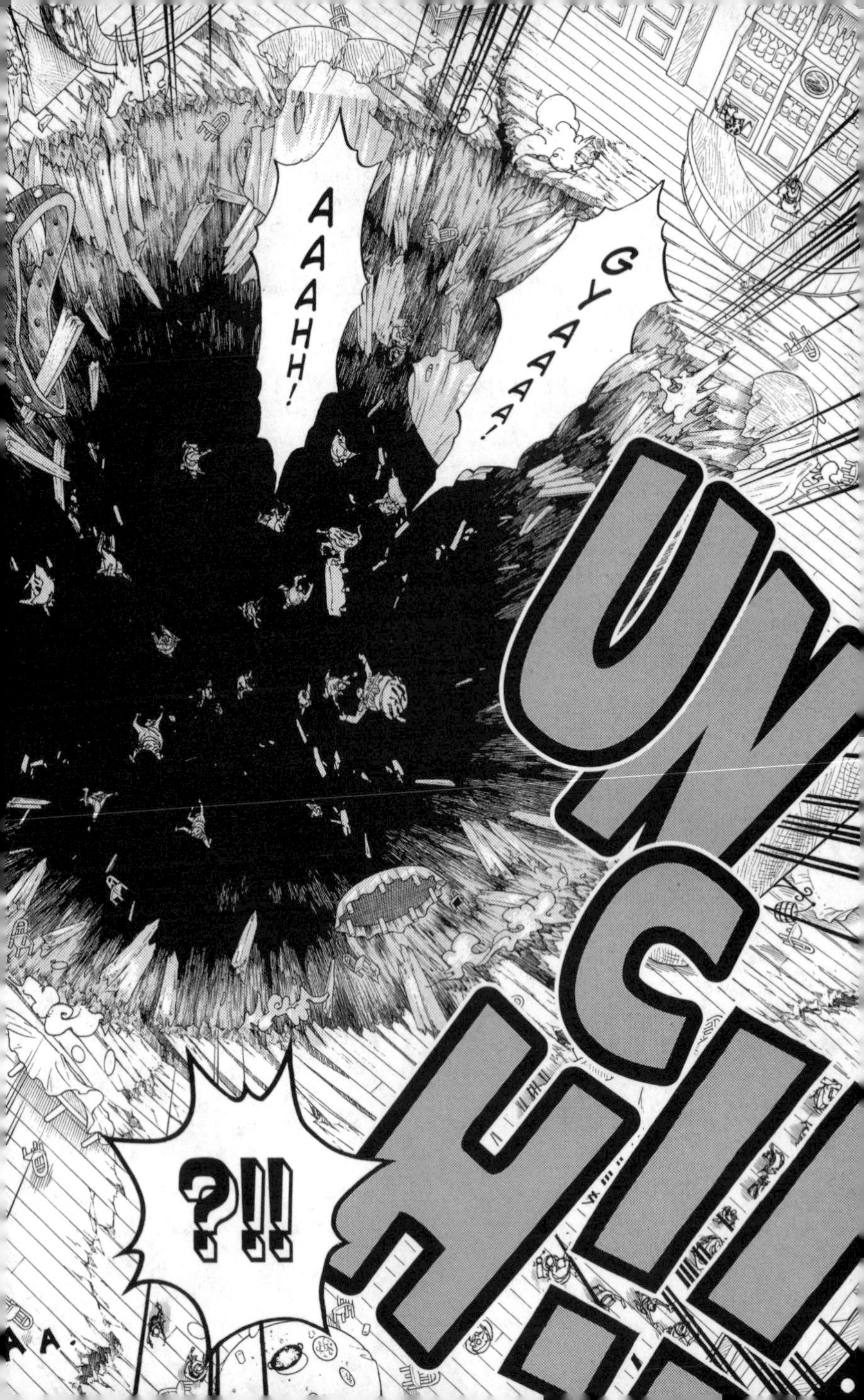
GYAAAAA!
AAAAHH!
?!!

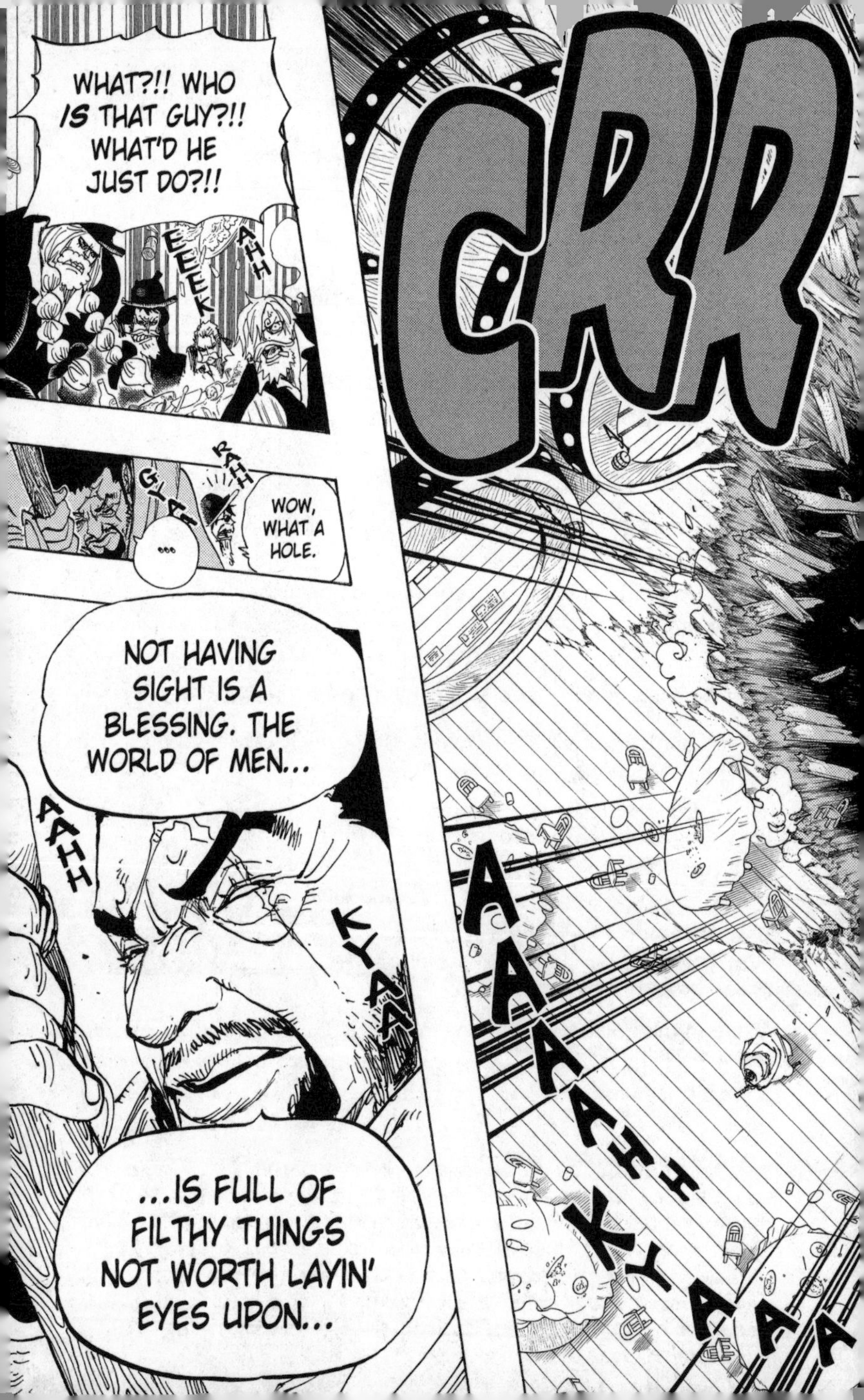
CRR
AAAAHH
KYAAAA
WHAT?!! WHO *IS* THAT GUY?!! WHAT'D HE JUST DO?!!
AHH
EEEEK
WOW, WHAT A HOLE.
RAHH
GYAA
...
NOT HAVING SIGHT IS A BLESSING. THE WORLD OF MEN...
KYAAA
AAHH
...IS FULL OF FILTHY THINGS NOT WORTH LAYIN' EYES UPON...

SBS Question Corner

エス
ビー
エス

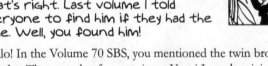

(Hippo Iron, Saitama)

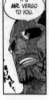

IT'S MR. VERGO TO YOU.

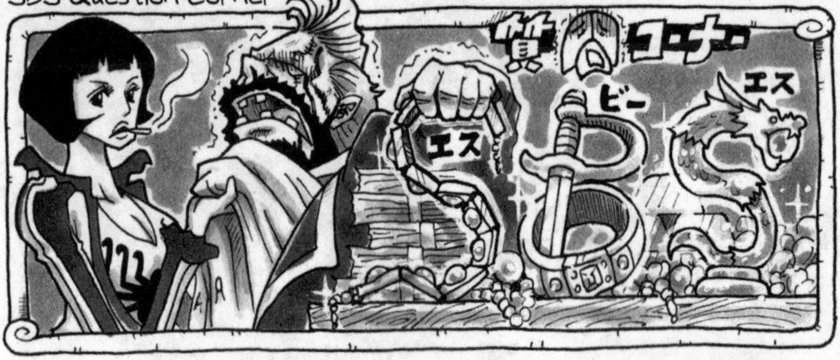

Oda(A): All right! Let's get ready, folks!
"Start!! The SBS!!"
Yahoo!

Question(Q): Take it back. That's Mr. SBS.

--Kimurin

A: Oh!! S...sorry... Start the...Mr. SBS...

Q: Question. Question for Odacchi. When did Franky become such a pervert? (^▽^)

--Arabiki Sausage

A: Franky was perverted since his previous life.

Q: I found him, Odacchi!!!!! In fact, it was surprisingly easy. It's him, Kandre!! Volume 57, page 108, third panel, second from the left! That has to be him!! If I'm wrong, then you have to be crazy. I'm totally right, aren't I?!!

--Teaguechikei

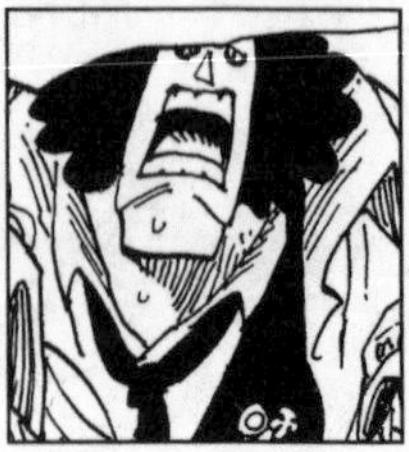

A: That's right. Last volume I told everyone to find him if they had the time. Well, you found him!

Q: Hello! In the Volume 70 SBS, you mentioned the twin brothers Andre/Kandre. That was also famous singer Yosui Inoue's original stage name upon his debut over 40 years ago, right? He even had an afro at the time.

--Was Once a Guitar Lad

A: Yes, that's right. I took the rhyming name from the same place, but as a matter of fact, I had no idea that it was referring to him. I'd just heard the name on TV once years ago. It says that your age is 56, Guitar Lad, so I guess that would explain it, eh? By the way, I originally named Andre after the wrestler Andre the Giant, because I thought they looked alike. Basically, I just make up my names on the spot, ha ha.

Chapter 702:
CORRIDA COLISEUM

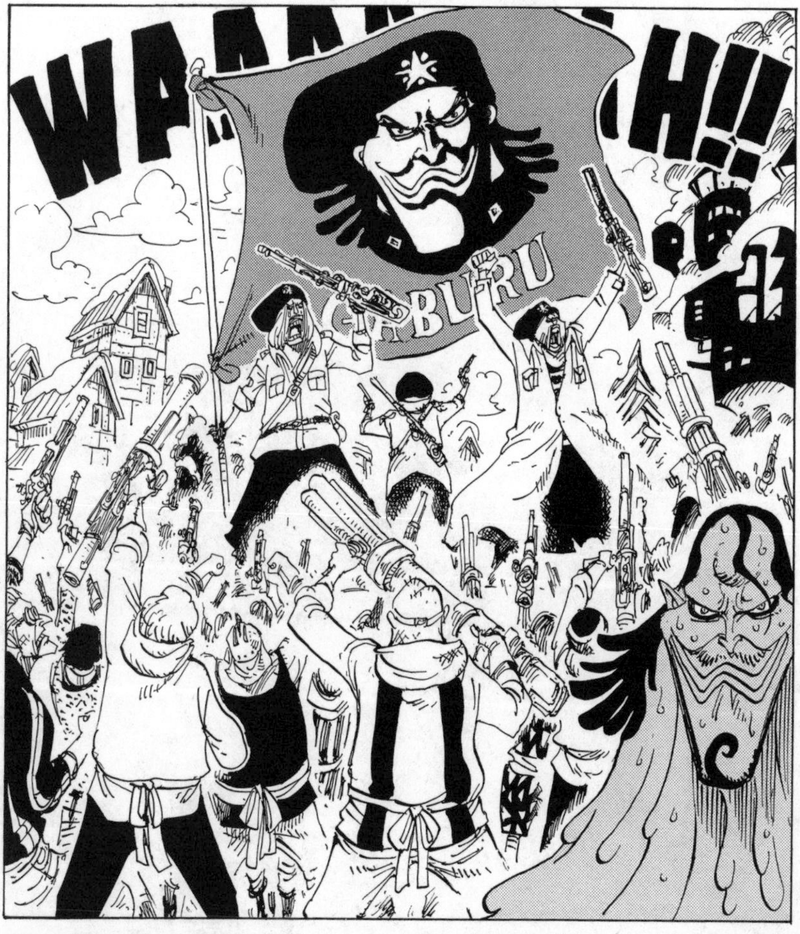

CARIBOU'S NEW WORLD KEE HEE HEE, VOL. 23: "PROLETARIATS, GRAB YOUR WEAPONS!! CAPTAIN GABURU, CHILD OF THE REVOLUTION, HAS RETURNED!!!"

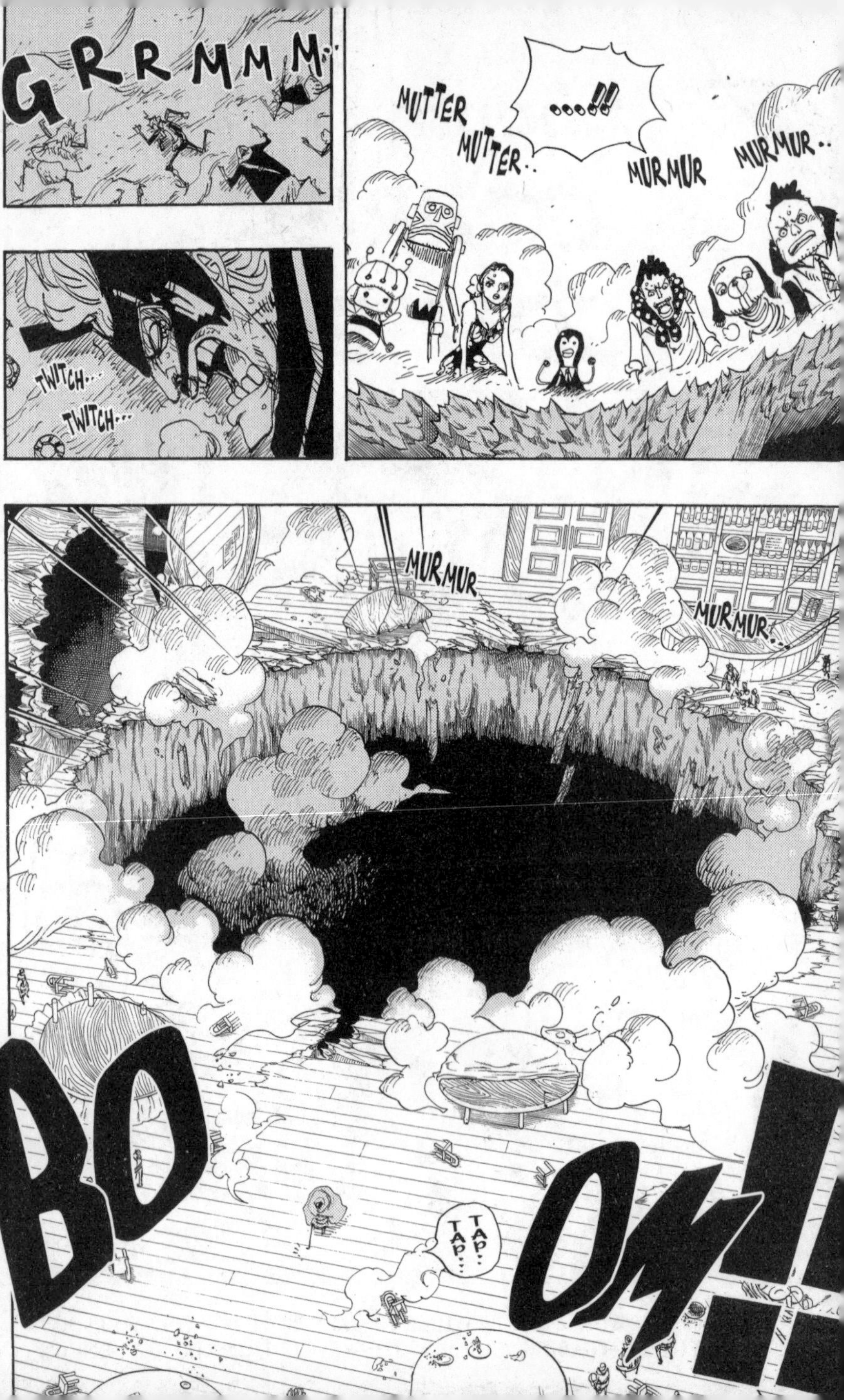
MURMUR..
MURMUR
...!!
MUTTER
MUTTER..
GRRMMM
TWITCH...
TWITCH...
MURMUR!
MURMUR
BOOM!!
TAP.. TAP...

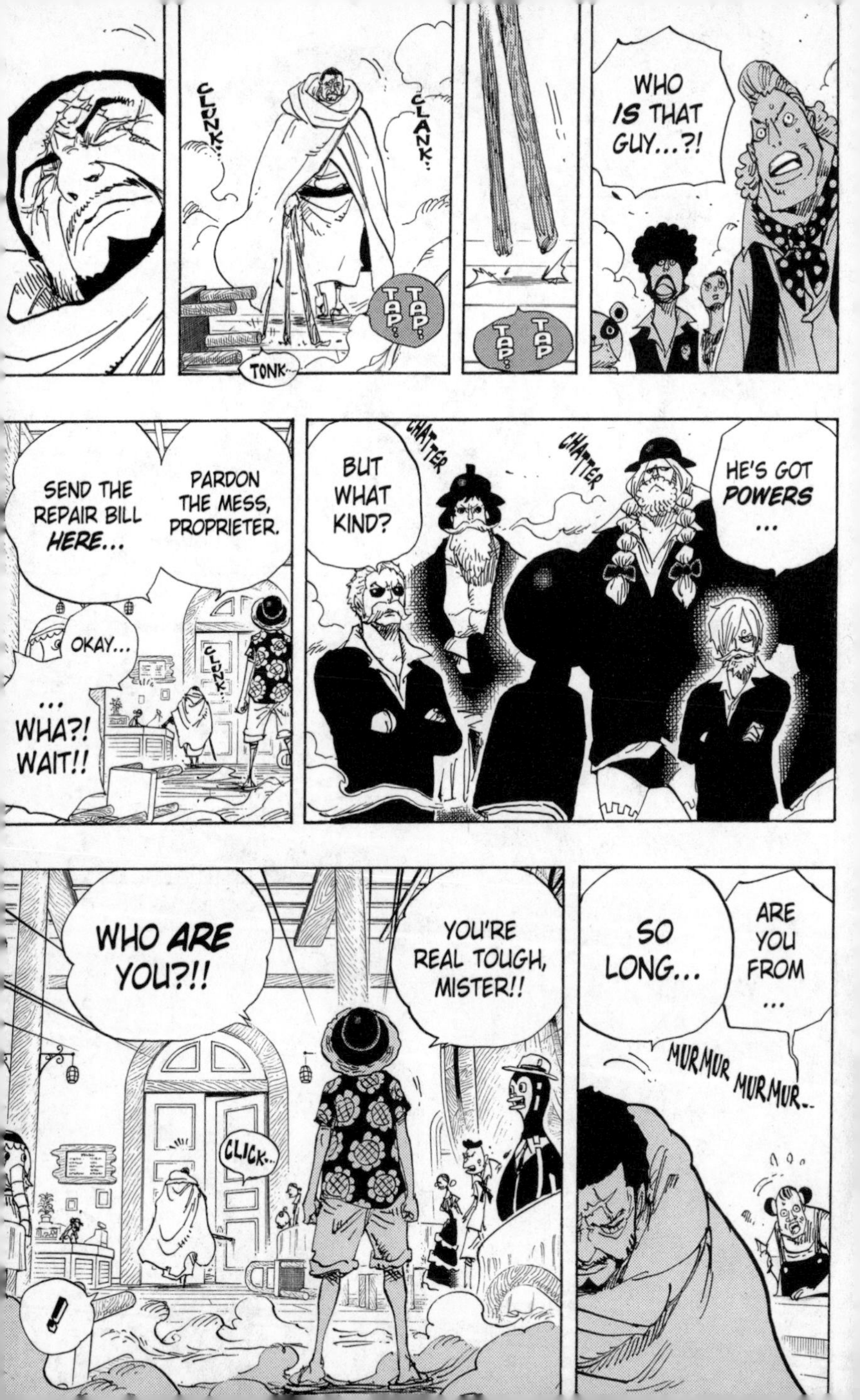
WHO IS THAT GUY...?!
TAP TAP
TAP TAP
CLANK
CLUNK
TAP TAP
TONK
HE'S GOT POWERS ...
CHATTER
CHATTER
BUT WHAT KIND?
PARDON THE MESS, PROPRIETER.
SEND THE REPAIR BILL HERE...
OKAY...
CLUNK
... WHA?! WAIT!!
ARE YOU FROM ...
SO LONG...
MURMUR MURMUR
YOU'RE REAL TOUGH, MISTER!!
WHO ARE YOU?!!
CLICK
!

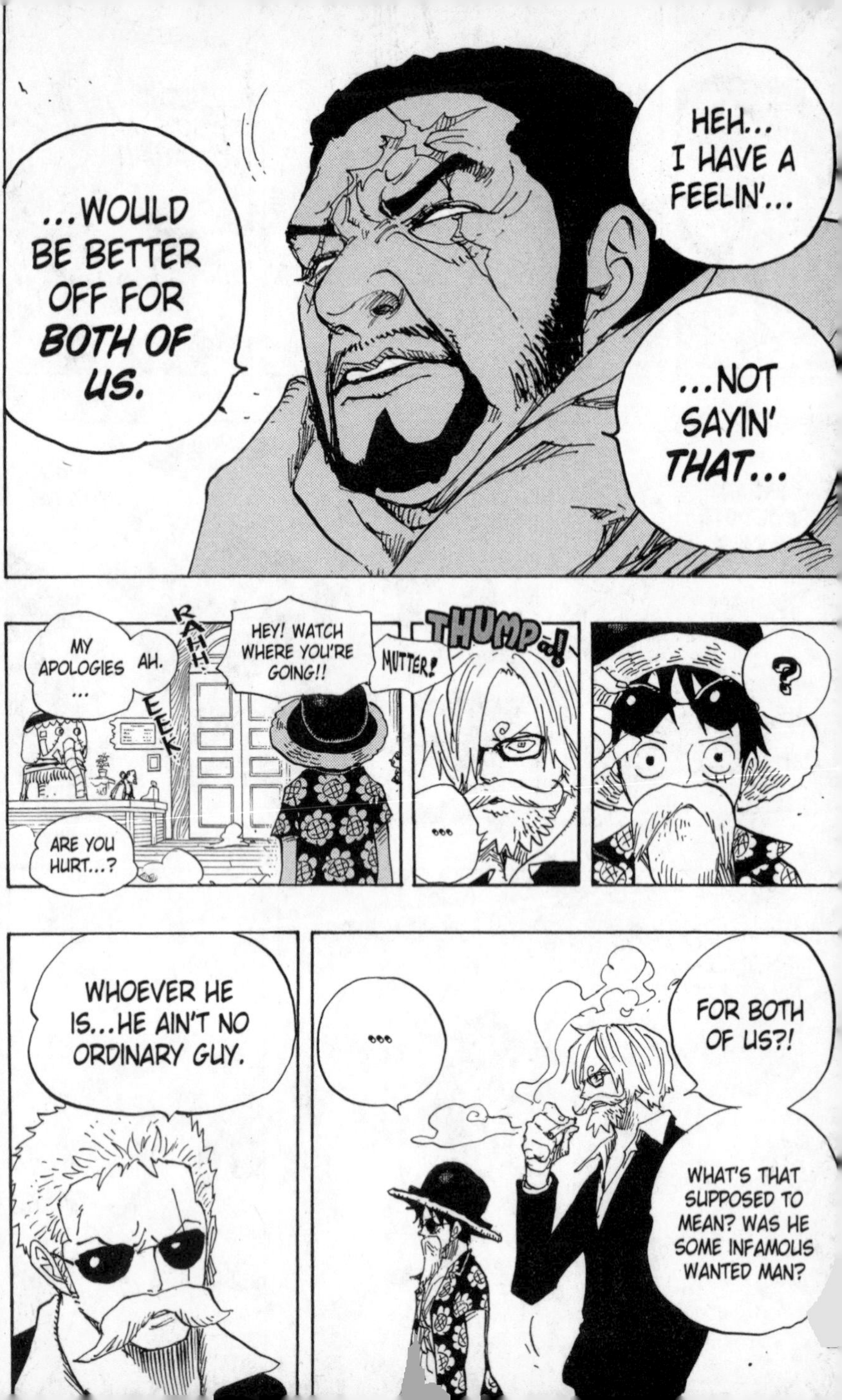
HEH... I HAVE A FEELIN'...
...NOT SAYIN' THAT...
...WOULD BE BETTER OFF FOR BOTH OF US.
?
THUMP
MUTTER!
...
HEY! WATCH WHERE YOU'RE GOING!!
RAHH
EEEK
AH.
MY APOLOGIES ...
ARE YOU HURT...?
FOR BOTH OF US?!
WHAT'S THAT SUPPOSED TO MEAN? WAS HE SOME INFAMOUS WANTED MAN?
...
WHOEVER HE IS...HE AIN'T NO ORDINARY GUY.

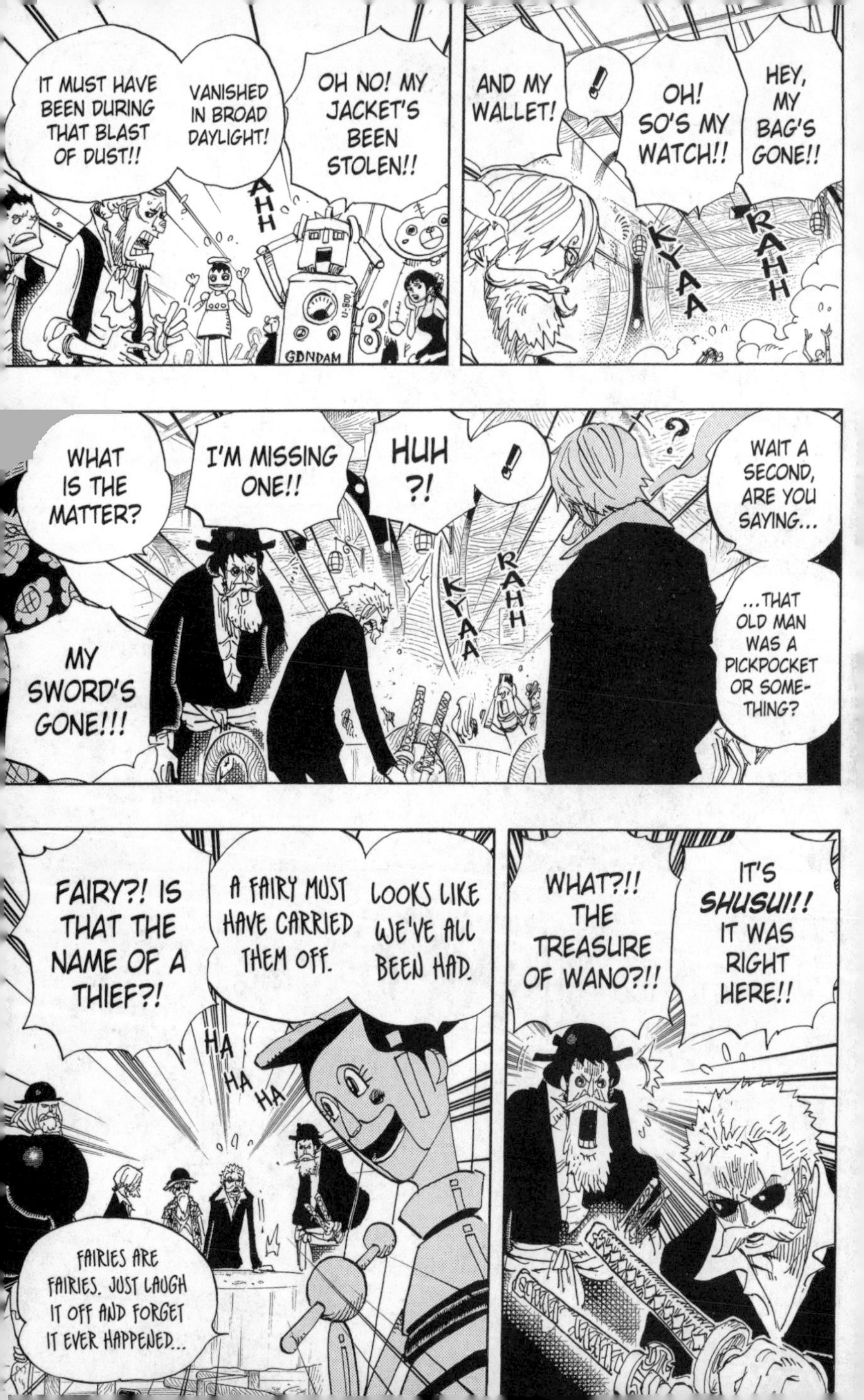
HEY, MY BAG'S GONE!!
OH! SO'S MY WATCH!!
!
AND MY WALLET!
RAHH
KYAA
OH NO! MY JACKET'S BEEN STOLEN!!
VANISHED IN BROAD DAYLIGHT!
IT MUST HAVE BEEN DURING THAT BLAST OF DUST!!
AHH
GDNDAM
WAIT A SECOND, ARE YOU SAYING...
...THAT OLD MAN WAS A PICKPOCKET OR SOMETHING?
?
!
HUH ?!
RAHH
KYAA
I'M MISSING ONE!!
WHAT IS THE MATTER?
MY SWORD'S GONE!!!
IT'S SHUSUI!! IT WAS RIGHT HERE!!
WHAT?!! THE TREASURE OF WANO?!!
LOOKS LIKE WE'VE ALL BEEN HAD.
A FAIRY MUST HAVE CARRIED THEM OFF.
FAIRY?! IS THAT THE NAME OF A THIEF?!
HA HA HA
FAIRIES ARE FAIRIES. JUST LAUGH IT OFF AND FORGET IT EVER HAPPENED...

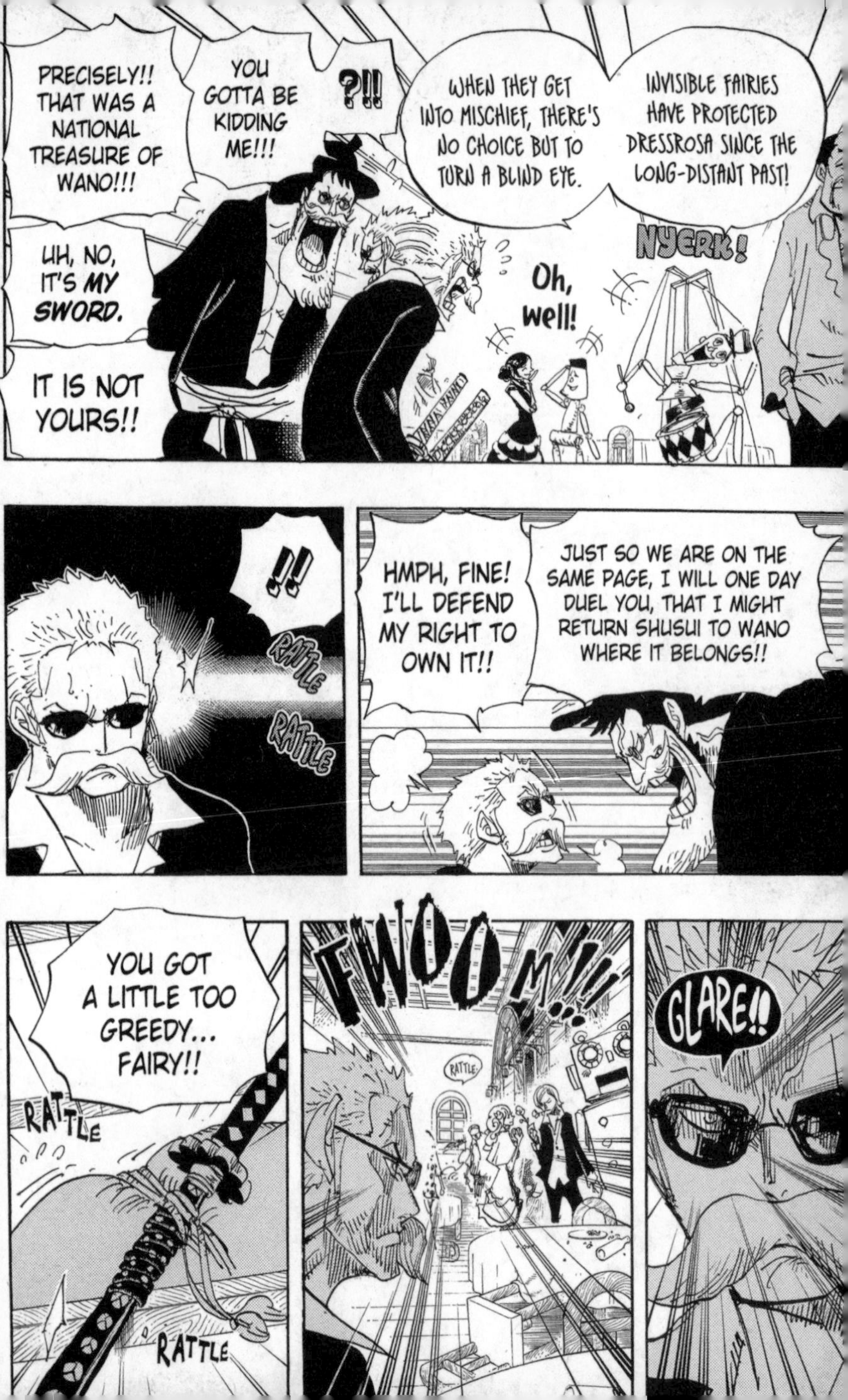
INVISIBLE FAIRIES HAVE PROTECTED DRESSROSA SINCE THE LONG-DISTANT PAST!
WHEN THEY GET INTO MISCHIEF, THERE'S NO CHOICE BUT TO TURN A BLIND EYE.
NYERK!
Oh, well!
?!!
YOU GOTTA BE KIDDING ME!!!
PRECISELY!! THAT WAS A NATIONAL TREASURE OF WANO!!!
UH, NO, IT'S MY SWORD.
IT IS NOT YOURS!!
JUST SO WE ARE ON THE SAME PAGE, I WILL ONE DAY DUEL YOU, THAT I MIGHT RETURN SHUSUI TO WANO WHERE IT BELONGS!!
HMPH, FINE! I'LL DEFEND MY RIGHT TO OWN IT!!
!!
RATTLE
RATTLE
GLARE!!
FWOOM!!!
RATTLE
YOU GOT A LITTLE TOO GREEDY... FAIRY!!
RATTLE
RATTLE

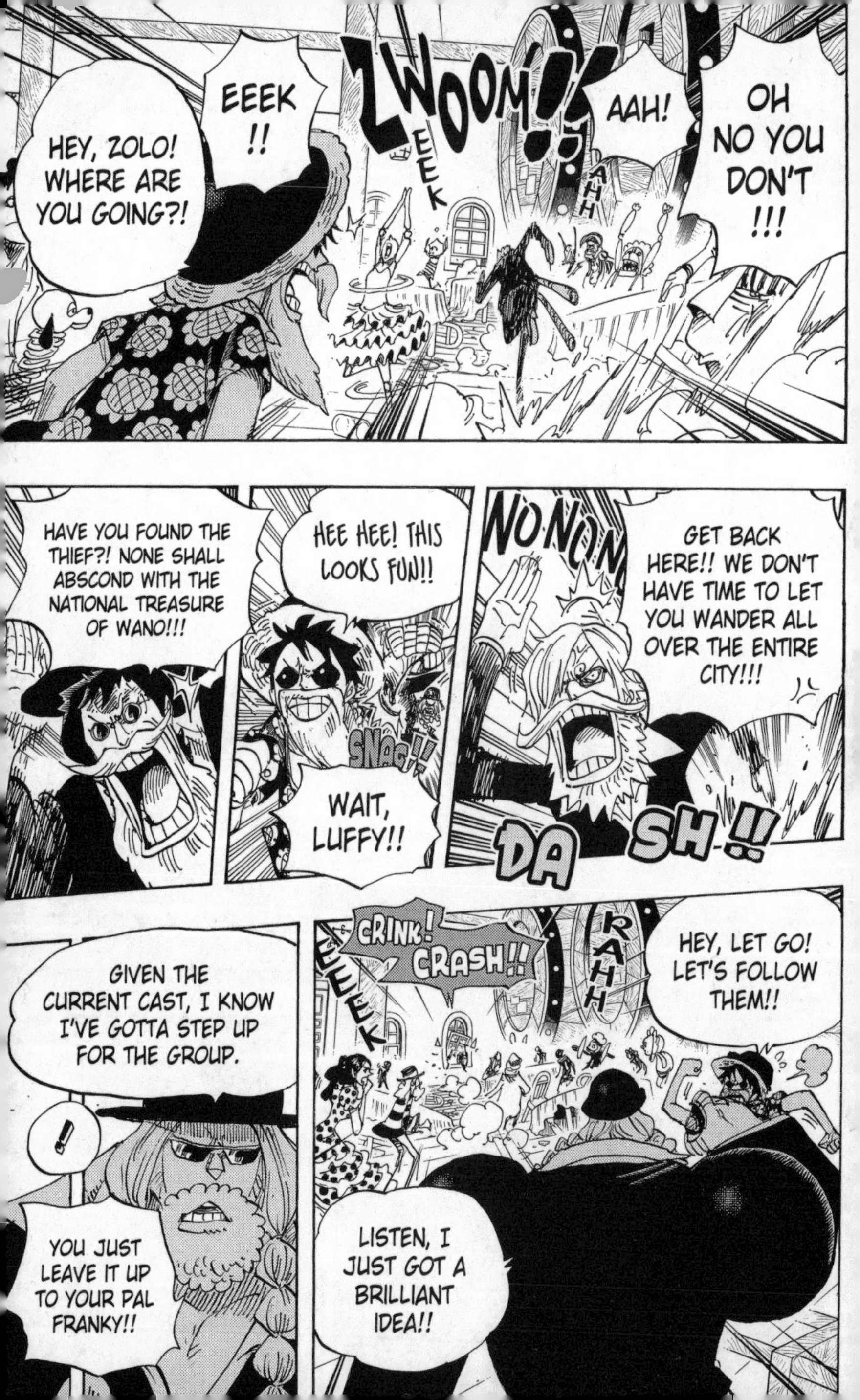
OH NO YOU DON'T!!!
AAH!
AHH
ZWOOM!!
EEEK
EEEK!!
HEY, ZOLO! WHERE ARE YOU GOING?!
GET BACK HERE!! WE DON'T HAVE TIME TO LET YOU WANDER ALL OVER THE ENTIRE CITY!!!
DASH!!
HEE HEE! THIS LOOKS FUN!!
SNAG!!
WAIT, LUFFY!!
HAVE YOU FOUND THE THIEF?! NONE SHALL ABSCOND WITH THE NATIONAL TREASURE OF WANO!!!
HEY, LET GO! LET'S FOLLOW THEM!!
RAHH
CRINK! CRASH!!
EEEEK
LISTEN, I JUST GOT A BRILLIANT IDEA!!
GIVEN THE CURRENT CAST, I KNOW I'VE GOTTA STEP UP FOR THE GROUP.
!
YOU JUST LEAVE IT UP TO YOUR PAL FRANKY!!

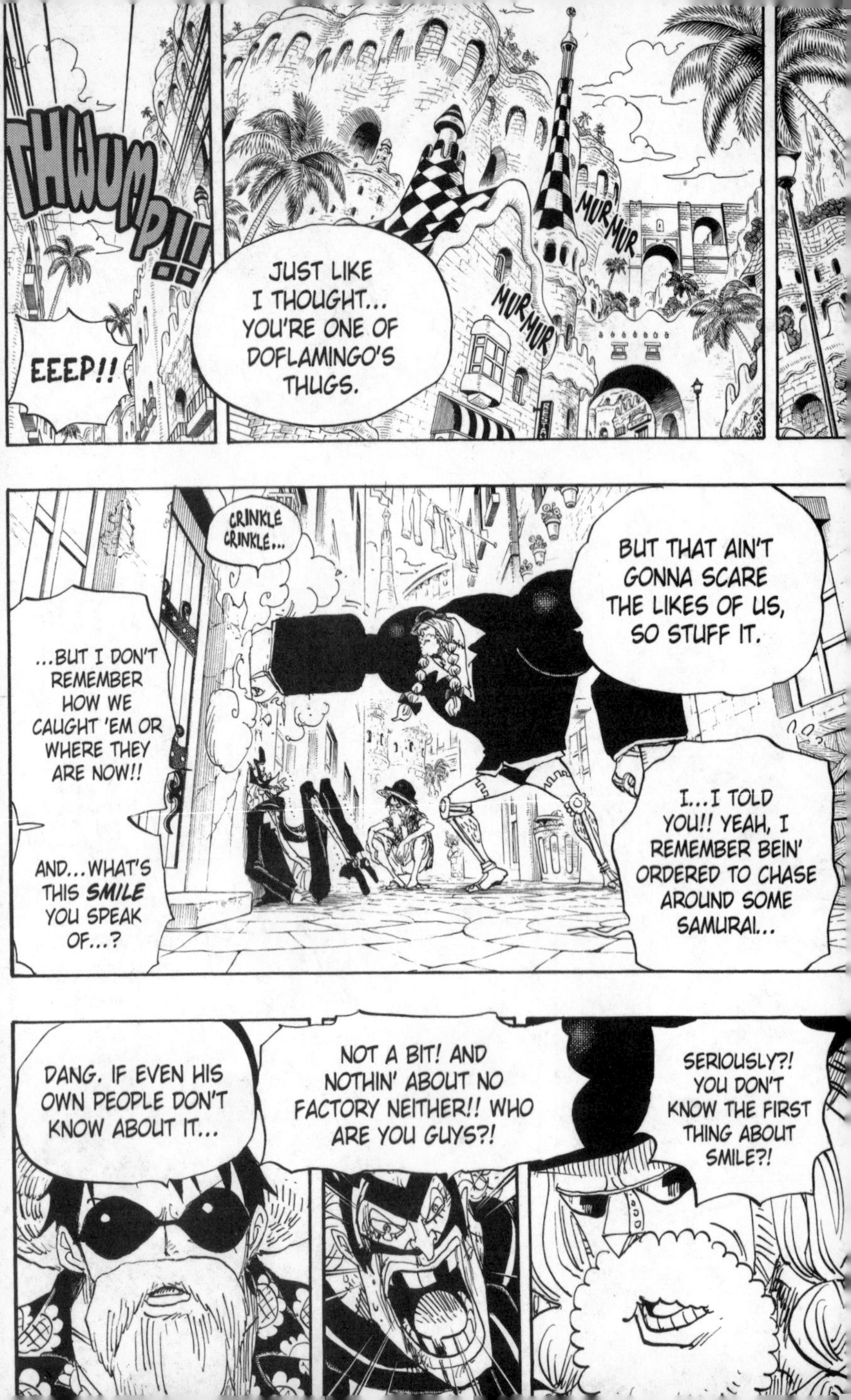
MUR MUR
MUR MUR
JUST LIKE I THOUGHT... YOU'RE ONE OF DOFLAMINGO'S THUGS.
THWUMP!!!
EEEP!!
BUT THAT AIN'T GONNA SCARE THE LIKES OF US, SO STUFF IT.
CRINKLE CRINKLE...
I...I TOLD YOU!! YEAH, I REMEMBER BEIN' ORDERED TO CHASE AROUND SOME SAMURAI...
...BUT I DON'T REMEMBER HOW WE CAUGHT 'EM OR WHERE THEY ARE NOW!!
AND...WHAT'S THIS *SMILE* YOU SPEAK OF...?
SERIOUSLY?! YOU DON'T KNOW THE FIRST THING ABOUT SMILE?!
NOT A BIT! AND NOTHIN' ABOUT NO FACTORY NEITHER!! WHO ARE YOU GUYS?!
DANG. IF EVEN HIS OWN PEOPLE DON'T KNOW ABOUT IT...

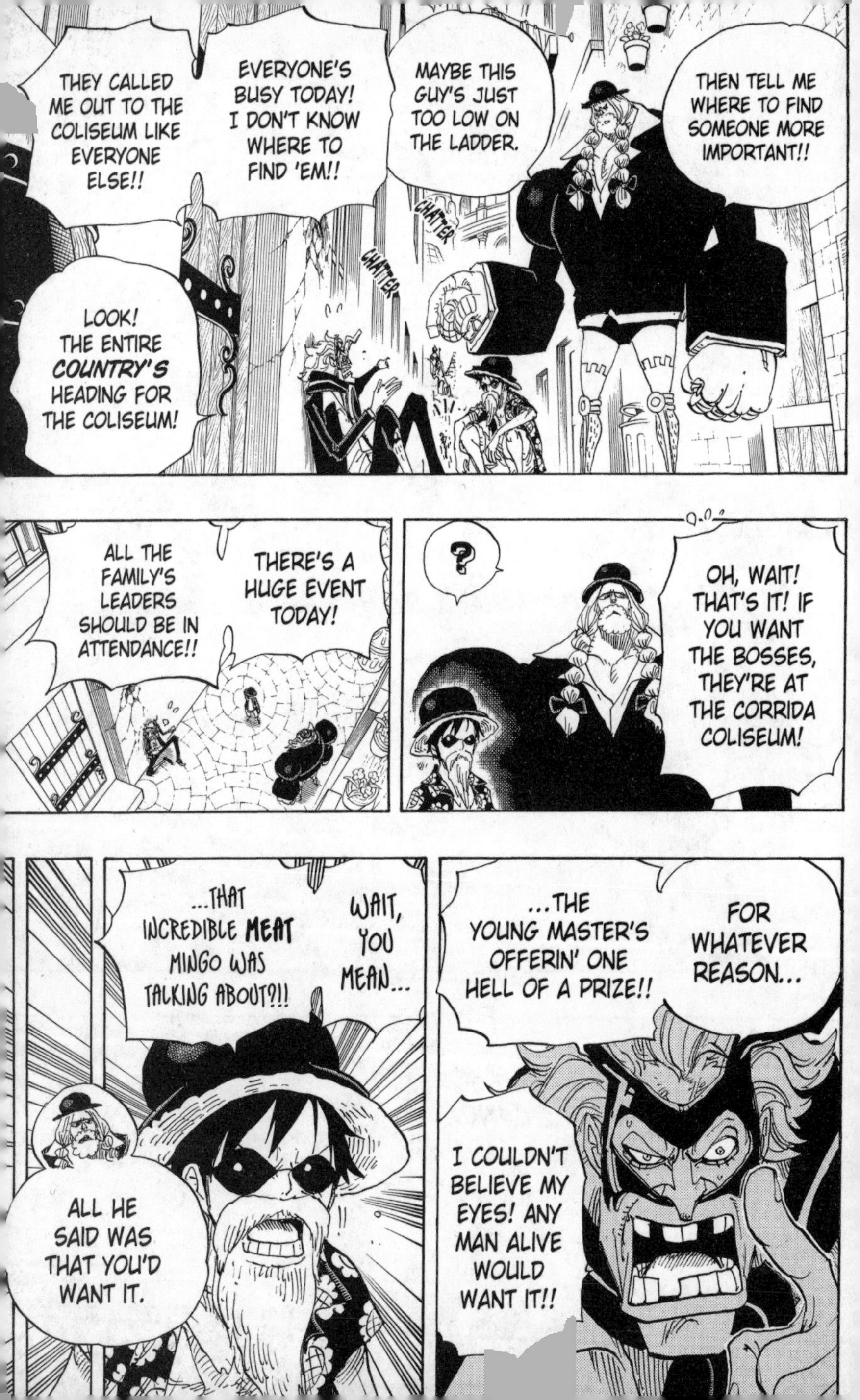
THEN TELL ME WHERE TO FIND SOMEONE MORE IMPORTANT!!
MAYBE THIS GUY'S JUST TOO LOW ON THE LADDER.
CHATTER
CHATTER
EVERYONE'S BUSY TODAY! I DON'T KNOW WHERE TO FIND 'EM!!
THEY CALLED ME OUT TO THE COLISEUM LIKE EVERYONE ELSE!!
LOOK! THE ENTIRE **COUNTRY'S** HEADING FOR THE COLISEUM!
?
OH, WAIT! THAT'S IT! IF YOU WANT THE BOSSES, THEY'RE AT THE CORRIDA COLISEUM!
THERE'S A HUGE EVENT TODAY!
ALL THE FAMILY'S LEADERS SHOULD BE IN ATTENDANCE!!
FOR WHATEVER REASON...
...THE YOUNG MASTER'S OFFERIN' ONE HELL OF A PRIZE!!
I COULDN'T BELIEVE MY EYES! ANY MAN ALIVE WOULD WANT IT!!
WAIT, YOU MEAN...
...THAT INCREDIBLE **MEAT** MINGO WAS TALKING ABOUT?!!
ALL HE SAID WAS THAT YOU'D WANT IT.

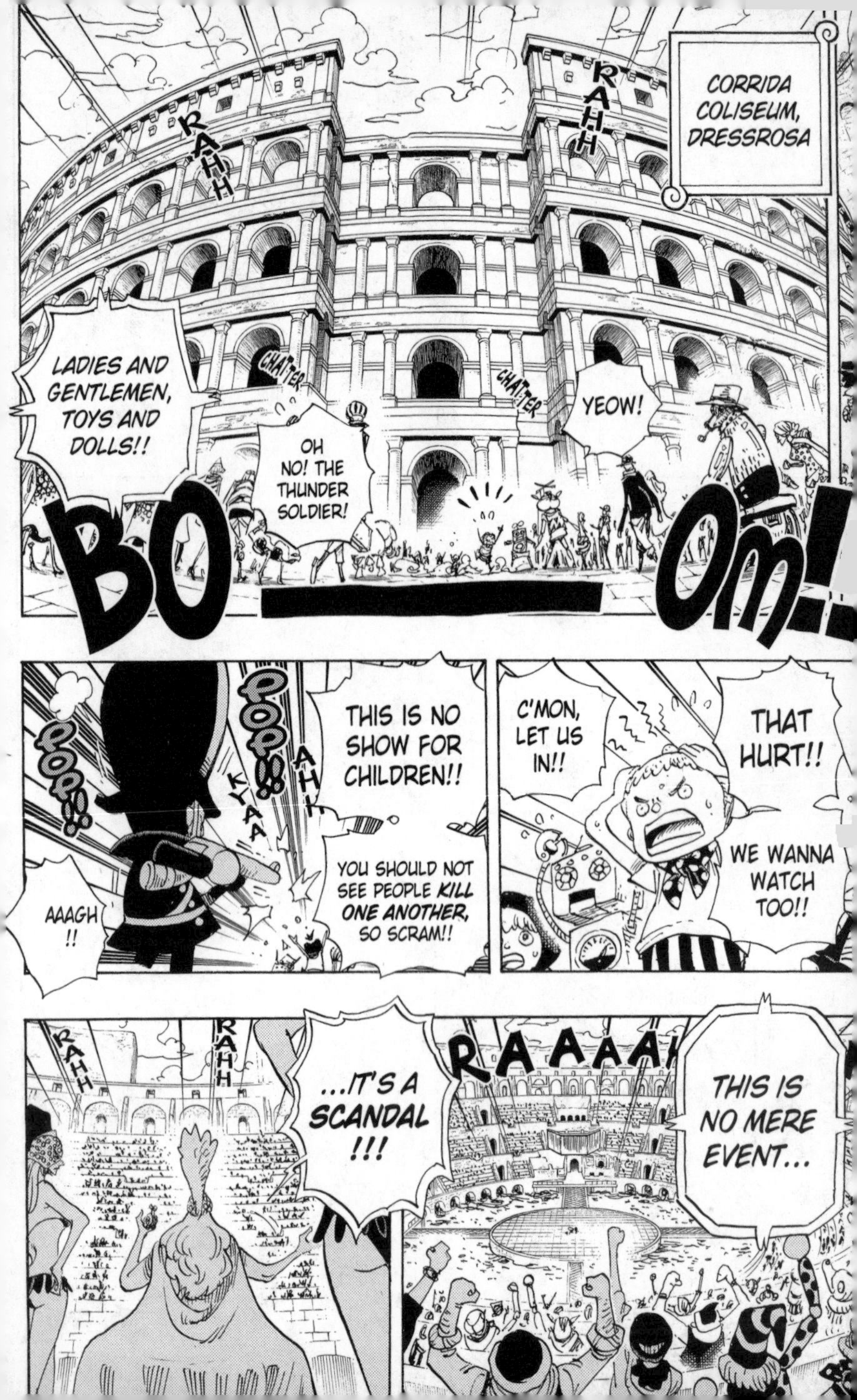
CORRIDA COLISEUM, DRESSROSA
RAHH
RAHH
YEOW!
CHATTER
OH NO! THE THUNDER SOLDIER!
CHATTER
LADIES AND GENTLEMEN, TOYS AND DOLLS!!
BO—OM!!
THAT HURT!!
C'MON, LET US IN!!
WE WANNA WATCH TOO!!
THIS IS NO SHOW FOR CHILDREN!!
AH
KYAA
POP!!
POP!!
YOU SHOULD NOT SEE PEOPLE KILL ONE ANOTHER, SO SCRAM!!
AAAGH!!
THIS IS NO MERE EVENT...
RAAAA
...IT'S A SCANDAL!!!
RAHH
RAHH

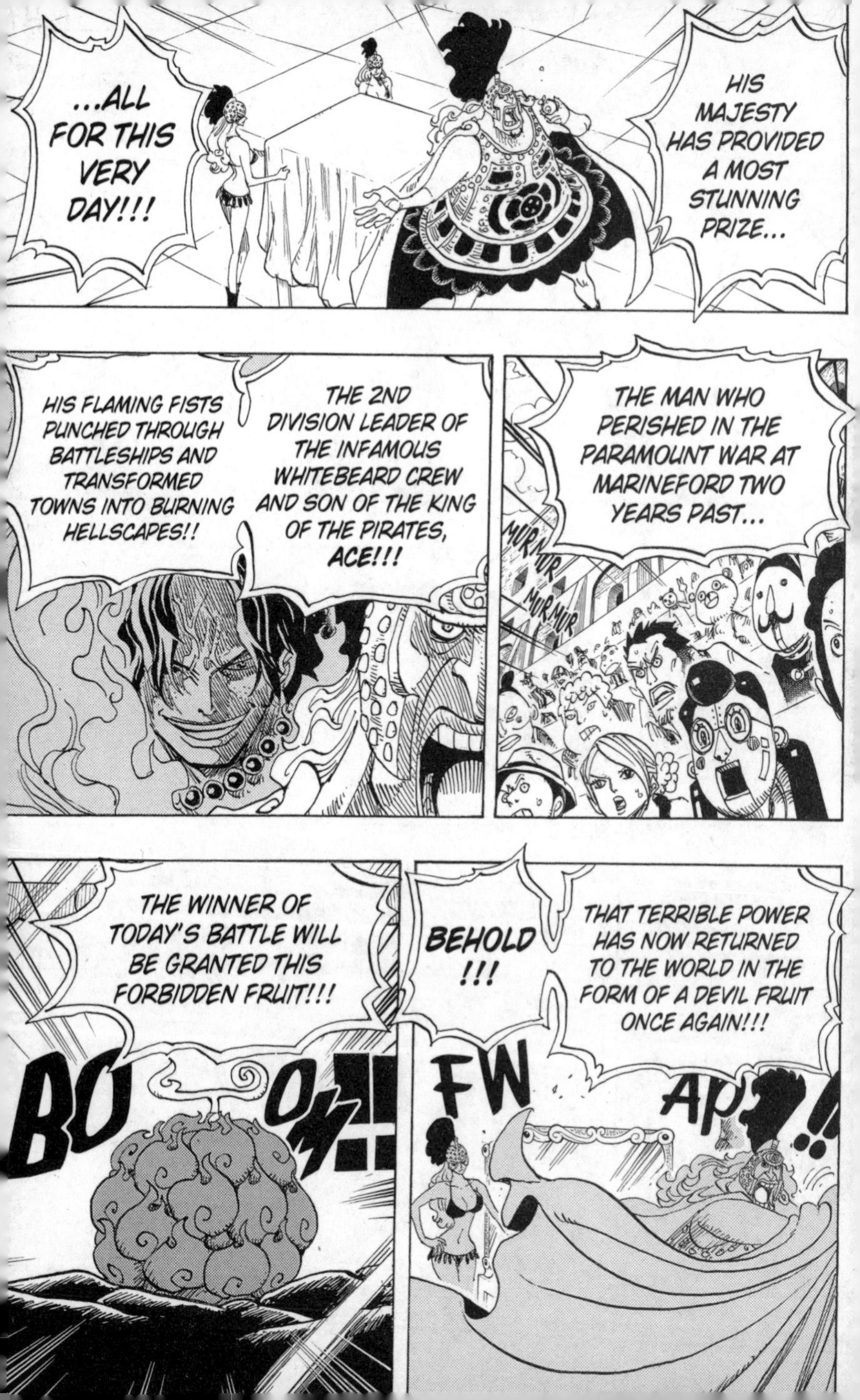
HIS MAJESTY HAS PROVIDED A MOST STUNNING PRIZE...
...ALL FOR THIS VERY DAY!!!
THE MAN WHO PERISHED IN THE PARAMOUNT WAR AT MARINEFORD TWO YEARS PAST...
MURMUR
MURMUR
THE 2ND DIVISION LEADER OF THE INFAMOUS WHITEBEARD CREW AND SON OF THE KING OF THE PIRATES, ACE!!!
HIS FLAMING FISTS PUNCHED THROUGH BATTLESHIPS AND TRANSFORMED TOWNS INTO BURNING HELLSCAPES!!
THAT TERRIBLE POWER HAS NOW RETURNED TO THE WORLD IN THE FORM OF A DEVIL FRUIT ONCE AGAIN!!!
BEHOLD!!!
FWAP!!
THE WINNER OF TODAY'S BATTLE WILL BE GRANTED THIS FORBIDDEN FRUIT!!!
BOOM!!

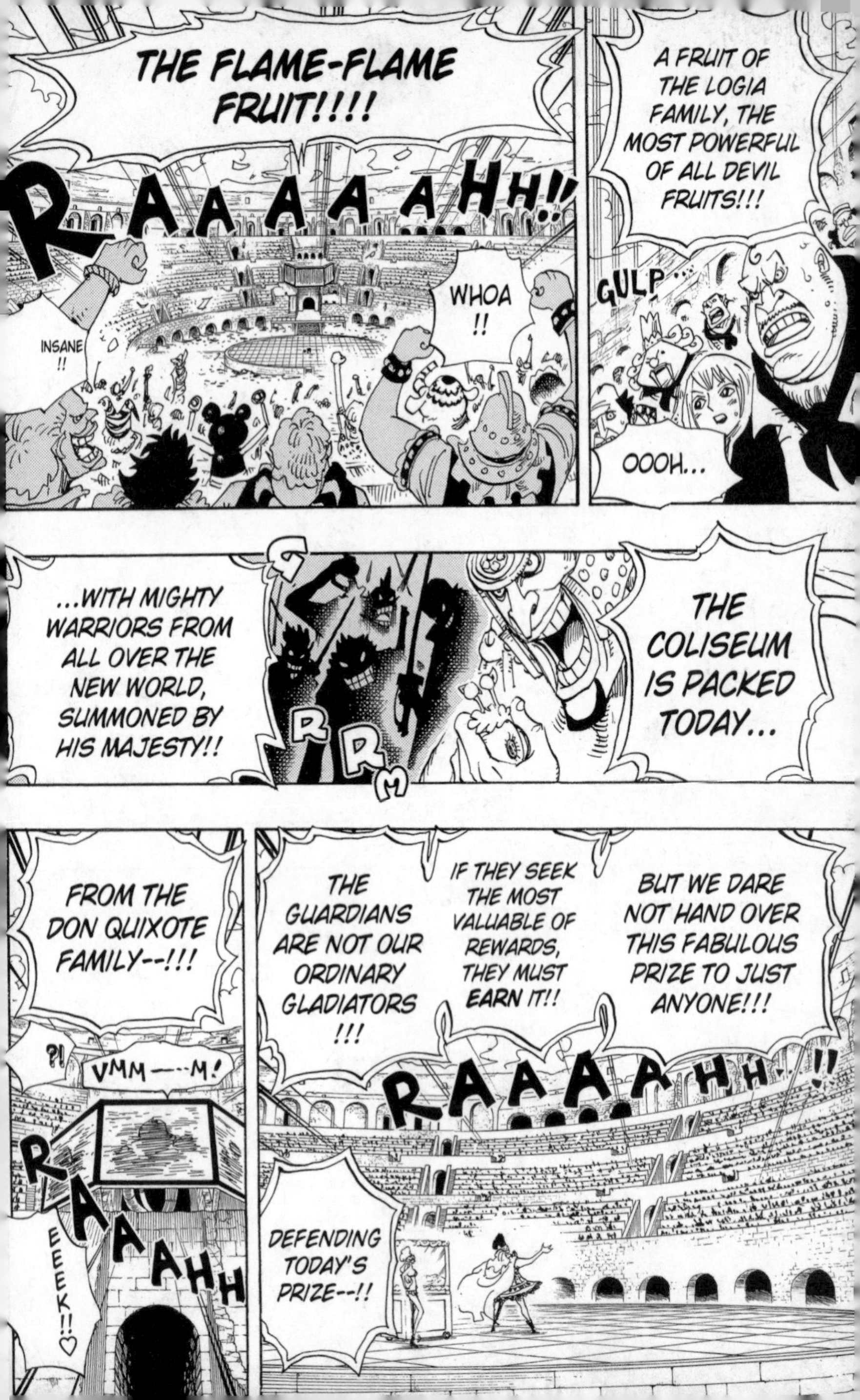
A FRUIT OF THE LOGIA FAMILY, THE MOST POWERFUL OF ALL DEVIL FRUITS!!!
GULP...
OOOH...
THE FLAME-FLAME FRUIT!!!!
RAAAAAHH!!
WHOA !!
INSANE !!
THE COLISEUM IS PACKED TODAY...
GRRRM
...WITH MIGHTY WARRIORS FROM ALL OVER THE NEW WORLD, SUMMONED BY HIS MAJESTY!!
BUT WE DARE NOT HAND OVER THIS FABULOUS PRIZE TO JUST ANYONE!!!
IF THEY SEEK THE MOST VALUABLE OF REWARDS, THEY MUST EARN IT!!
THE GUARDIANS ARE NOT OUR ORDINARY GLADIATORS !!!
RAAAAAHH!!
DEFENDING TODAY'S PRIZE--!!
FROM THE DON QUIXOTE FAMILY--!!!
VMM---M!
?!
RAAAHH
EEEEK!!♡

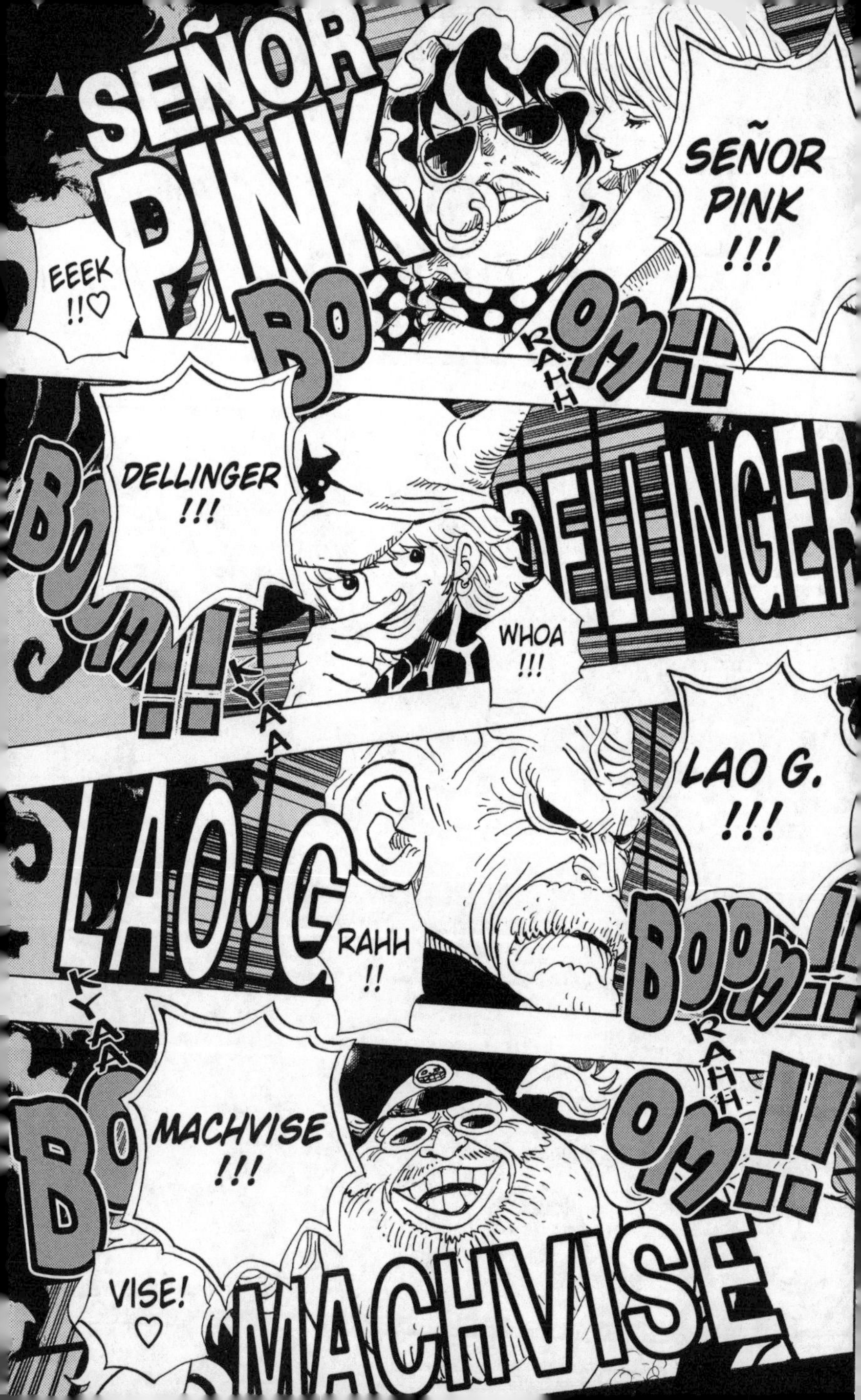
SEÑOR PINK !!!
SEÑOR PINK
BOOM!!
RAHH
EEEK !!♡
DELLINGER
WHOA !!!
DELLINGER !!!
BOOM!!
KYAA
LAO G. !!!
BOOM!!
RAHH
LAO G
RAHH !!
KYAA
BOOM!!
RAHH
MACHVISE !!!
MACHVISE
VISE! ♡

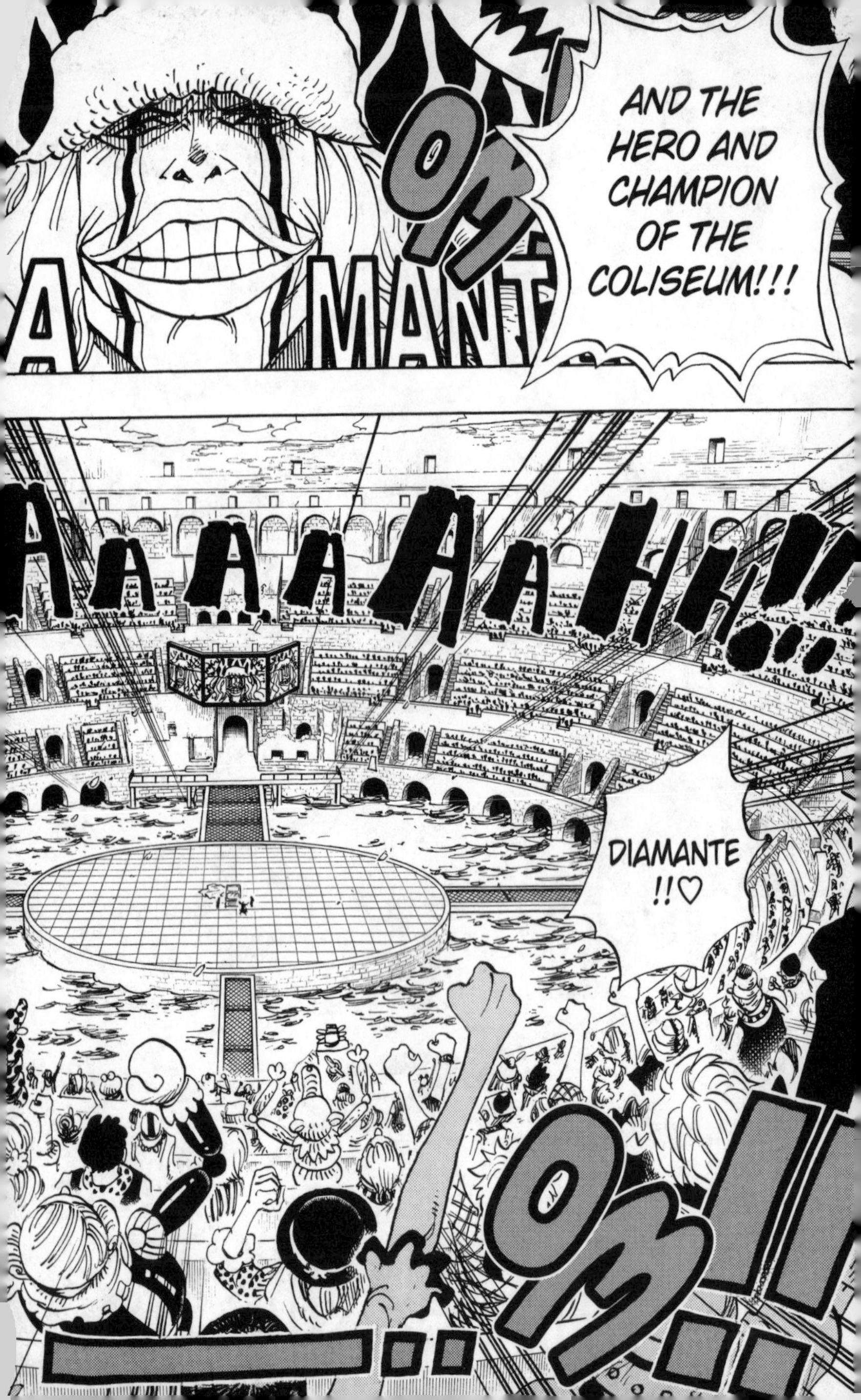
AND THE HERO AND CHAMPION OF THE COLISEUM!!!
OH
A MANT
AAAAAAHH!!...
DIAMANTE !!♡
OH!!...

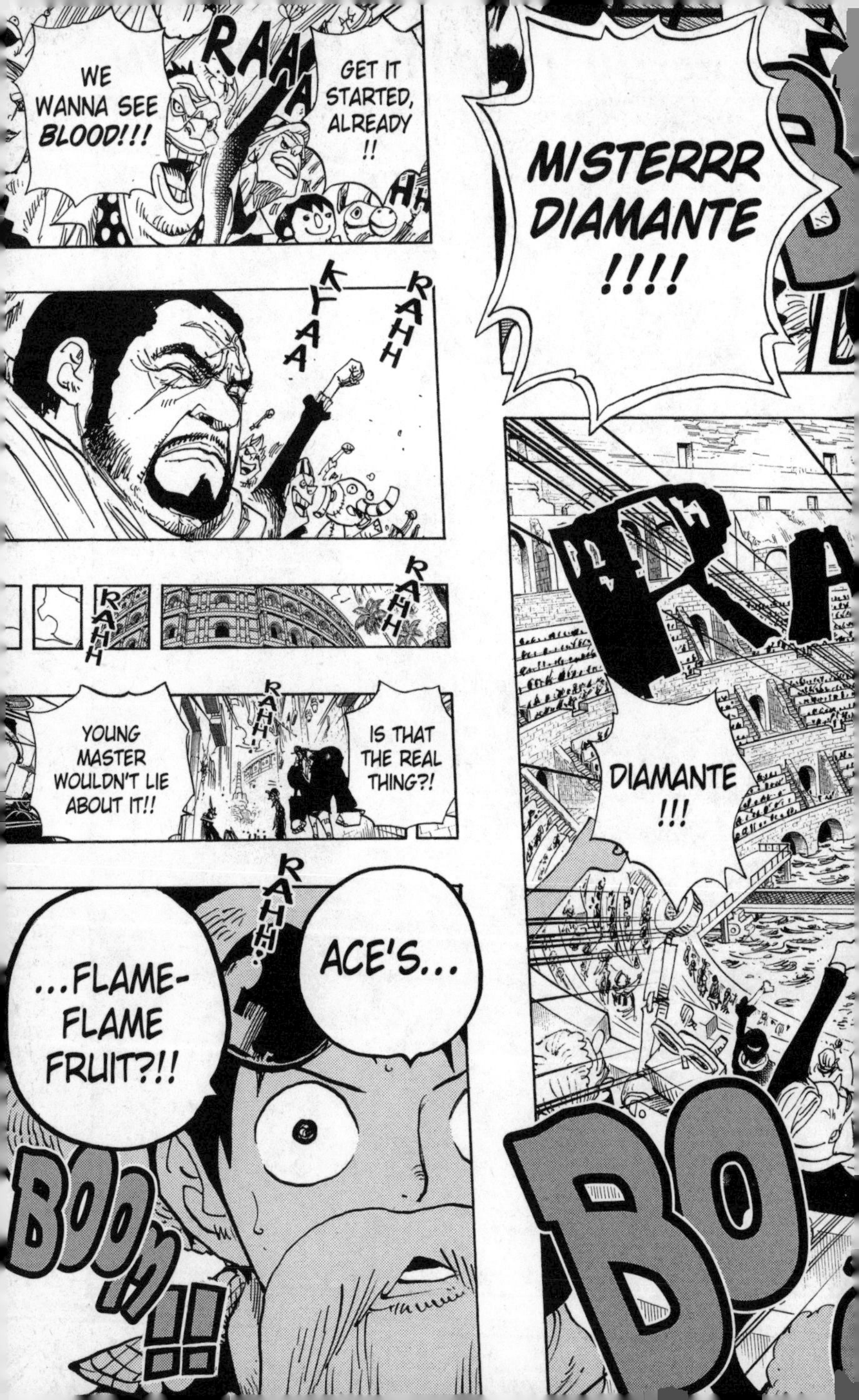
MISTERRR DIAMANTE !!!!
BRA
DIAMANTE !!!
BO
GET IT STARTED, ALREADY !!
RAAA
WE WANNA SEE BLOOD!!!
RAHH
KYAA
RAHH
RAHH
IS THAT THE REAL THING?!
RAHH!
YOUNG MASTER WOULDN'T LIE ABOUT IT!!
RAHH
ACE'S...
...FLAME-FLAME FRUIT?!!
BOOM!!

Chapter 703: WAITING ROOM

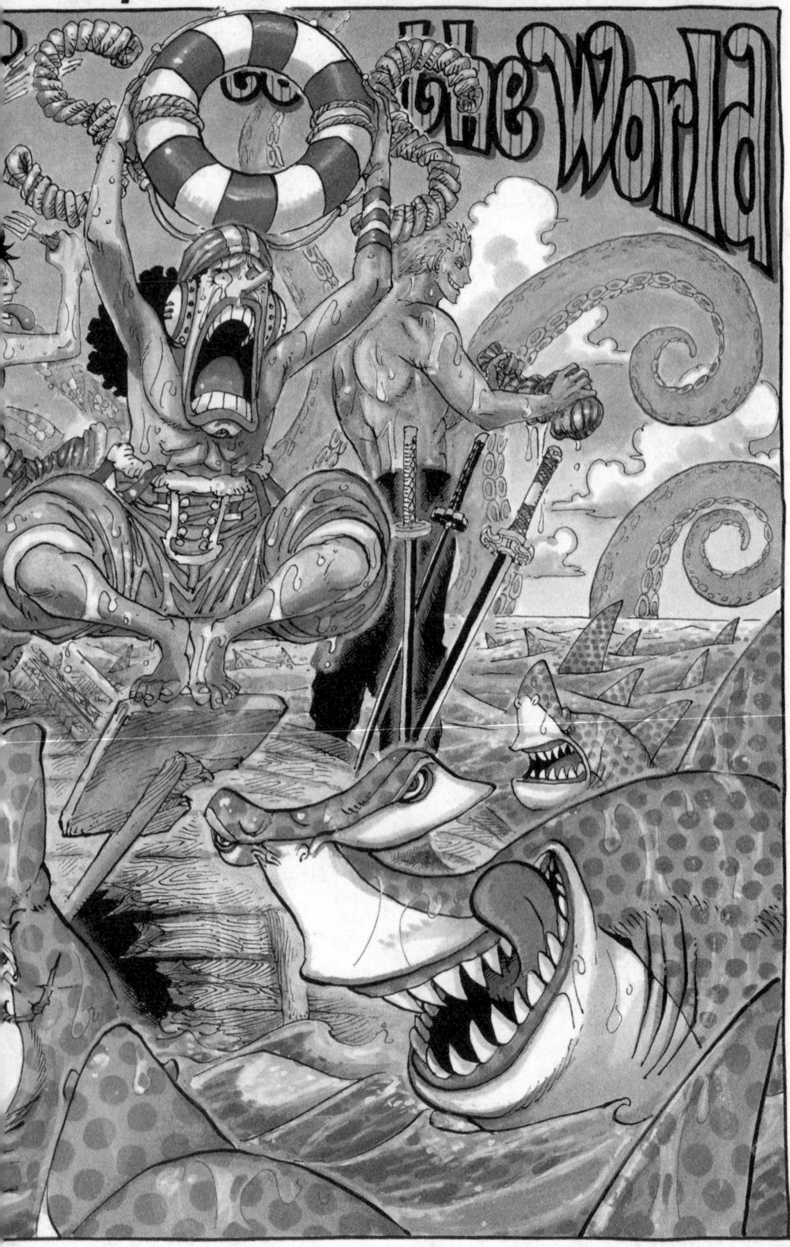

the World

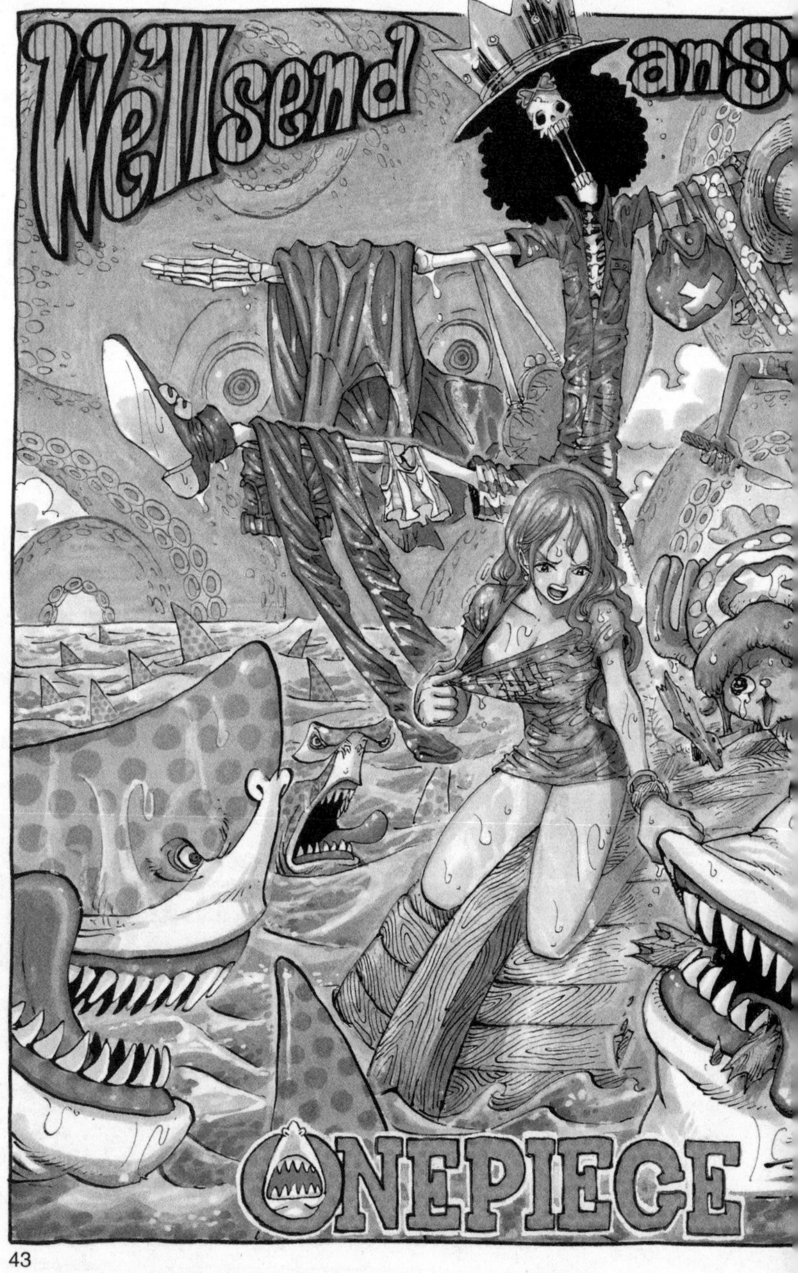
We'll send an
ONE PIECE

vol. 71

ONE PIECE

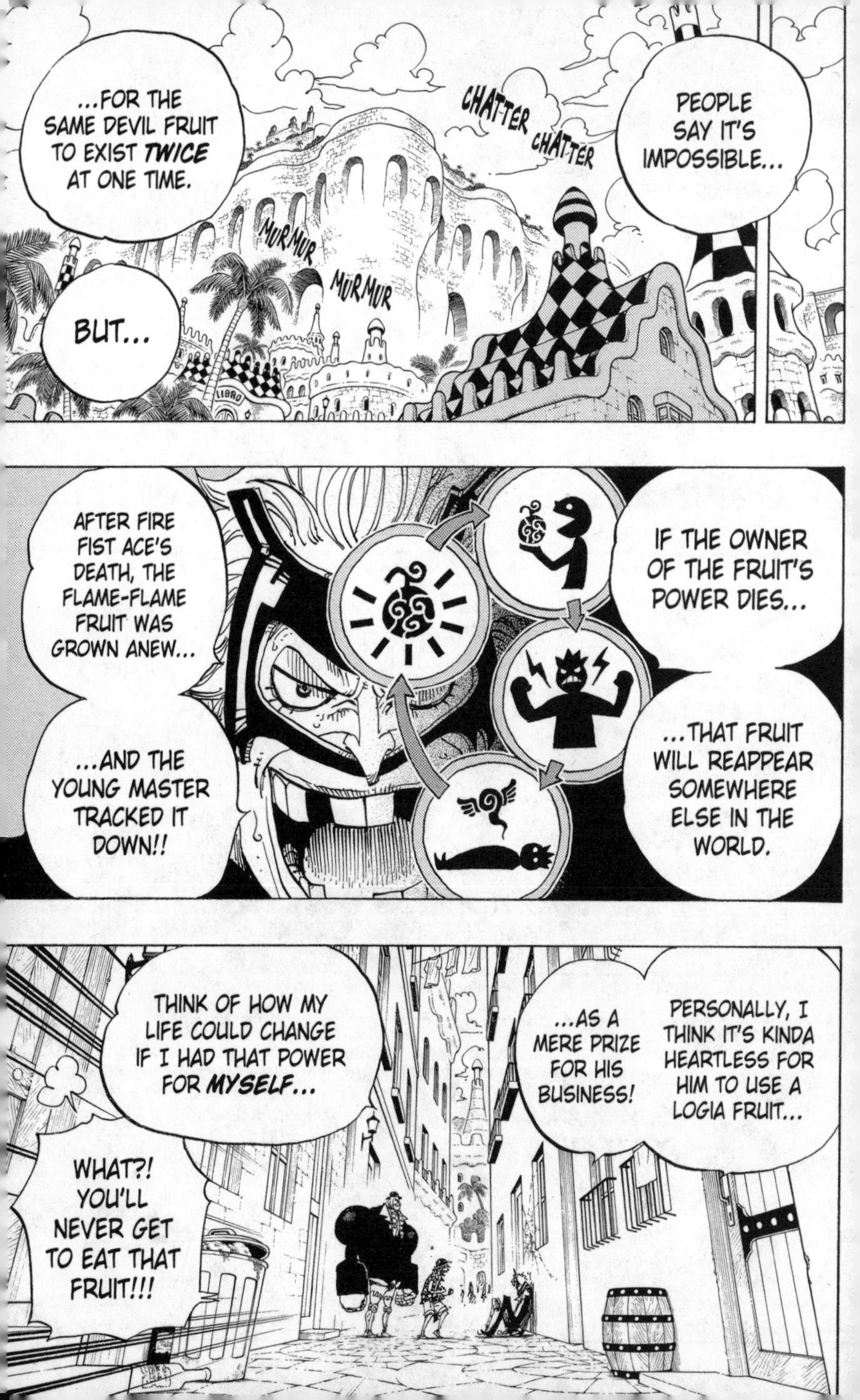
PEOPLE SAY IT'S IMPOSSIBLE...
CHATTER CHATTER
...FOR THE SAME DEVIL FRUIT TO EXIST ***TWICE*** AT ONE TIME.
MURMUR MURMUR
BUT...
IF THE OWNER OF THE FRUIT'S POWER DIES...
...THAT FRUIT WILL REAPPEAR SOMEWHERE ELSE IN THE WORLD.
AFTER FIRE FIST ACE'S DEATH, THE FLAME-FLAME FRUIT WAS GROWN ANEW...
...AND THE YOUNG MASTER TRACKED IT DOWN!!
PERSONALLY, I THINK IT'S KINDA HEARTLESS FOR HIM TO USE A LOGIA FRUIT...
...AS A MERE PRIZE FOR HIS BUSINESS!
THINK OF HOW MY LIFE COULD CHANGE IF I HAD THAT POWER FOR ***MYSELF***...
WHAT?! YOU'LL NEVER GET TO EAT THAT FRUIT!!!

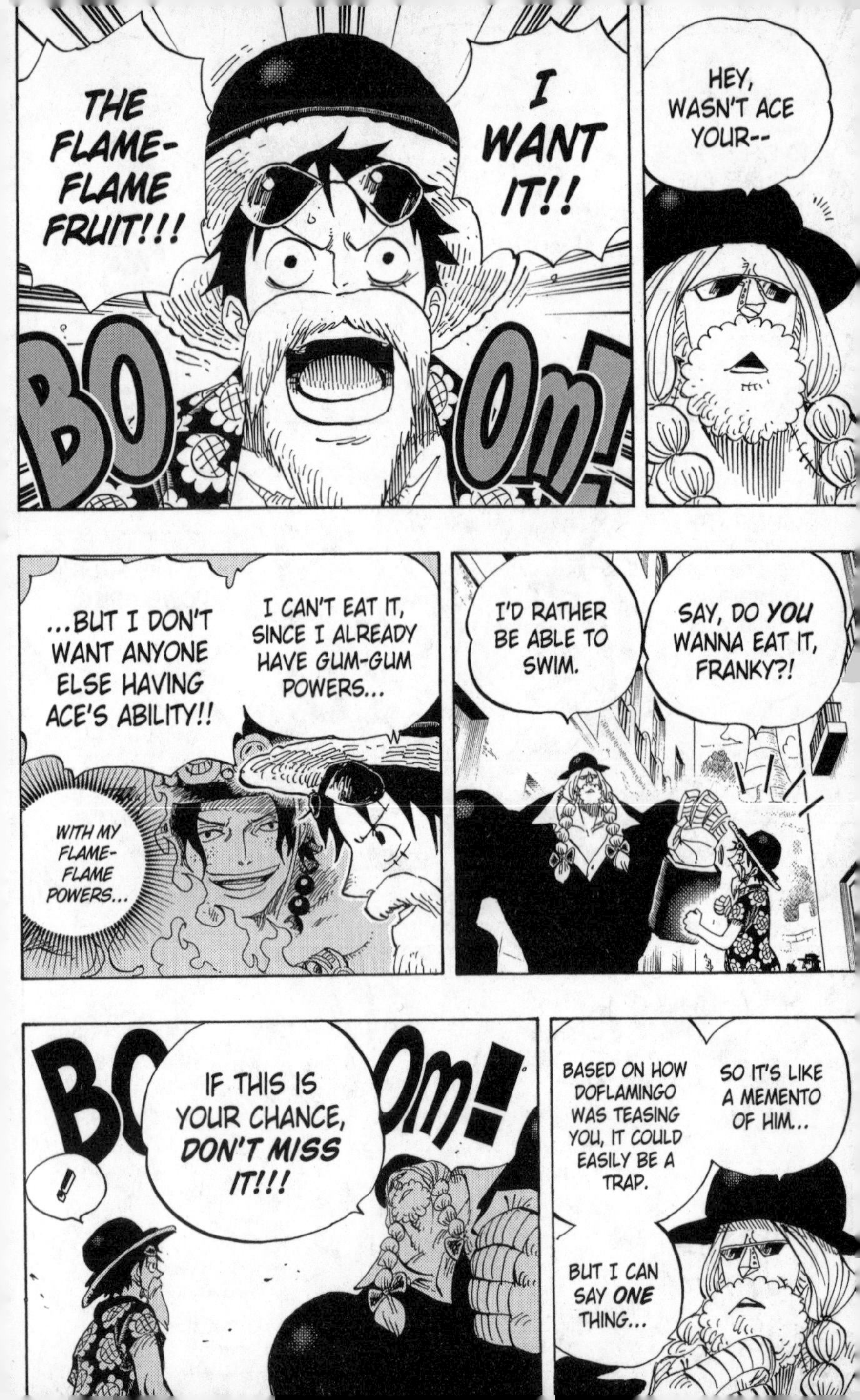
HEY, WASN'T ACE YOUR--
I WANT IT!!
THE FLAME-FLAME FRUIT!!!
BOOM!
SAY, DO YOU WANNA EAT IT, FRANKY?!
I'D RATHER BE ABLE TO SWIM.
I CAN'T EAT IT, SINCE I ALREADY HAVE GUM-GUM POWERS...
...BUT I DON'T WANT ANYONE ELSE HAVING ACE'S ABILITY!!
WITH MY FLAME-FLAME POWERS...
SO IT'S LIKE A MEMENTO OF HIM...
BASED ON HOW DOFLAMINGO WAS TEASING YOU, IT COULD EASILY BE A TRAP.
BUT I CAN SAY ONE THING...
BOOM!
IF THIS IS YOUR CHANCE, DON'T MISS IT!!!
!

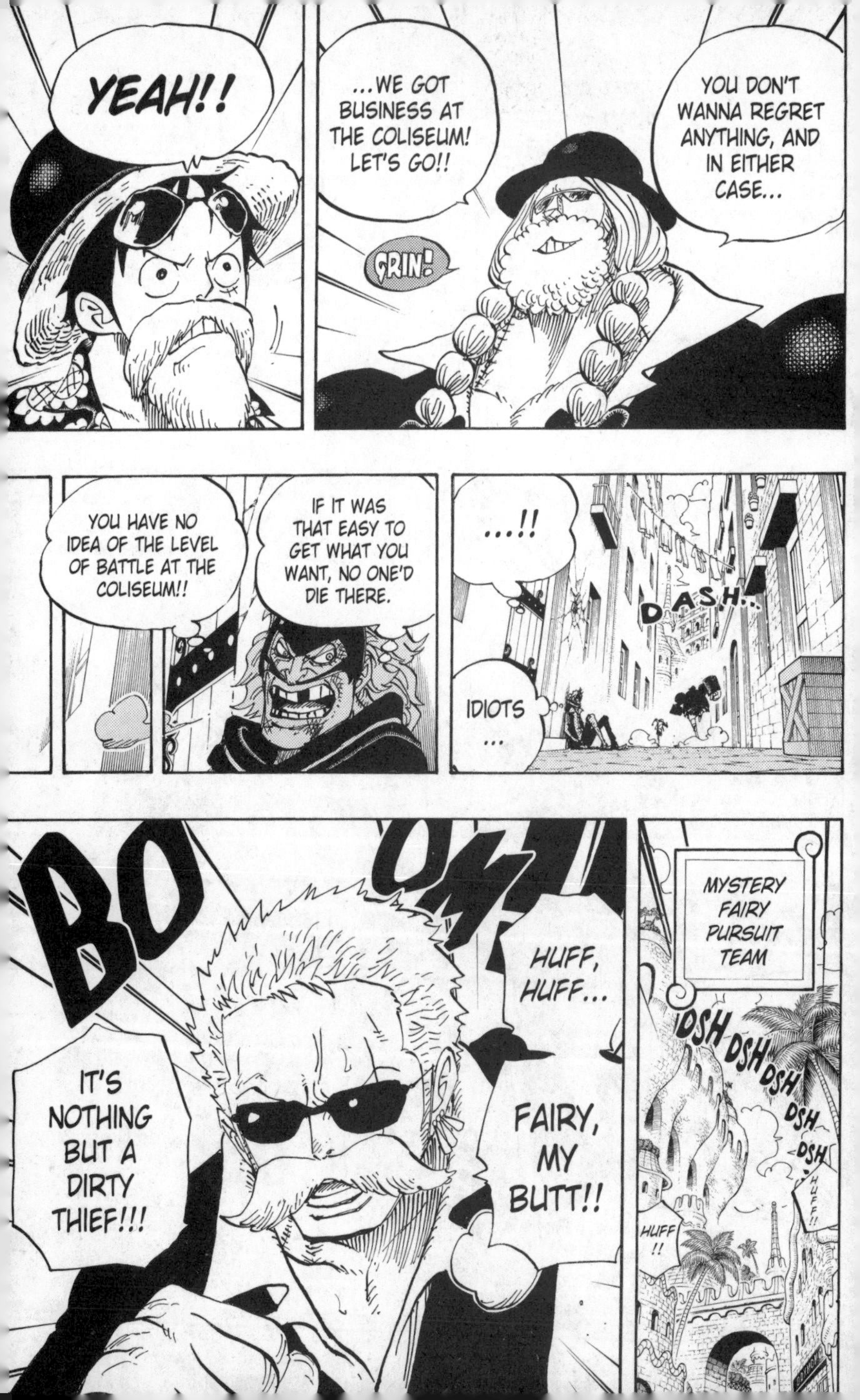
YOU DON'T WANNA REGRET ANYTHING, AND IN EITHER CASE...
...WE GOT BUSINESS AT THE COLISEUM! LET'S GO!!
GRIN!
YEAH!!
...!!
DASH..
IDIOTS ...
IF IT WAS THAT EASY TO GET WHAT YOU WANT, NO ONE'D DIE THERE.
YOU HAVE NO IDEA OF THE LEVEL OF BATTLE AT THE COLISEUM!!
MYSTERY FAIRY PURSUIT TEAM
DSH DSH DSH DSH DSH
HUFF!!
HUFF!!
BOOM
HUFF, HUFF...
FAIRY, MY BUTT!!
IT'S NOTHING BUT A DIRTY THIEF!!!

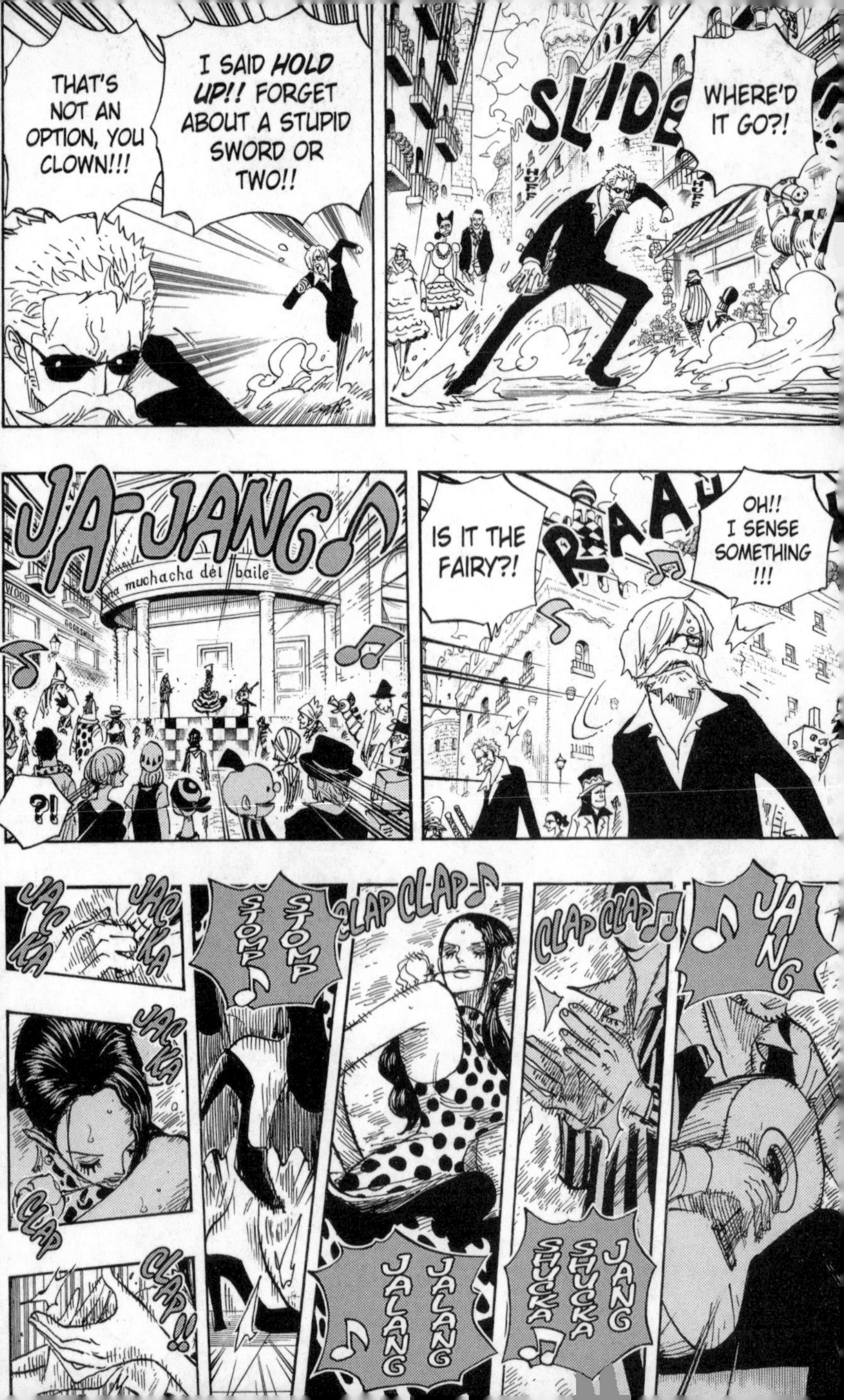

SLIDE
HUFF
HUFF
WHERE'D IT GO?!
I SAID **HOLD UP!!** FORGET ABOUT A STUPID SWORD OR TWO!!
THAT'S NOT AN OPTION, YOU CLOWN!!!
OH!! I SENSE SOMETHING!!!
RAAA
IS IT THE FAIRY?!
JA-JANG♪
muchacha del baile
?!
JANG
CLAP CLAP♫
JANG SHUCKA SHUCKA
CLAP CLAP♪
JALANG JALANG
STOMP STOMP
JACKA
JACKA
JACKA
CLAP
CLAP!!

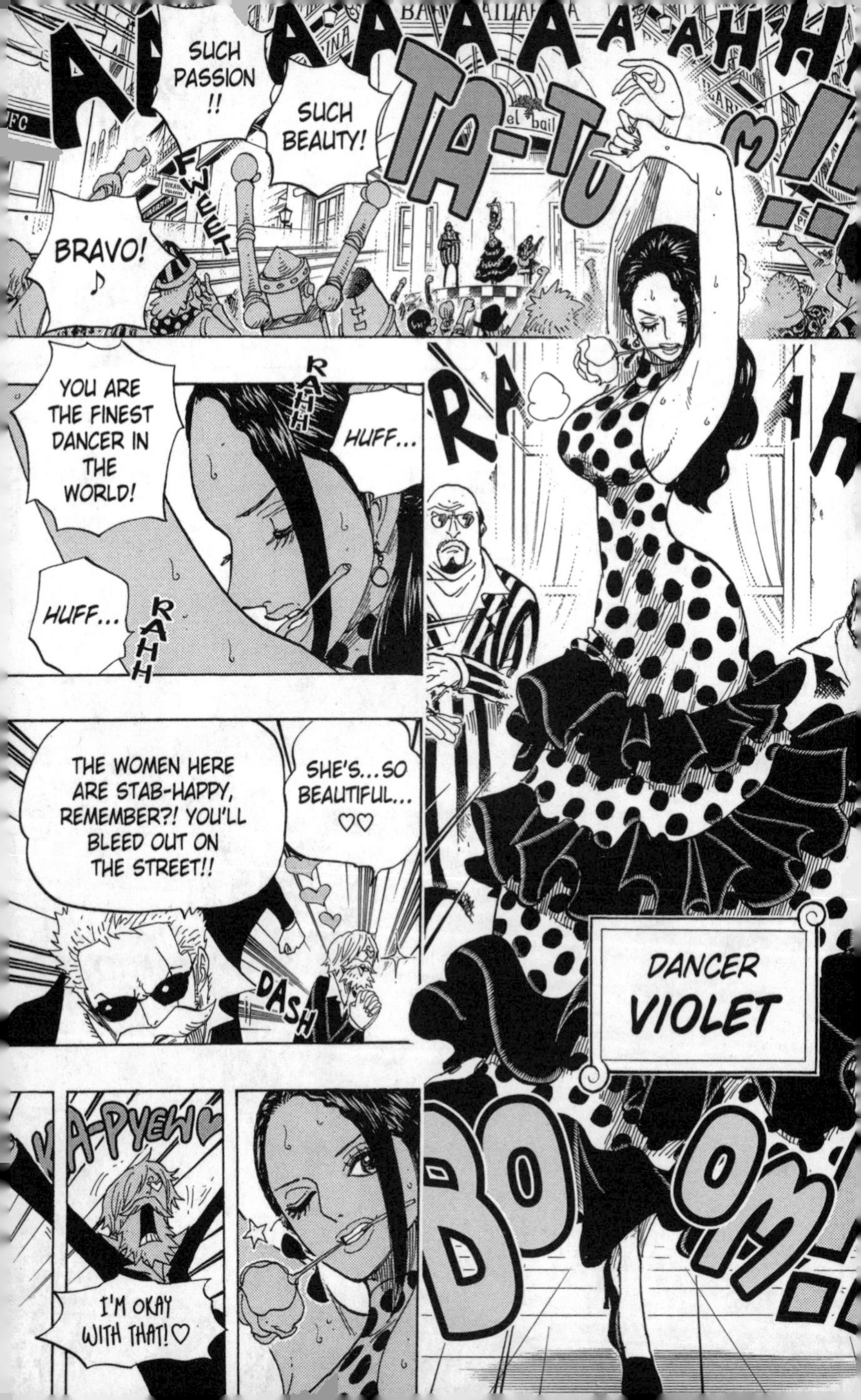

AAAAAAAHH
TA-TUM!!
SUCH BEAUTY!
SUCH PASSION!!
FWEET
BRAVO! ♪
el bail
RAAH
DANCER VIOLET
BOOM!!
YOU ARE THE FINEST DANCER IN THE WORLD!
RAHH
HUFF...
HUFF...
RAHH
SHE'S...SO BEAUTIFUL... ♡♡
THE WOMEN HERE ARE STAB-HAPPY, REMEMBER?! YOU'LL BLEED OUT ON THE STREET!!
DASH
A-PYEW♡
I'M OKAY WITH THAT!♡

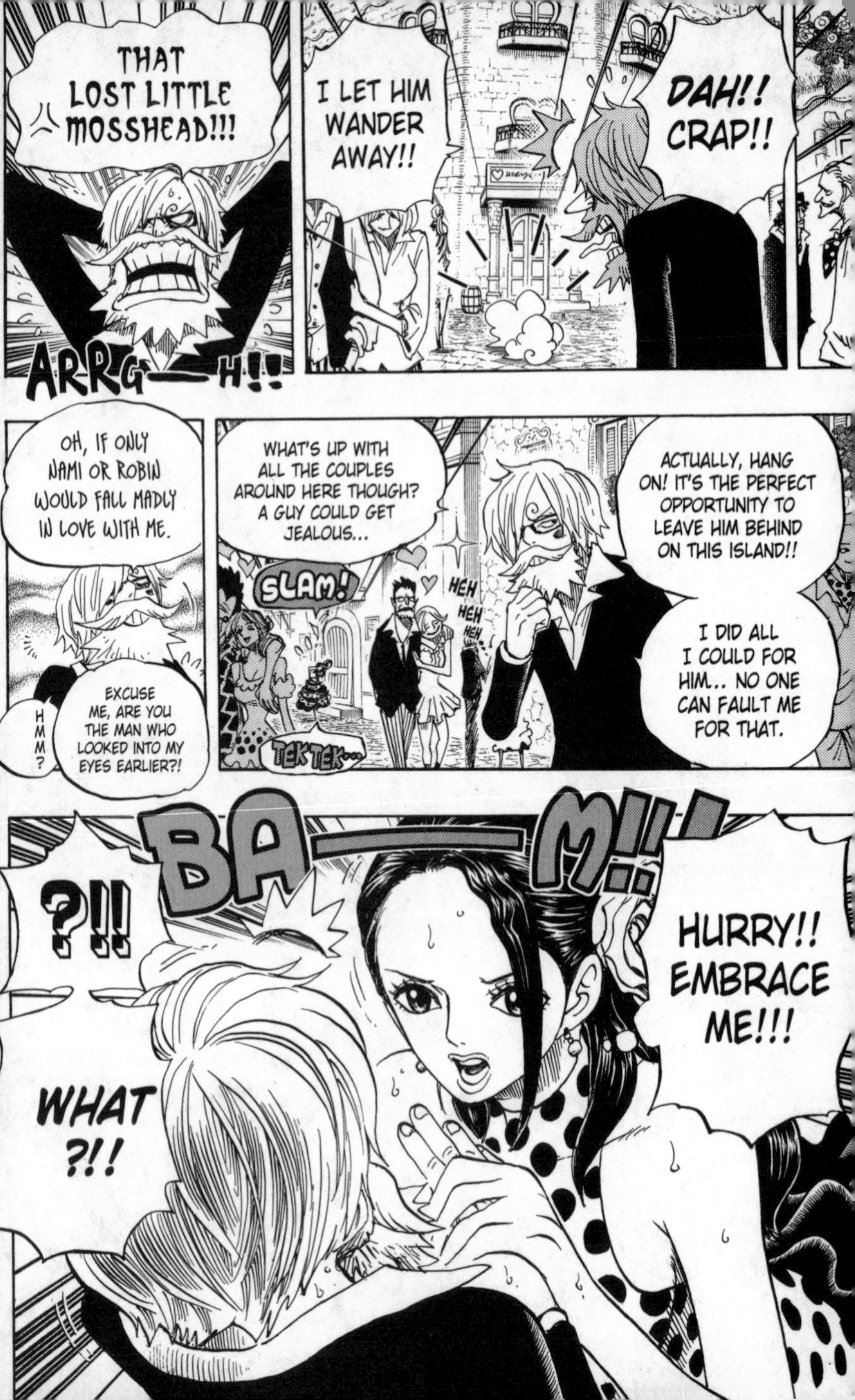
DAH!! CRAP!!
I LET HIM WANDER AWAY!!
THAT LOST LITTLE MOSSHEAD!!!
ARRG—H!!
ACTUALLY, HANG ON! IT'S THE PERFECT OPPORTUNITY TO LEAVE HIM BEHIND ON THIS ISLAND!!
I DID ALL I COULD FOR HIM... NO ONE CAN FAULT ME FOR THAT.
WHAT'S UP WITH ALL THE COUPLES AROUND HERE THOUGH? A GUY COULD GET JEALOUS...
HEH HEH HEH
SLAM!
TEK TEK...
OH, IF ONLY NAMI OR ROBIN WOULD FALL MADLY IN LOVE WITH ME.
EXCUSE ME, ARE YOU THE MAN WHO LOOKED INTO MY EYES EARLIER?!
HMM?
BA—M!!!
HURRY!! EMBRACE ME!!!
?!!
WHAT?!!

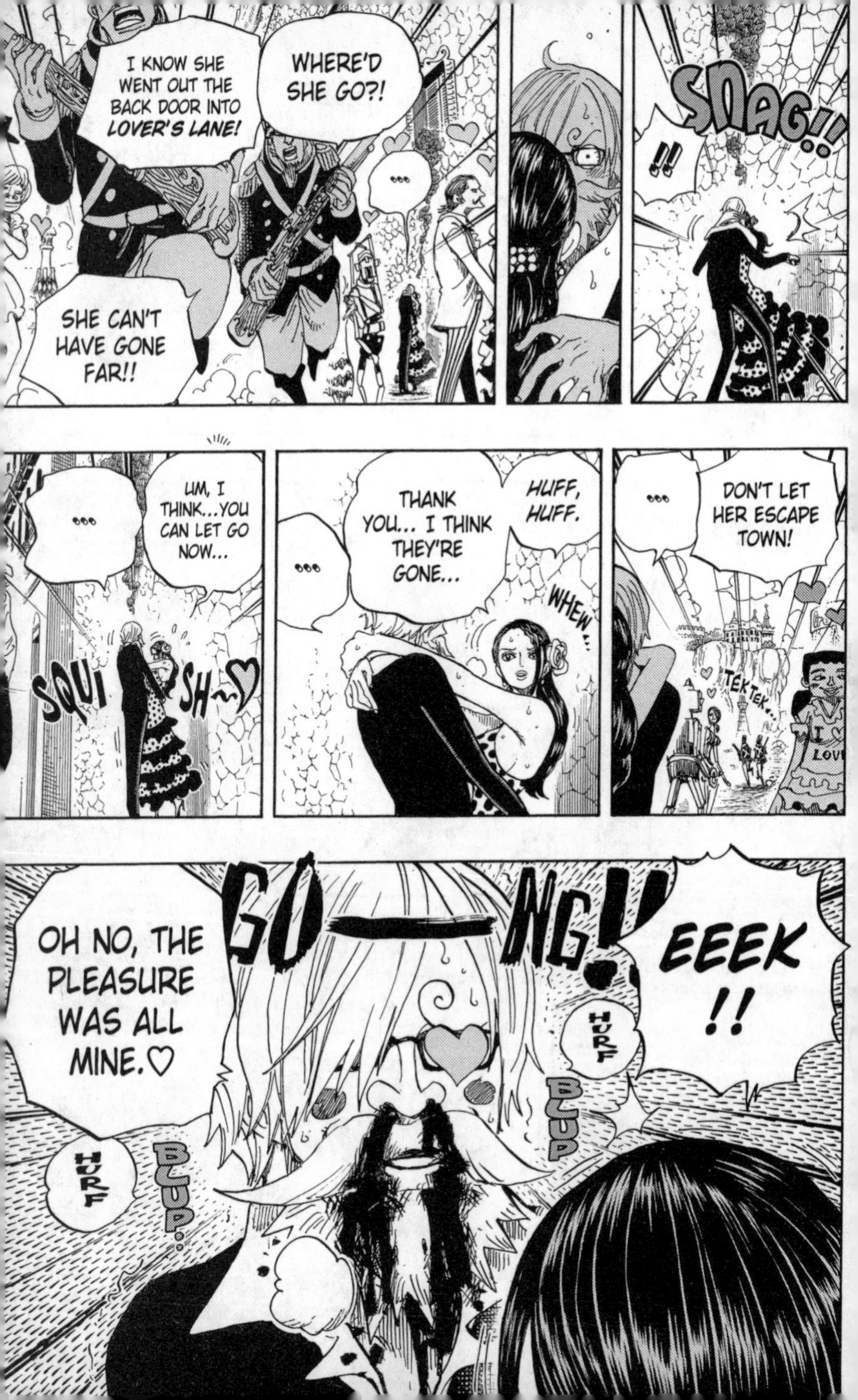
SNAG!!
!!
WHERE'D SHE GO?!
I KNOW SHE WENT OUT THE BACK DOOR INTO LOVER'S LANE!
...
SHE CAN'T HAVE GONE FAR!!
DON'T LET HER ESCAPE TOWN!
...
TEKTEK...
HUFF, HUFF.
THANK YOU... I THINK THEY'RE GONE...
...
WHEW...
UM, I THINK...YOU CAN LET GO NOW...
...
SQUISH~♡
EEEK!!
GO—NG!
OH NO, THE PLEASURE WAS ALL MINE.♡
HURF
BLUP
HURF
BLUP..

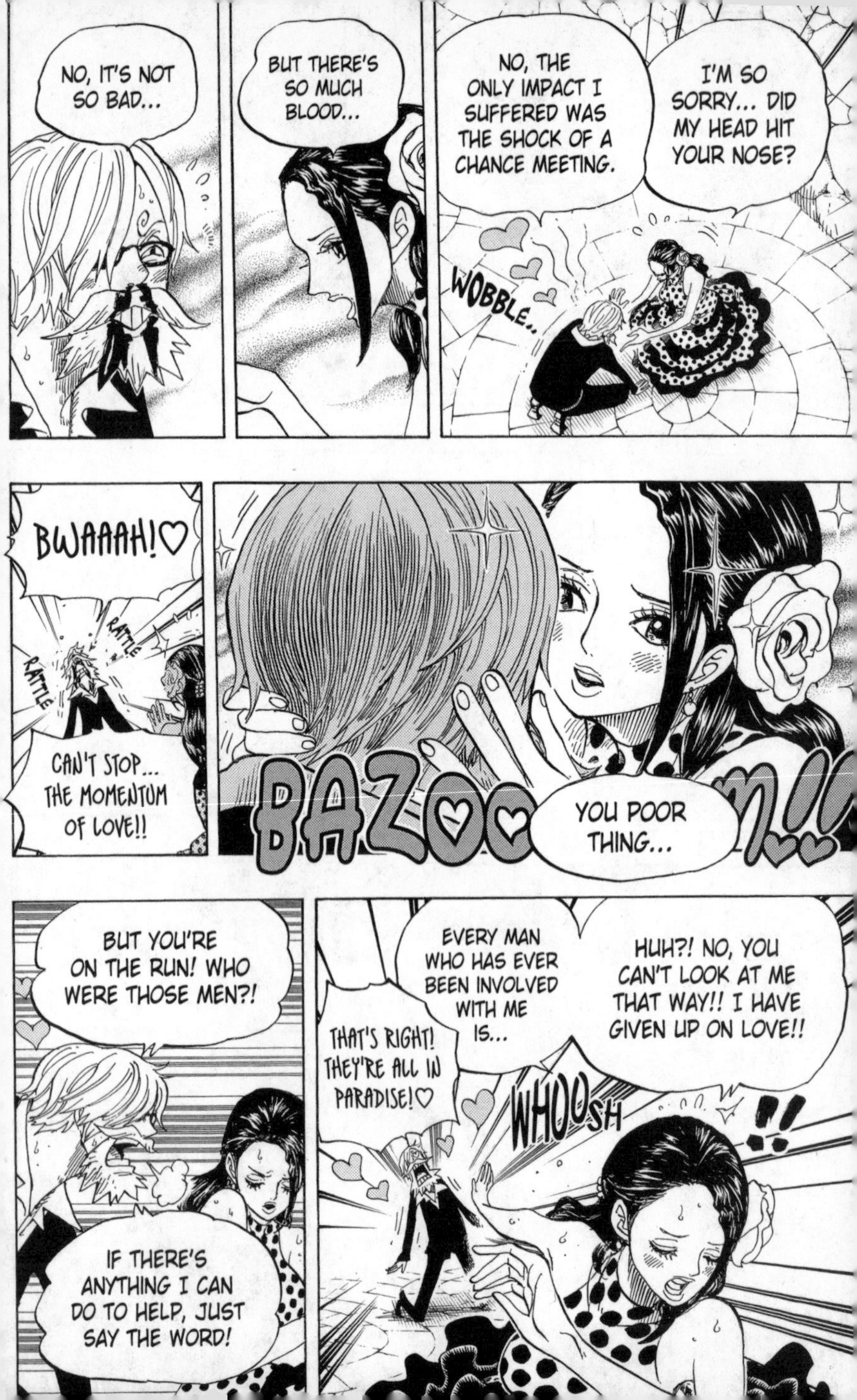
I'M SO SORRY... DID MY HEAD HIT YOUR NOSE?
NO, THE ONLY IMPACT I SUFFERED WAS THE SHOCK OF A CHANCE MEETING.
WOBBLE...
BUT THERE'S SO MUCH BLOOD...
NO, IT'S NOT SO BAD...
YOU POOR THING...
BWAAAH!♡
RATTLE
RATTLE
CAN'T STOP... THE MOMENTUM OF LOVE!!
HUH?! NO, YOU CAN'T LOOK AT ME THAT WAY!! I HAVE GIVEN UP ON LOVE!!
EVERY MAN WHO HAS EVER BEEN INVOLVED WITH ME IS...
THAT'S RIGHT! THEY'RE ALL IN PARADISE!♡
WHOOSH
BUT YOU'RE ON THE RUN! WHO WERE THOSE MEN?!
IF THERE'S ANYTHING I CAN DO TO HELP, JUST SAY THE WORD!

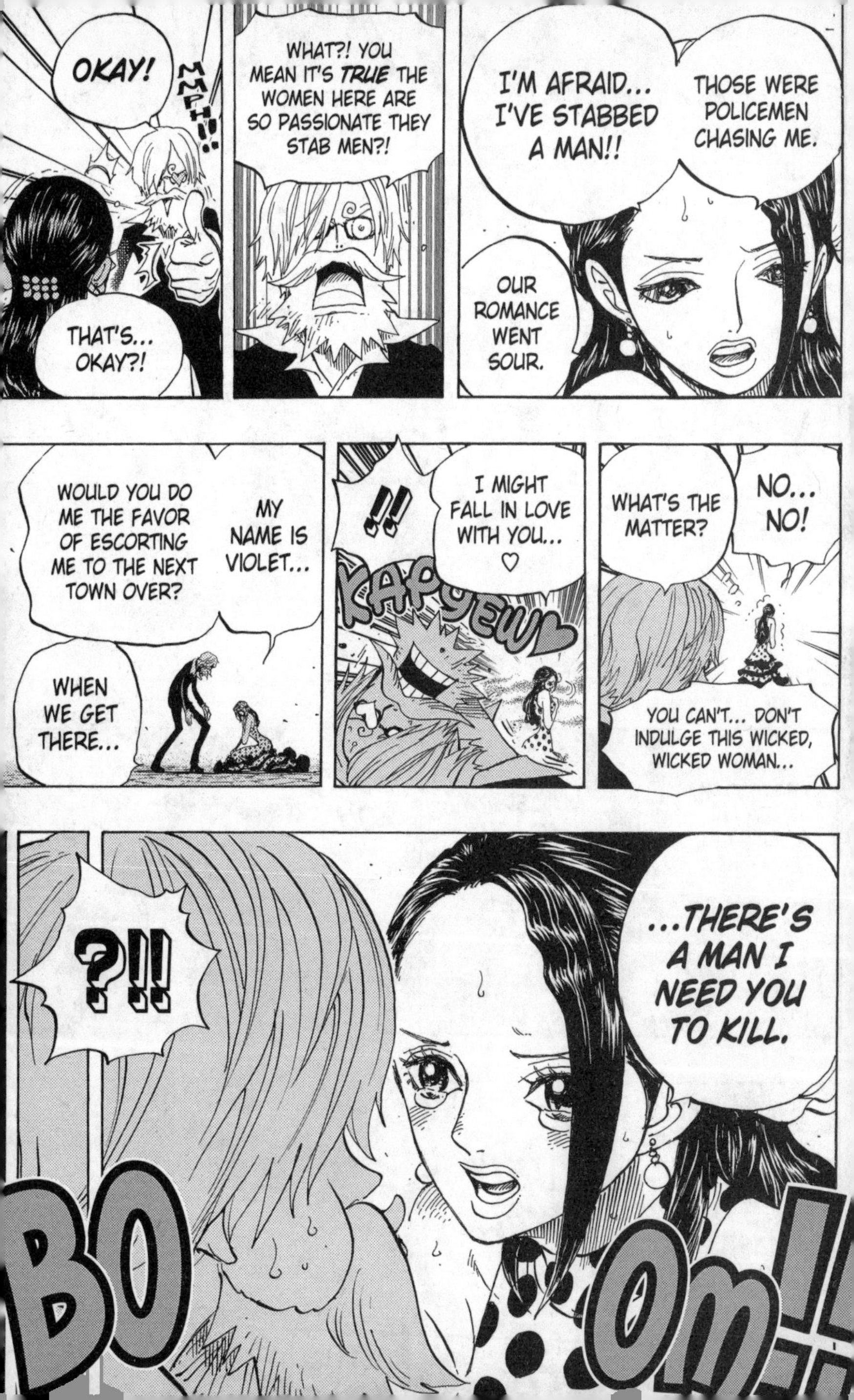
THOSE WERE POLICEMEN CHASING ME.
I'M AFRAID... I'VE STABBED A MAN!!
OUR ROMANCE WENT SOUR.
WHAT?! YOU MEAN IT'S TRUE THE WOMEN HERE ARE SO PASSIONATE THEY STAB MEN?!
MMMPH!!
OKAY!
THAT'S... OKAY?!
NO... NO!
WHAT'S THE MATTER?
YOU CAN'T... DON'T INDULGE THIS WICKED, WICKED WOMAN...
I MIGHT FALL IN LOVE WITH YOU... ♡
!!
KAPYEW
MY NAME IS VIOLET...
WOULD YOU DO ME THE FAVOR OF ESCORTING ME TO THE NEXT TOWN OVER?
WHEN WE GET THERE...
...THERE'S A MAN I NEED YOU TO KILL.
?!!
BOOM!!

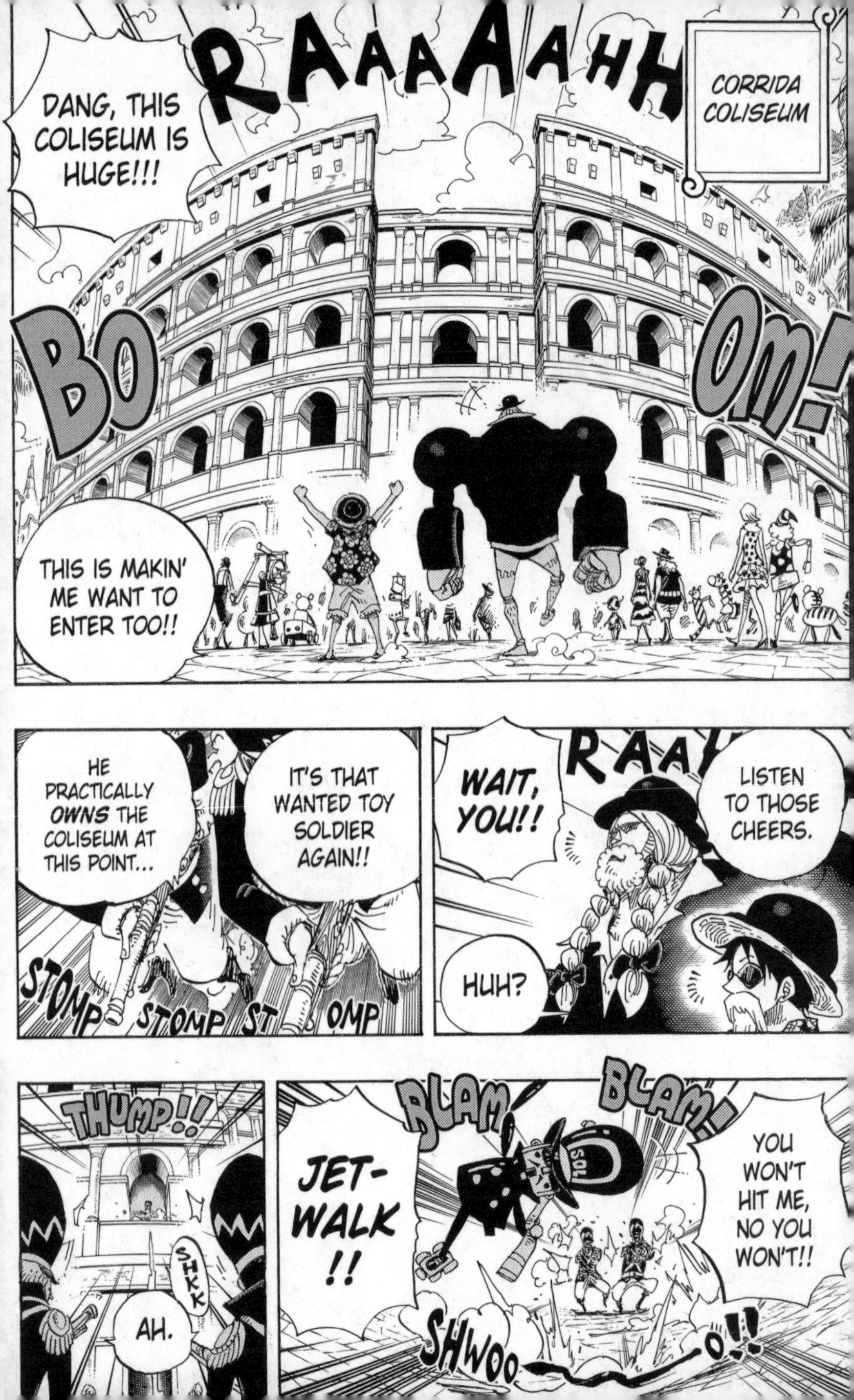
CORRIDA COLISEUM
RAAAAAHH
DANG, THIS COLISEUM IS HUGE!!!
BOOM!!
THIS IS MAKIN' ME WANT TO ENTER TOO!!
RAA
LISTEN TO THOSE CHEERS.
WAIT, YOU!!
HUH?
IT'S THAT WANTED TOY SOLDIER AGAIN!!
HE PRACTICALLY OWNS THE COLISEUM AT THIS POINT...
STOMP STOMP STOMP
BLAM BLAM!
YOU WON'T HIT ME, NO YOU WON'T!!
JET-WALK!!
SHWOO—O!!
THUMP!!
SHKK
AH.

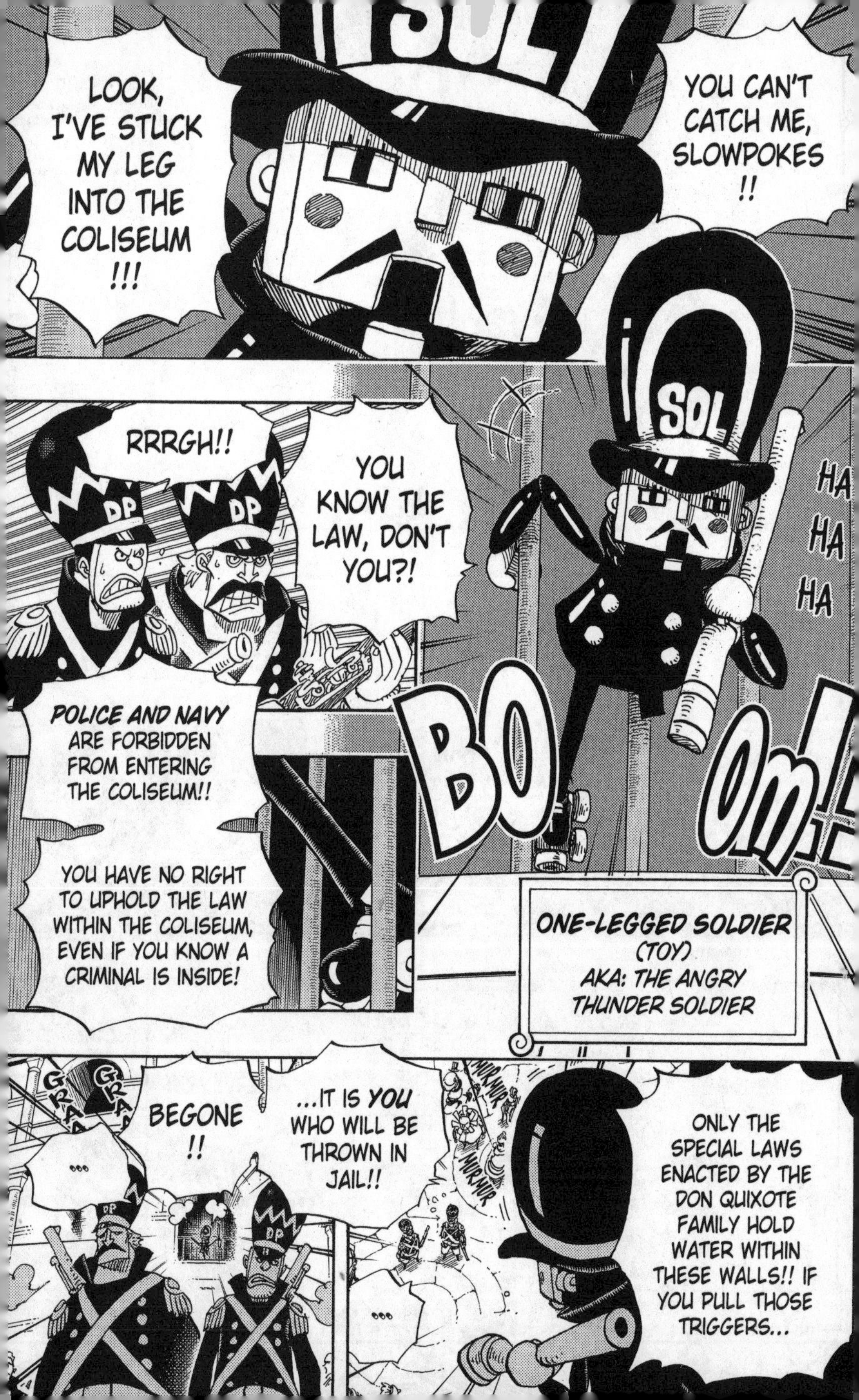
YOU CAN'T CATCH ME, SLOWPOKES!!
LOOK, I'VE STUCK MY LEG INTO THE COLISEUM!!!
HA HA HA
BOOM!
ONE-LEGGED SOLDIER (TOY) AKA: THE ANGRY THUNDER SOLDIER
RRRGH!!
YOU KNOW THE LAW, DON'T YOU?!
POLICE AND NAVY ARE FORBIDDEN FROM ENTERING THE COLISEUM!!
YOU HAVE NO RIGHT TO UPHOLD THE LAW WITHIN THE COLISEUM, EVEN IF YOU KNOW A CRIMINAL IS INSIDE!
ONLY THE SPECIAL LAWS ENACTED BY THE DON QUIXOTE FAMILY HOLD WATER WITHIN THESE WALLS!! IF YOU PULL THOSE TRIGGERS...
...IT IS YOU WHO WILL BE THROWN IN JAIL!!
MURMUR
MURMUR
...
BEGONE!!
...
GRAA
GRAA

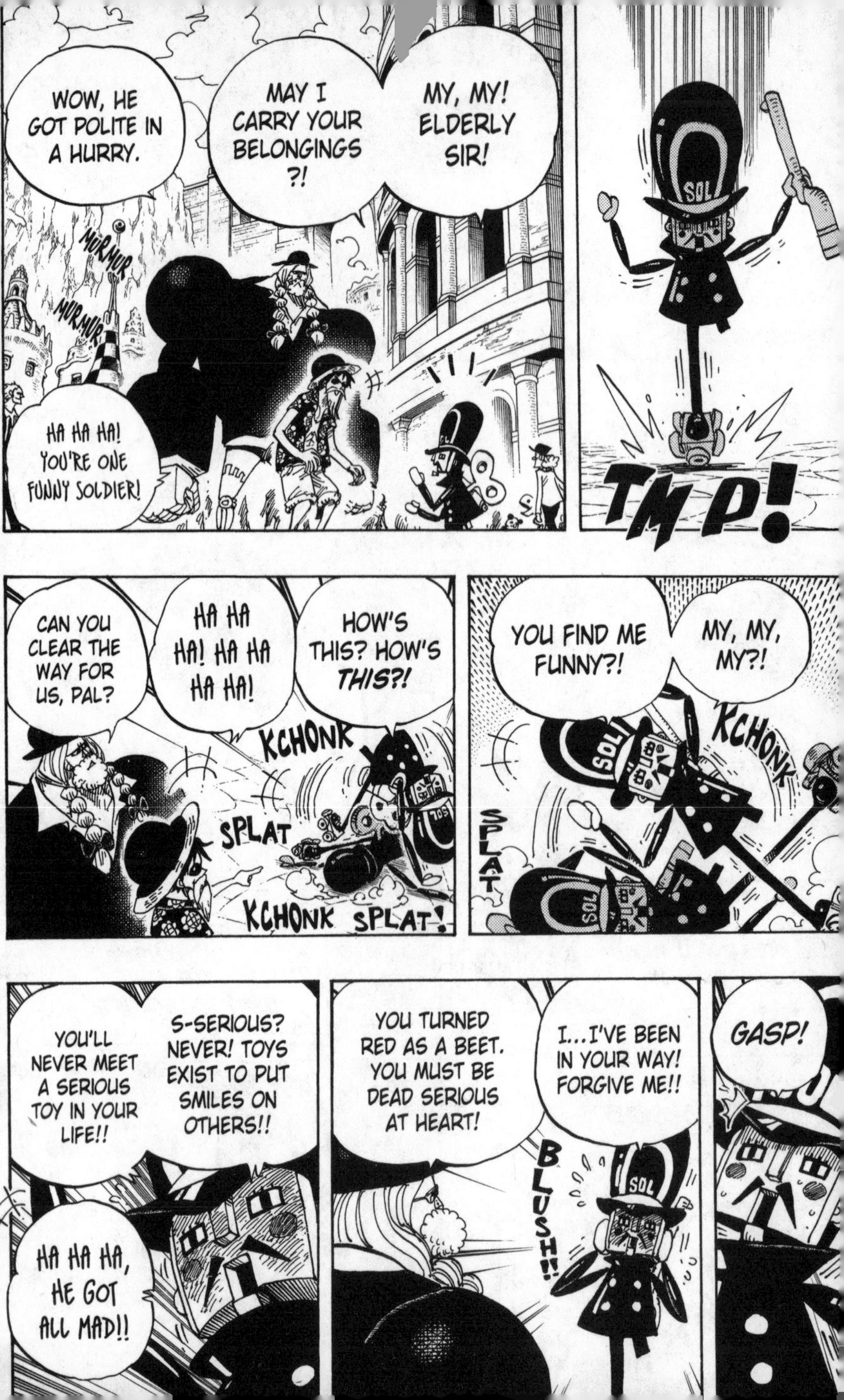
TMP!
MY, MY! ELDERLY SIR!
MAY I CARRY YOUR BELONGINGS ?!
WOW, HE GOT POLITE IN A HURRY.
MURMUR
MURMUR
HA HA HA! YOU'RE ONE FUNNY SOLDIER!
MY, MY, MY?!
YOU FIND ME FUNNY?!
KCHONK
SPLAT
HOW'S THIS? HOW'S THIS?!
HA HA HA! HA HA HA HA HA!
CAN YOU CLEAR THE WAY FOR US, PAL?
KCHONK
SPLAT
KCHONK SPLAT!
GASP!
I...I'VE BEEN IN YOUR WAY! FORGIVE ME!!
YOU TURNED RED AS A BEET. YOU MUST BE DEAD SERIOUS AT HEART!
BLUSH!!
S-SERIOUS? NEVER! TOYS EXIST TO PUT SMILES ON OTHERS!!
YOU'LL NEVER MEET A SERIOUS TOY IN YOUR LIFE!!
HA HA HA, HE GOT ALL MAD!!

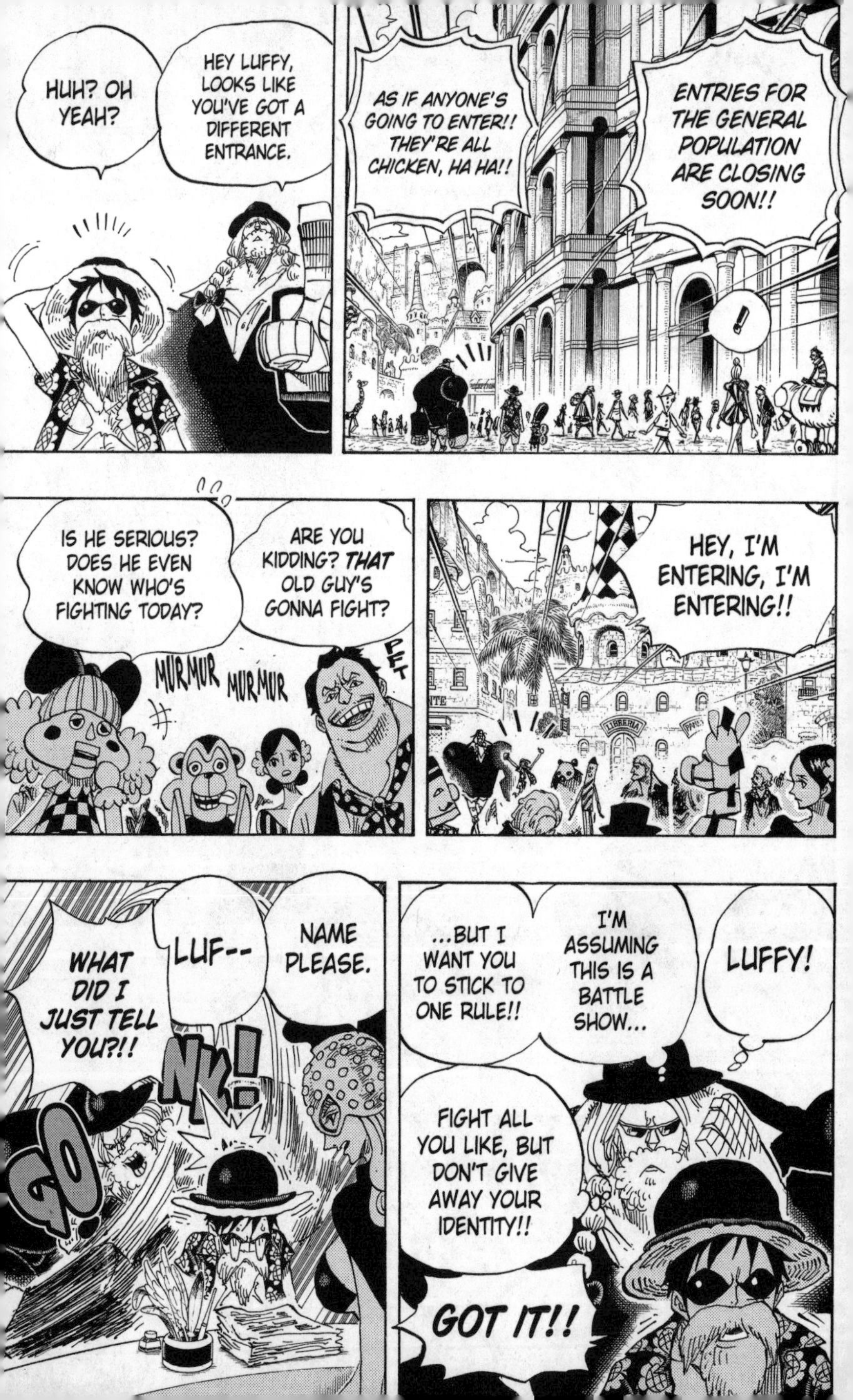
ENTRIES FOR THE GENERAL POPULATION ARE CLOSING SOON!!
AS IF ANYONE'S GOING TO ENTER!! THEY'RE ALL CHICKEN, HA HA!!
!
HEY LUFFY, LOOKS LIKE YOU'VE GOT A DIFFERENT ENTRANCE.
HUH? OH YEAH?
HEY, I'M ENTERING, I'M ENTERING!!
LIBRERIA
ARE YOU KIDDING? THAT OLD GUY'S GONNA FIGHT?
PFT
IS HE SERIOUS? DOES HE EVEN KNOW WHO'S FIGHTING TODAY?
MURMUR MURMUR
LUFFY!
I'M ASSUMING THIS IS A BATTLE SHOW...
...BUT I WANT YOU TO STICK TO ONE RULE!!
FIGHT ALL YOU LIKE, BUT DON'T GIVE AWAY YOUR IDENTITY!!
GOT IT!!
NAME PLEASE.
LUF--
WHAT DID I JUST TELL YOU?!!
GONK!

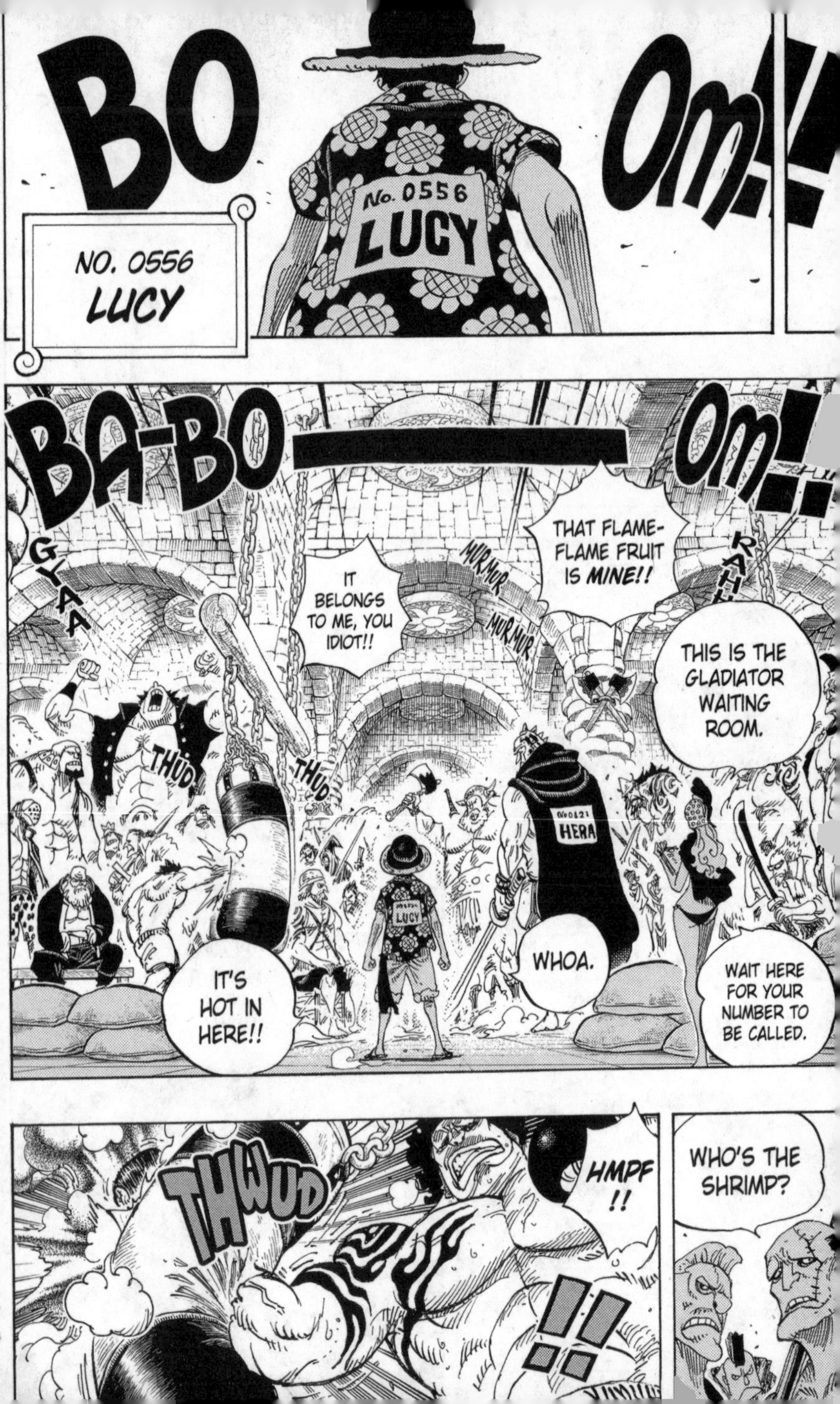
BO
OM!!
NO. 0556
LUCY
No. 0556
LUCY
BA-BO——OM!!
RAHH
THAT FLAME-FLAME FRUIT IS MINE!!
MURMUR
MURMUR
IT BELONGS TO ME, YOU IDIOT!!
GYAA
THIS IS THE GLADIATOR WAITING ROOM.
HERA
WAIT HERE FOR YOUR NUMBER TO BE CALLED.
WHOA.
LUCY
THUD
THUD
IT'S HOT IN HERE!!
WHO'S THE SHRIMP?
HMPF!!
THWUD
!!

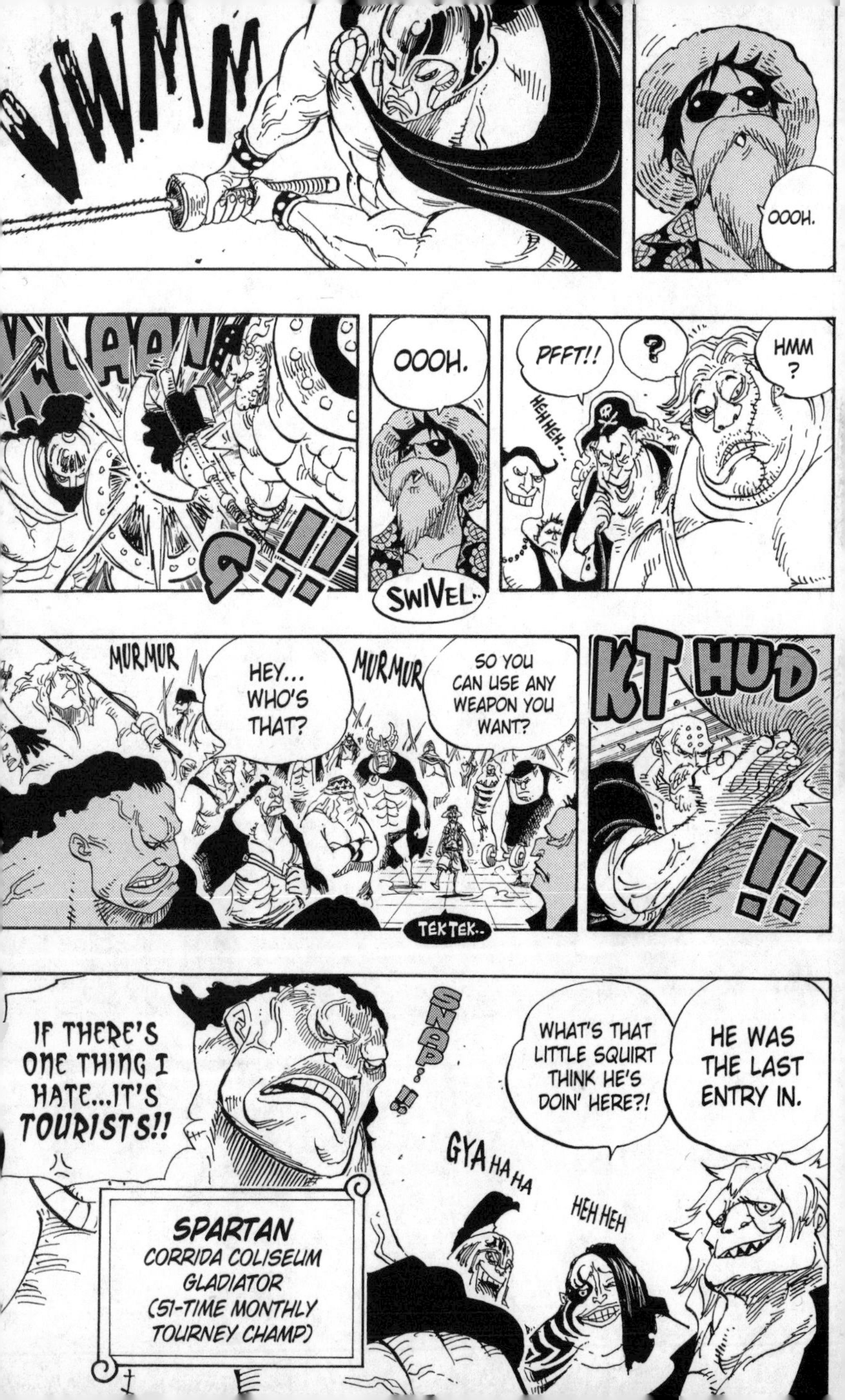
OOOH.
VWMM
HMM ?
?
PFFT!!
HEH HEH...
OOOH.
SWIVEL..
KTHUD
!!
SO YOU CAN USE ANY WEAPON YOU WANT?
MURMUR
HEY... WHO'S THAT?
MURMUR
TEKTEK..
HE WAS THE LAST ENTRY IN.
WHAT'S THAT LITTLE SQUIRT THINK HE'S DOIN' HERE?!
HEH HEH
GYA HA HA
SNAP!!
IF THERE'S ONE THING I HATE...IT'S TOURISTS!!
SPARTAN
CORRIDA COLISEUM GLADIATOR
(51-TIME MONTHLY TOURNEY CHAMP)

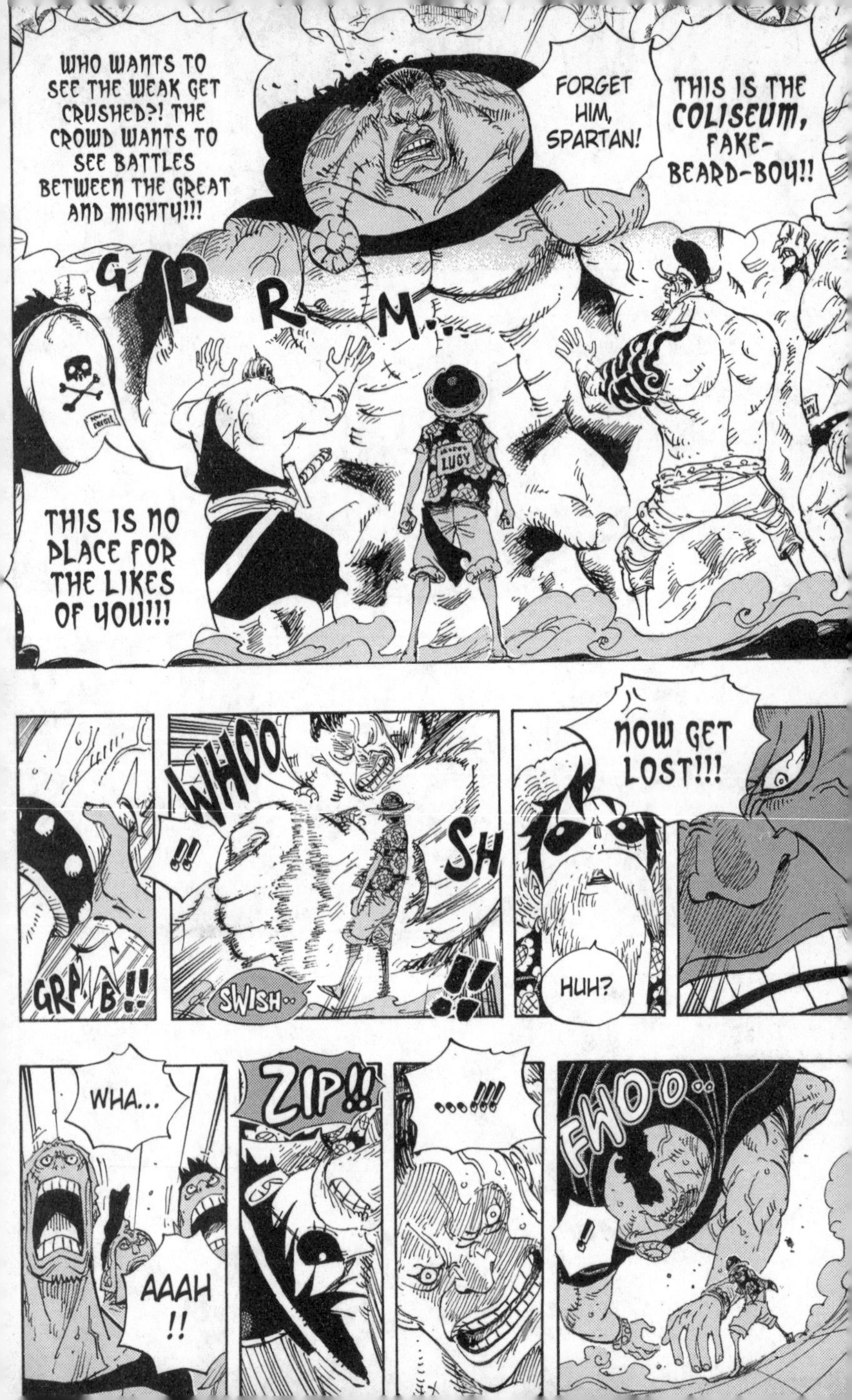
THIS IS THE COLISEUM, FAKE-BEARD-BOY!!
FORGET HIM, SPARTAN!
WHO WANTS TO SEE THE WEAK GET CRUSHED?! THE CROWD WANTS TO SEE BATTLES BETWEEN THE GREAT AND MIGHTY!!!
GRRM...
THIS IS NO PLACE FOR THE LIKES OF YOU!!!
NOW GET LOST!!!
HUH?
WHOOSH
!!
!!
SWISH..
GRAB!!
FWOO..
!
...!!!
ZIP!!
WHA...
AAAH!!

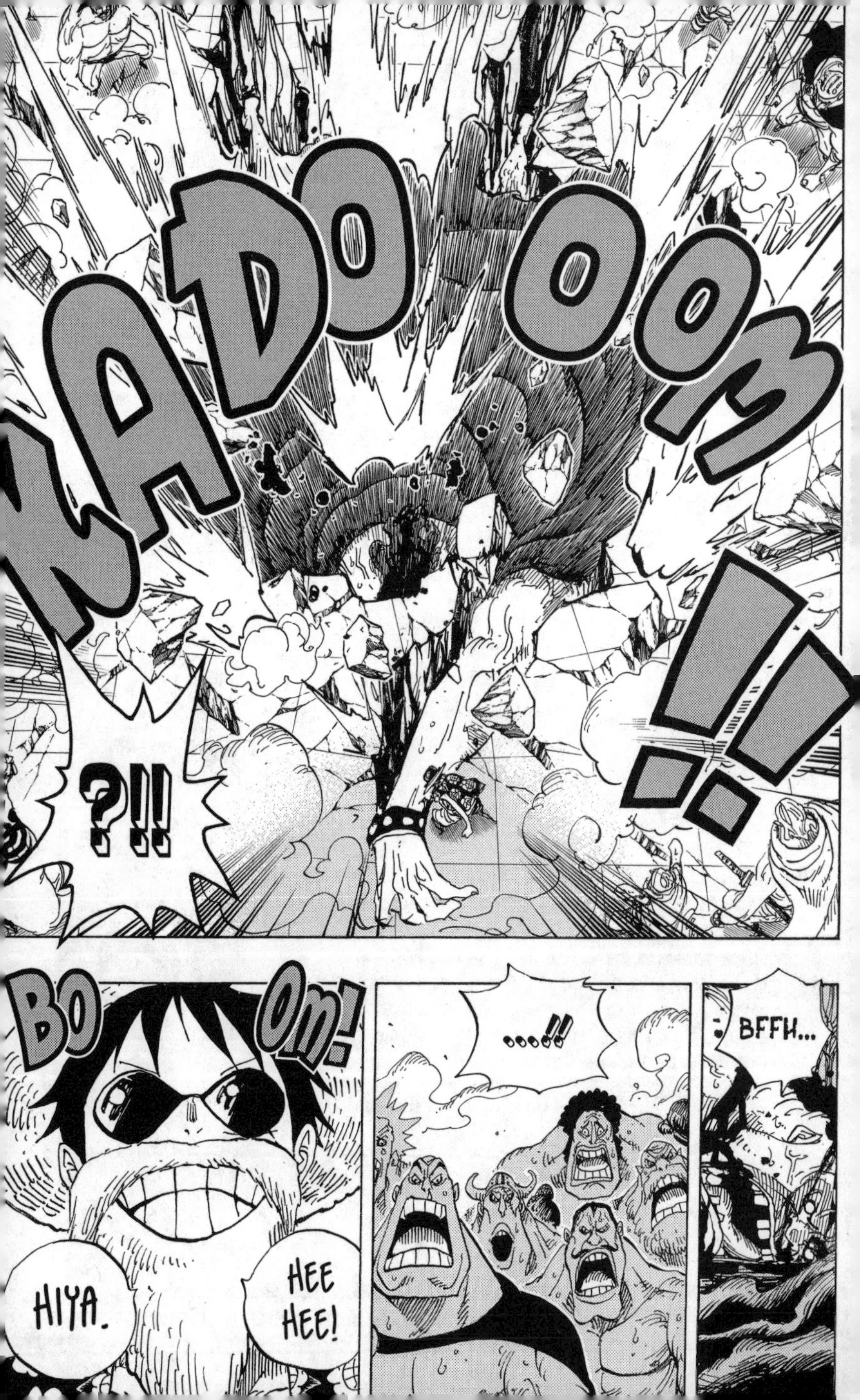
KADOOOM!!
?!!
BFFH...
....!!
BOOM!
HEE HEE!
HIYA.

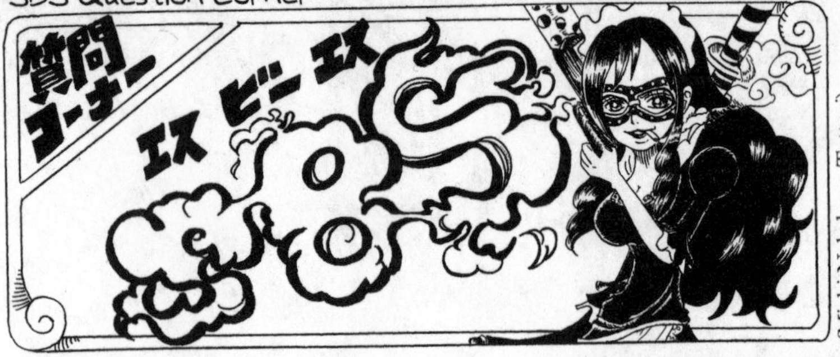
質問コーナー
エス ビー エス

(Michi Nakahara, Tottori)

Q: In Chapter 700--oh! Good evening, Odacchi. In Chapter 700, when Luffy's crew is sailing to Dress~~rosa~~olga, the waves of the sea look like rabbits, but what does Law like to eat aside from rice balls?

--Hasumomo

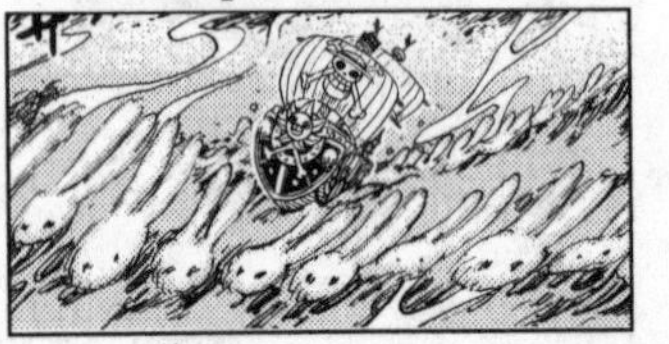

A: Ah, he likes, um...grilled fish! Next question.

Q: I'm curious about something. Robin likes to say scary things out loud. But in her imagination, she's usually thinking of fun, cute things like cats or old ladies in frilly dresses. Why doesn't Robin try to cheer everyone up with her fantasies? That's what I like about Robin.

--Y.O.

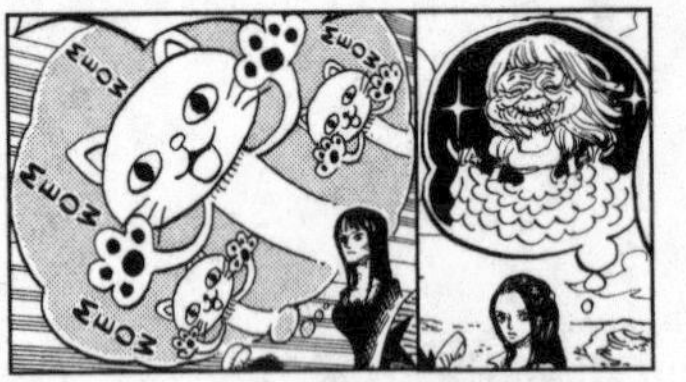

A: Ahh, I see. Yes, good point. Given that she scolded Franky for making weird faces in Chopper's body at Punk Hazard, Robin must really like cute faces. But she's a bit socially clumsy, and her attempts to paint a picture with words end up on the creepy side. She's just one of those ladies.

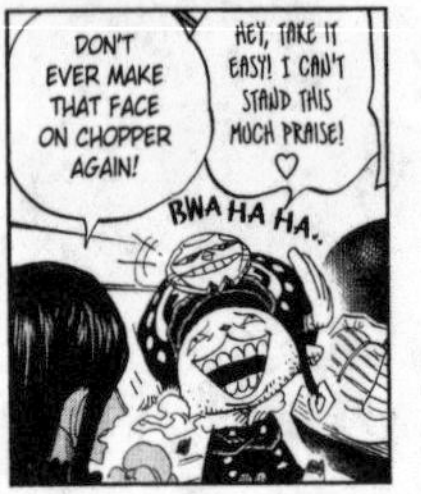
HEY, TAKE IT EASY! I CAN'T STAND THIS MUCH PRAISE! ♡
DON'T EVER MAKE THAT FACE ON CHOPPER AGAIN!
BWA HA HA..

Q: So, who in the Straw Hat Crew can use Haki? I'm so curious, I can't even cause any love hurricanes.

--Kakuharu

A: It's these three. Inside the parentheses are the types they specialize in.

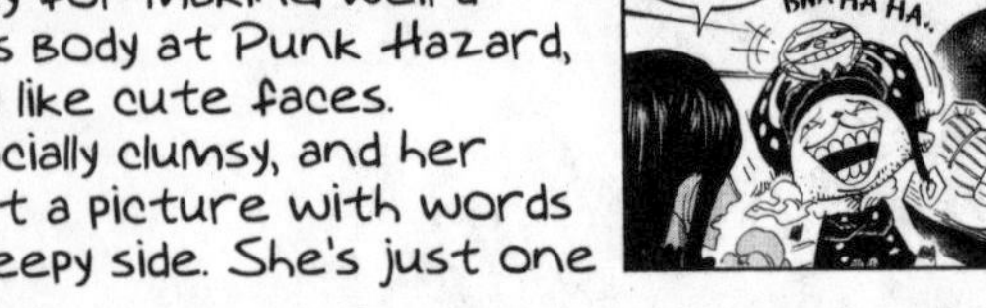

(Supreme King) (Armament) (Observation)

Chapter 704:
LUCY AND THE STATUE OF KYROS

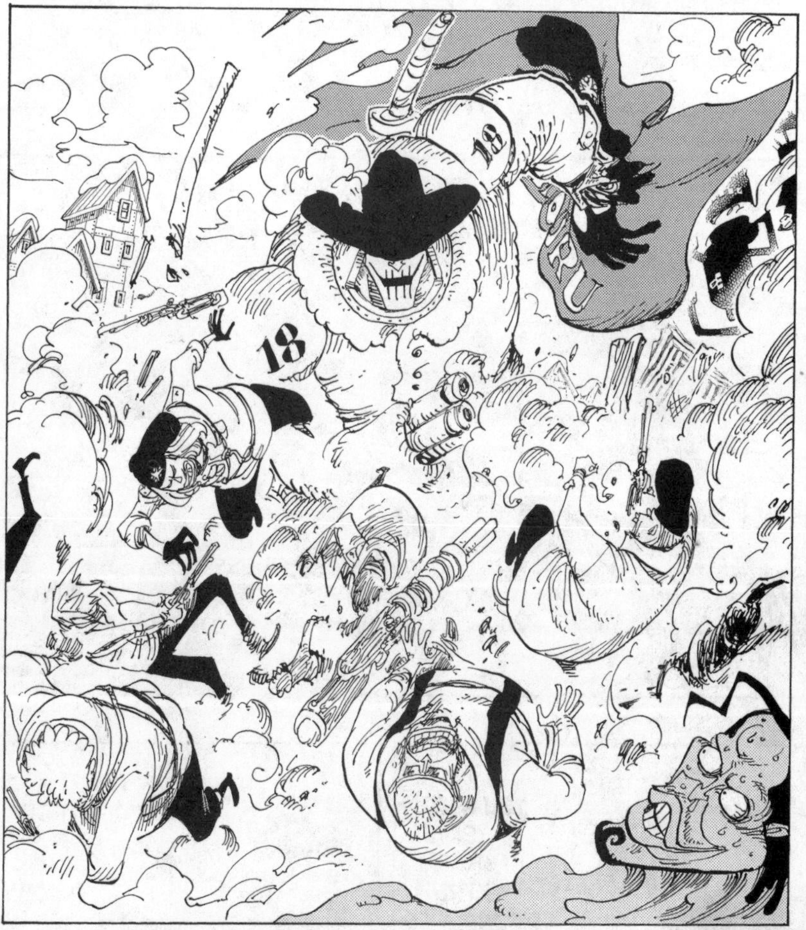

CARIBOU'S NEW WORLD KEE HEE HEE, VOL. 24
"PROLETARIAT RIOT SUPPRESSED"

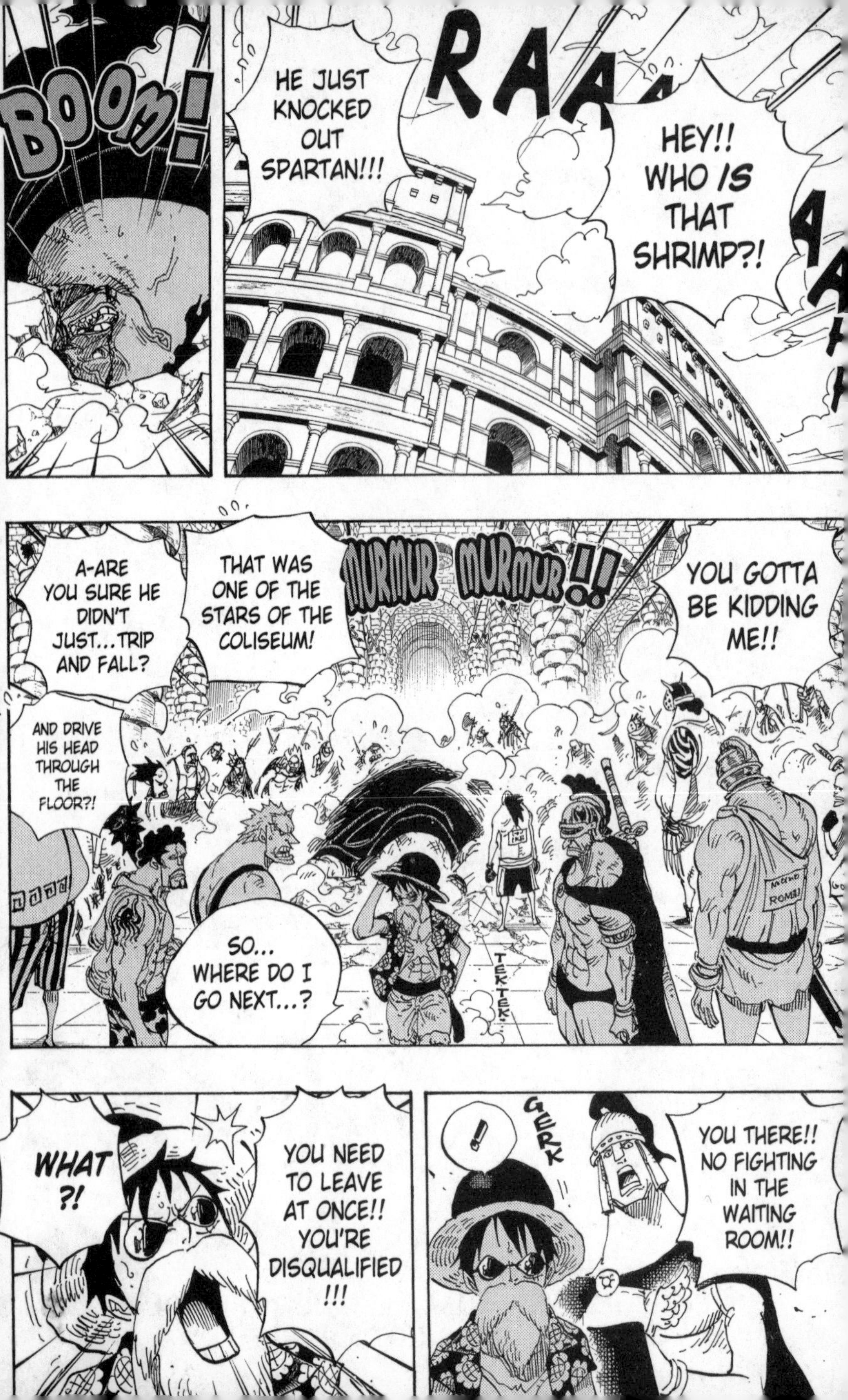
RAAAAAH
HEY!! WHO *IS* THAT SHRIMP?!
HE JUST KNOCKED OUT SPARTAN!!!
BOOM!
YOU GOTTA BE KIDDING ME!!
MURMUR MURMUR!!
THAT WAS ONE OF THE STARS OF THE COLISEUM!
A-ARE YOU SURE HE DIDN'T JUST...TRIP AND FALL?
AND DRIVE HIS HEAD THROUGH THE FLOOR?!
SO... WHERE DO I GO NEXT...?
TEK TEK...
YOU THERE!! NO FIGHTING IN THE WAITING ROOM!!
GERK
!
YOU NEED TO LEAVE AT ONCE!! YOU'RE DISQUALIFIED!!!
WHAT?!

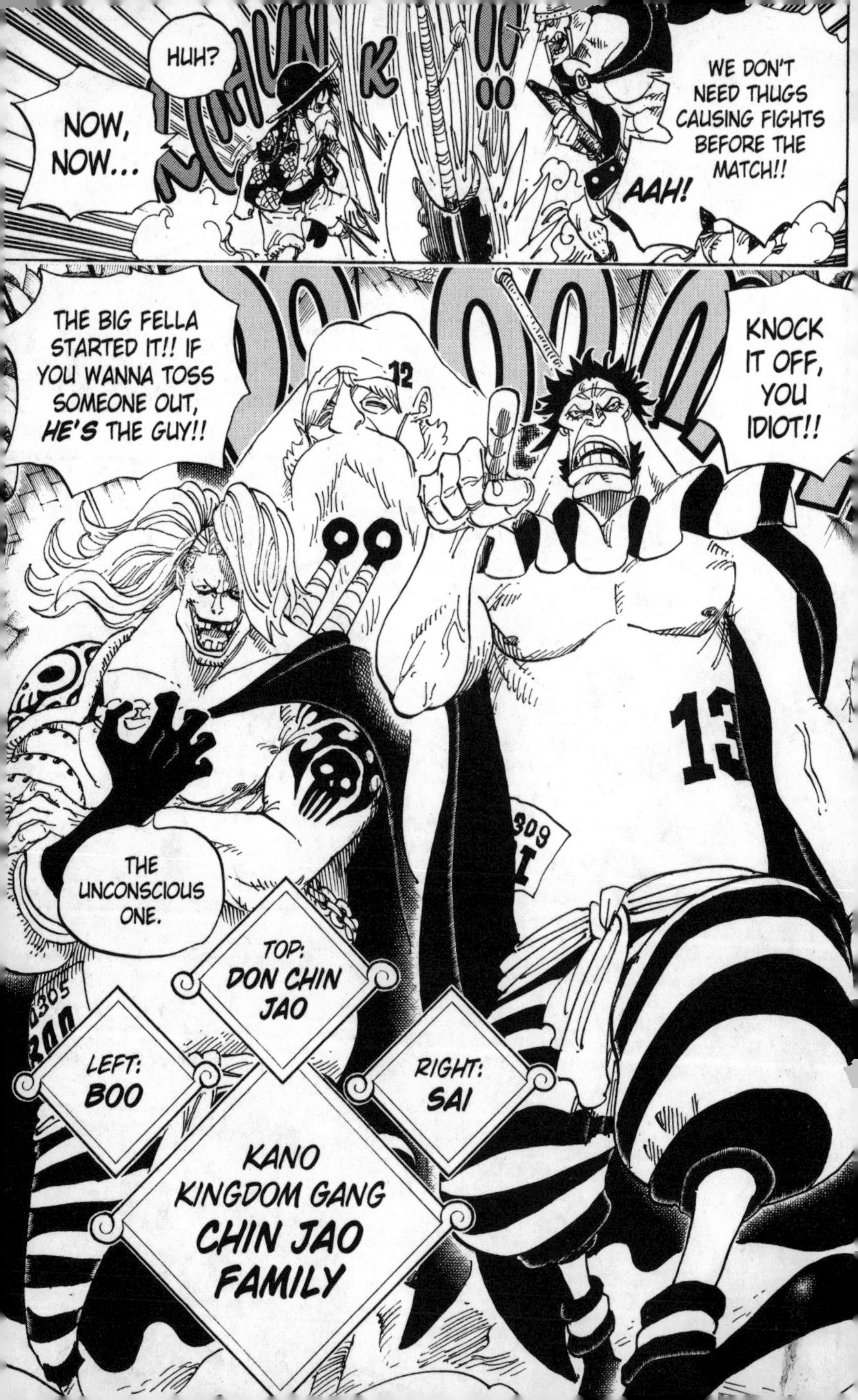

WE DON'T NEED THUGS CAUSING FIGHTS BEFORE THE MATCH!!
AAH!
WHUNK!!
HUH?
NOW, NOW...
KNOCK IT OFF, YOU IDIOT!!
THE BIG FELLA STARTED IT!! IF YOU WANNA TOSS SOMEONE OUT, ***HE'S*** THE GUY!!
THE UNCONSCIOUS ONE.
TOP: DON CHIN JAO
RIGHT: SAI
LEFT: BOO
KANO KINGDOM GANG **CHIN JAO FAMILY**

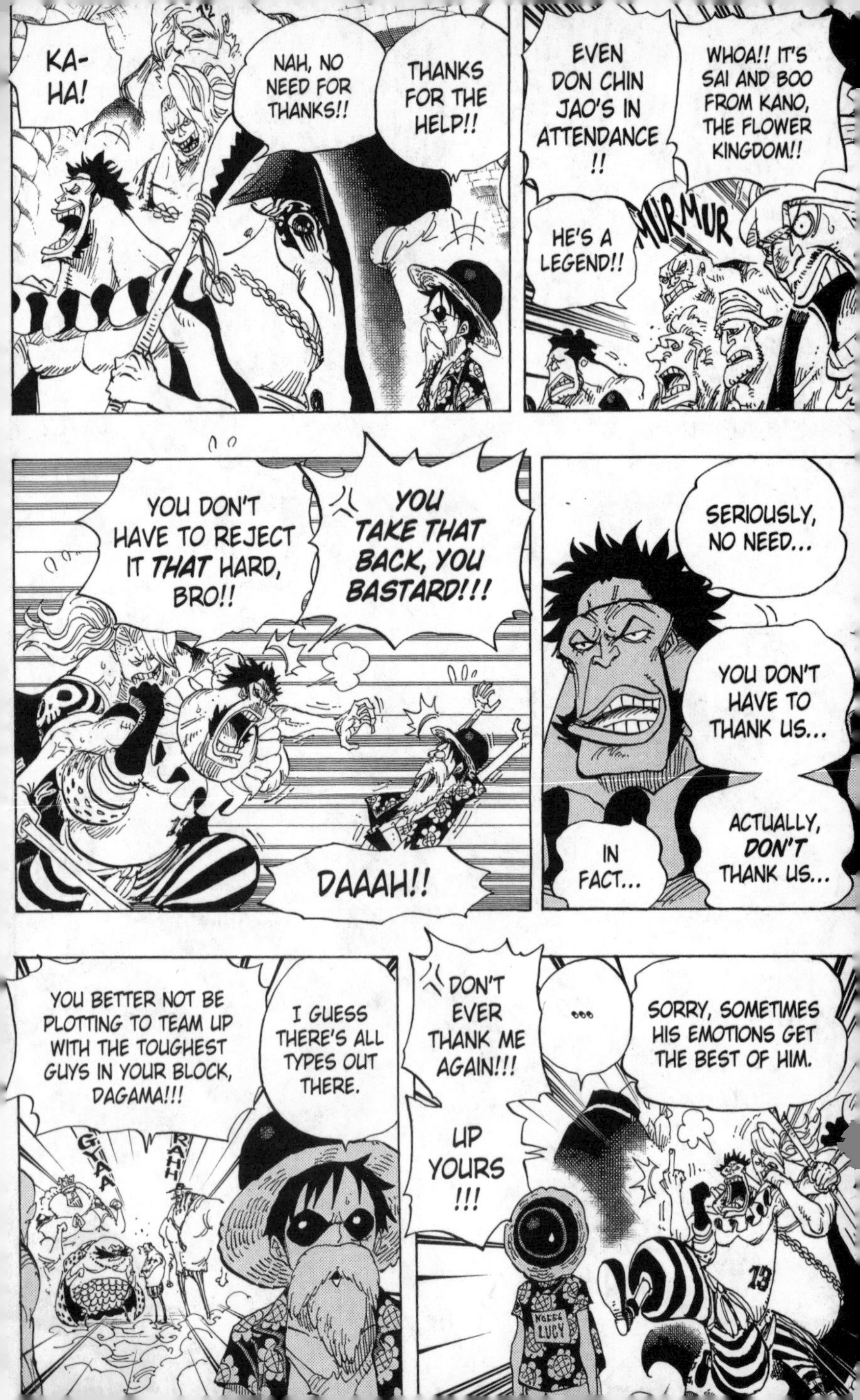
WHOA!! IT'S SAI AND BOO FROM KANO, THE FLOWER KINGDOM!!
EVEN DON CHIN JAO'S IN ATTENDANCE!!
MURMUR
HE'S A LEGEND!!
THANKS FOR THE HELP!!
NAH, NO NEED FOR THANKS!!
KA-HA!
SERIOUSLY, NO NEED...
YOU DON'T HAVE TO THANK US...
ACTUALLY, ***DON'T*** THANK US...
IN FACT...
YOU TAKE THAT BACK, YOU BASTARD!!!
YOU DON'T HAVE TO REJECT IT ***THAT*** HARD, BRO!!
DAAAH!!
SORRY, SOMETIMES HIS EMOTIONS GET THE BEST OF HIM.
...
DON'T EVER THANK ME AGAIN!!!
UP YOURS!!!
LUCY
I GUESS THERE'S ALL TYPES OUT THERE.
YOU BETTER NOT BE PLOTTING TO TEAM UP WITH THE TOUGHEST GUYS IN YOUR BLOCK, DAGAMA!!!
GYAA
RAHH

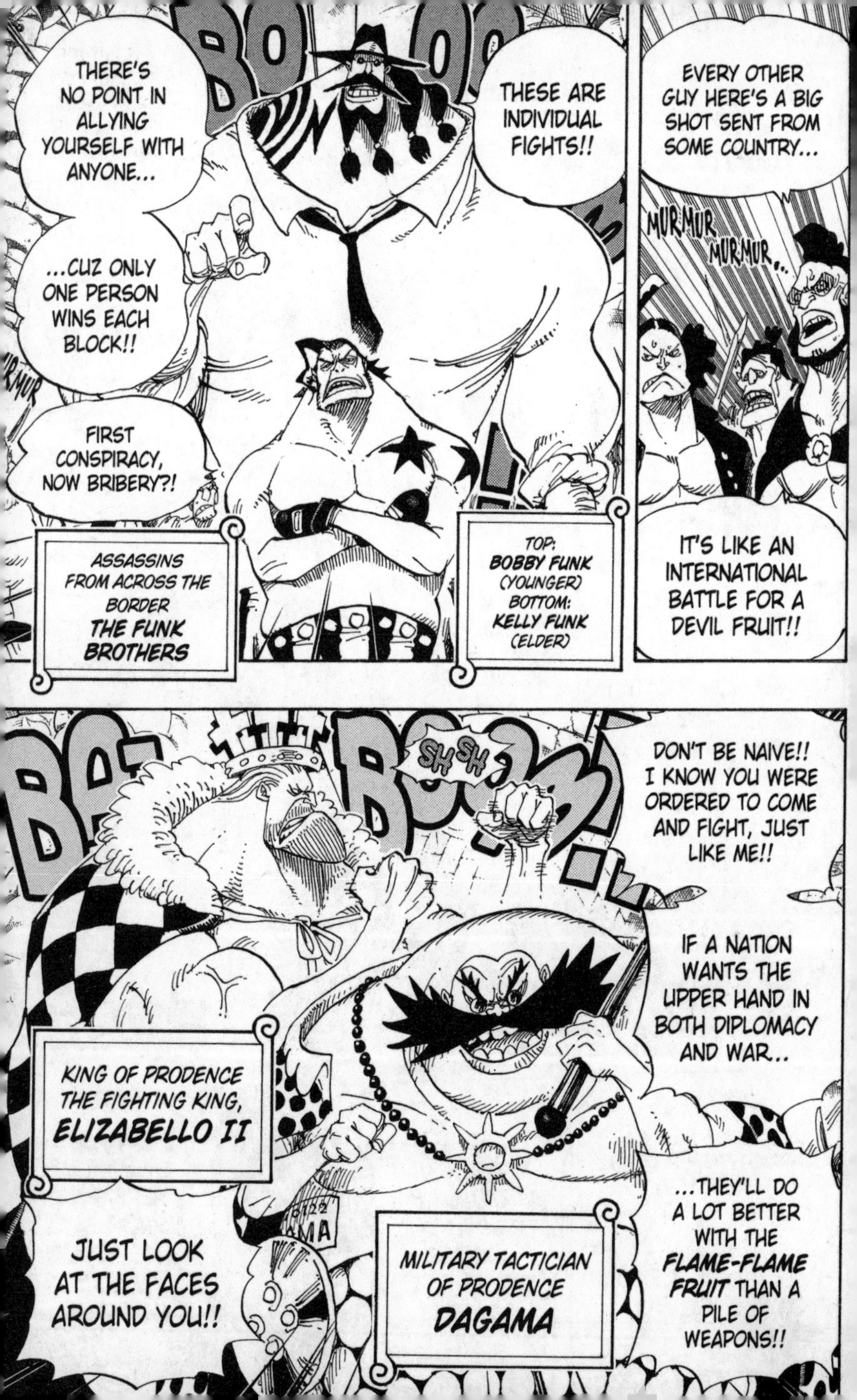
EVERY OTHER GUY HERE'S A BIG SHOT SENT FROM SOME COUNTRY...
MURMUR MURMUR...
IT'S LIKE AN INTERNATIONAL BATTLE FOR A DEVIL FRUIT!!
THESE ARE INDIVIDUAL FIGHTS!!
TOP: BOBBY FUNK (YOUNGER) BOTTOM: KELLY FUNK (ELDER)
THERE'S NO POINT IN ALLYING YOURSELF WITH ANYONE...
...CUZ ONLY ONE PERSON WINS EACH BLOCK!!
FIRST CONSPIRACY, NOW BRIBERY?!
ASSASSINS FROM ACROSS THE BORDER THE FUNK BROTHERS
DON'T BE NAIVE!! I KNOW YOU WERE ORDERED TO COME AND FIGHT, JUST LIKE ME!!
IF A NATION WANTS THE UPPER HAND IN BOTH DIPLOMACY AND WAR...
...THEY'LL DO A LOT BETTER WITH THE FLAME-FLAME FRUIT THAN A PILE OF WEAPONS!!
MILITARY TACTICIAN OF PRODENCE DAGAMA
SH SH
KING OF PRODENCE THE FIGHTING KING, ELIZABELLO II
JUST LOOK AT THE FACES AROUND YOU!!

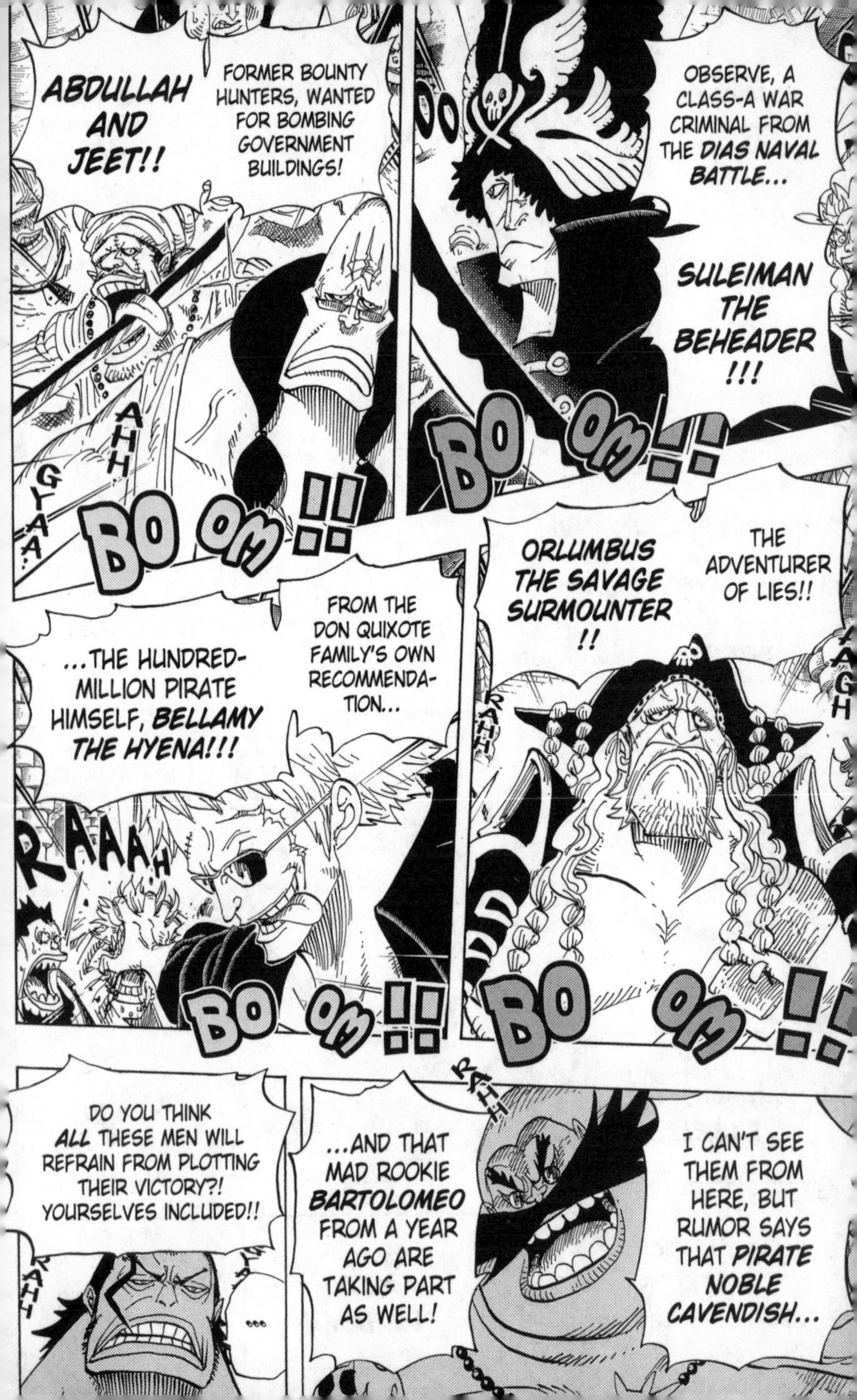
OBSERVE, A CLASS-A WAR CRIMINAL FROM THE DIAS NAVAL BATTLE...
SULEIMAN THE BEHEADER!!!
BOOM!!
FORMER BOUNTY HUNTERS, WANTED FOR BOMBING GOVERNMENT BUILDINGS!
ABDULLAH AND JEET!!
AHH
GYAAA
BOOM!!
THE ADVENTURER OF LIES!!
ORLUMBUS THE SAVAGE SURMOUNTER!!
AAGH
RAHH
BOOM!!
FROM THE DON QUIXOTE FAMILY'S OWN RECOMMENDATION...
...THE HUNDRED-MILLION PIRATE HIMSELF, BELLAMY THE HYENA!!!
RAAAAH
BOOM!!
I CAN'T SEE THEM FROM HERE, BUT RUMOR SAYS THAT PIRATE NOBLE CAVENDISH...
...AND THAT MAD ROOKIE BARTOLOMEO FROM A YEAR AGO ARE TAKING PART AS WELL!
RAHH
DO YOU THINK ALL THESE MEN WILL REFRAIN FROM PLOTTING THEIR VICTORY?! YOURSELVES INCLUDED!!
RAHH
...

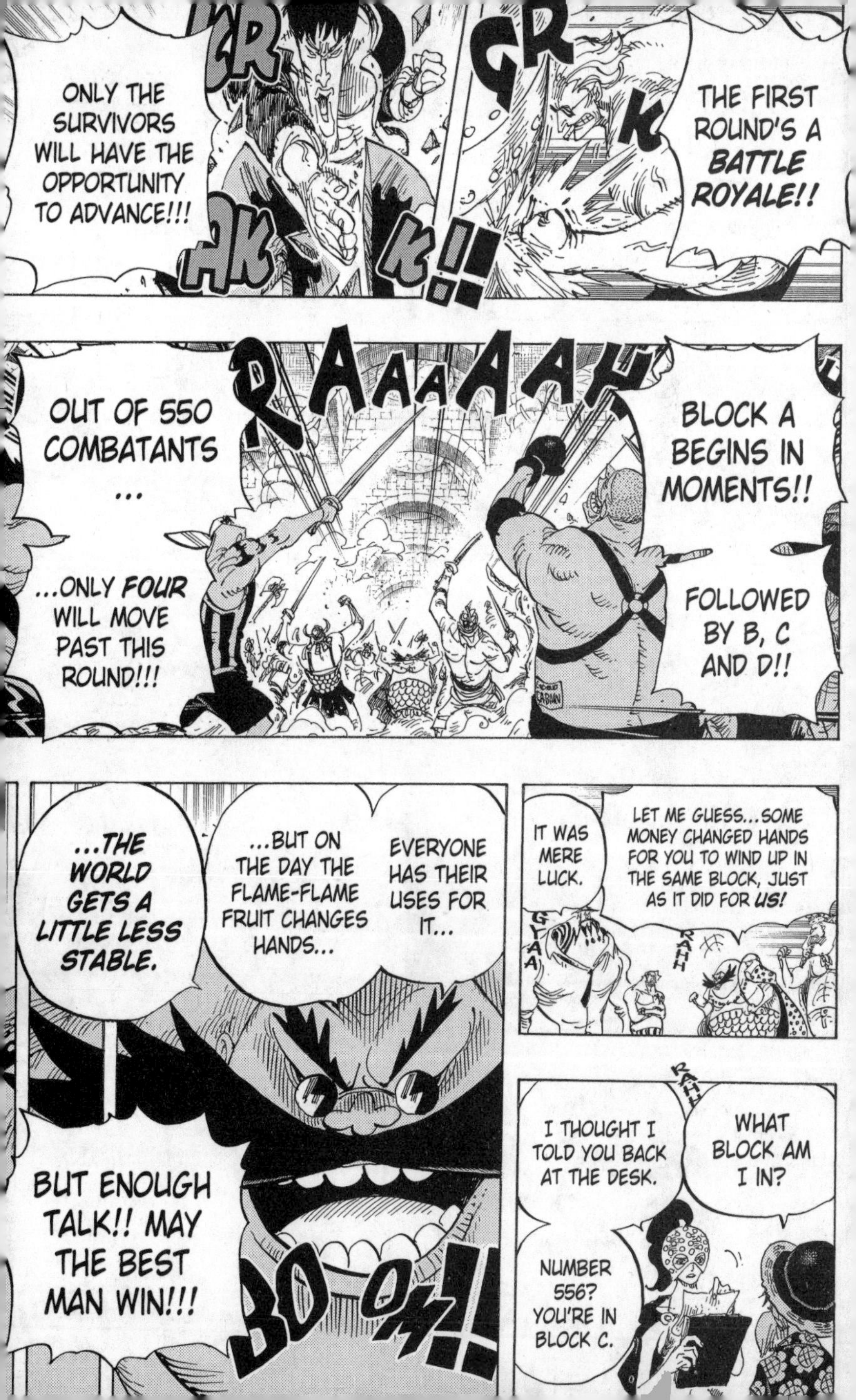

GR
K
THE FIRST ROUND'S A *BATTLE ROYALE!!*
CR
AK K!!
ONLY THE SURVIVORS WILL HAVE THE OPPORTUNITY TO ADVANCE!!!
BLOCK A BEGINS IN MOMENTS!!
FOLLOWED BY B, C AND D!!
RAAAAAH
OUT OF 550 COMBATANTS ...
...ONLY *FOUR* WILL MOVE PAST THIS ROUND!!!
LET ME GUESS...SOME MONEY CHANGED HANDS FOR YOU TO WIND UP IN THE SAME BLOCK, JUST AS IT DID FOR *US!*
IT WAS MERE LUCK.
GYAA
RAHH
RAHH
WHAT BLOCK AM I IN?
I THOUGHT I TOLD YOU BACK AT THE DESK.
NUMBER 556? YOU'RE IN BLOCK C.
EVERYONE HAS THEIR USES FOR IT...
...BUT ON THE DAY THE FLAME-FLAME FRUIT CHANGES HANDS...
...THE WORLD GETS A LITTLE LESS STABLE.
BUT ENOUGH TALK!! MAY THE BEST MAN WIN!!!
BOOM!!

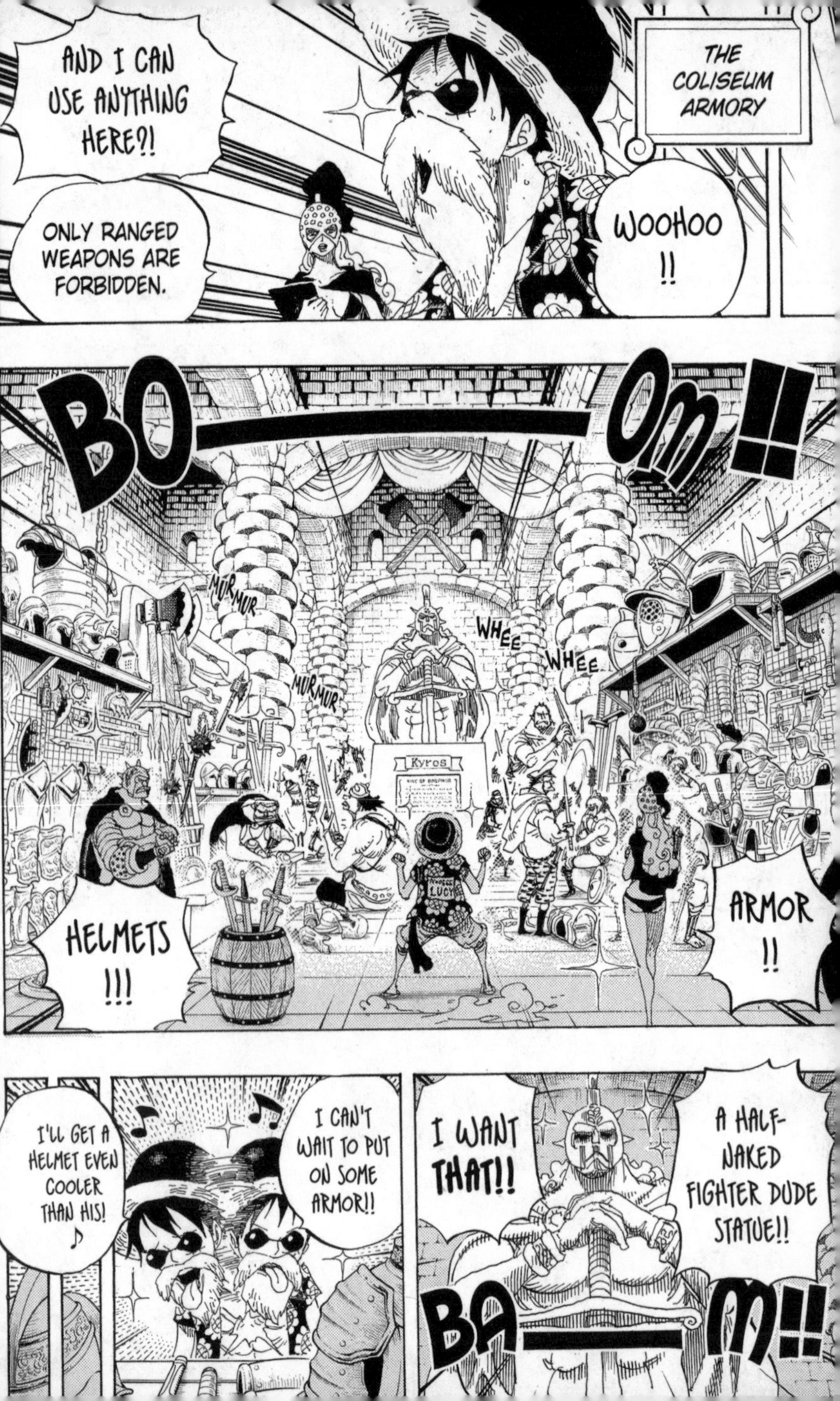
THE COLISEUM ARMORY
AND I CAN USE ANYTHING HERE?!
ONLY RANGED WEAPONS ARE FORBIDDEN.
WOOHOO!!
BO—OM!!
MURMUR
MURMUR
WHEE
WHEE
Kyros
LUCY
ARMOR!!
HELMETS!!!
A HALF-NAKED FIGHTER DUDE STATUE!!
I WANT THAT!!
BA—M!!
I CAN'T WAIT TO PUT ON SOME ARMOR!!
I'LL GET A HELMET EVEN COOLER THAN HIS! ♪

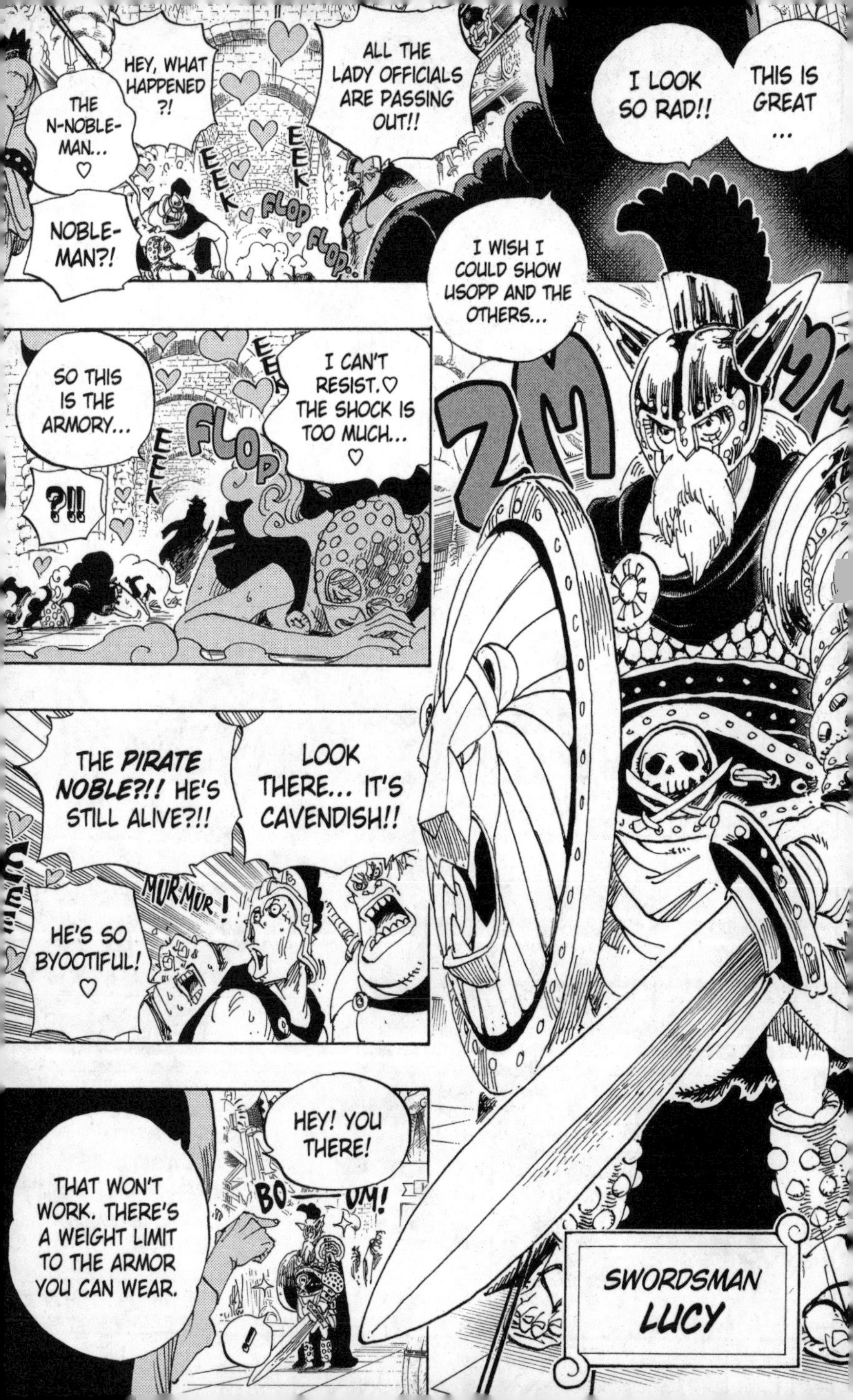

THIS IS GREAT...
I LOOK SO RAD!!
I WISH I COULD SHOW USOPP AND THE OTHERS...
ZM
SWORDSMAN LUCY
ALL THE LADY OFFICIALS ARE PASSING OUT!!
HEY, WHAT HAPPENED?!
THE N-NOBLEMAN... ♡
EEK EEK
FLOP FLOP
NOBLEMAN?!
I CAN'T RESIST.♡ THE SHOCK IS TOO MUCH... ♡
EEK
FLOP
SO THIS IS THE ARMORY...
EEK
?!!
LOOK THERE... IT'S CAVENDISH!!
THE PIRATE NOBLE?!! HE'S STILL ALIVE?!!
MURMUR!
HE'S SO BYOOTIFUL! ♡
HEY! YOU THERE!
BOOM!
THAT WON'T WORK. THERE'S A WEIGHT LIMIT TO THE ARMOR YOU CAN WEAR.
!

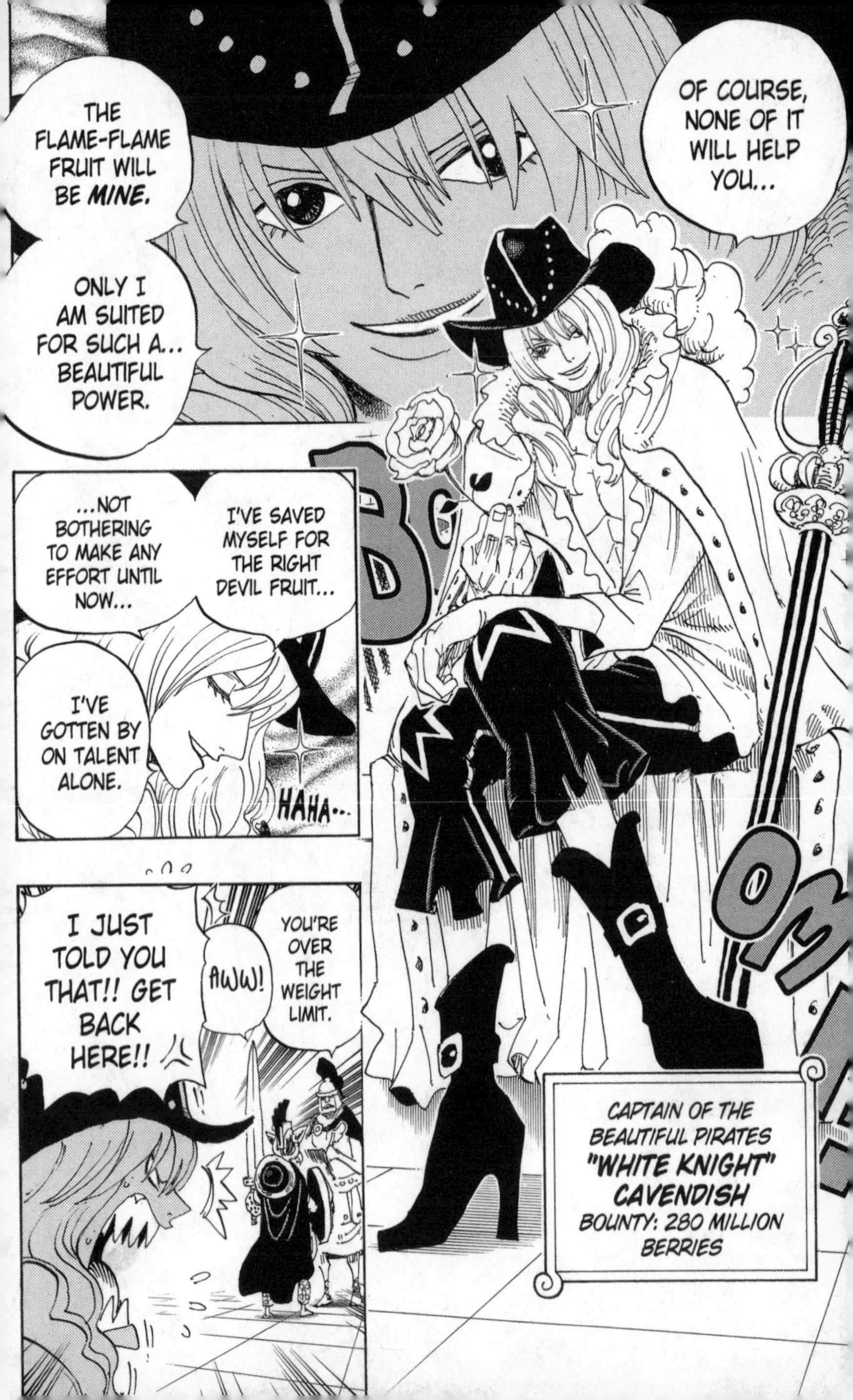

OF COURSE, NONE OF IT WILL HELP YOU...
THE FLAME-FLAME FRUIT WILL BE *MINE.*
ONLY I AM SUITED FOR SUCH A... BEAUTIFUL POWER.
BOOM!
CAPTAIN OF THE BEAUTIFUL PIRATES **"WHITE KNIGHT" CAVENDISH** BOUNTY: 280 MILLION BERRIES
I'VE SAVED MYSELF FOR THE RIGHT DEVIL FRUIT...
...NOT BOTHERING TO MAKE ANY EFFORT UNTIL NOW...
I'VE GOTTEN BY ON TALENT ALONE.
HAHA...
YOU'RE OVER THE WEIGHT LIMIT.
AWW!
I JUST TOLD YOU THAT!! GET BACK HERE!!

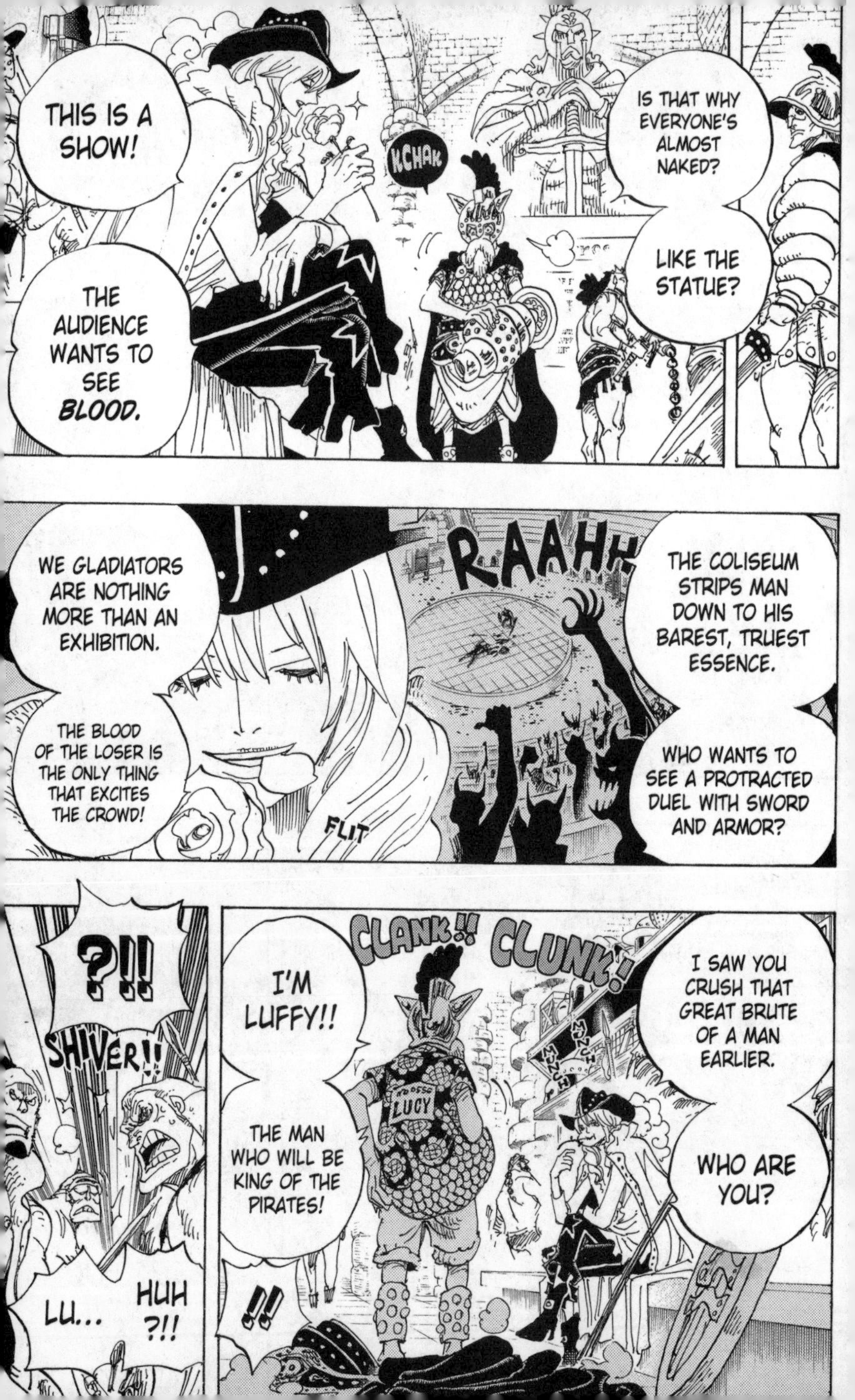
IS THAT WHY EVERYONE'S ALMOST NAKED?
LIKE THE STATUE?
KCHAK
THIS IS A SHOW!
THE AUDIENCE WANTS TO SEE BLOOD.
THE COLISEUM STRIPS MAN DOWN TO HIS BAREST, TRUEST ESSENCE.
WHO WANTS TO SEE A PROTRACTED DUEL WITH SWORD AND ARMOR?
RAAHH
WE GLADIATORS ARE NOTHING MORE THAN AN EXHIBITION.
THE BLOOD OF THE LOSER IS THE ONLY THING THAT EXCITES THE CROWD!
FLIT
I SAW YOU CRUSH THAT GREAT BRUTE OF A MAN EARLIER.
WHO ARE YOU?
MUNCH
MUNCH
CLANK!! CLUNK!
I'M LUFFY!!
THE MAN WHO WILL BE KING OF THE PIRATES!
LUCY
!!
?!!
SHIVER!!
HUH ?!!
LU...

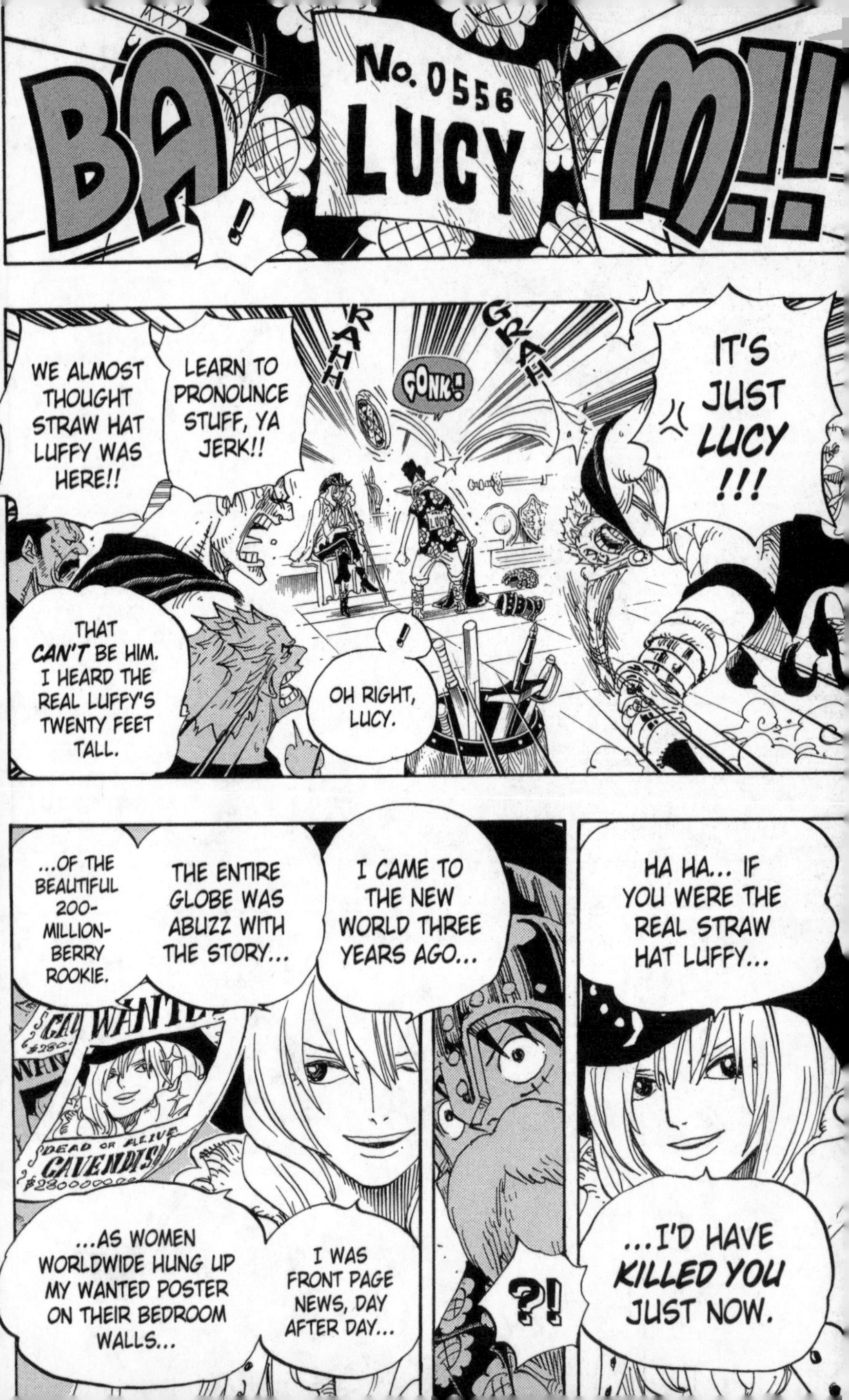
BAM!!
No. 0556
LUCY
!
IT'S JUST LUCY!!!
GRAH
GONK!
RAHH
LEARN TO PRONOUNCE STUFF, YA JERK!!
WE ALMOST THOUGHT STRAW HAT LUFFY WAS HERE!!
!
OH RIGHT, LUCY.
THAT CAN'T BE HIM. I HEARD THE REAL LUFFY'S TWENTY FEET TALL.
HA HA... IF YOU WERE THE REAL STRAW HAT LUFFY...
...I'D HAVE KILLED YOU JUST NOW.
?!
I CAME TO THE NEW WORLD THREE YEARS AGO...
THE ENTIRE GLOBE WAS ABUZZ WITH THE STORY...
...OF THE BEAUTIFUL 200-MILLION-BERRY ROOKIE.
DEAD OR ALIVE
I WAS FRONT PAGE NEWS, DAY AFTER DAY...
...AS WOMEN WORLDWIDE HUNG UP MY WANTED POSTER ON THEIR BEDROOM WALLS...

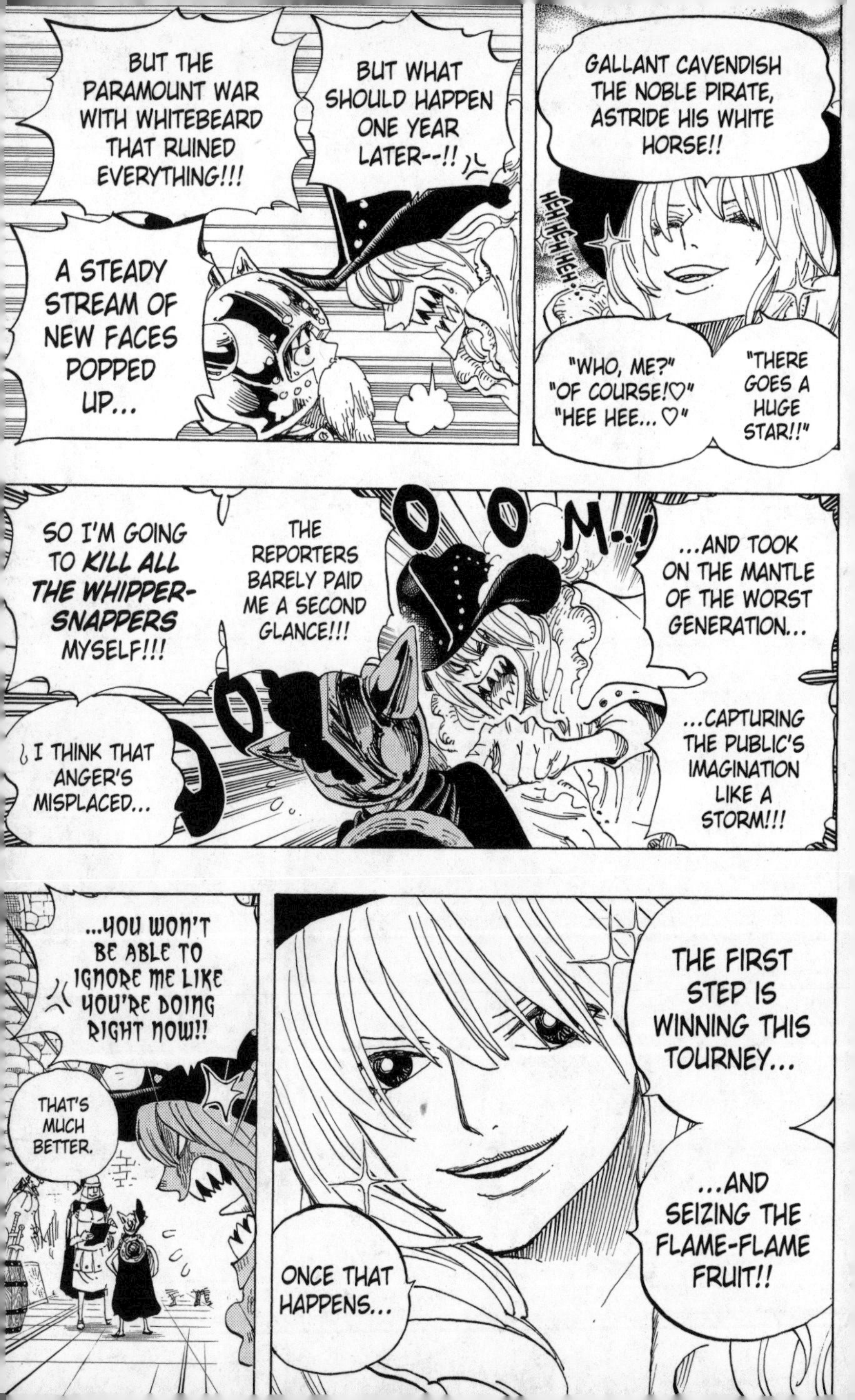
GALLANT CAVENDISH THE NOBLE PIRATE, ASTRIDE HIS WHITE HORSE!!
HEH HEH HEH...
"THERE GOES A HUGE STAR!!"
"WHO, ME?" "OF COURSE!♡" "HEE HEE...♡"
BUT WHAT SHOULD HAPPEN ONE YEAR LATER--!!
BUT THE PARAMOUNT WAR WITH WHITEBEARD THAT RUINED EVERYTHING!!!
A STEADY STREAM OF NEW FACES POPPED UP...
...AND TOOK ON THE MANTLE OF THE WORST GENERATION...
...CAPTURING THE PUBLIC'S IMAGINATION LIKE A STORM!!!
DOOM..!
THE REPORTERS BARELY PAID ME A SECOND GLANCE!!!
SO I'M GOING TO **KILL ALL THE WHIPPER-SNAPPERS** MYSELF!!!
I THINK THAT ANGER'S MISPLACED...
THE FIRST STEP IS WINNING THIS TOURNEY...
...AND SEIZING THE FLAME-FLAME FRUIT!!
ONCE THAT HAPPENS...
...YOU WON'T BE ABLE TO IGNORE ME LIKE YOU'RE DOING RIGHT NOW!!
THAT'S MUCH BETTER.

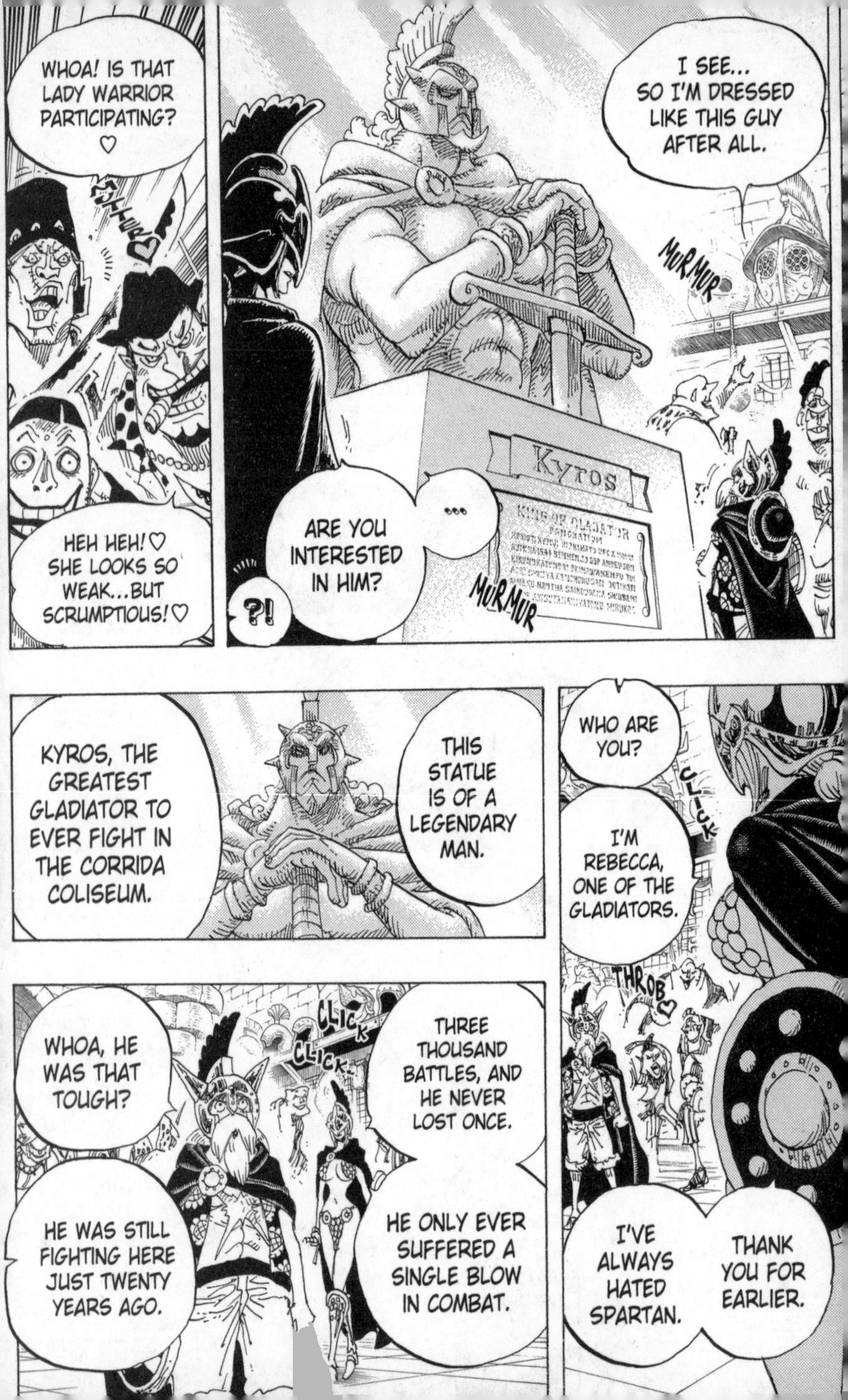
I SEE... SO I'M DRESSED LIKE THIS GUY AFTER ALL.
MURMUR
...
Kyros
ARE YOU INTERESTED IN HIM?
?!
MURMUR
WHOA! IS THAT LADY WARRIOR PARTICIPATING? ♡
HEH HEH! ♡ SHE LOOKS SO WEAK...BUT SCRUMPTIOUS! ♡
WHO ARE YOU?
CLICK
I'M REBECCA, ONE OF THE GLADIATORS.
THROB ♡
THANK YOU FOR EARLIER.
I'VE ALWAYS HATED SPARTAN.
THIS STATUE IS OF A LEGENDARY MAN.
KYROS, THE GREATEST GLADIATOR TO EVER FIGHT IN THE CORRIDA COLISEUM.
THREE THOUSAND BATTLES, AND HE NEVER LOST ONCE.
CLICK
CLICK
WHOA, HE WAS THAT TOUGH?
HE ONLY EVER SUFFERED A SINGLE BLOW IN COMBAT.
HE WAS STILL FIGHTING HERE JUST TWENTY YEARS AGO.

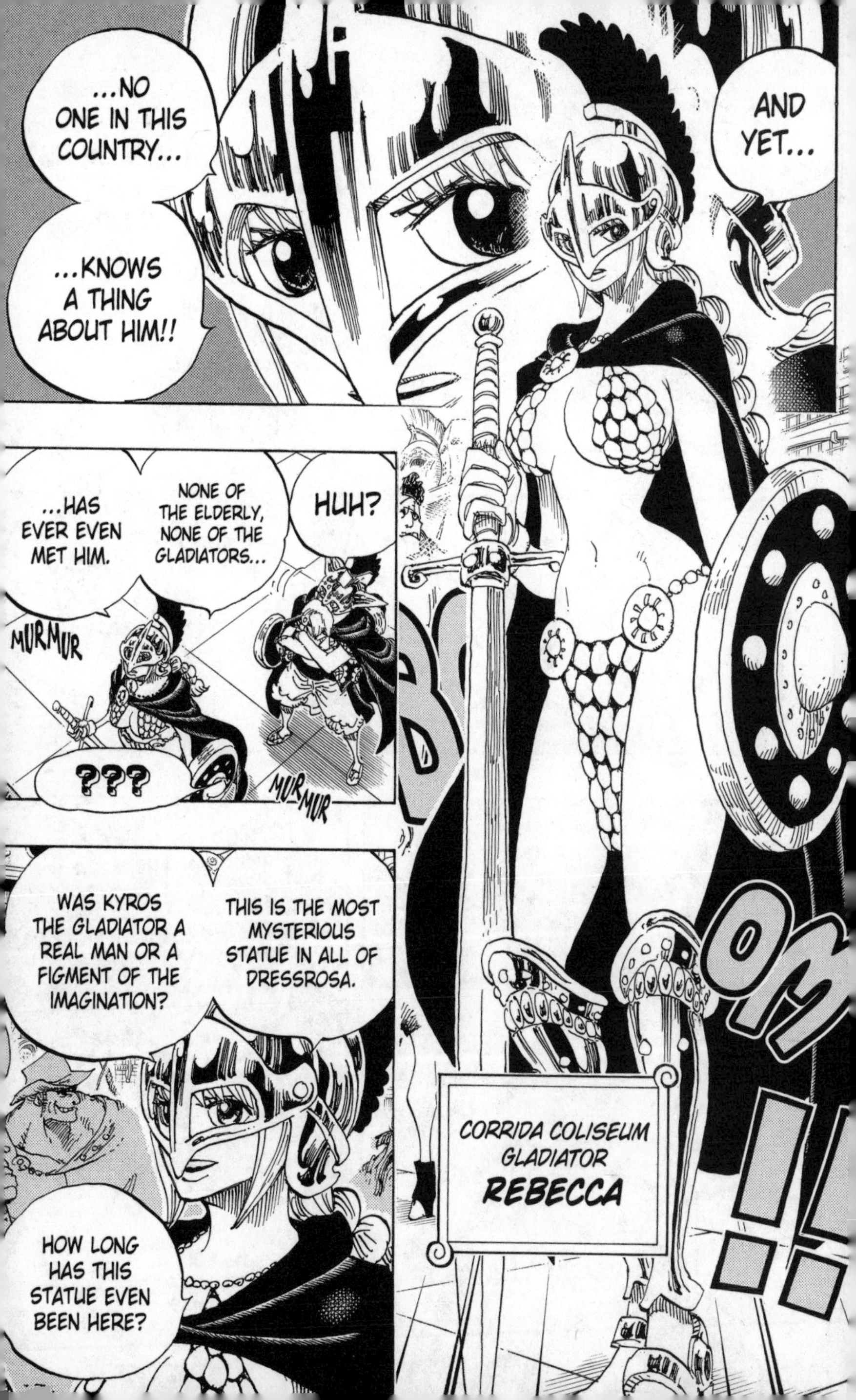
AND YET...
CORRIDA COLISEUM GLADIATOR REBECCA
OM!!
...NO ONE IN THIS COUNTRY...
...KNOWS A THING ABOUT HIM!!
HUH?
NONE OF THE ELDERLY, NONE OF THE GLADIATORS...
...HAS EVER EVEN MET HIM.
MURMUR
MURMUR
???
THIS IS THE MOST MYSTERIOUS STATUE IN ALL OF DRESSROSA.
WAS KYROS THE GLADIATOR A REAL MAN OR A FIGMENT OF THE IMAGINATION?
HOW LONG HAS THIS STATUE EVEN BEEN HERE?

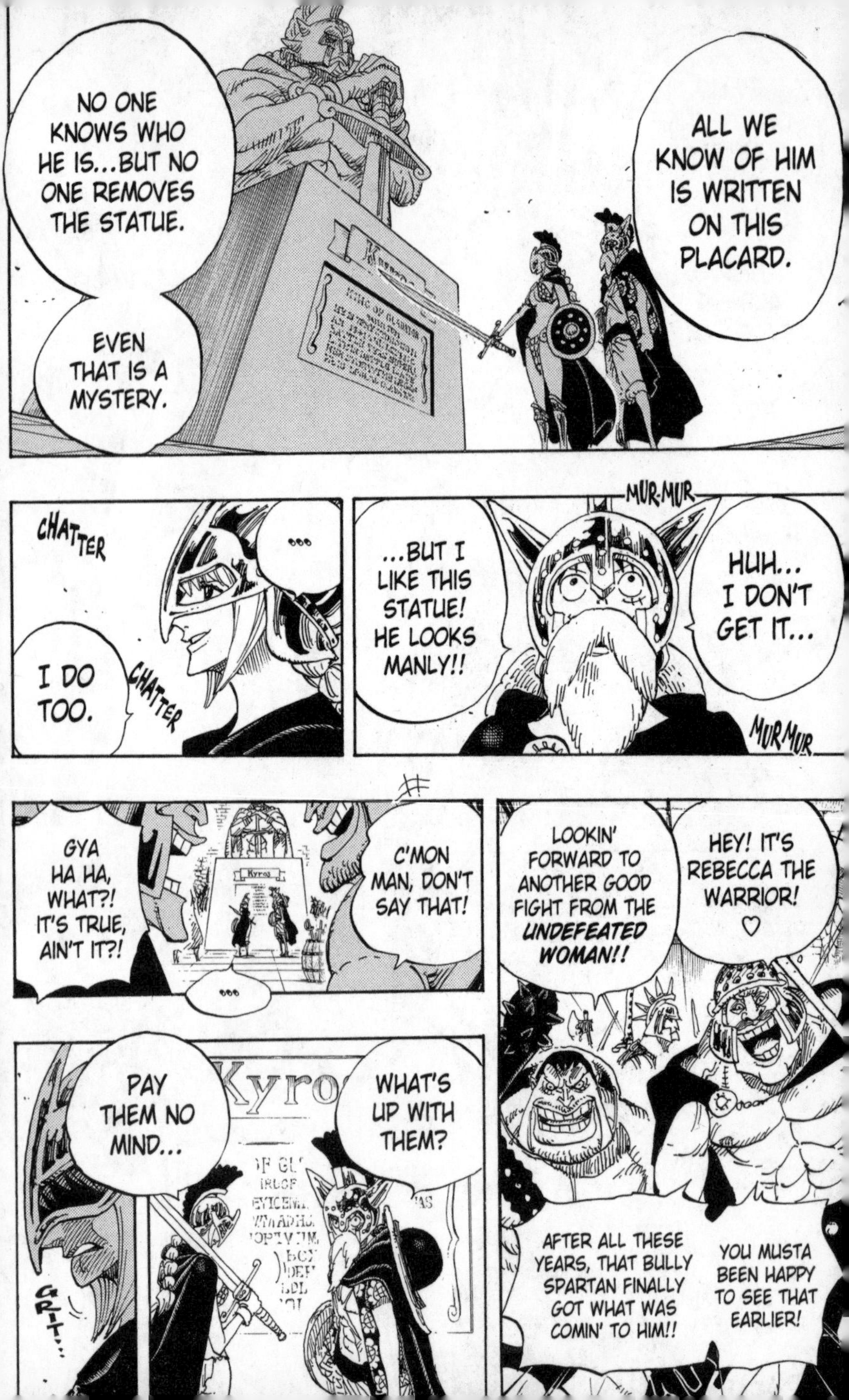
ALL WE KNOW OF HIM IS WRITTEN ON THIS PLACARD.
NO ONE KNOWS WHO HE IS...BUT NO ONE REMOVES THE STATUE.
EVEN THAT IS A MYSTERY.
MUR-MUR
HUH... I DON'T GET IT...
...BUT I LIKE THIS STATUE! HE LOOKS MANLY!!
MUR MUR
...
CHATTER
I DO TOO.
CHATTER
HEY! IT'S REBECCA THE WARRIOR! ♡
LOOKIN' FORWARD TO ANOTHER GOOD FIGHT FROM THE *UNDEFEATED WOMAN!!*
YOU MUSTA BEEN HAPPY TO SEE THAT EARLIER!
AFTER ALL THESE YEARS, THAT BULLY SPARTAN FINALLY GOT WHAT WAS COMIN' TO HIM!!
C'MON MAN, DON'T SAY THAT!
GYA HA HA, WHAT?! IT'S TRUE, AIN'T IT?!
Kyros
...
WHAT'S UP WITH THEM?
PAY THEM NO MIND...
Kyros
GRIT...

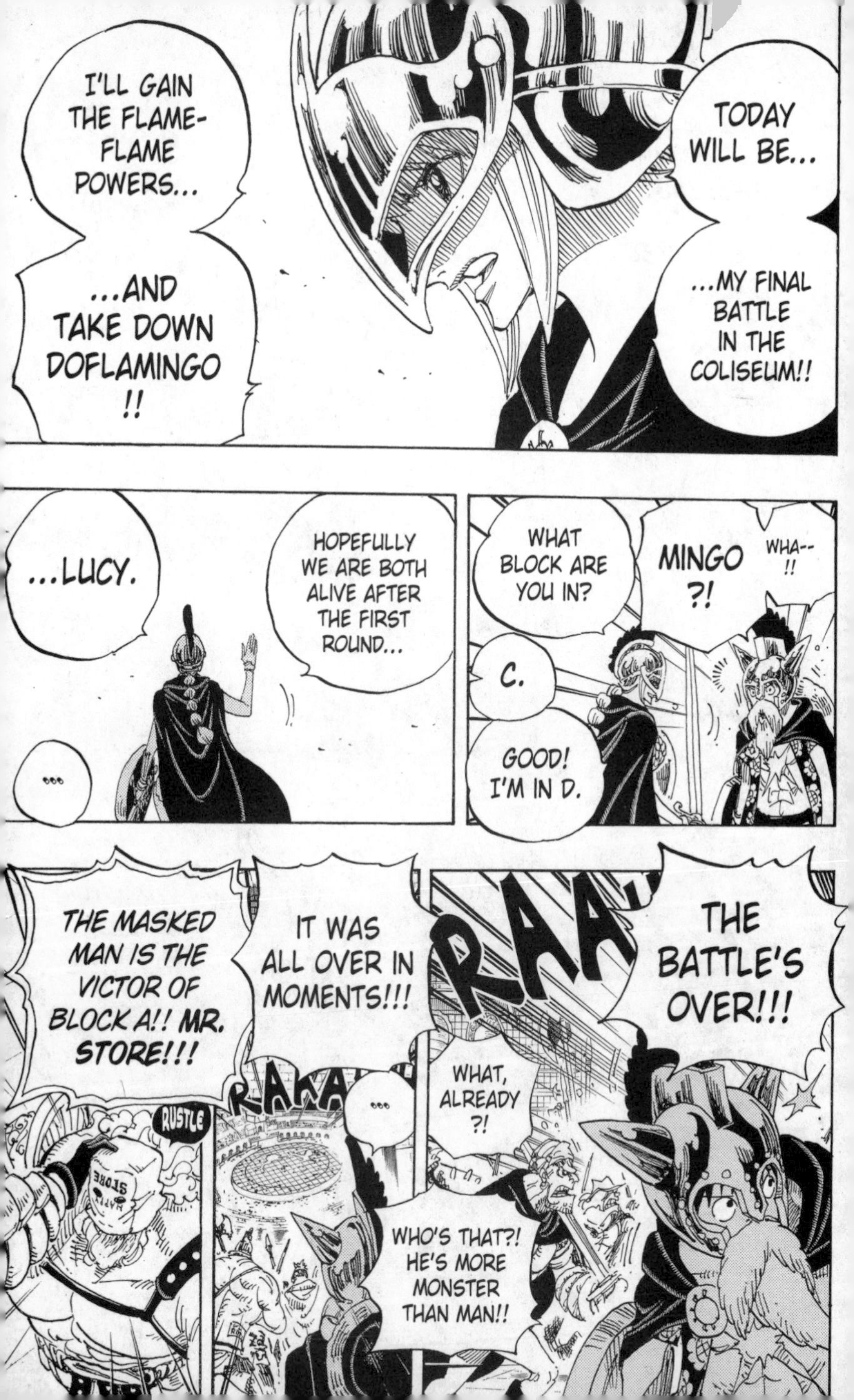
TODAY WILL BE...
...MY FINAL BATTLE IN THE COLISEUM!!
I'LL GAIN THE FLAME-FLAME POWERS...
...AND TAKE DOWN DOFLAMINGO!!
WHA-- !!
MINGO ?!
WHAT BLOCK ARE YOU IN?
C.
GOOD! I'M IN D.
HOPEFULLY WE ARE BOTH ALIVE AFTER THE FIRST ROUND...
...LUCY.
...
THE BATTLE'S OVER!!!
RAA
IT WAS ALL OVER IN MOMENTS!!!
WHAT, ALREADY ?!
WHO'S THAT?! HE'S MORE MONSTER THAN MAN!!
...
RAKA
THE MASKED MAN IS THE VICTOR OF BLOCK A!! MR. STORE!!!
RUSTLE

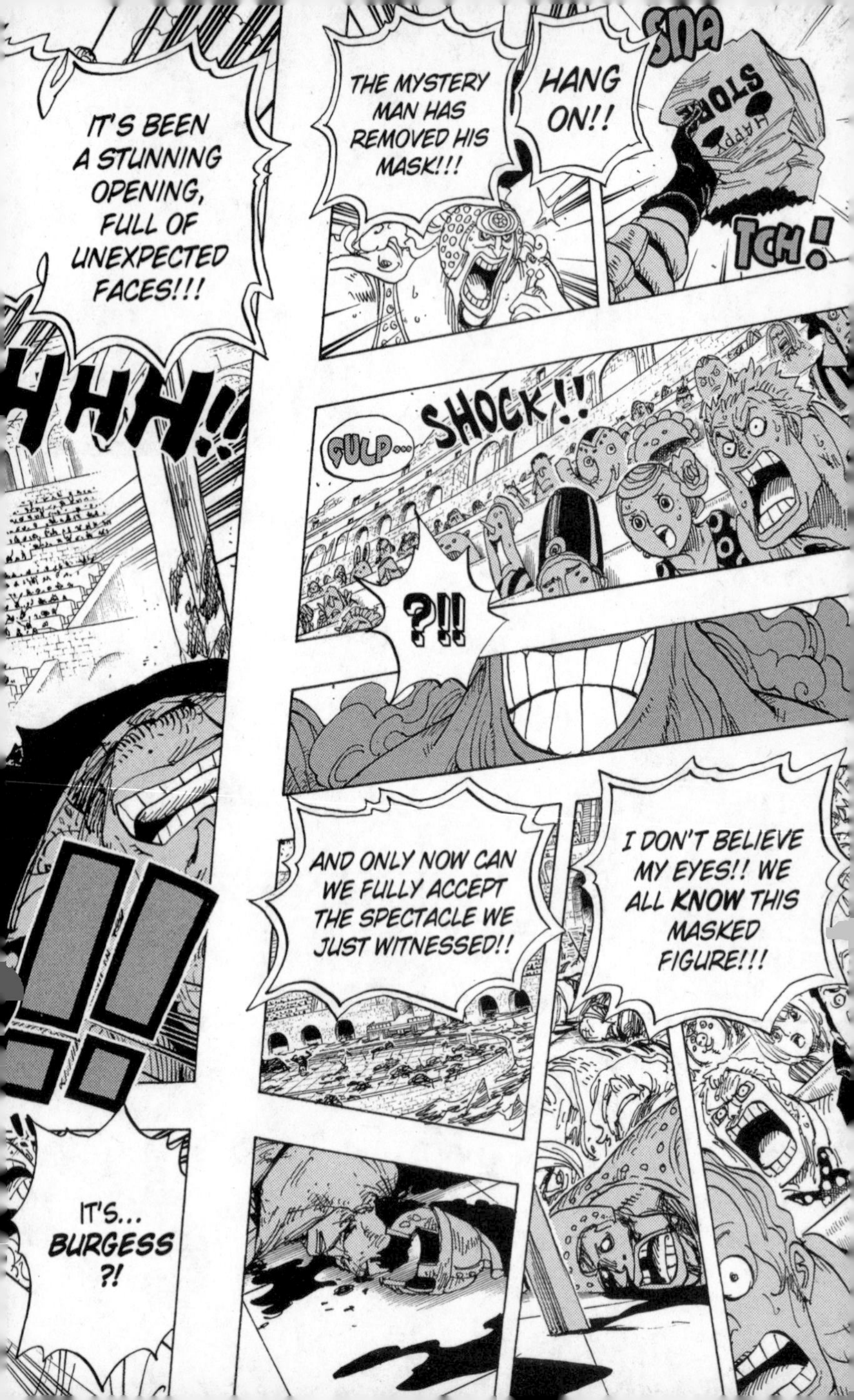

SNA
HANG ON!!
TCH!
THE MYSTERY MAN HAS REMOVED HIS MASK!!!
SHOCK!!
GULP...
?!!
I DON'T BELIEVE MY EYES!! WE ALL KNOW THIS MASKED FIGURE!!!
AND ONLY NOW CAN WE FULLY ACCEPT THE SPECTACLE WE JUST WITNESSED!!
IT'S BEEN A STUNNING OPENING, FULL OF UNEXPECTED FACES!!!
HHH!!
!!
IT'S... BURGESS ?!

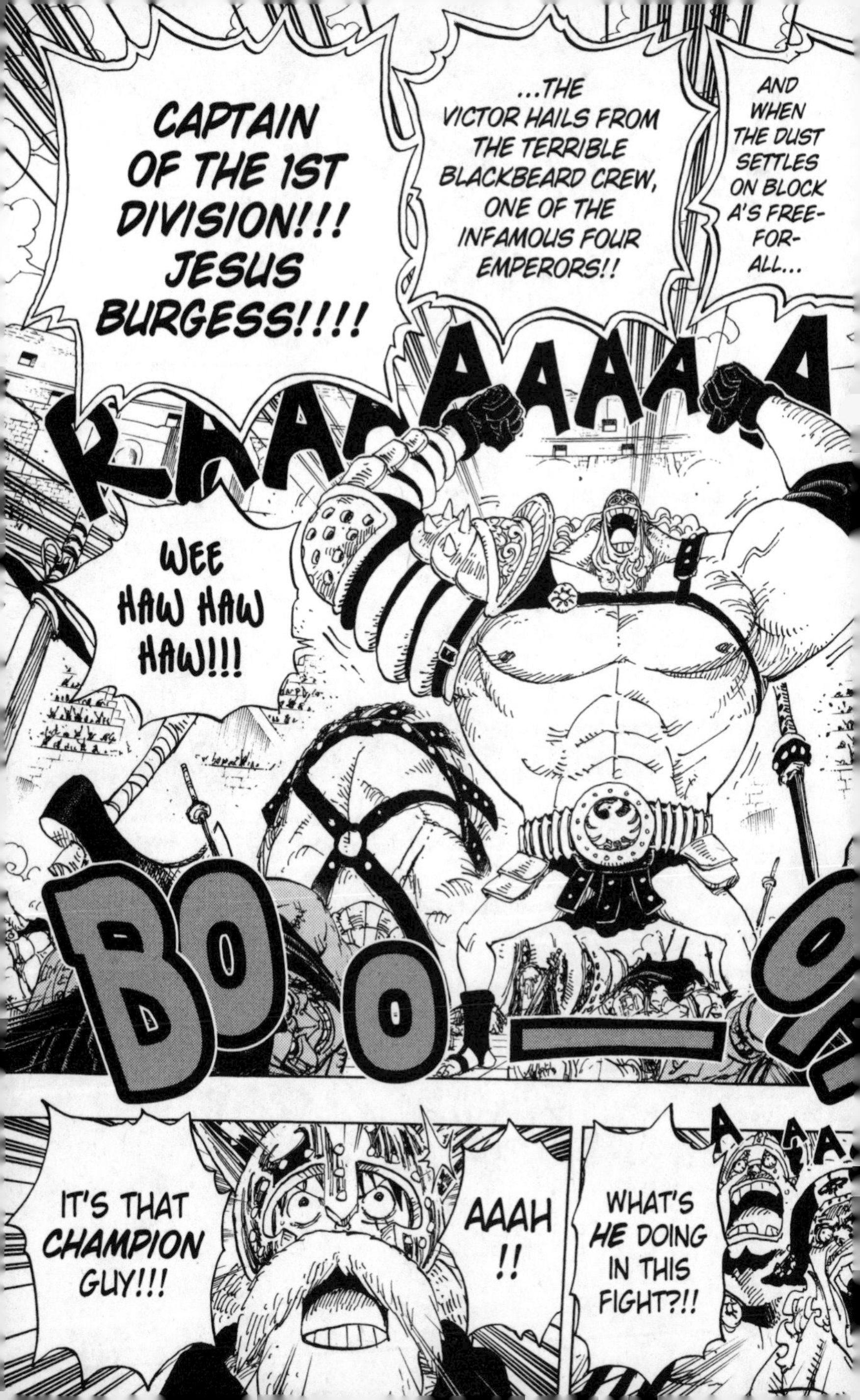
AND WHEN THE DUST SETTLES ON BLOCK A'S FREE-FOR-ALL...
...THE VICTOR HAILS FROM THE TERRIBLE BLACKBEARD CREW, ONE OF THE INFAMOUS FOUR EMPERORS!!
CAPTAIN OF THE 1ST DIVISION!!! JESUS BURGESS!!!!
KAAAAAAAA
WEE HAW HAW HAW!!!
BOO—O
WHAT'S HE DOING IN THIS FIGHT?!!
AAAH !!
IT'S THAT CHAMPION GUY!!!

SBS Question Corner

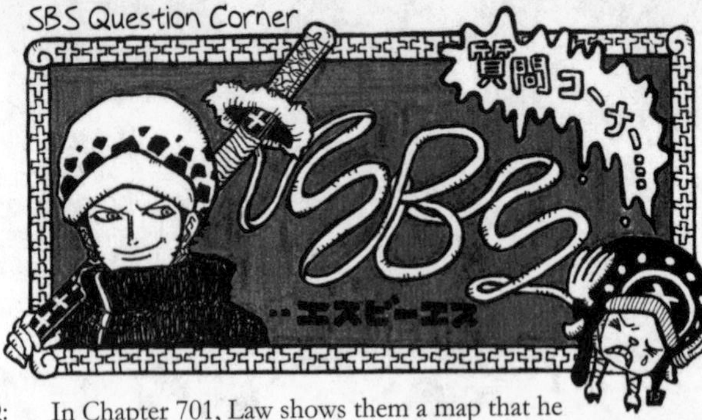

質問コーナー…
SBS
エスビーエス

(Lily, Kanagawa)

Greenbit
Dressrosa
THE TEAM THAT GOES TO DELIVER CAESAR...
GREEN BIT
DRESS ROSA
Present Location

Q: In Chapter 701, Law shows them a map that he claims his crew prepared for him! Could that be referring to Bepo?!! I mean, that does look like a paw print in the corner, doesn't it?

--T. Takaaki

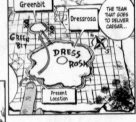

A: Yes, it does. And of course, Bepo is the navigator of the Heart Pirates. He drew the map.

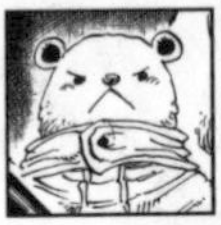

Q: Odacchi! In Volume 70, Chapter 700, Sanji made three rice balls for Law, who hates bread. What was inside each of them?

--Natsuki

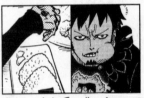

A: Well, the first one was tuna and mayonnaise. The next one was okaka (dried and ground bonito fish with soy sauce), and the last was a super-sour dried plum! By the way, Law also hates sour plums. He had a fight with Sanji a few minutes after that scene.

Q: What's the name of Law's sword? How many tattoos does Law have?! Can you draw all of his tattoos for us, Odacchi?!!! (≧ロ≦)

A: Sure thing. These are from my original sketch notebook. ➡ There's definitely a heart motif going on there. Wonder what's up with that? His katana's name is Kikoku, meaning "demon wail." No special category for it. It's a cursed blade.

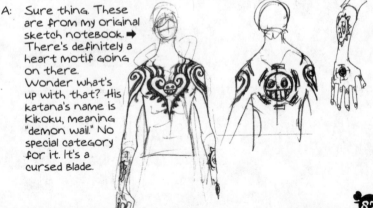

Chapter 705:

MAYNARD THE PURSUER

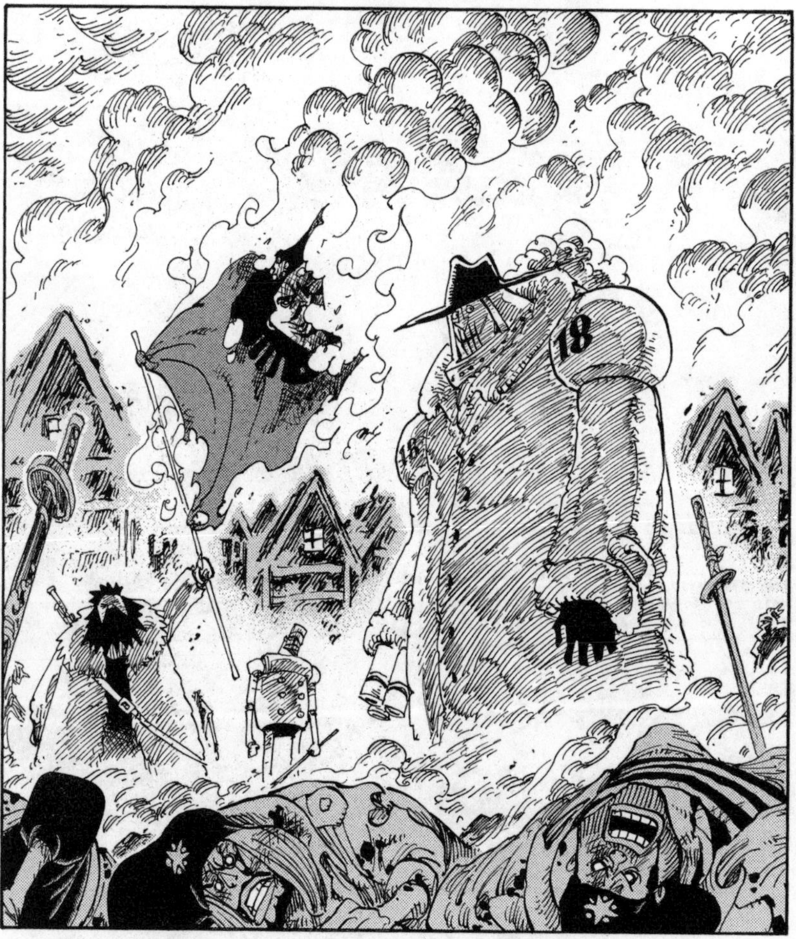
18

CARIBOU'S NEW WORLD KEE HEE HEE, VOL. 25
"AN EXAMPLE TO THE OTHERS"

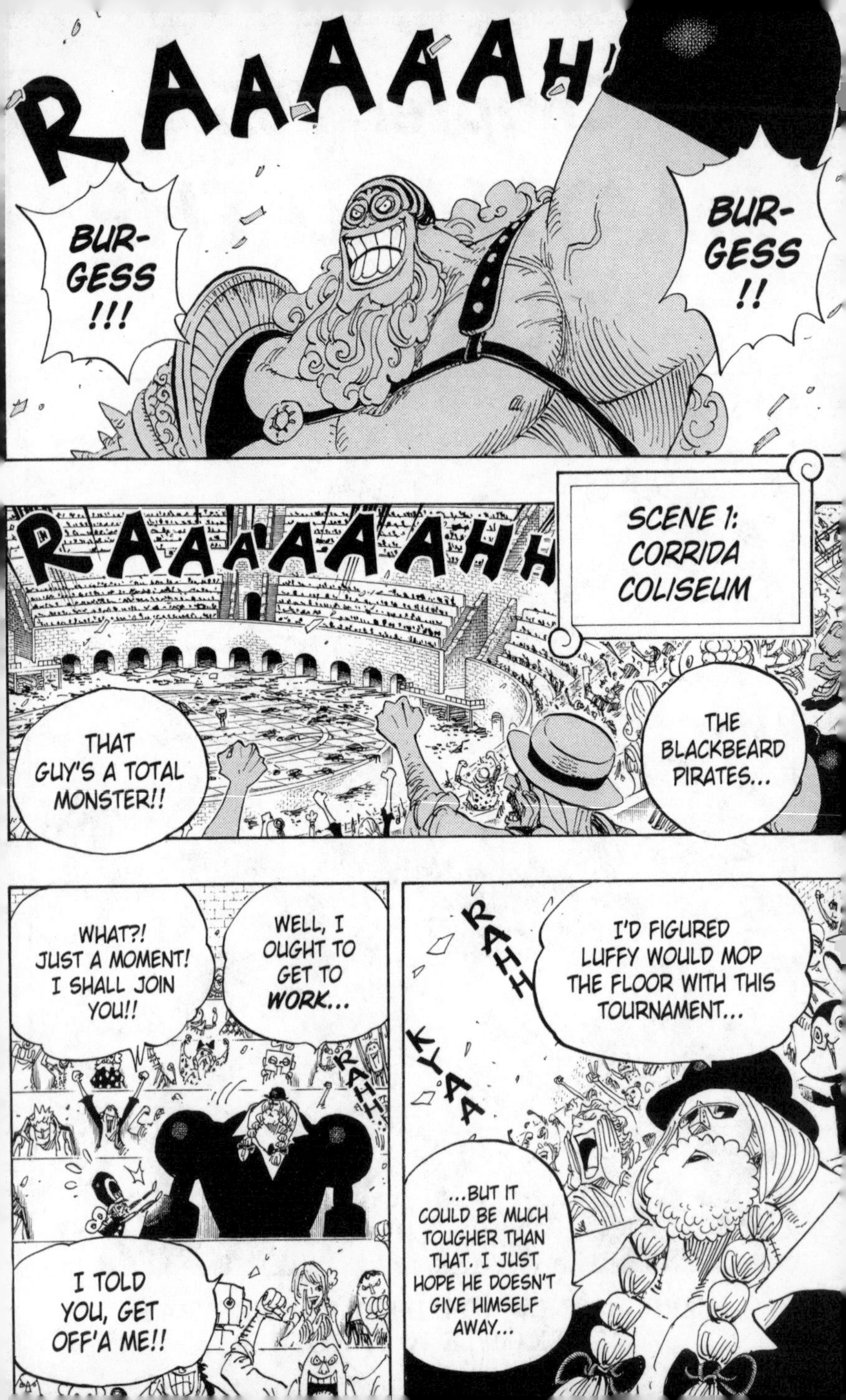
RAAAAAH
BUR-GESS !!
BUR-GESS !!!
SCENE 1: CORRIDA COLISEUM
RAAAAAHH
THE BLACKBEARD PIRATES...
THAT GUY'S A TOTAL MONSTER!!
I'D FIGURED LUFFY WOULD MOP THE FLOOR WITH THIS TOURNAMENT...
RAHH
KYAA
...BUT IT COULD BE MUCH TOUGHER THAN THAT. I JUST HOPE HE DOESN'T GIVE HIMSELF AWAY...
WELL, I OUGHT TO GET TO WORK...
WHAT?! JUST A MOMENT! I SHALL JOIN YOU!!
RAHH
I TOLD YOU, GET OFF'A ME!!

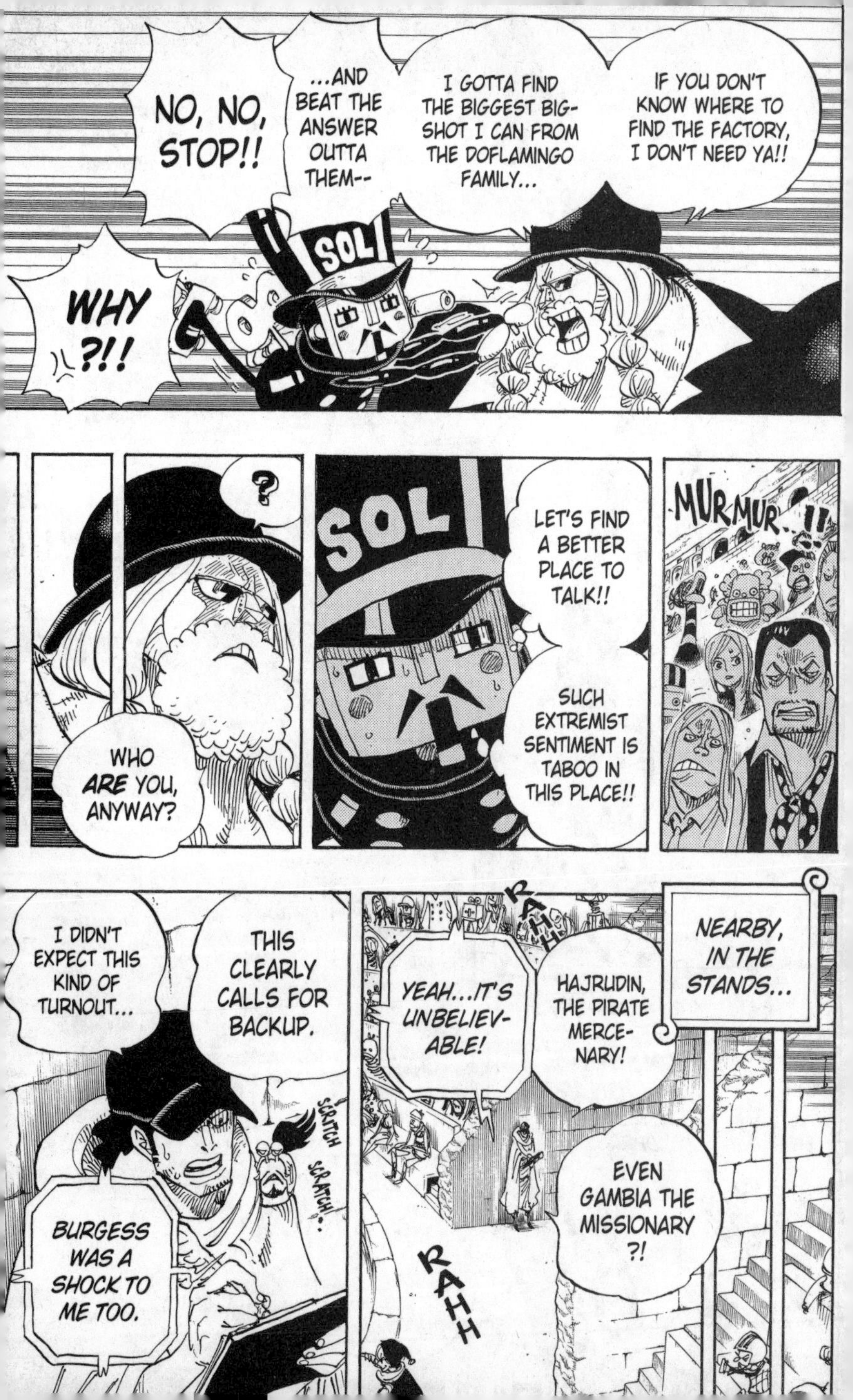
IF YOU DON'T KNOW WHERE TO FIND THE FACTORY, I DON'T NEED YA!!
I GOTTA FIND THE BIGGEST BIG-SHOT I CAN FROM THE DOFLAMINGO FAMILY...
...AND BEAT THE ANSWER OUTTA THEM--
NO, NO, STOP!!
SOL
WHY ?!!
MURMUR...!!
SOL
LET'S FIND A BETTER PLACE TO TALK!!
SUCH EXTREMIST SENTIMENT IS TABOO IN THIS PLACE!!
?
WHO ARE YOU, ANYWAY?
NEARBY, IN THE STANDS...
RAHH
HAJRUDIN, THE PIRATE MERCENARY!
YEAH...IT'S UNBELIEVABLE!
EVEN GAMBIA THE MISSIONARY ?!
RAHH
THIS CLEARLY CALLS FOR BACKUP.
I DIDN'T EXPECT THIS KIND OF TURNOUT...
SCRATCH
SCRATCH
BURGESS WAS A SHOCK TO ME TOO.

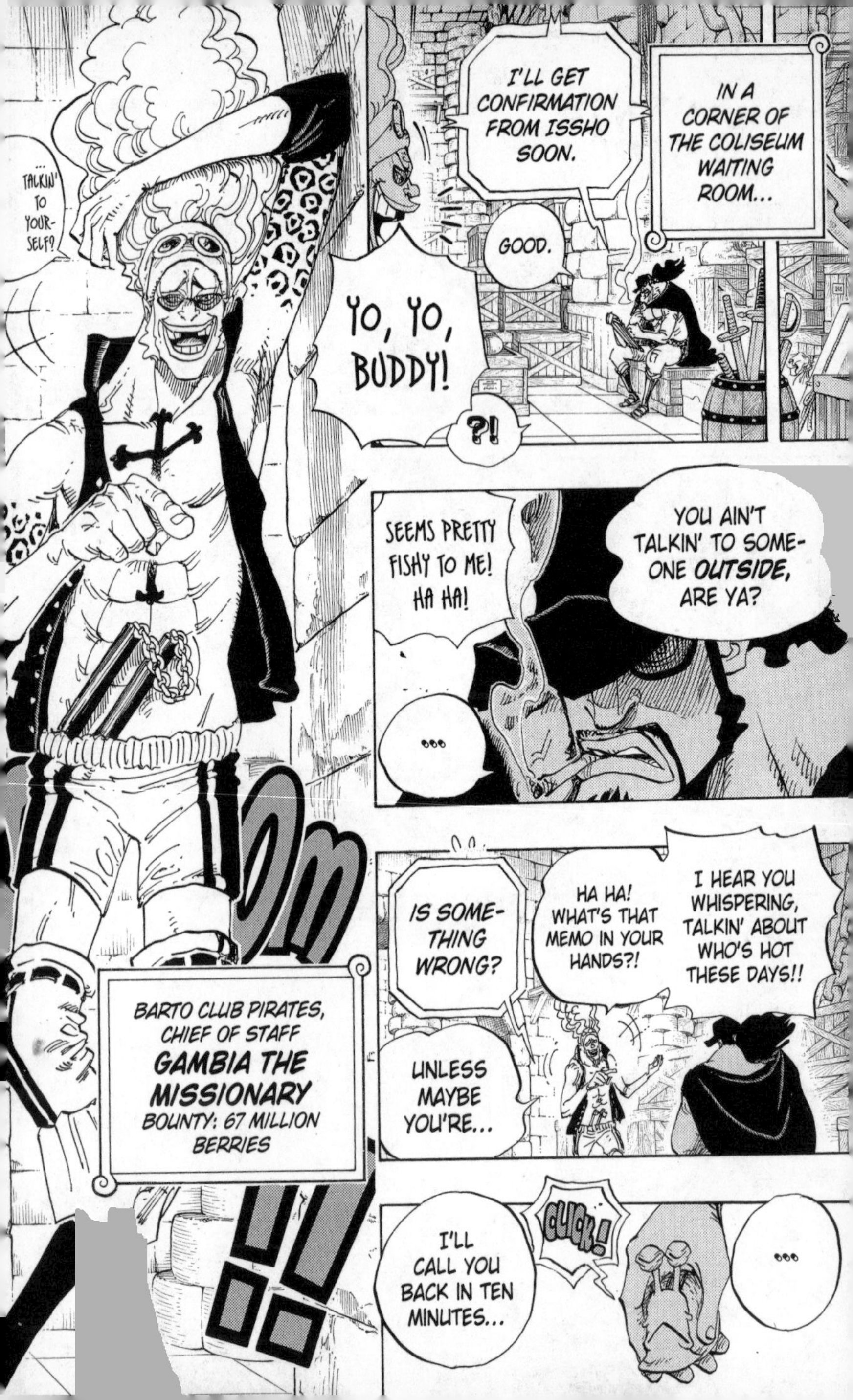

IN A CORNER OF THE COLISEUM WAITING ROOM...
I'LL GET CONFIRMATION FROM ISSHO SOON.
GOOD.
YOU AIN'T TALKIN' TO SOME-ONE OUTSIDE, ARE YA?
SEEMS PRETTY FISHY TO ME! HA HA!
...
I HEAR YOU WHISPERING, TALKIN' ABOUT WHO'S HOT THESE DAYS!!
HA HA! WHAT'S THAT MEMO IN YOUR HANDS?!
IS SOME-THING WRONG?
UNLESS MAYBE YOU'RE...
...
CLICK!
I'LL CALL YOU BACK IN TEN MINUTES...
YO, YO, BUDDY!
?!
... TALKIN' TO YOUR-SELF?
BARTO CLUB PIRATES, CHIEF OF STAFF
GAMBIA THE MISSIONARY
BOUNTY: 67 MILLION BERRIES

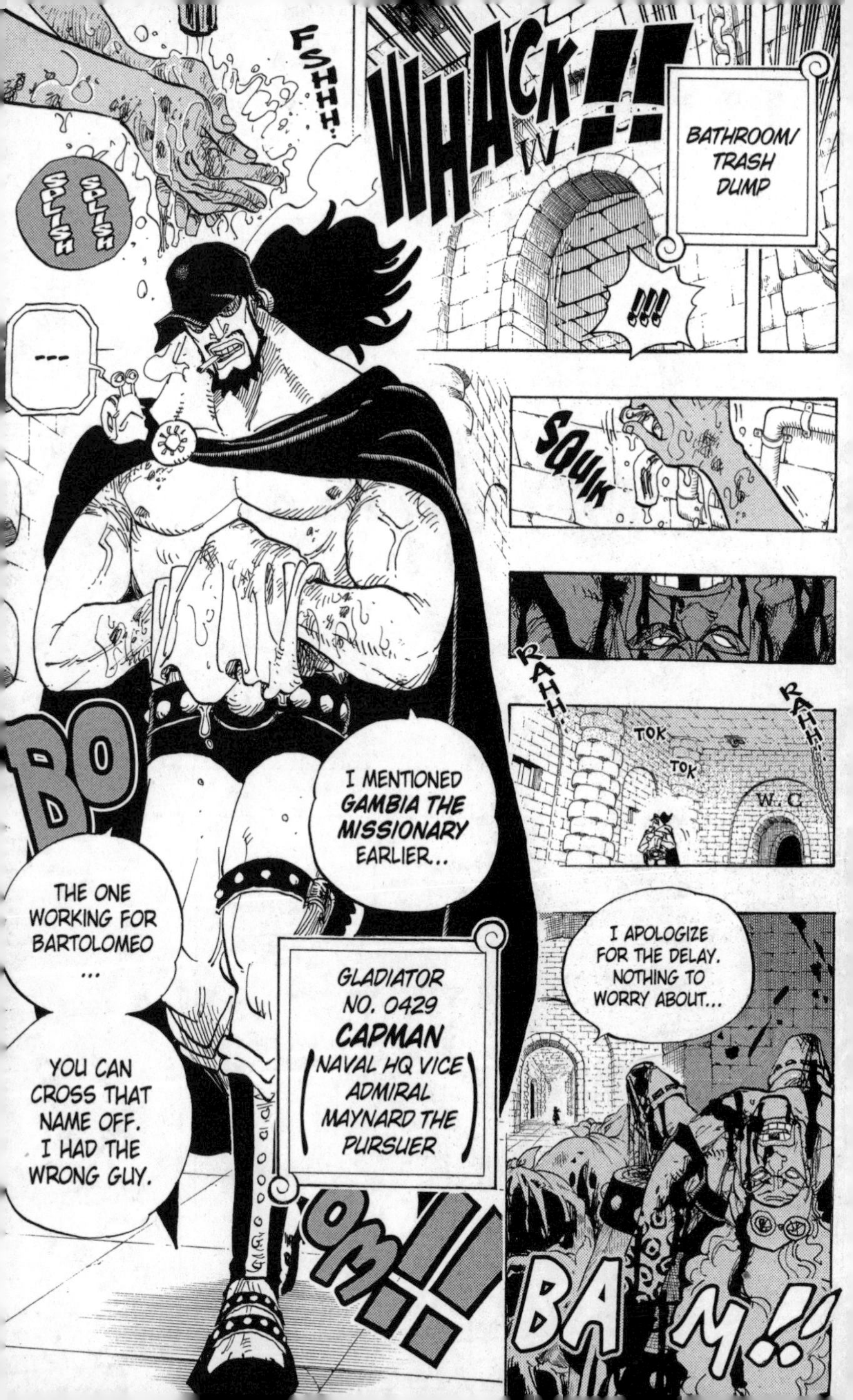
WHACK!!
BATHROOM/ TRASH DUMP
!!!
SQUIK
RAHH
RAHH
TOK
TOK
W.C
I APOLOGIZE FOR THE DELAY. NOTHING TO WORRY ABOUT...
BAM!!
FSHHH
SPLISH SPLISH
...
BOOM!!
I MENTIONED GAMBIA THE MISSIONARY EARLIER...
GLADIATOR NO. 0429 CAPMAN (NAVAL HQ VICE ADMIRAL MAYNARD THE PURSUER)
THE ONE WORKING FOR BARTOLOMEO ...
YOU CAN CROSS THAT NAME OFF. I HAD THE WRONG GUY.

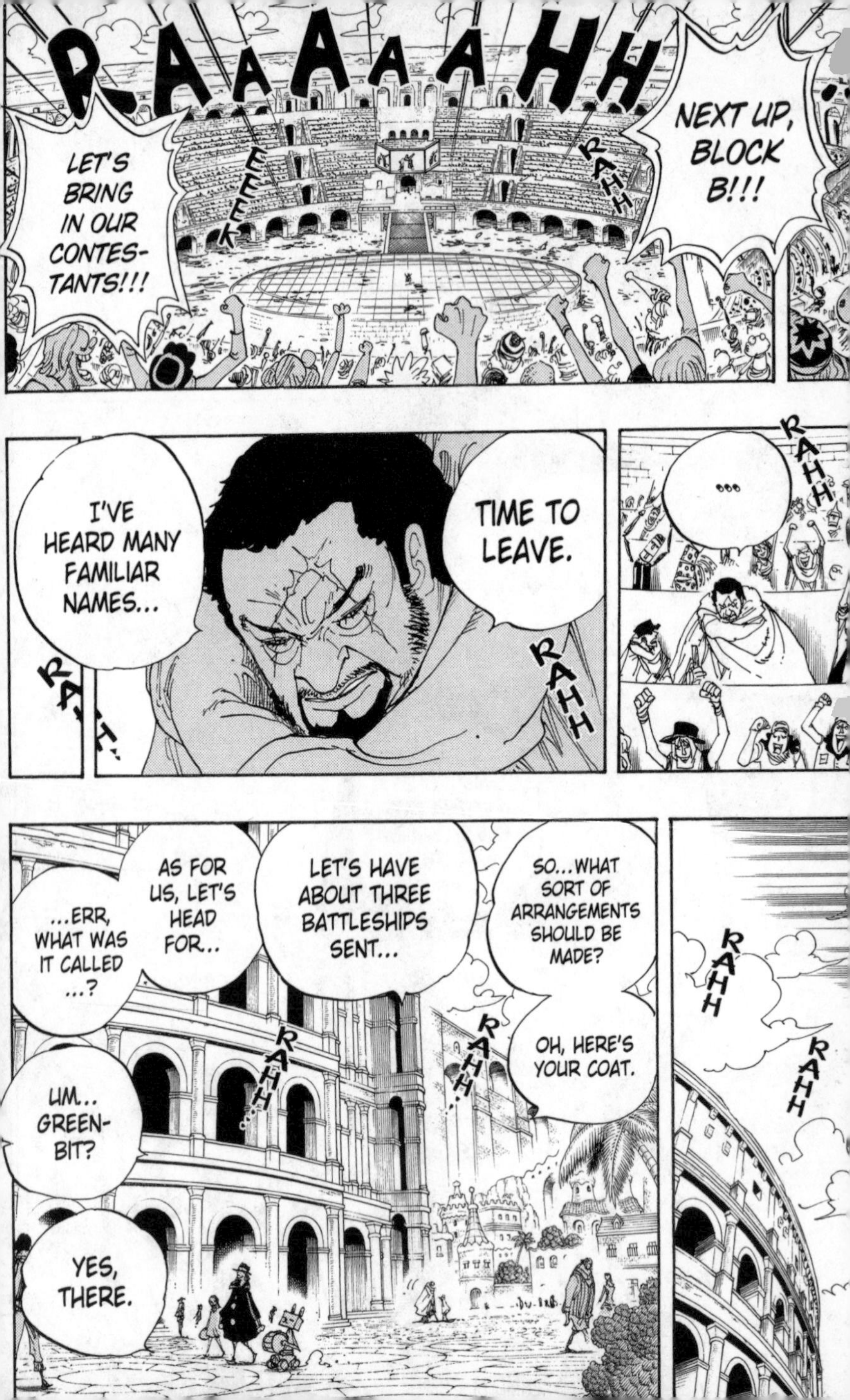
RAAAAAHH
NEXT UP, BLOCK B!!!
RAHH
EEEEK
LET'S BRING IN OUR CONTES-TANTS!!!
...
RAHH
TIME TO LEAVE.
RAHH
I'VE HEARD MANY FAMILIAR NAMES...
RAH..
RAHH
RAHH
SO...WHAT SORT OF ARRANGEMENTS SHOULD BE MADE?
OH, HERE'S YOUR COAT.
RAHH..
LET'S HAVE ABOUT THREE BATTLESHIPS SENT...
AS FOR US, LET'S HEAD FOR...
RAHH..
...ERR, WHAT WAS IT CALLED ...?
UM.. GREEN-BIT?
YES, THERE.

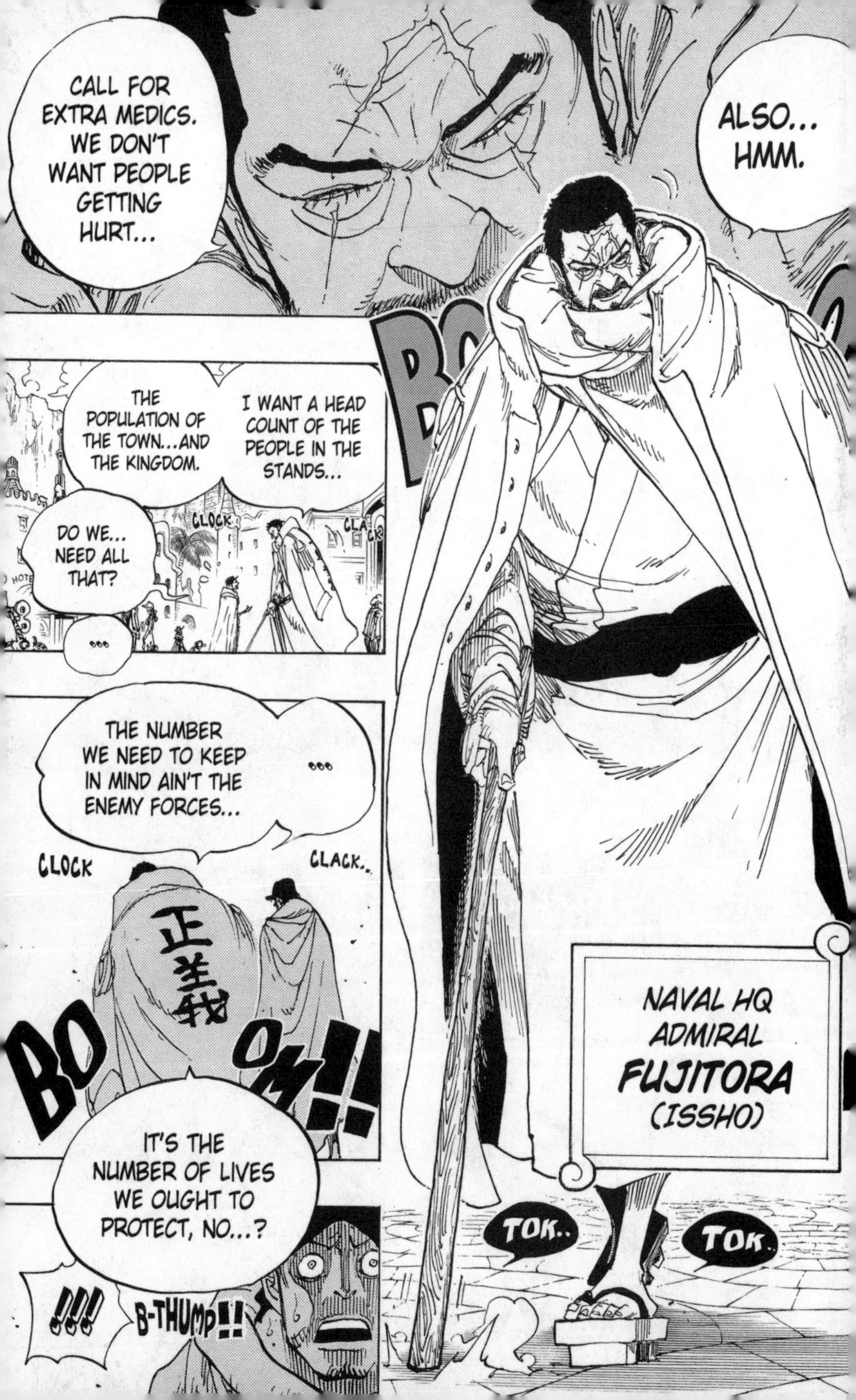
ALSO... HMM.
CALL FOR EXTRA MEDICS. WE DON'T WANT PEOPLE GETTING HURT...
BO
NAVAL HQ ADMIRAL FUJITORA (ISSHO)
TOK..
TOK..
I WANT A HEAD COUNT OF THE PEOPLE IN THE STANDS...
THE POPULATION OF THE TOWN...AND THE KINGDOM.
CLOCK
CLACK
DO WE... NEED ALL THAT?
...
...
THE NUMBER WE NEED TO KEEP IN MIND AIN'T THE ENEMY FORCES...
CLACK..
CLOCK
正義
BOOM!!
IT'S THE NUMBER OF LIVES WE OUGHT TO PROTECT, NO...?
B-THUMP!!
!!!

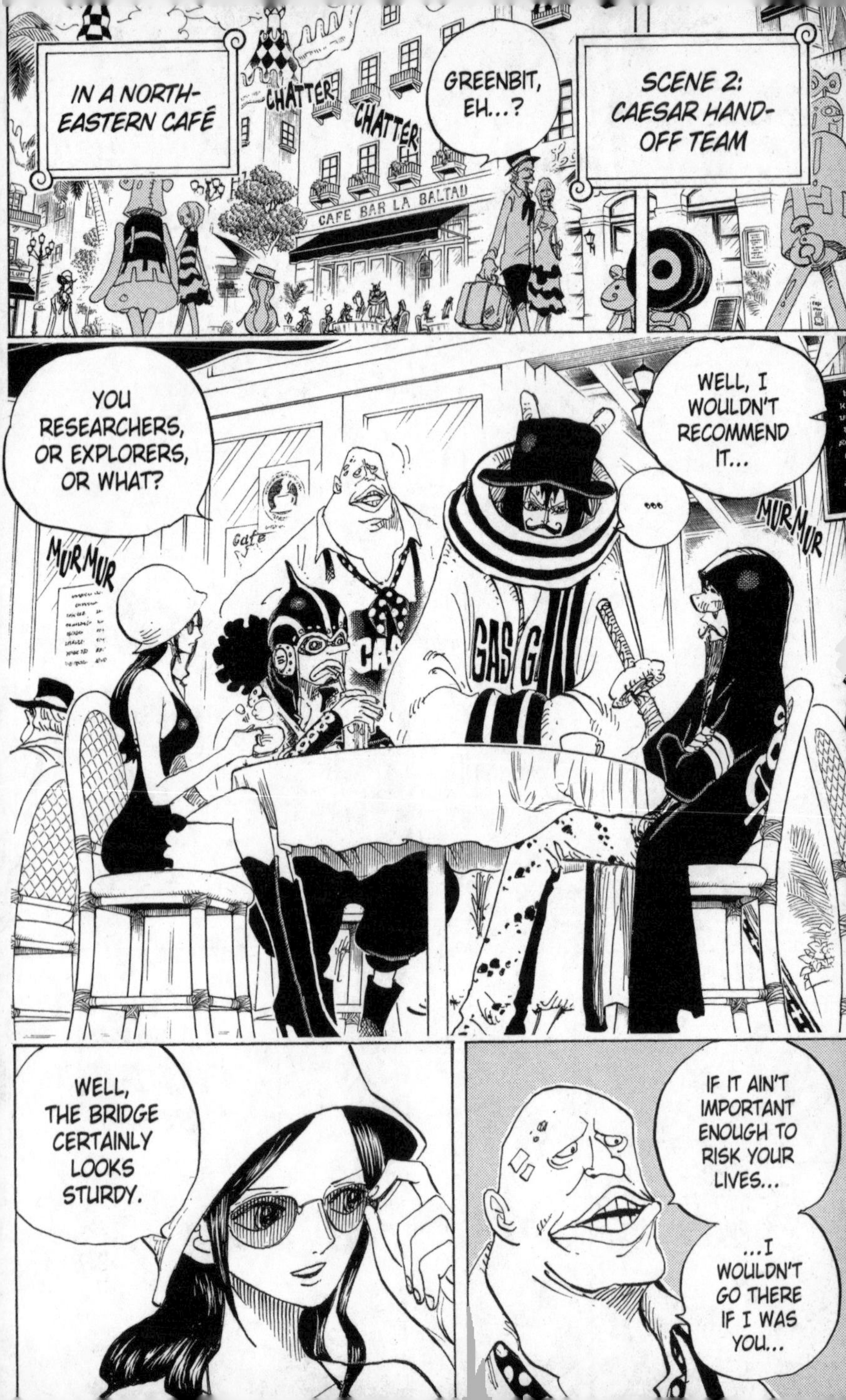
SCENE 2: CAESAR HAND-OFF TEAM
GREENBIT, EH...?
CHATTER
CHATTER
IN A NORTH-EASTERN CAFÉ
CAFE BAR LA BALTAU
WELL, I WOULDN'T RECOMMEND IT...
MURMUR
...
YOU RESEARCHERS, OR EXPLORERS, OR WHAT?
MURMUR
IF IT AIN'T IMPORTANT ENOUGH TO RISK YOUR LIVES...
...I WOULDN'T GO THERE IF I WAS YOU...
WELL, THE BRIDGE CERTAINLY LOOKS STURDY.

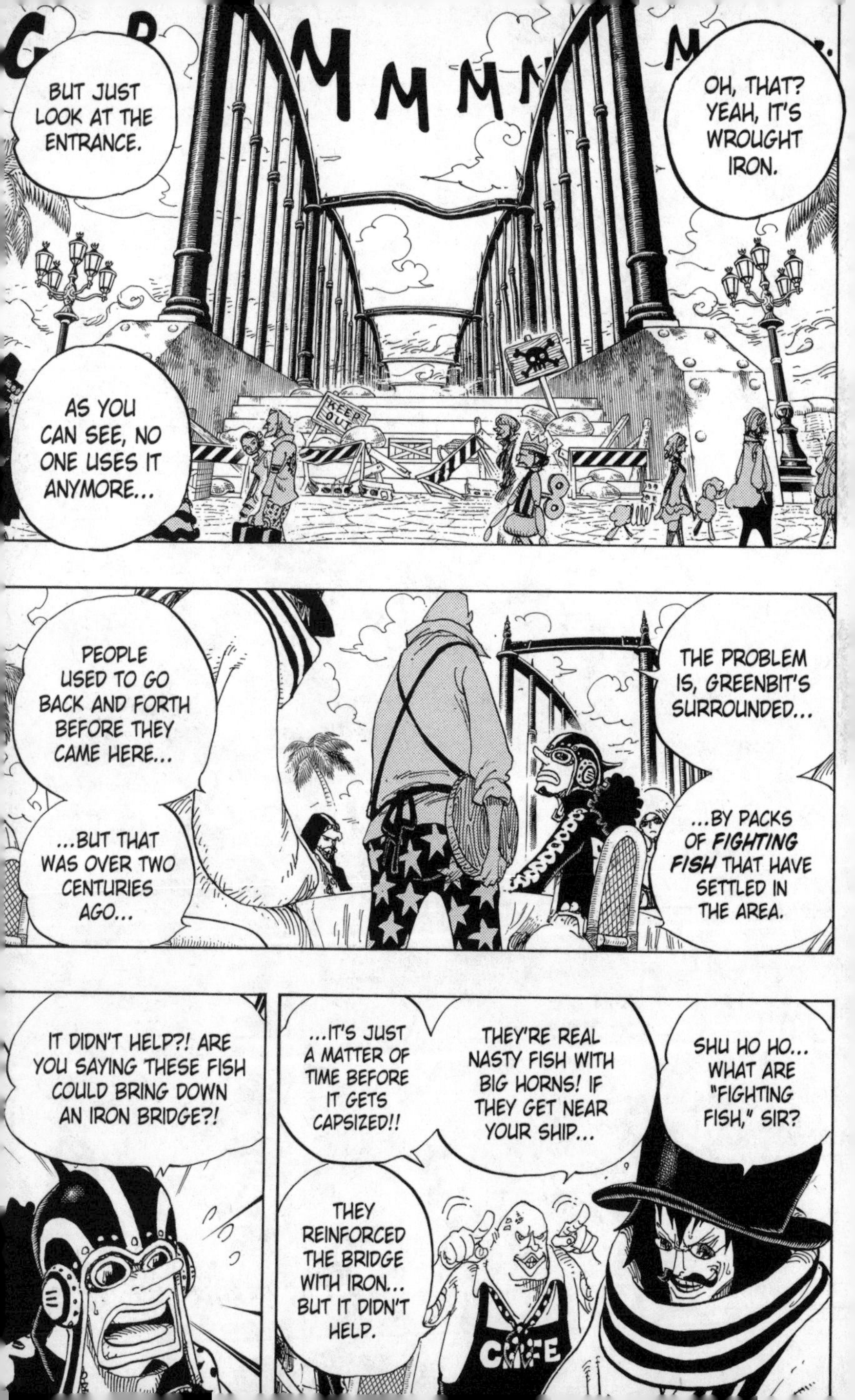
GRMMMMN...
OH, THAT? YEAH, IT'S WROUGHT IRON.
BUT JUST LOOK AT THE ENTRANCE.
KEEP OUT
AS YOU CAN SEE, NO ONE USES IT ANYMORE...
THE PROBLEM IS, GREENBIT'S SURROUNDED...
...BY PACKS OF *FIGHTING FISH* THAT HAVE SETTLED IN THE AREA.
PEOPLE USED TO GO BACK AND FORTH BEFORE THEY CAME HERE...
...BUT THAT WAS OVER TWO CENTURIES AGO...
SHU HO HO... WHAT ARE "FIGHTING FISH," SIR?
THEY'RE REAL NASTY FISH WITH BIG HORNS! IF THEY GET NEAR YOUR SHIP...
...IT'S JUST A MATTER OF TIME BEFORE IT GETS CAPSIZED!!
THEY REINFORCED THE BRIDGE WITH IRON... BUT IT DIDN'T HELP.
CAFE
IT DIDN'T HELP?! ARE YOU SAYING THESE FISH COULD BRING DOWN AN IRON BRIDGE?!

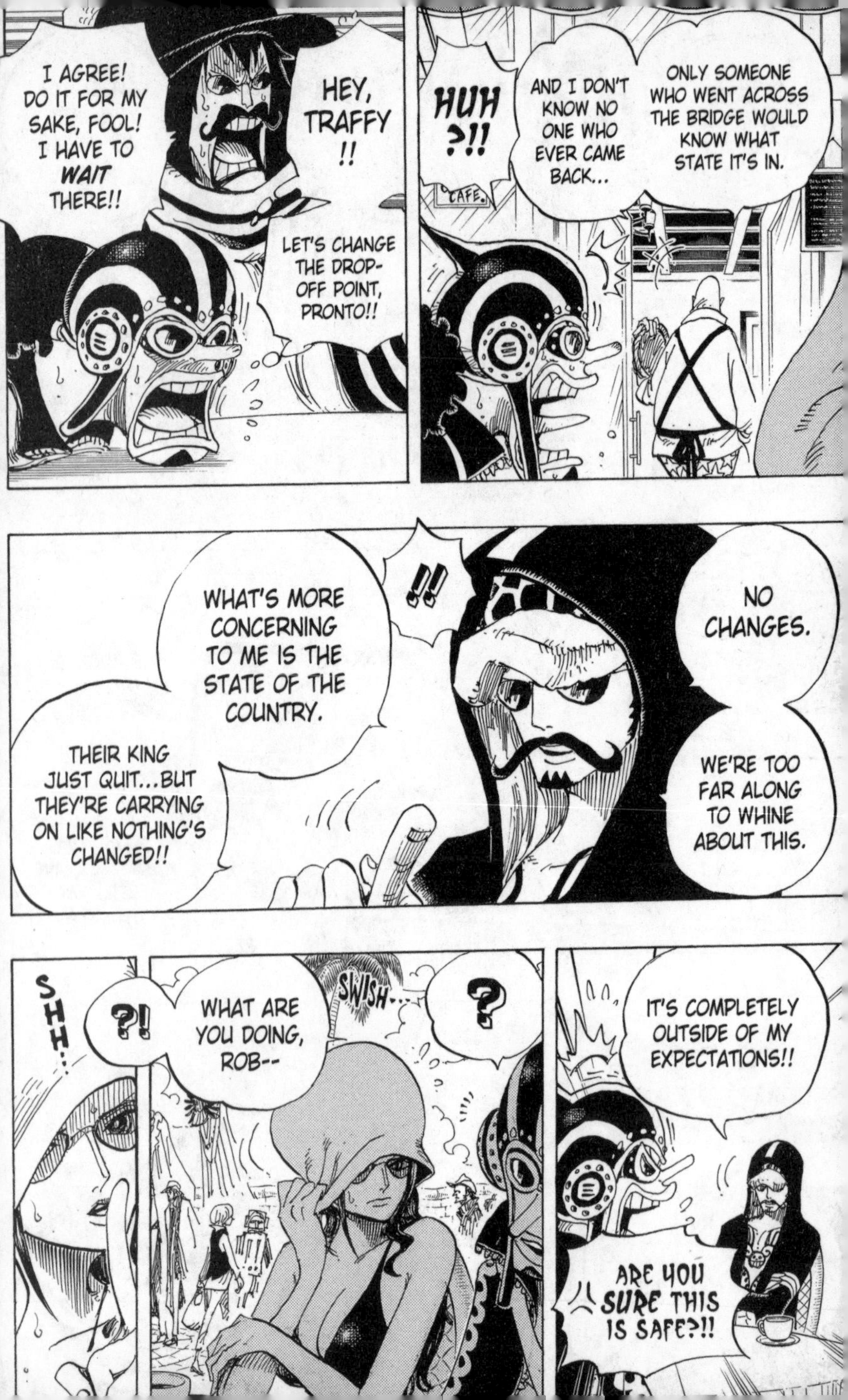
ONLY SOMEONE WHO WENT ACROSS THE BRIDGE WOULD KNOW WHAT STATE IT'S IN.
AND I DON'T KNOW NO ONE WHO EVER CAME BACK...
HUH ?!!
CAFE.
HEY, TRAFFY !!
I AGREE! DO IT FOR MY SAKE, FOOL! I HAVE TO WAIT THERE!!
LET'S CHANGE THE DROP-OFF POINT, PRONTO!!
NO CHANGES.
WE'RE TOO FAR ALONG TO WHINE ABOUT THIS.
!!
WHAT'S MORE CONCERNING TO ME IS THE STATE OF THE COUNTRY.
THEIR KING JUST QUIT...BUT THEY'RE CARRYING ON LIKE NOTHING'S CHANGED!!
IT'S COMPLETELY OUTSIDE OF MY EXPECTATIONS!!
ARE YOU SURE THIS IS SAFE?!!
?
SWISH...
WHAT ARE YOU DOING, ROB--
?!
SHH...

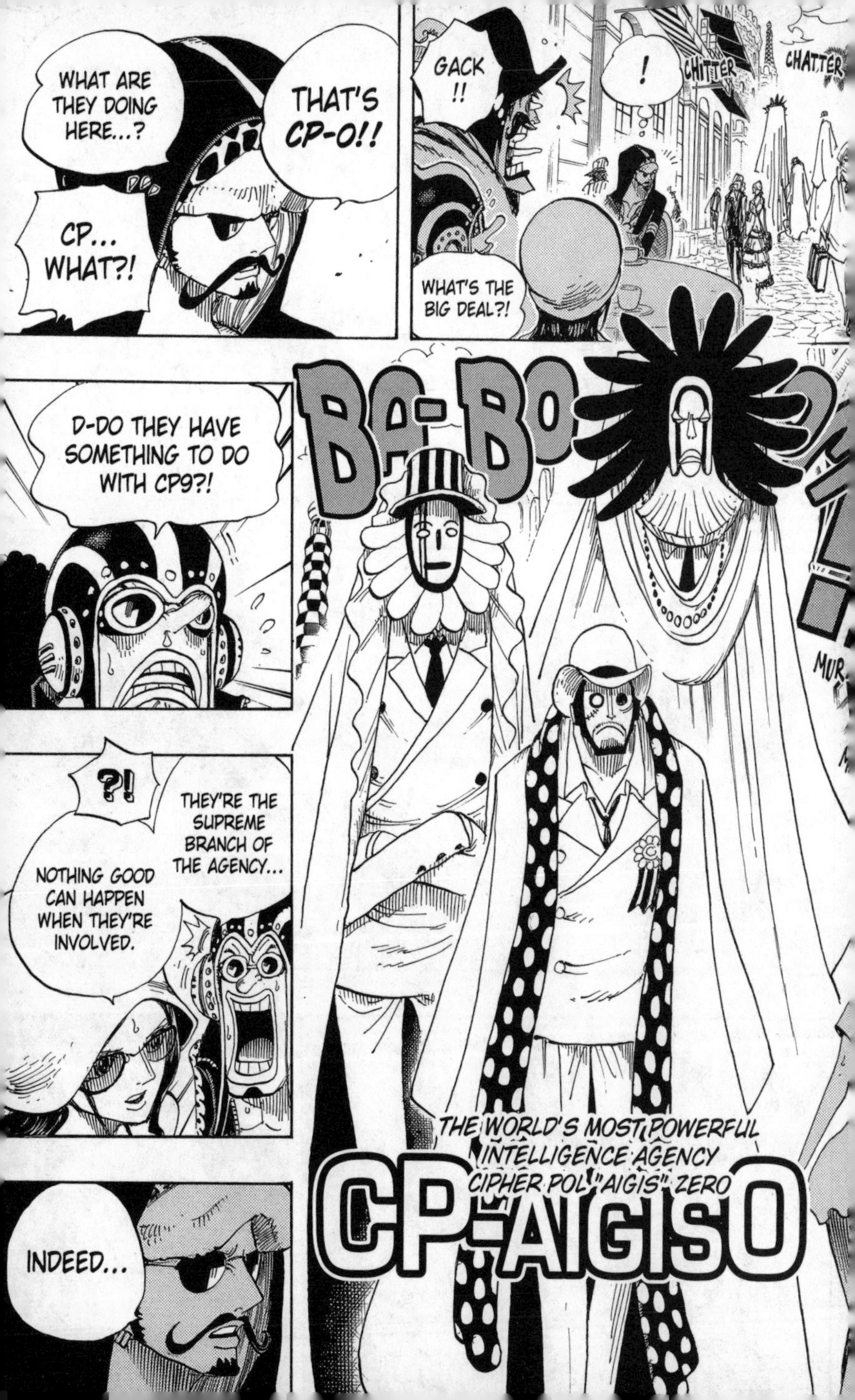
GACK !!
!
CHITTER
CHATTER
WHAT'S THE BIG DEAL?!
THAT'S CP-0!!
WHAT ARE THEY DOING HERE...?
CP... WHAT?!
BA-BO
?!
MUR
THE WORLD'S MOST POWERFUL INTELLIGENCE AGENCY CIPHER POL "AIGIS" ZERO
CP-AIGIS0
D-DO THEY HAVE SOMETHING TO DO WITH CP9?!
?!
THEY'RE THE SUPREME BRANCH OF THE AGENCY...
NOTHING GOOD CAN HAPPEN WHEN THEY'RE INVOLVED.
INDEED...

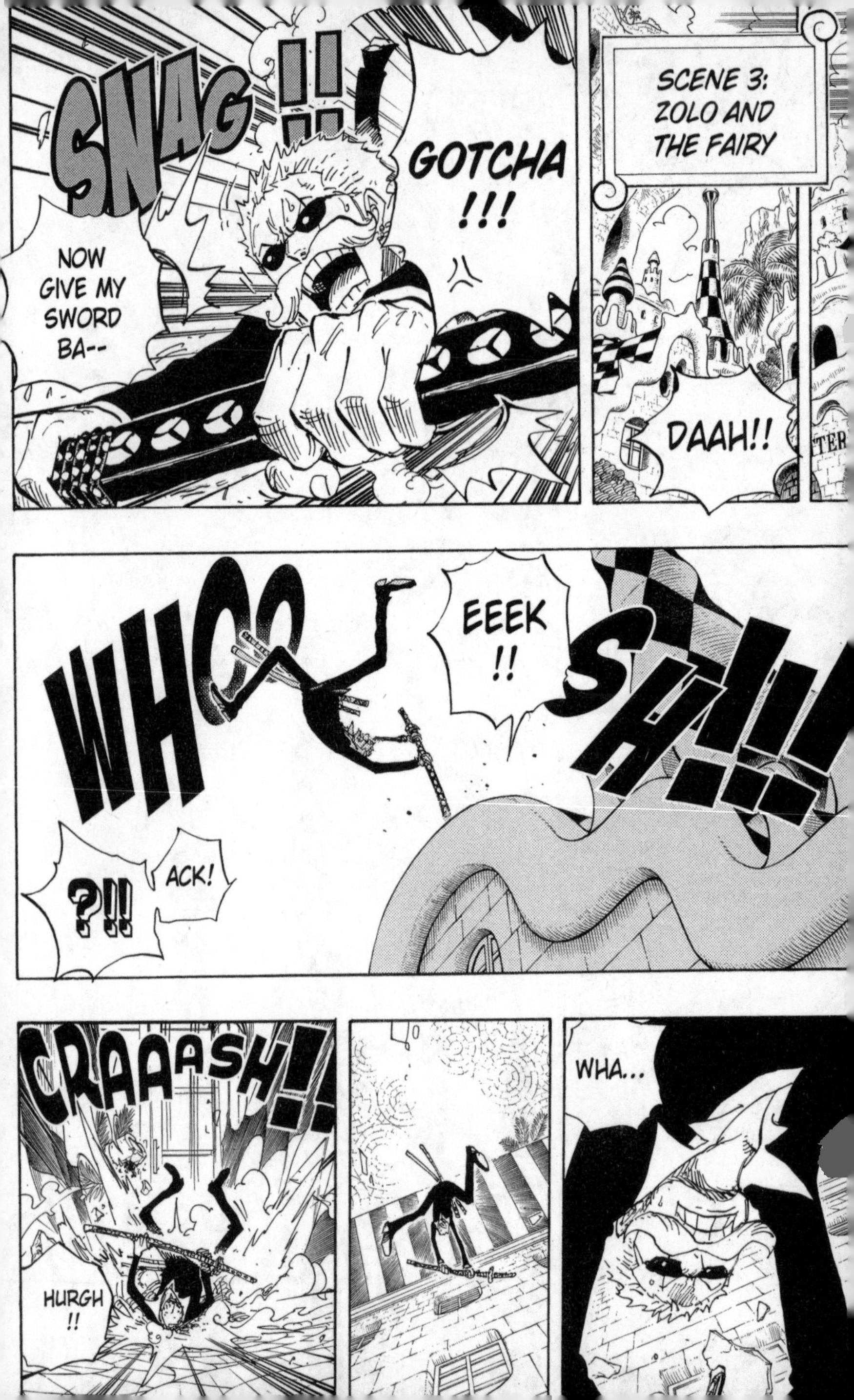
SCENE 3: ZOLO AND THE FAIRY
DAAH!!
SNAG!!
GOTCHA!!!
NOW GIVE MY SWORD BA--
SH!!
EEEK!!
WHOO
ACK!
?!!
WHA...
CRAAASH!!
HURGH!!

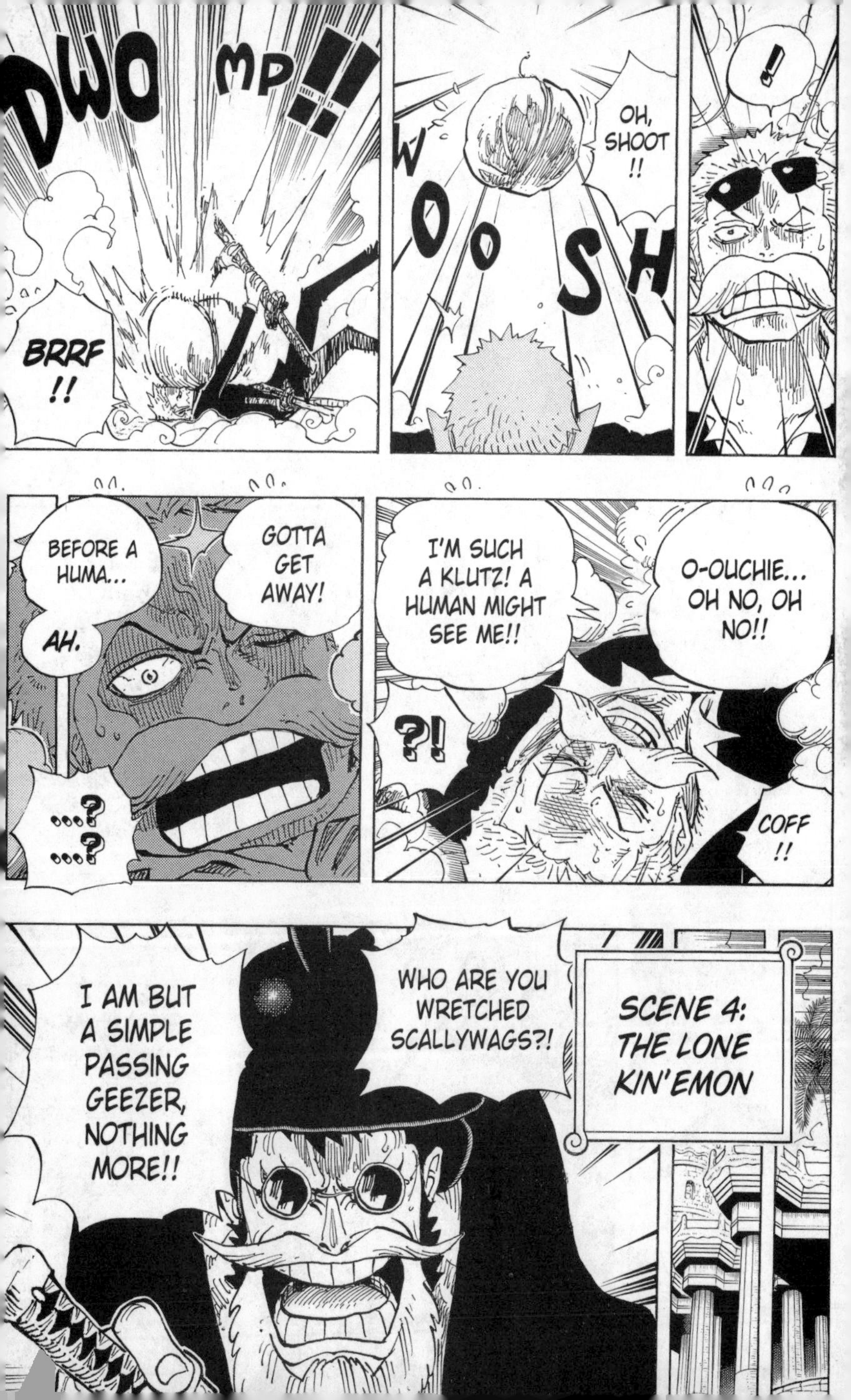
!
OH, SHOOT !!
WOOSH
DWOMP!!
BRRF !!
O-OUCHIE... OH NO, OH NO!!
I'M SUCH A KLUTZ! A HUMAN MIGHT SEE ME!!
?!
COFF !!
GOTTA GET AWAY!
BEFORE A HUMA...
AH.
...? ...?
SCENE 4: THE LONE KIN'EMON
WHO ARE YOU WRETCHED SCALLYWAGS?!
I AM BUT A SIMPLE PASSING GEEZER, NOTHING MORE!!

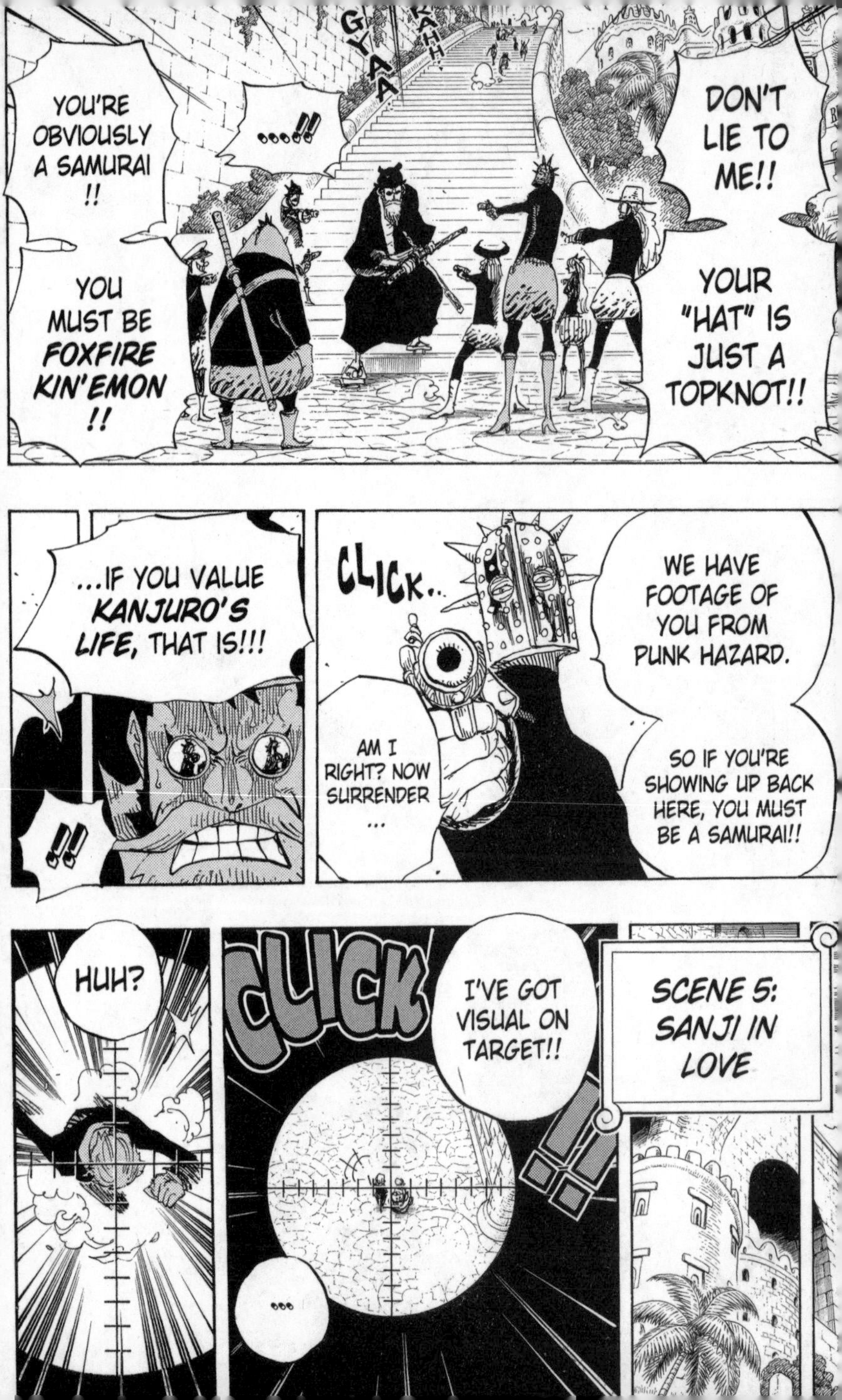
GYAA
KAHH
DON'T LIE TO ME!!
YOUR "HAT" IS JUST A TOPKNOT!!
...!!
YOU'RE OBVIOUSLY A SAMURAI !!
YOU MUST BE FOXFIRE KIN'EMON !!
WE HAVE FOOTAGE OF YOU FROM PUNK HAZARD.
SO IF YOU'RE SHOWING UP BACK HERE, YOU MUST BE A SAMURAI!!
CLICK...
AM I RIGHT? NOW SURRENDER ...
...IF YOU VALUE KANJURO'S LIFE, THAT IS!!!
!!
SCENE 5: SANJI IN LOVE
CLICK
I'VE GOT VISUAL ON TARGET!!
!!
...
HUH?

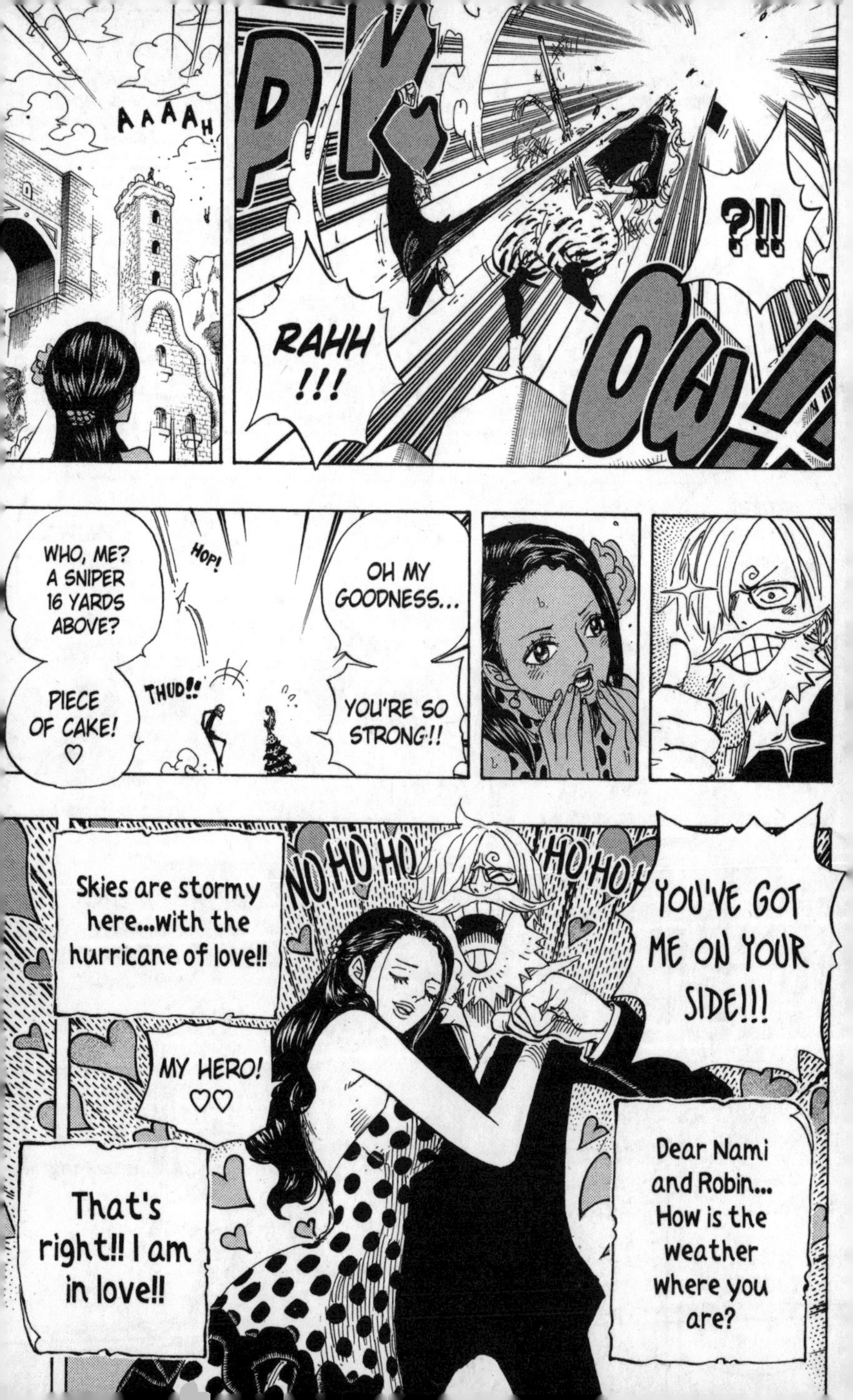
?!!
OW!!
RAHH !!!
AAAAH
OH MY GOODNESS...
YOU'RE SO STRONG!!
HOP!
WHO, ME? A SNIPER 16 YARDS ABOVE?
THUD!!
PIECE OF CAKE! ♡
YOU'VE GOT ME ON YOUR SIDE!!!
HO HO H
NO HO HO
Dear Nami and Robin... How is the weather where you are?
Skies are stormy here...with the hurricane of love!!
MY HERO! ♡♡
That's right!! I am in love!!

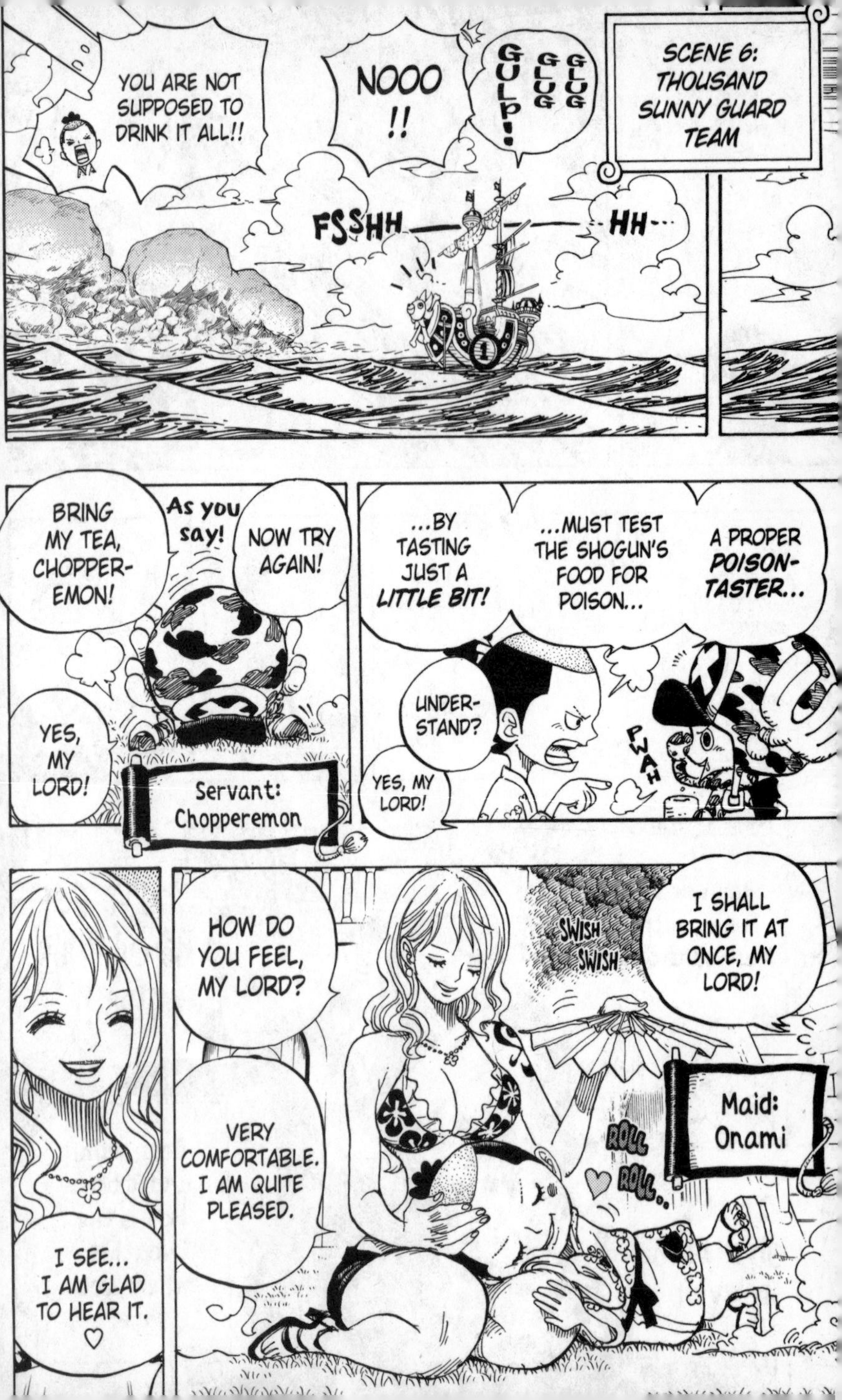
GULP!
GLUG GLUG
NOOO!!
YOU ARE NOT SUPPOSED TO DRINK IT ALL!!
FSSHH—HH...
SCENE 6: THOUSAND SUNNY GUARD TEAM
A PROPER POISON-TASTER...
...MUST TEST THE SHOGUN'S FOOD FOR POISON...
...BY TASTING JUST A LITTLE BIT!
UNDERSTAND?
PWAH
YES, MY LORD!
NOW TRY AGAIN!
As you say!
BRING MY TEA, CHOPPER-EMON!
YES, MY LORD!
Servant: Chopperemon
I SHALL BRING IT AT ONCE, MY LORD!
SWISH SWISH
Maid: Onami
ROLL ROLL..
HOW DO YOU FEEL, MY LORD?
VERY COMFORTABLE. I AM QUITE PLEASED.
I SEE... I AM GLAD TO HEAR IT. ♡

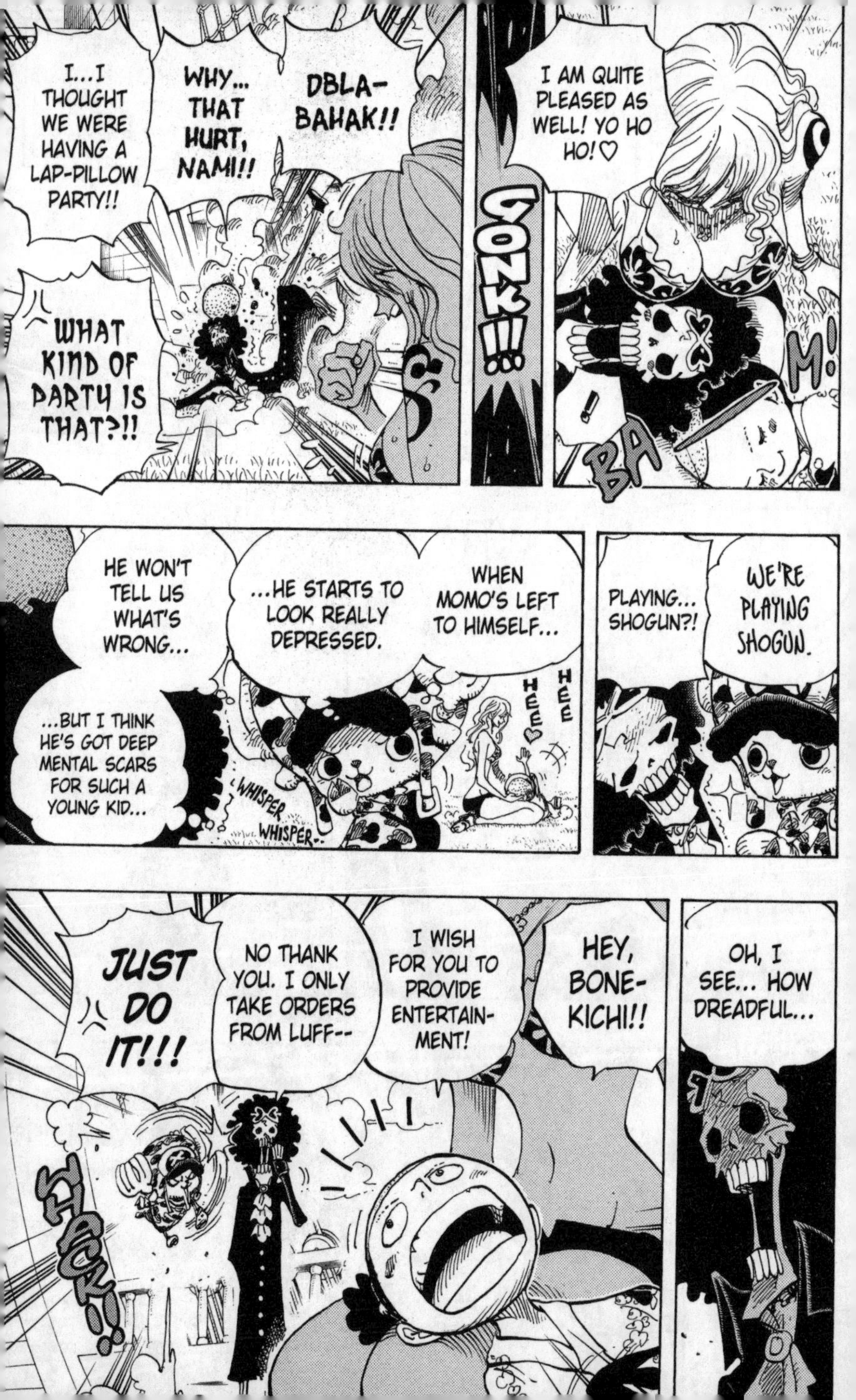
I AM QUITE PLEASED AS WELL! YO HO HO!♡
M!
BA
!
GONK!!!
DBLA-BAHAK!!
WHY... THAT HURT, NAMI!!
I...I THOUGHT WE WERE HAVING A LAP-PILLOW PARTY!!
WHAT KIND OF PARTY IS THAT?!!
WE'RE PLAYING SHOGUN.
PLAYING... SHOGUN?!
WHEN MOMO'S LEFT TO HIMSELF...
HEE HEE
...HE STARTS TO LOOK REALLY DEPRESSED.
HE WON'T TELL US WHAT'S WRONG...
...BUT I THINK HE'S GOT DEEP MENTAL SCARS FOR SUCH A YOUNG KID...
WHISPER WHISPER
OH, I SEE... HOW DREADFUL...
HEY, BONE-KICHI!!
I WISH FOR YOU TO PROVIDE ENTERTAIN-MENT!
NO THANK YOU. I ONLY TAKE ORDERS FROM LUFF--
JUST DO IT!!!
THACK!!

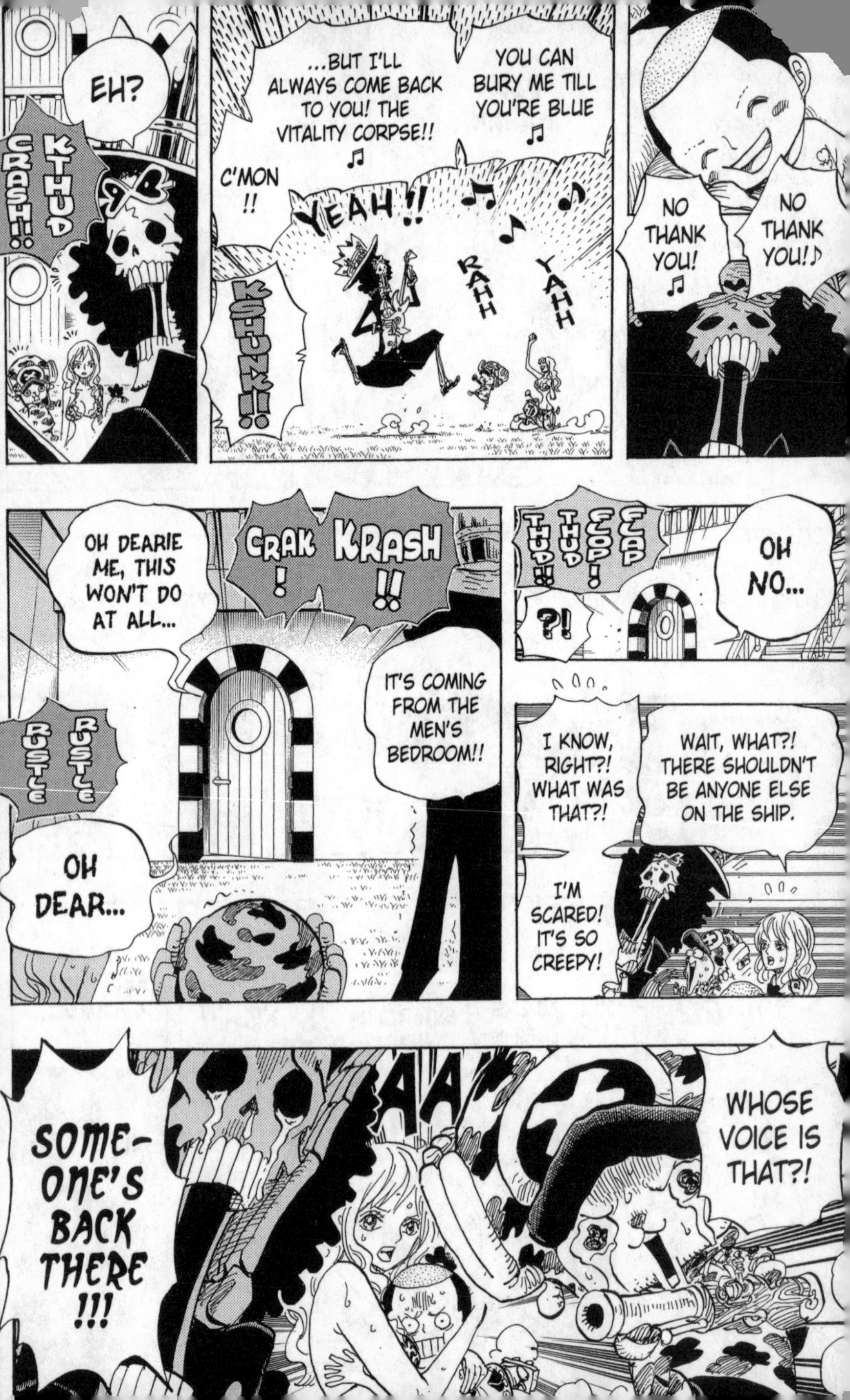
NO THANK YOU!♪
NO THANK YOU! ♫
YOU CAN BURY ME TILL YOU'RE BLUE ♫
...BUT I'LL ALWAYS COME BACK TO YOU! THE VITALITY CORPSE!! ♫
C'MON !!
YEAH!!
YAHH
RAHH
KSHUNK!!
EH?
KTHUD
CRASH!!
OH NO...
FLAP
FLOP!
THUD!!
THUD!!
?!
WAIT, WHAT?! THERE SHOULDN'T BE ANYONE ELSE ON THE SHIP.
I KNOW, RIGHT?! WHAT WAS THAT?!
I'M SCARED! IT'S SO CREEPY!
KRASH!!
CRAK!
OH DEARIE ME, THIS WON'T DO AT ALL...
IT'S COMING FROM THE MEN'S BEDROOM!!
RUSTLE
RUSTLE
OH DEAR...
WHOSE VOICE IS THAT?!
AAA
SOME-ONE'S BACK THERE!!!

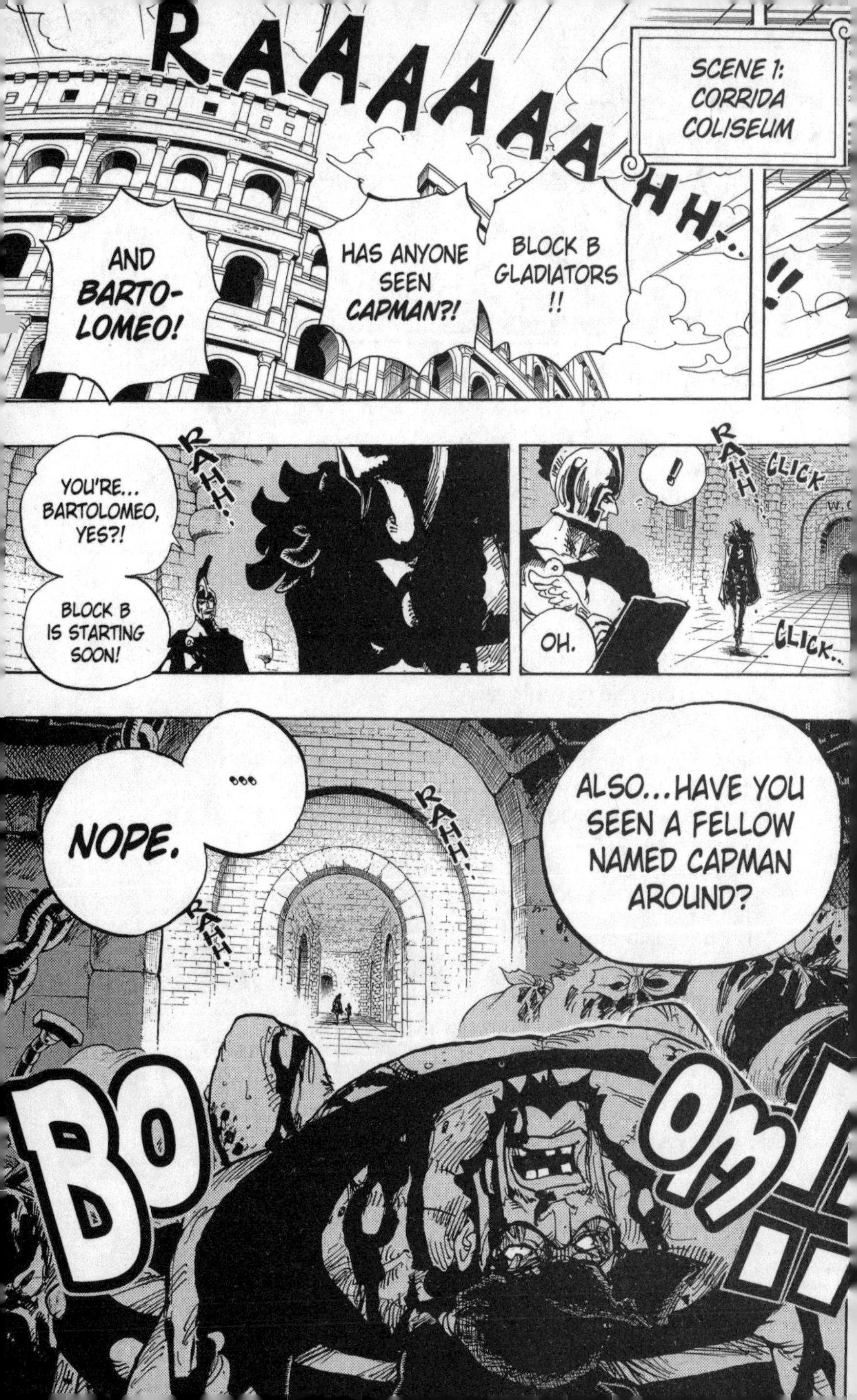
SCENE 1: CORRIDA COLISEUM
RAAAAAAAHH..!!
BLOCK B GLADIATORS!!
HAS ANYONE SEEN CAPMAN?!
AND BARTOLOMEO!
RAHH..
CLICK
!
OH.
CLICK..
RAHH..
YOU'RE... BARTOLOMEO, YES?!
BLOCK B IS STARTING SOON!
ALSO...HAVE YOU SEEN A FELLOW NAMED CAPMAN AROUND?
RAHH..
...
NOPE.
RAHH..
BOOM!!

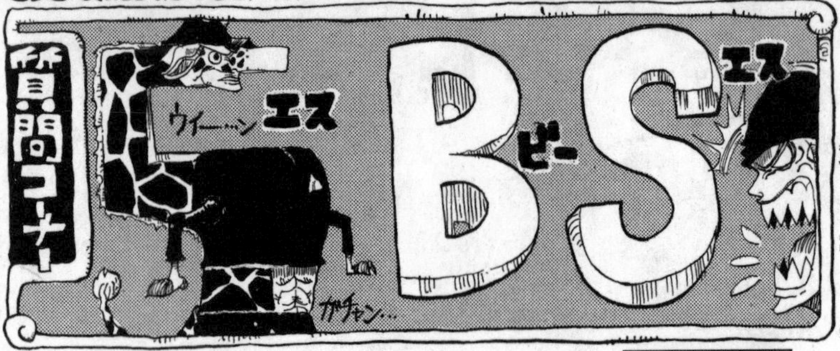
質問コーナー
ウイーン…ン エス
B
ビー
S
エス
ガチャン…

(Satomo, Yamanashi)

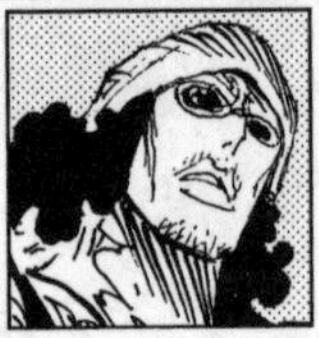

Q: Could you make shaved ice out of Aokiji?

--Dumb Dog

A: Yes, you certainly could. He's ice, after all. But would you really want to eat him? He'd turn back into Aokiji in your tummy, and BOOM! You're possessed.

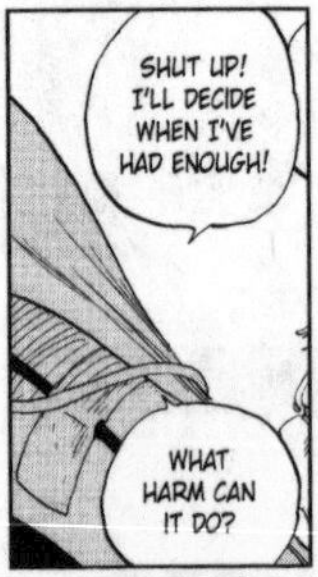
SHUT UP! I'LL DECIDE WHEN I'VE HAD ENOUGH!
WHAT HARM CAN IT DO?

Q: Our dad loves Whitebeard. Every night, he comes home drunk, and Mom scolds him. He always says, "I'll decide when I've had enough, gurarara!" But then the next morning, he grovels on the ground before her. How can our dad be cool again?

--Piro&Akke

A: Hmm. Well, he's cool partway through your story, but he's not in the morning. Here's an idea. How about if your mom becomes Whitebeard too, and forgives him by saying, "You may be a fool, but I still love you." Would that work?

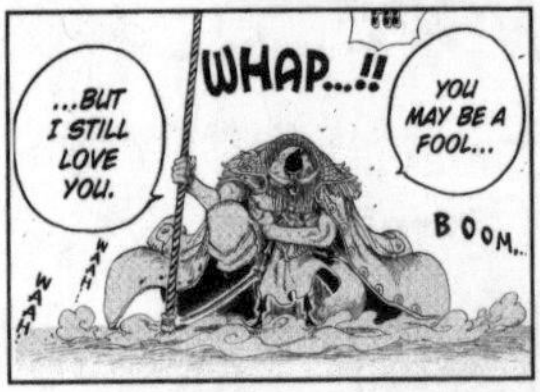
YOU MAY BE A FOOL...
WHAP...!!
...BUT I STILL LOVE YOU.
BOOM..

Q: My cat is really cute; he loves to hop up on your lap out of nowhere. My father (59) likes to lay his head on my mother's lap to get his ears cleaned, but she hates that. What is it about men and lap-pillows?

--Neko Robin

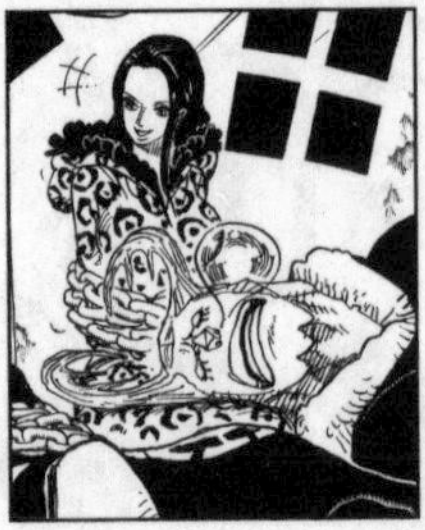

A: It's bumming me out to see so many pathetic dad letters. My theory is that the lap-pillow is a kind of dream, a source of passion. It's like when a climber sees a new mountain to climb. In fact, that's not a theory, it's real!!

Chapter 706:
I AIN'T GONNA LAUGH AT YA

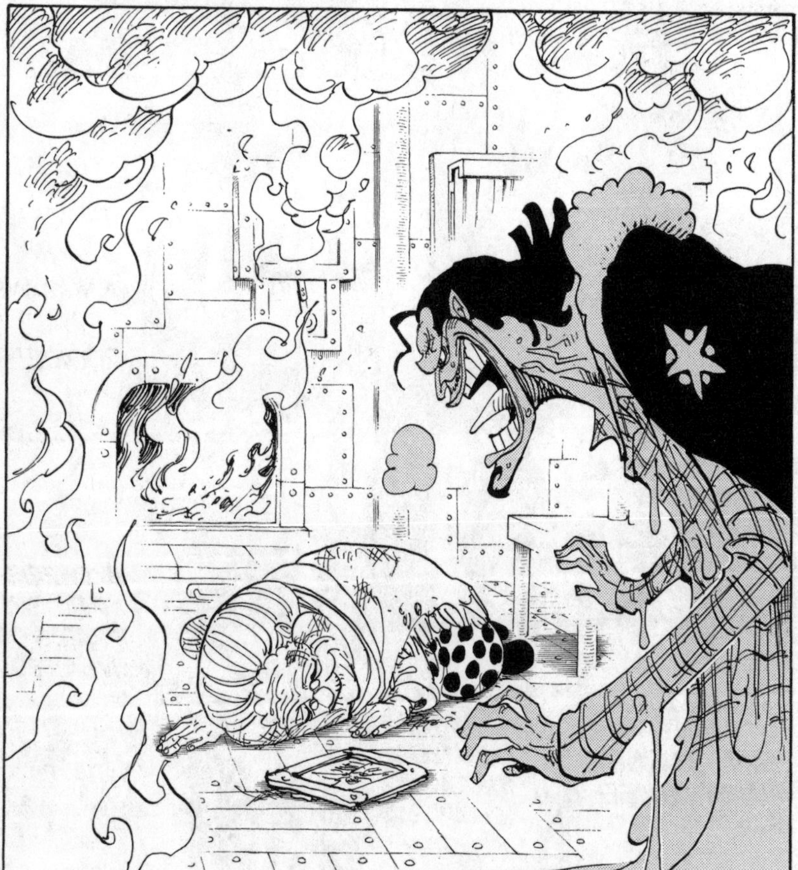

CARIBOU'S NEW WORLD KEE HEE HEE, VOL. 26
"THE OLD HAG LEFT BEHIND WITH A PHOTOGRAPH"

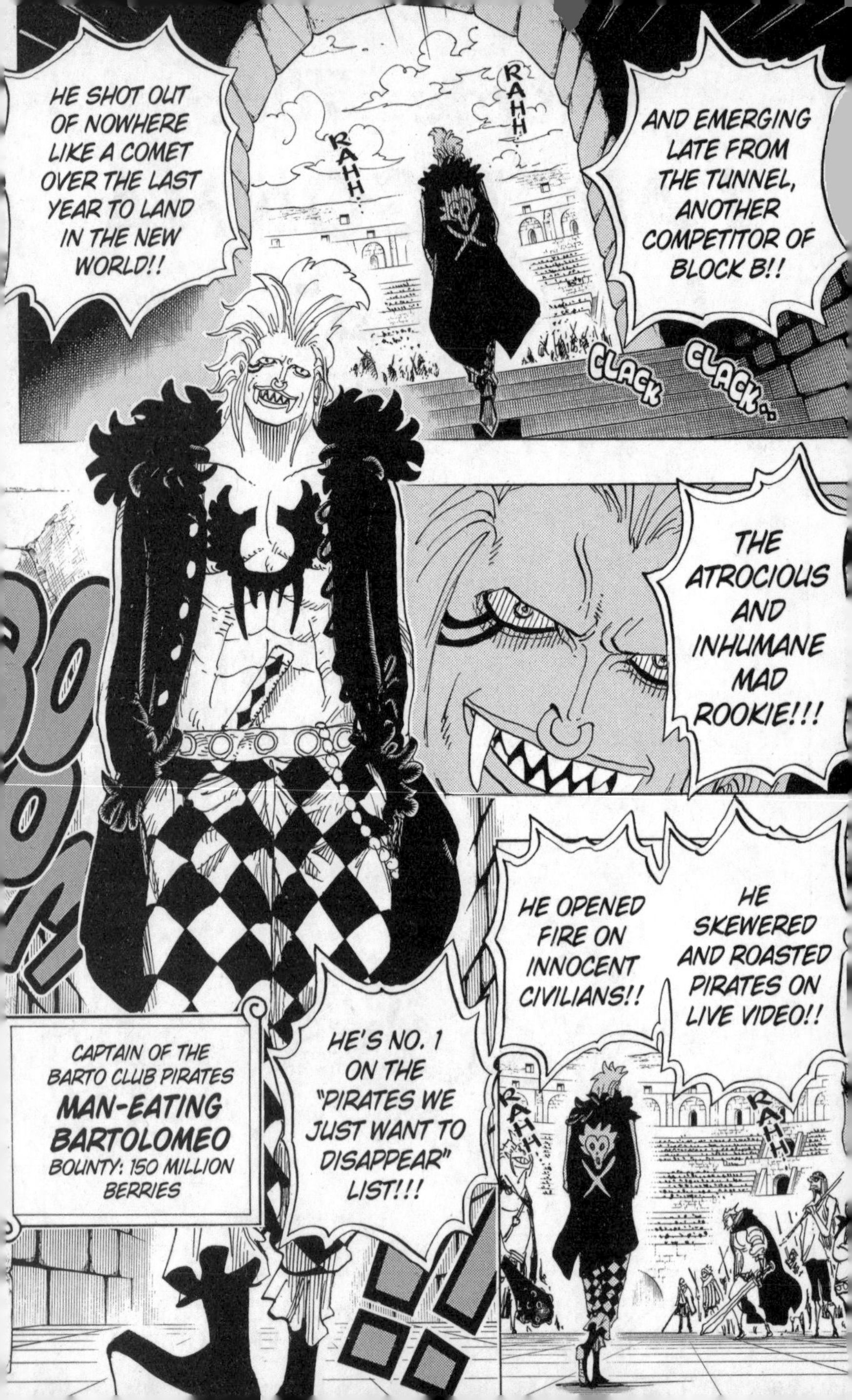
AND EMERGING LATE FROM THE TUNNEL, ANOTHER COMPETITOR OF BLOCK B!!
HE SHOT OUT OF NOWHERE LIKE A COMET OVER THE LAST YEAR TO LAND IN THE NEW WORLD!!
RAHH...
RAHH...
CLACK
CLACK..
THE ATROCIOUS AND INHUMANE MAD ROOKIE!!!
HE SKEWERED AND ROASTED PIRATES ON LIVE VIDEO!!
HE OPENED FIRE ON INNOCENT CIVILIANS!!
HE'S NO. 1 ON THE "PIRATES WE JUST WANT TO DISAPPEAR" LIST!!!
RAHH...
RAHH...
CAPTAIN OF THE BARTO CLUB PIRATES
MAN-EATING BARTOLOMEO
BOUNTY: 150 MILLION BERRIES

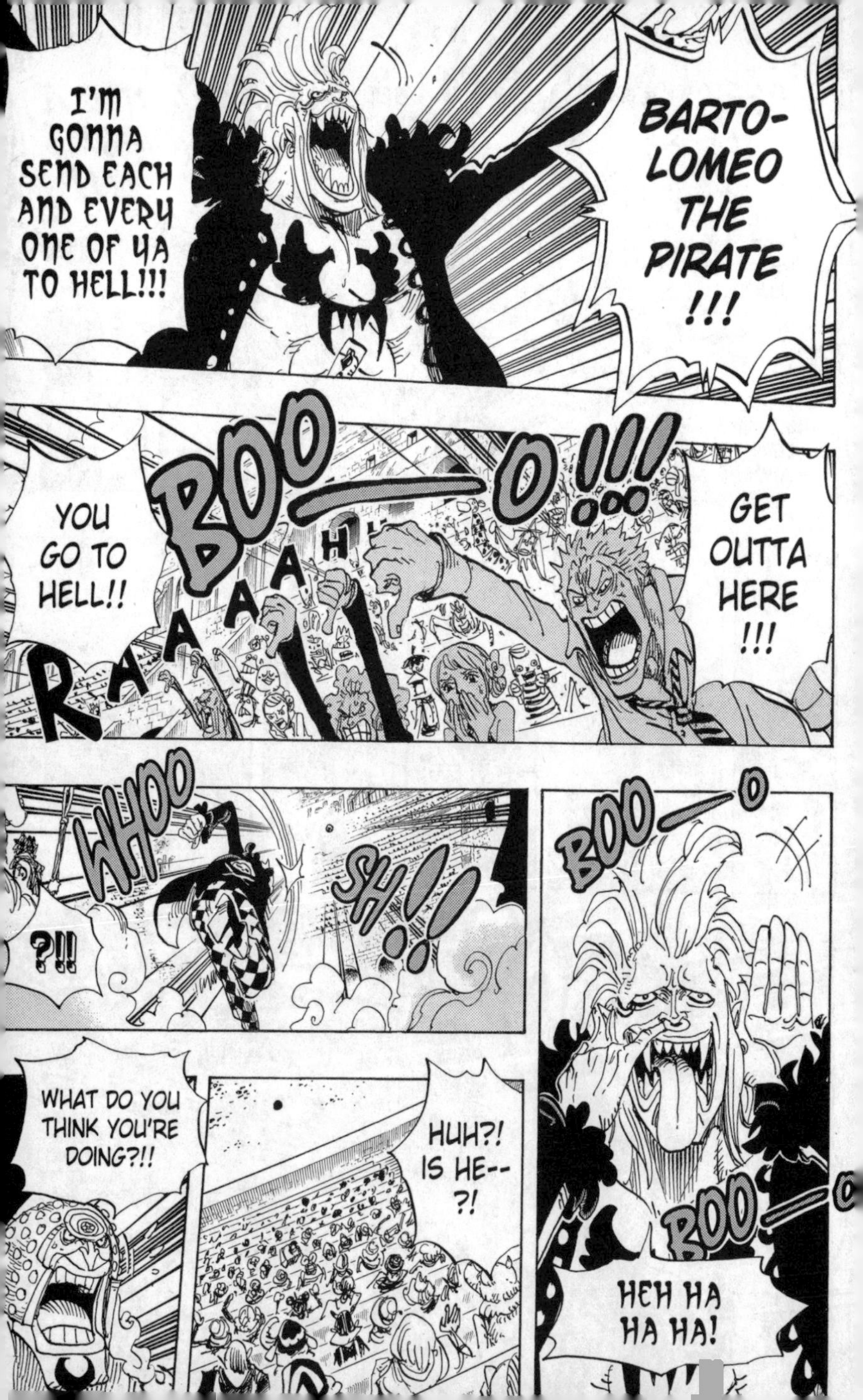
BARTO-LOMEO THE PIRATE!!!
I'M GONNA SEND EACH AND EVERY ONE OF YA TO HELL!!!
GET OUTTA HERE!!!
BOO—O!!!
RAAAAAH
YOU GO TO HELL!!
BOO—O
BOO—O
HEH HA HA HA!
WHOOSH!!
?!!
HUH?! IS HE--?!
WHAT DO YOU THINK YOU'RE DOING?!!

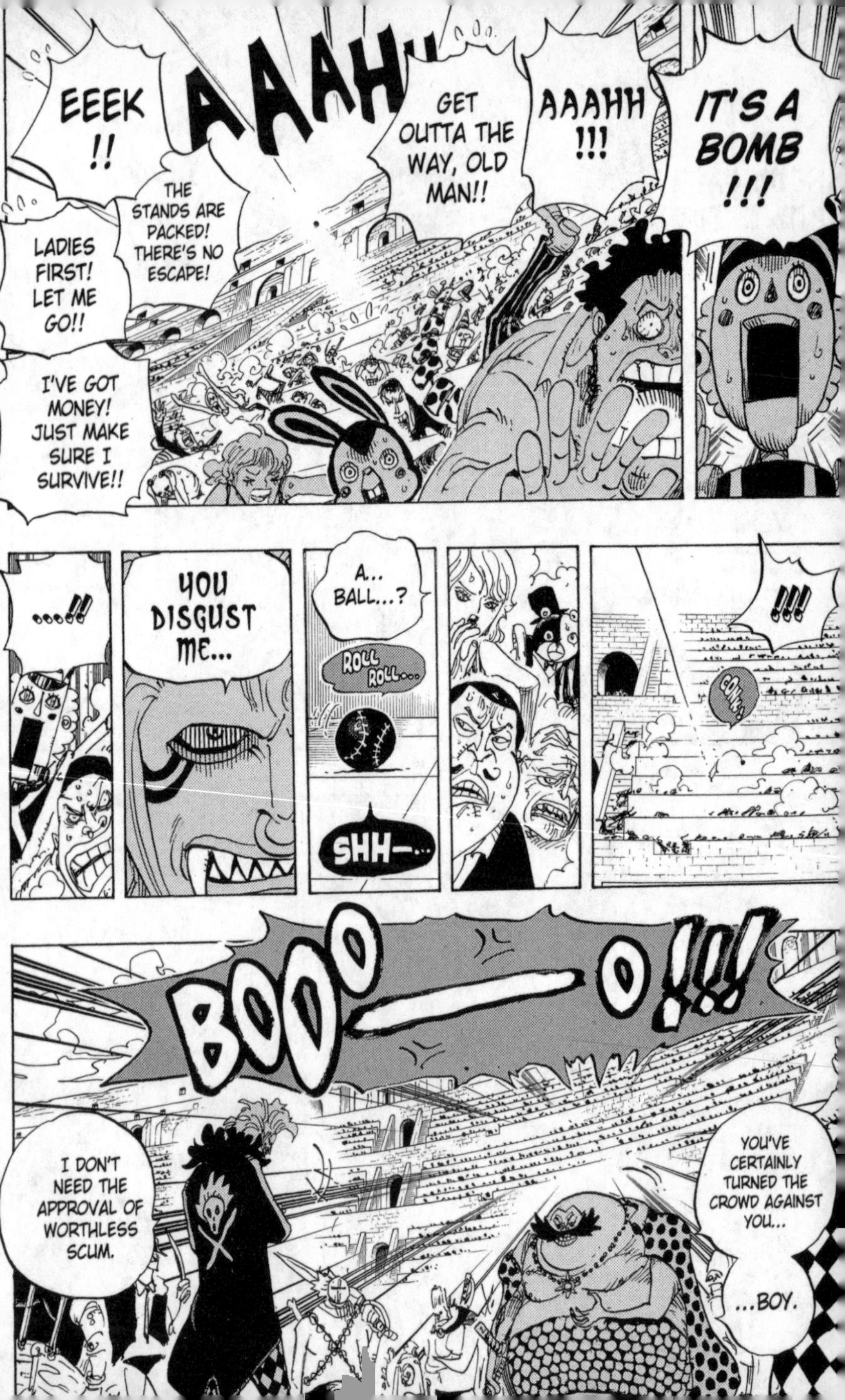
IT'S A BOMB!!!
AAAHH!!!
GET OUTTA THE WAY, OLD MAN!!
AAAH
EEEK!!
THE STANDS ARE PACKED! THERE'S NO ESCAPE!
LADIES FIRST! LET ME GO!!
I'VE GOT MONEY! JUST MAKE SURE I SURVIVE!!
!!!
A.. BALL...?
ROLL ROLL...
SHH—...
YOU DISGUST ME...
....!!
BOOO—O!!!
YOU'VE CERTAINLY TURNED THE CROWD AGAINST YOU...
...BOY.
I DON'T NEED THE APPROVAL OF WORTHLESS SCUM.

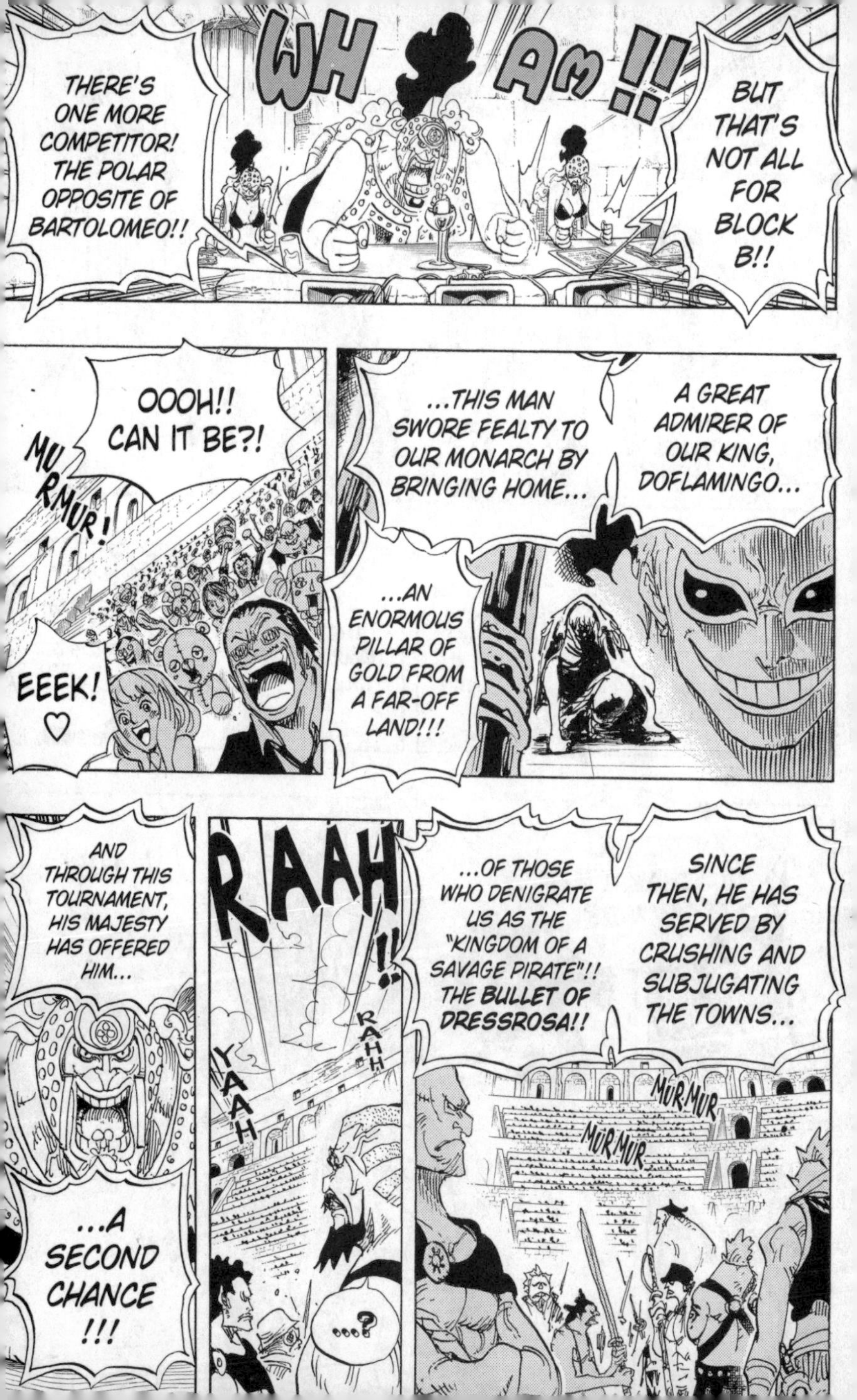

WHAM!!
BUT THAT'S NOT ALL FOR BLOCK B!!
THERE'S ONE MORE COMPETITOR! THE POLAR OPPOSITE OF BARTOLOMEO!!
A GREAT ADMIRER OF OUR KING, DOFLAMINGO...
...THIS MAN SWORE FEALTY TO OUR MONARCH BY BRINGING HOME...
...AN ENORMOUS PILLAR OF GOLD FROM A FAR-OFF LAND!!!
OOOH!! CAN IT BE?!
MURMUR!
EEEK! ♡
SINCE THEN, HE HAS SERVED BY CRUSHING AND SUBJUGATING THE TOWNS...
...OF THOSE WHO DENIGRATE US AS THE "KINGDOM OF A SAVAGE PIRATE"!! THE BULLET OF DRESSROSA!!
MURMUR
MURMUR
...?
RAAH!!
RAHH
YAAAH
AND THROUGH THIS TOURNAMENT, HIS MAJESTY HAS OFFERED HIM...
...A SECOND CHANCE!!!

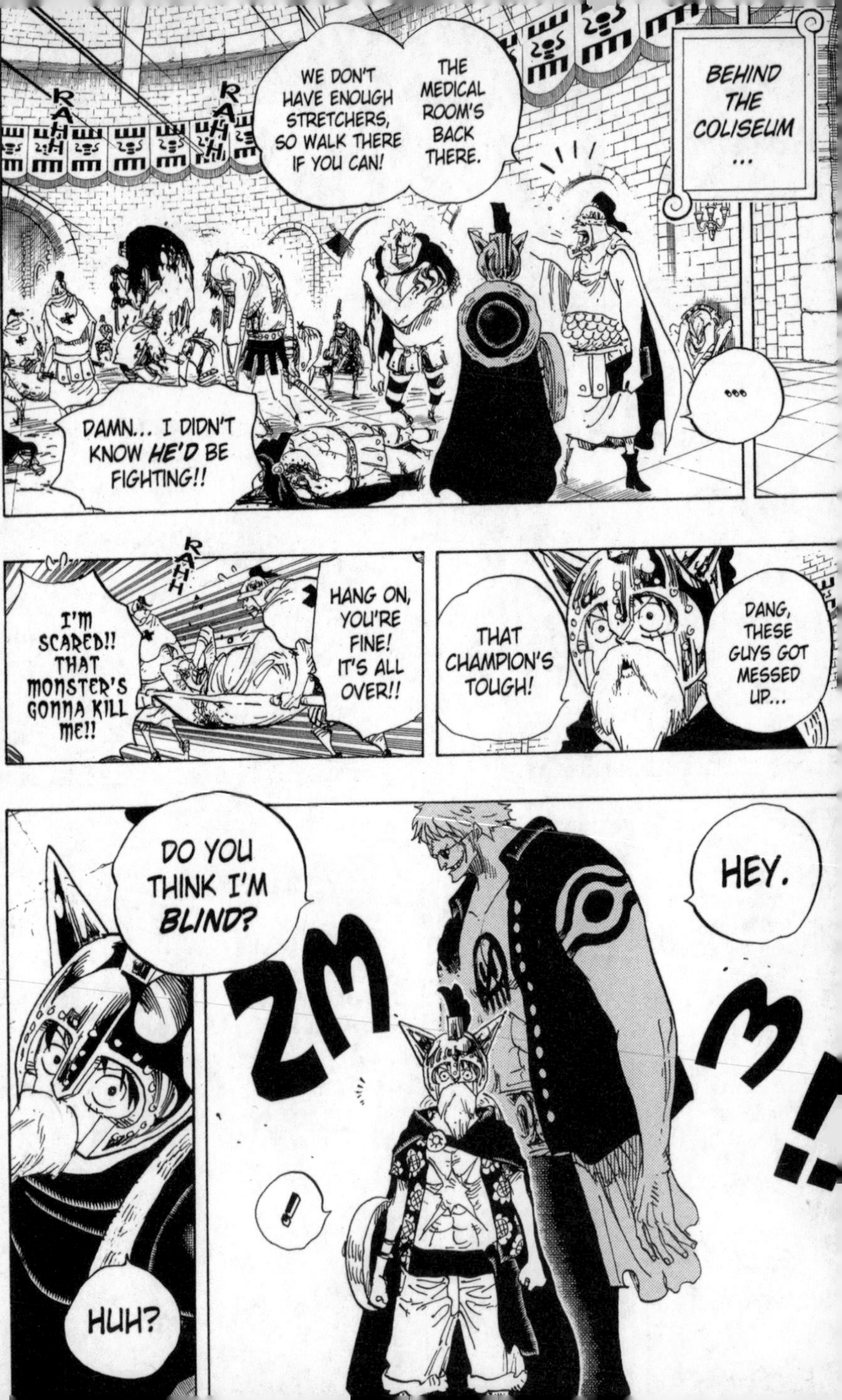
BEHIND THE COLISEUM...
THE MEDICAL ROOM'S BACK THERE.
WE DON'T HAVE ENOUGH STRETCHERS, SO WALK THERE IF YOU CAN!
RAHH
RAHH
...
DAMN... I DIDN'T KNOW *HE'D* BE FIGHTING!!
DANG, THESE GUYS GOT MESSED UP...
THAT CHAMPION'S TOUGH!
RAHH
HANG ON, YOU'RE FINE! IT'S ALL OVER!!
I'M SCARED!! THAT MONSTER'S GONNA KILL ME!!
HEY.
ZM
M!!
!
DO YOU THINK I'M *BLIND?*
HUH?

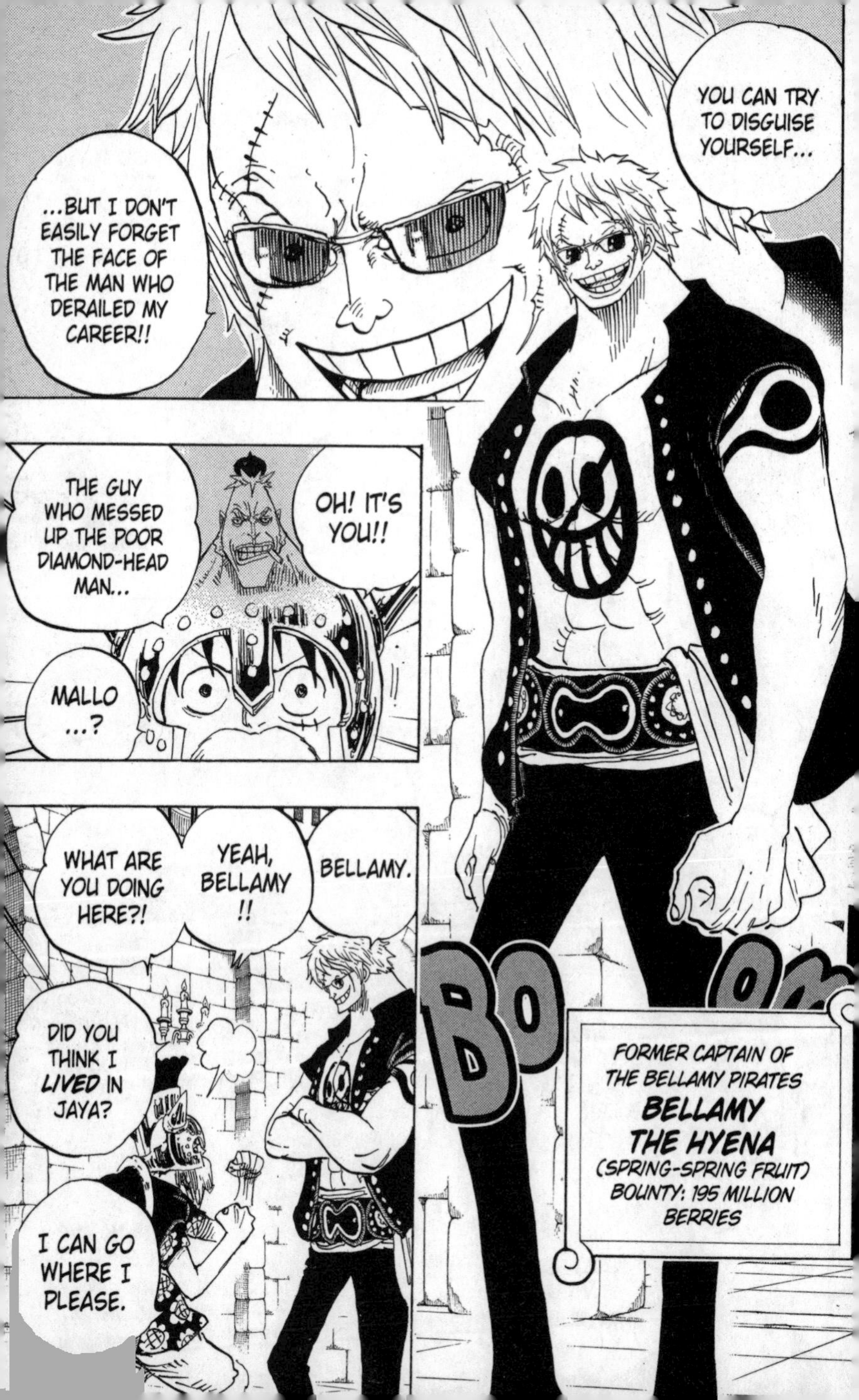
YOU CAN TRY TO DISGUISE YOURSELF...
...BUT I DON'T EASILY FORGET THE FACE OF THE MAN WHO DERAILED MY CAREER!!
BOOM
FORMER CAPTAIN OF THE BELLAMY PIRATES
BELLAMY THE HYENA
(SPRING-SPRING FRUIT)
BOUNTY: 195 MILLION BERRIES
OH! IT'S YOU!!
THE GUY WHO MESSED UP THE POOR DIAMOND-HEAD MAN...
MALLO ...?
BELLAMY.
YEAH, BELLAMY !!
WHAT ARE YOU DOING HERE?!
DID YOU THINK I *LIVED* IN JAYA?
I CAN GO WHERE I PLEASE.

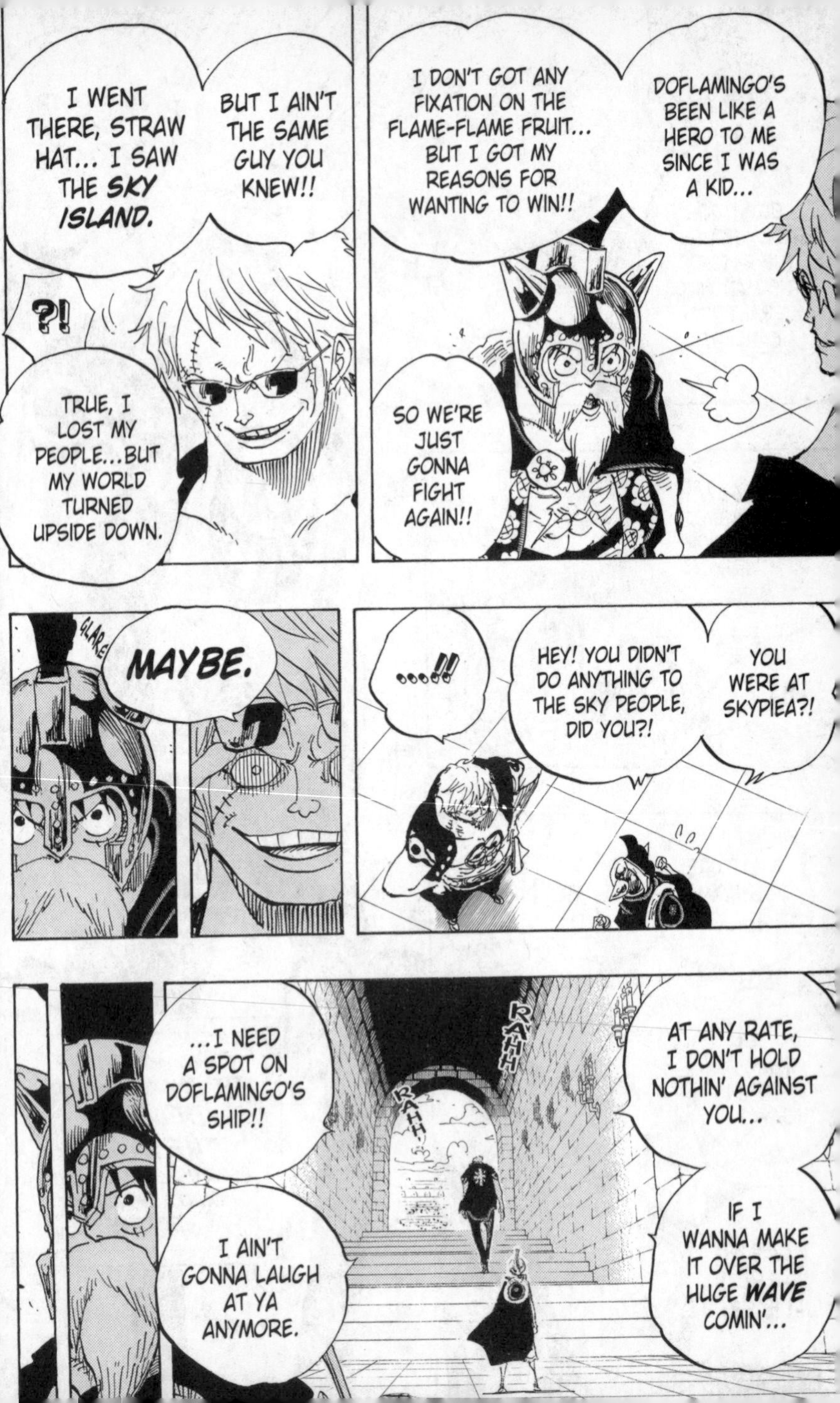
DOFLAMINGO'S BEEN LIKE A HERO TO ME SINCE I WAS A KID...
I DON'T GOT ANY FIXATION ON THE FLAME-FLAME FRUIT... BUT I GOT MY REASONS FOR WANTING TO WIN!!
SO WE'RE JUST GONNA FIGHT AGAIN!!
BUT I AIN'T THE SAME GUY YOU KNEW!!
I WENT THERE, STRAW HAT... I SAW THE ***SKY ISLAND.***
?!
TRUE, I LOST MY PEOPLE...BUT MY WORLD TURNED UPSIDE DOWN.
YOU WERE AT SKYPIEA?!
HEY! YOU DIDN'T DO ANYTHING TO THE SKY PEOPLE, DID YOU?!
...!!
GLARE
MAYBE.
RAHHH
AT ANY RATE, I DON'T HOLD NOTHIN' AGAINST YOU...
RAHH
IF I WANNA MAKE IT OVER THE HUGE ***WAVE*** COMIN'...
...I NEED A SPOT ON DOFLAMINGO'S SHIP!!
I AIN'T GONNA LAUGH AT YA ANYMORE.

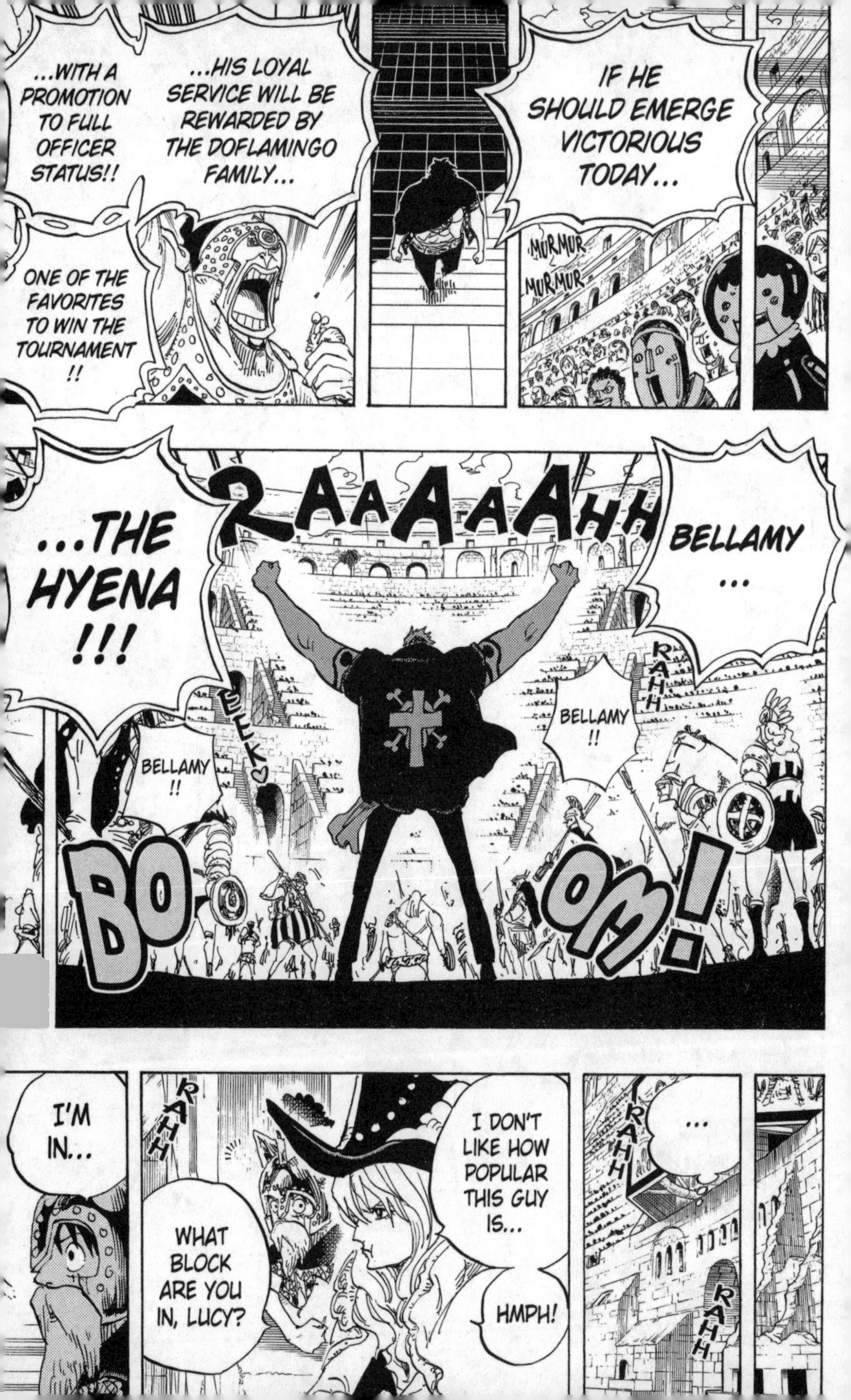
IF HE SHOULD EMERGE VICTORIOUS TODAY...
MURMUR
MURMUR
...HIS LOYAL SERVICE WILL BE REWARDED BY THE DOFLAMINGO FAMILY...
...WITH A PROMOTION TO FULL OFFICER STATUS!!
ONE OF THE FAVORITES TO WIN THE TOURNAMENT !!
BELLAMY ...
RAAAAAHH
...THE HYENA !!!
RAHH
BELLAMY !!
EEEK♡
BELLAMY !!
BOOM!
...
RAHH
RAHH
I DON'T LIKE HOW POPULAR THIS GUY IS...
HMPH!
RAHH
WHAT BLOCK ARE YOU IN, LUCY?
I'M IN...

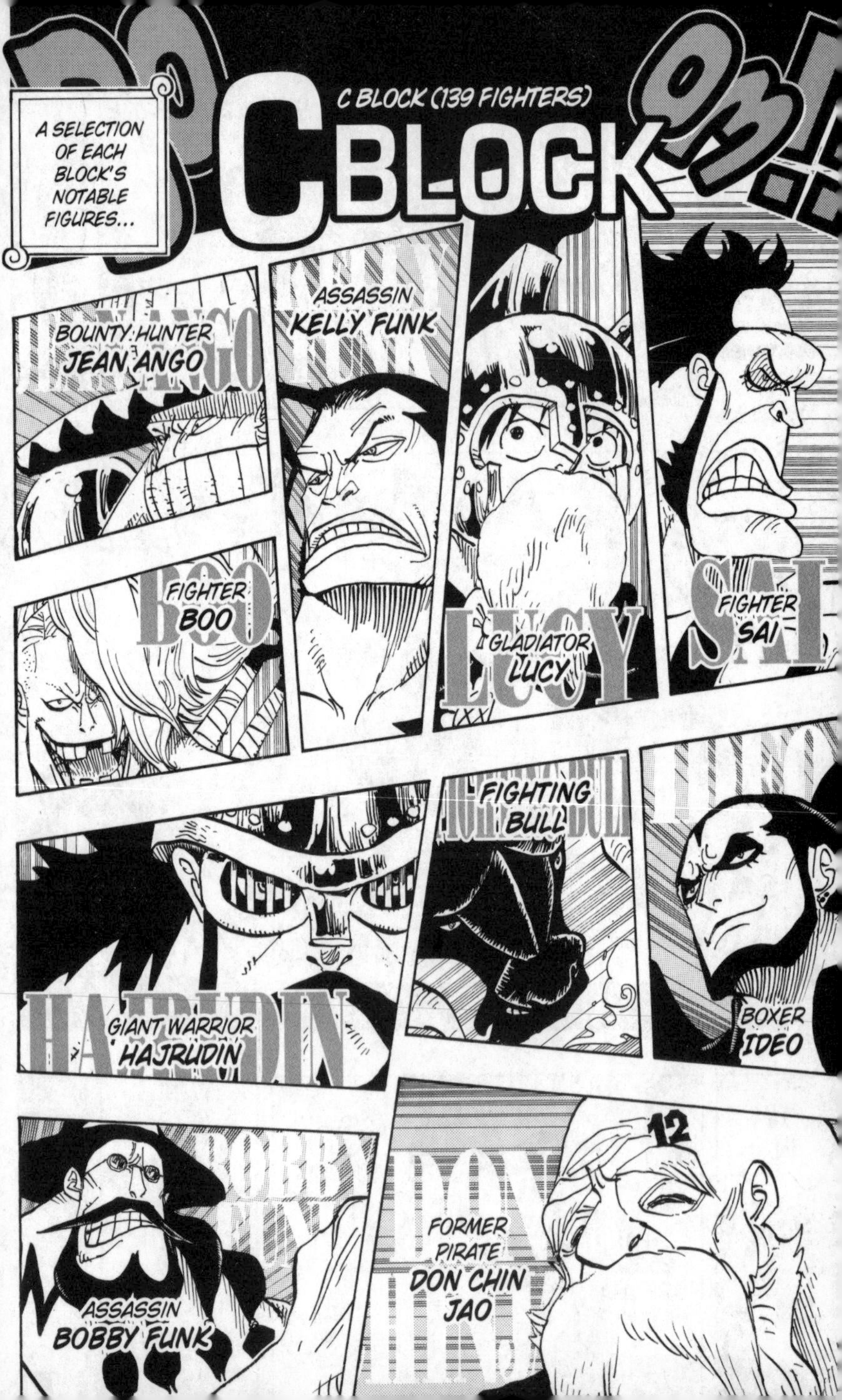
C BLOCK (139 FIGHTERS)
C BLOCK
A SELECTION OF EACH BLOCK'S NOTABLE FIGURES...
FIGHTER SAI
GLADIATOR LUCY
ASSASSIN KELLY FUNK
BOUNTY HUNTER JEAN ANGO
FIGHTER BOO
BOXER IDEO
FIGHTING BULL
GIANT WARRIOR HAJRUDIN
12
FORMER PIRATE DON CHIN JAO
ASSASSIN BOBBY FUNK

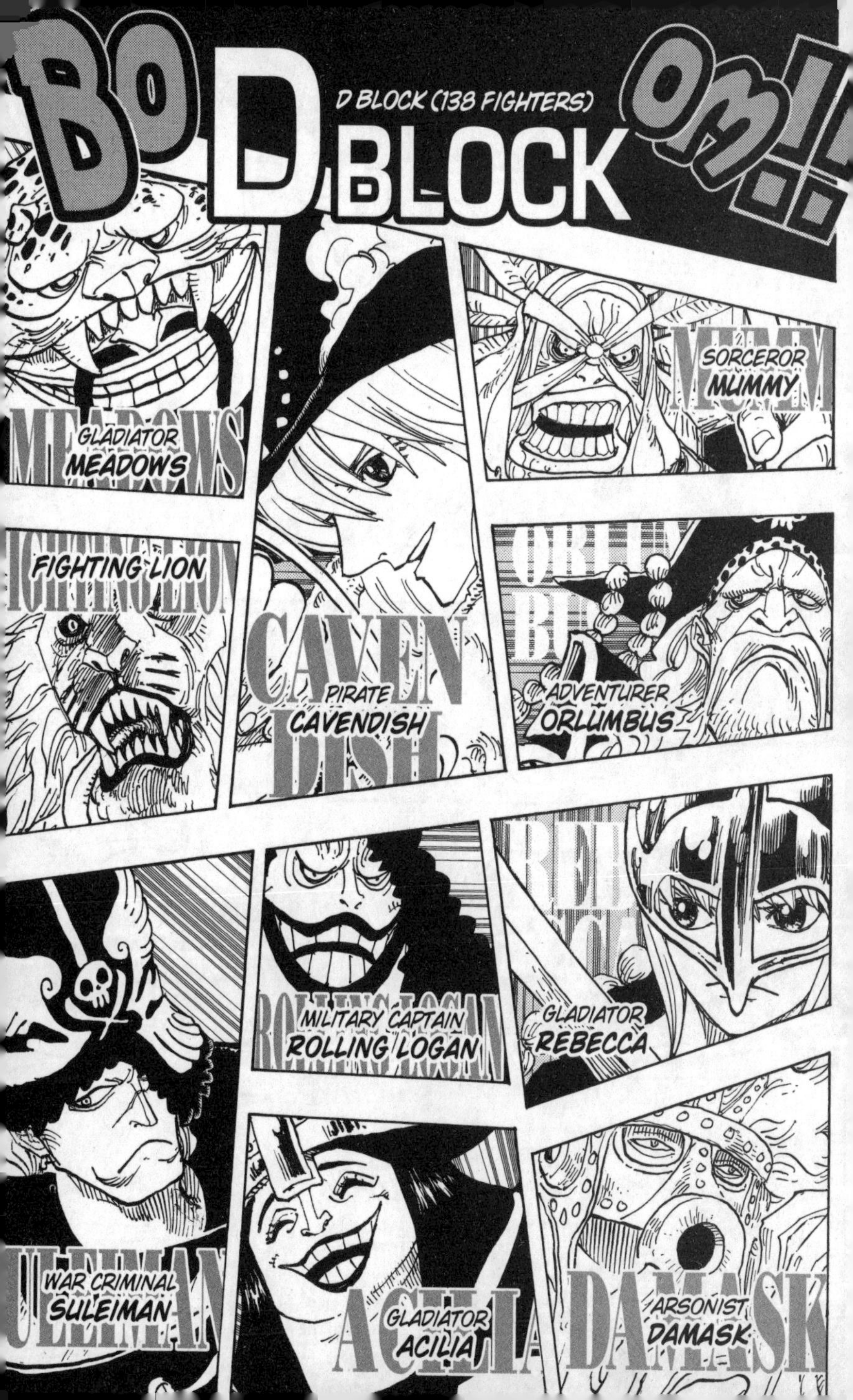

BOOM!!
D BLOCK (138 FIGHTERS)
D BLOCK
SORCEROR MUMMY
ADVENTURER ORLUMBUS
PIRATE CAVENDISH
GLADIATOR MEADOWS
FIGHTING LION
GLADIATOR REBECCA
ARSONIST DAMASK
MILITARY CAPTAIN ROLLING LOGAN
GLADIATOR ACILIA
WAR CRIMINAL SULEIMAN

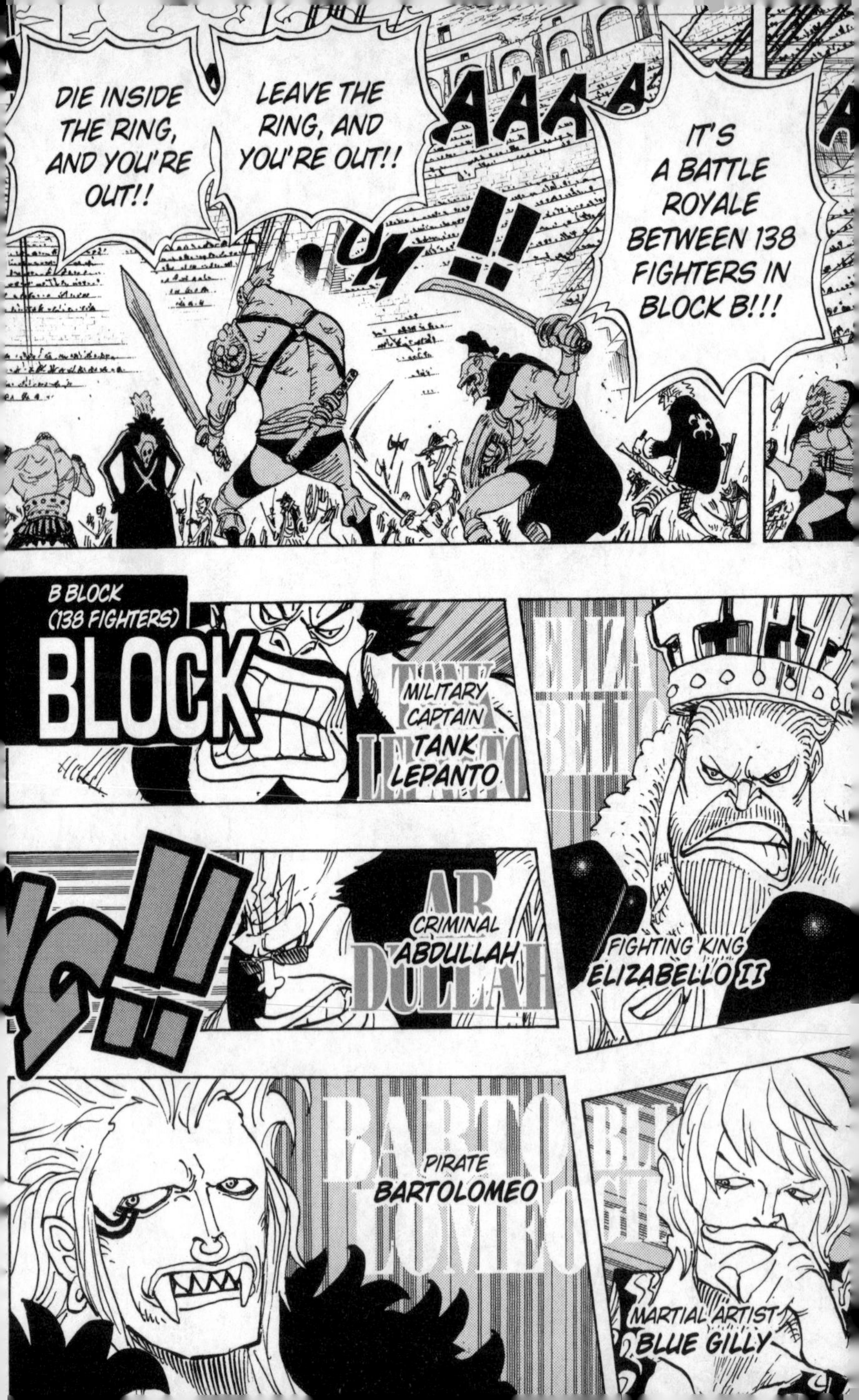
IT'S A BATTLE ROYALE BETWEEN 138 FIGHTERS IN BLOCK B!!!
AAAA
UOH!!
LEAVE THE RING, AND YOU'RE OUT!!
DIE INSIDE THE RING, AND YOU'RE OUT!!
FIGHTING KING ELIZABELLO II
B BLOCK (138 FIGHTERS)
BLOCK
MILITARY CAPTAIN TANK LEPANTO
CRIMINAL ABDULLAH
MARTIAL ARTIST BLUE GILLY
PIRATE BARTOLOMEO

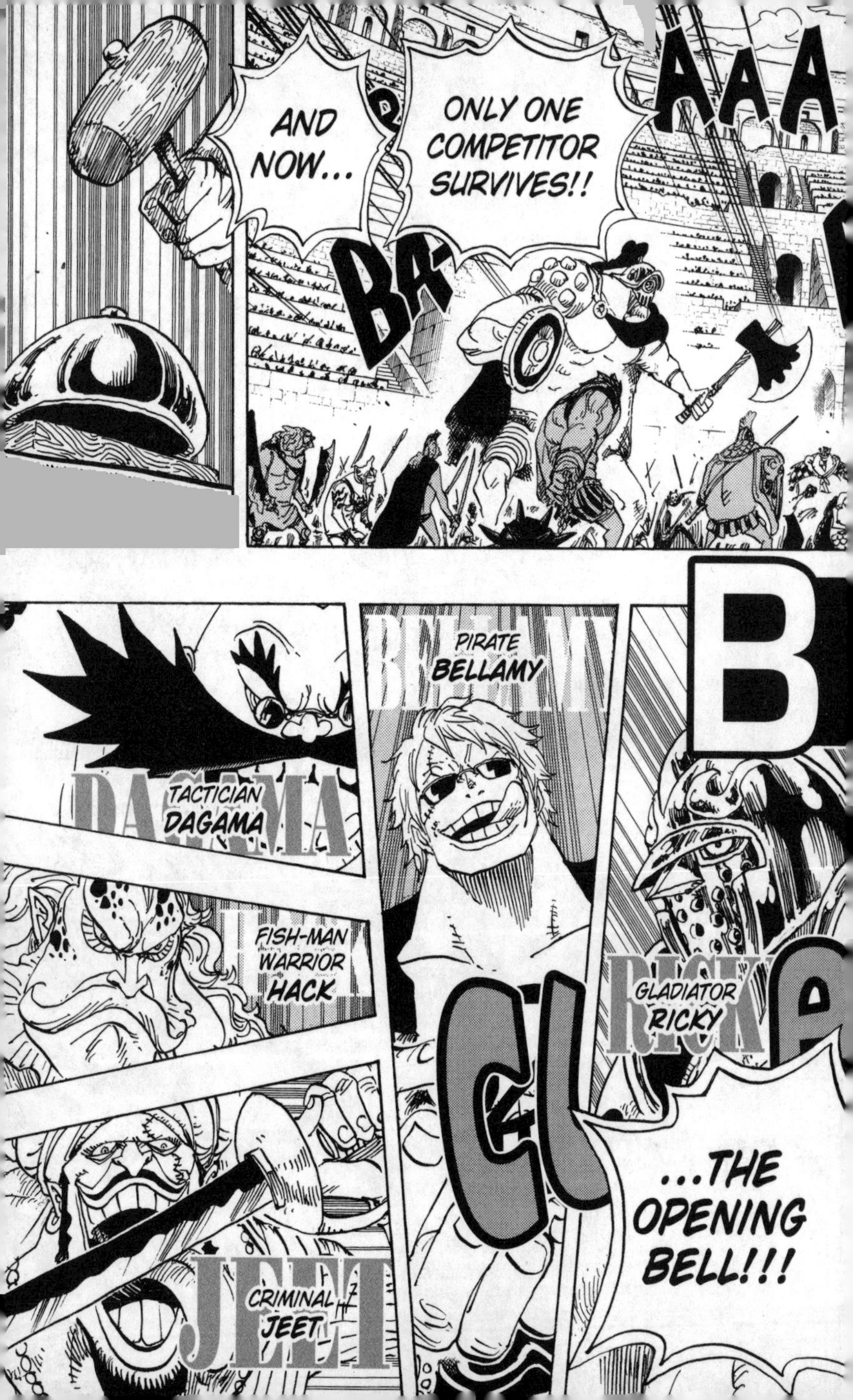

ONLY ONE COMPETITOR SURVIVES!!
BA-
AAA
AND NOW...
B
A
GLADIATOR RICKY
...THE OPENING BELL!!!
PIRATE BELLAMY
TACTICIAN DAGAMA
FISH-MAN WARRIOR HACK
CRIMINAL JEET

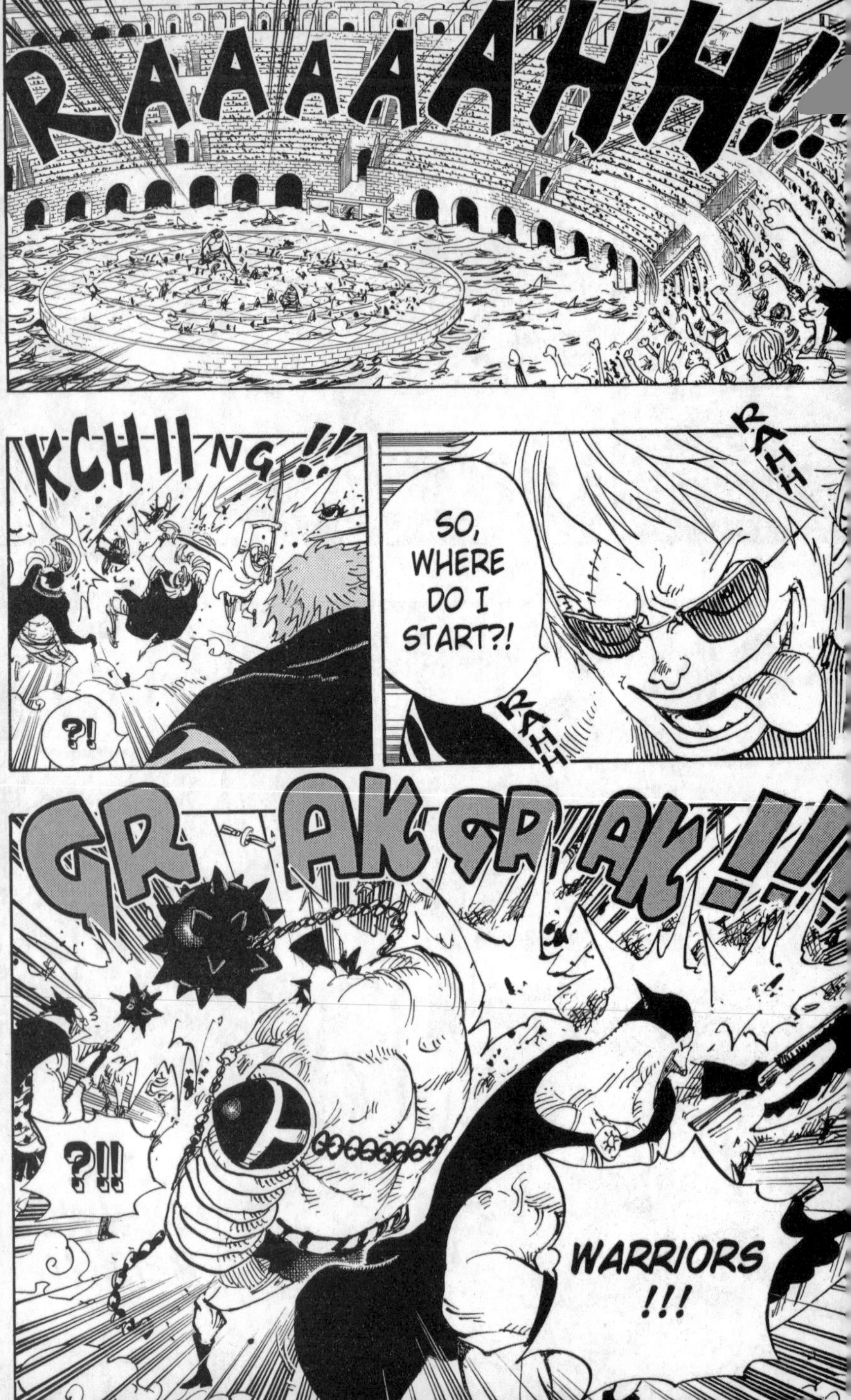
RAAAAAHH!!
RAHH
SO, WHERE DO I START?!
RAHH
KCHIING!!
?!
GRAK GRAK!!!
WARRIORS !!!
?!!

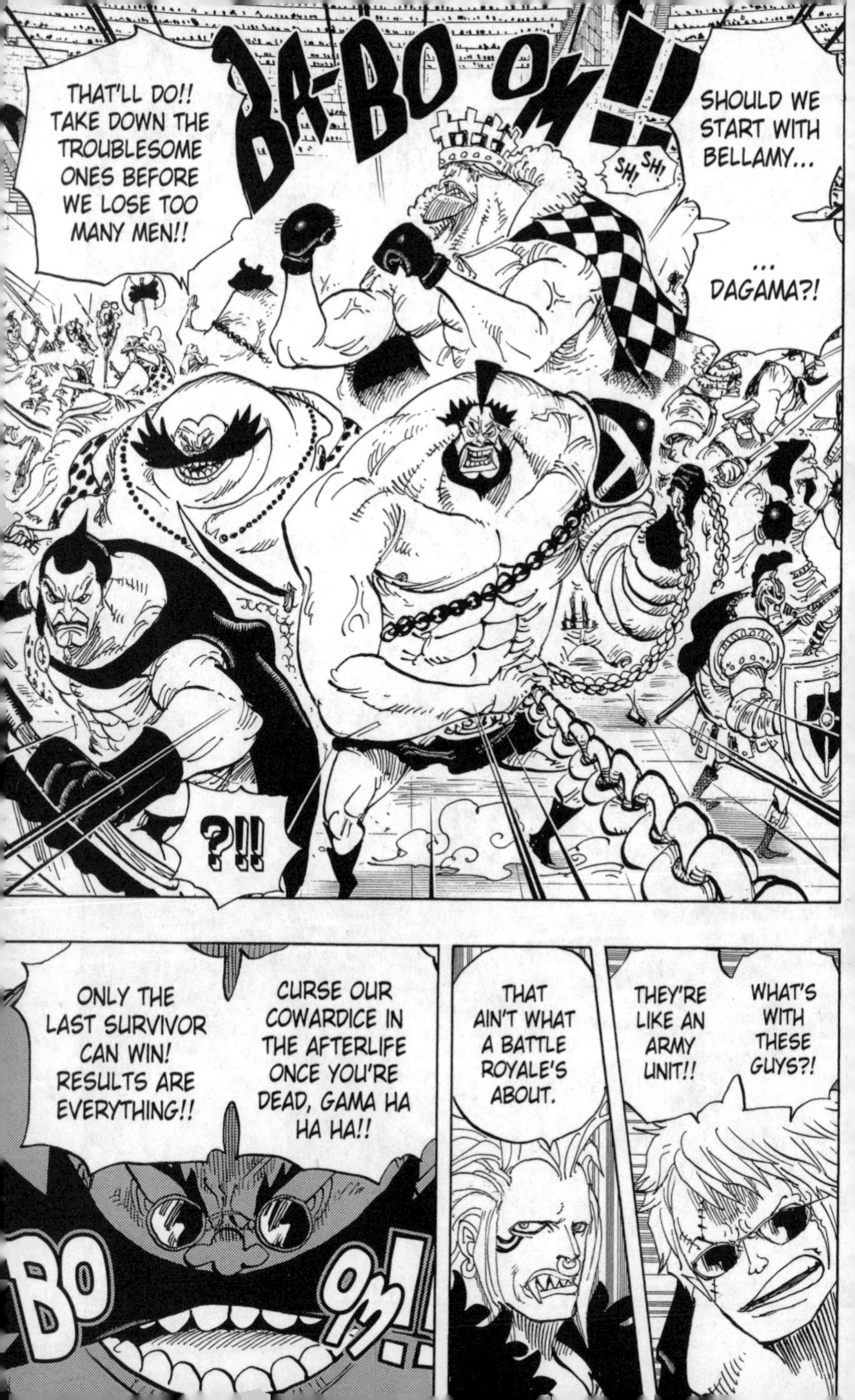
SHOULD WE START WITH BELLAMY...
...DAGAMA?!
SH! SH!
BA-BO OM!!
THAT'LL DO!! TAKE DOWN THE TROUBLESOME ONES BEFORE WE LOSE TOO MANY MEN!!
?!!
WHAT'S WITH THESE GUYS?!
THEY'RE LIKE AN ARMY UNIT!!
THAT AIN'T WHAT A BATTLE ROYALE'S ABOUT.
CURSE OUR COWARDICE IN THE AFTERLIFE ONCE YOU'RE DEAD, GAMA HA HA HA!!
ONLY THE LAST SURVIVOR CAN WIN! RESULTS ARE EVERYTHING!!
BO OM!!

Chapter 707: BLOCK B

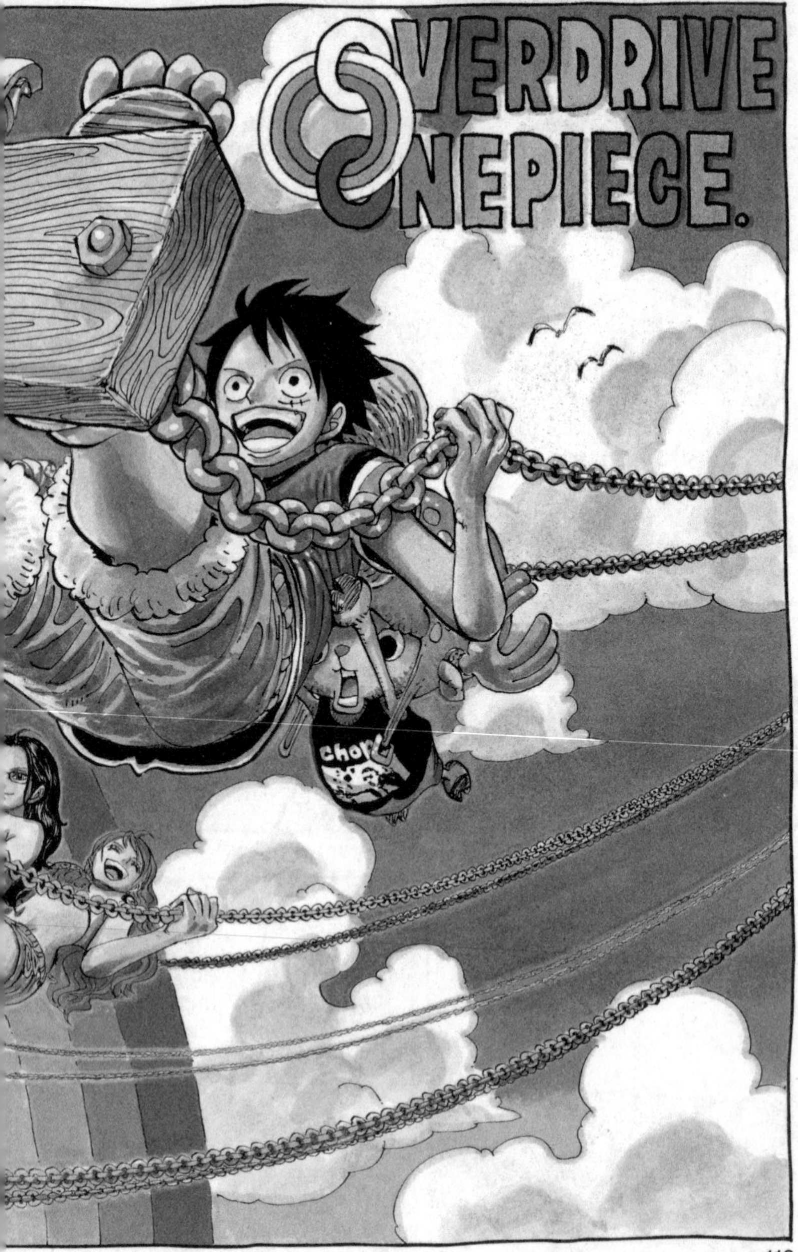
OVERDRIVE
ONEPIECE.
chop

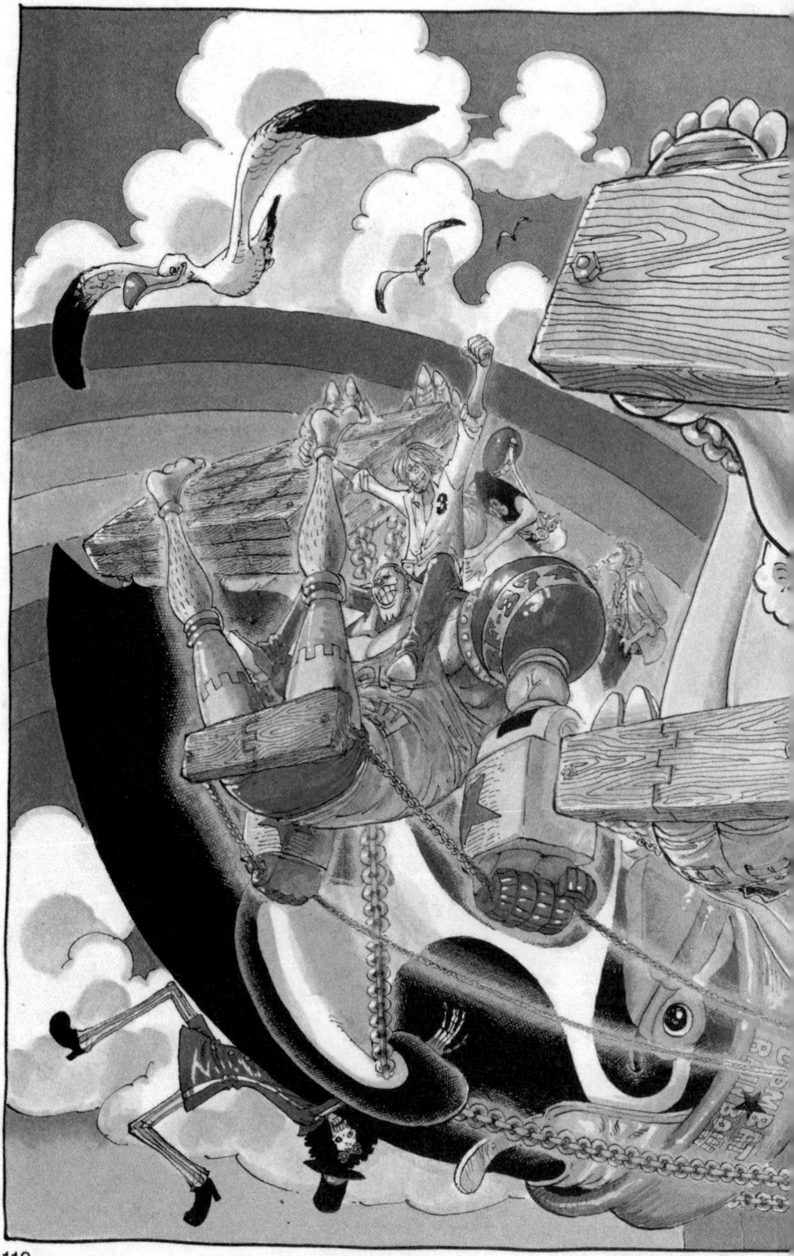

vol. 71
ONE PIECE

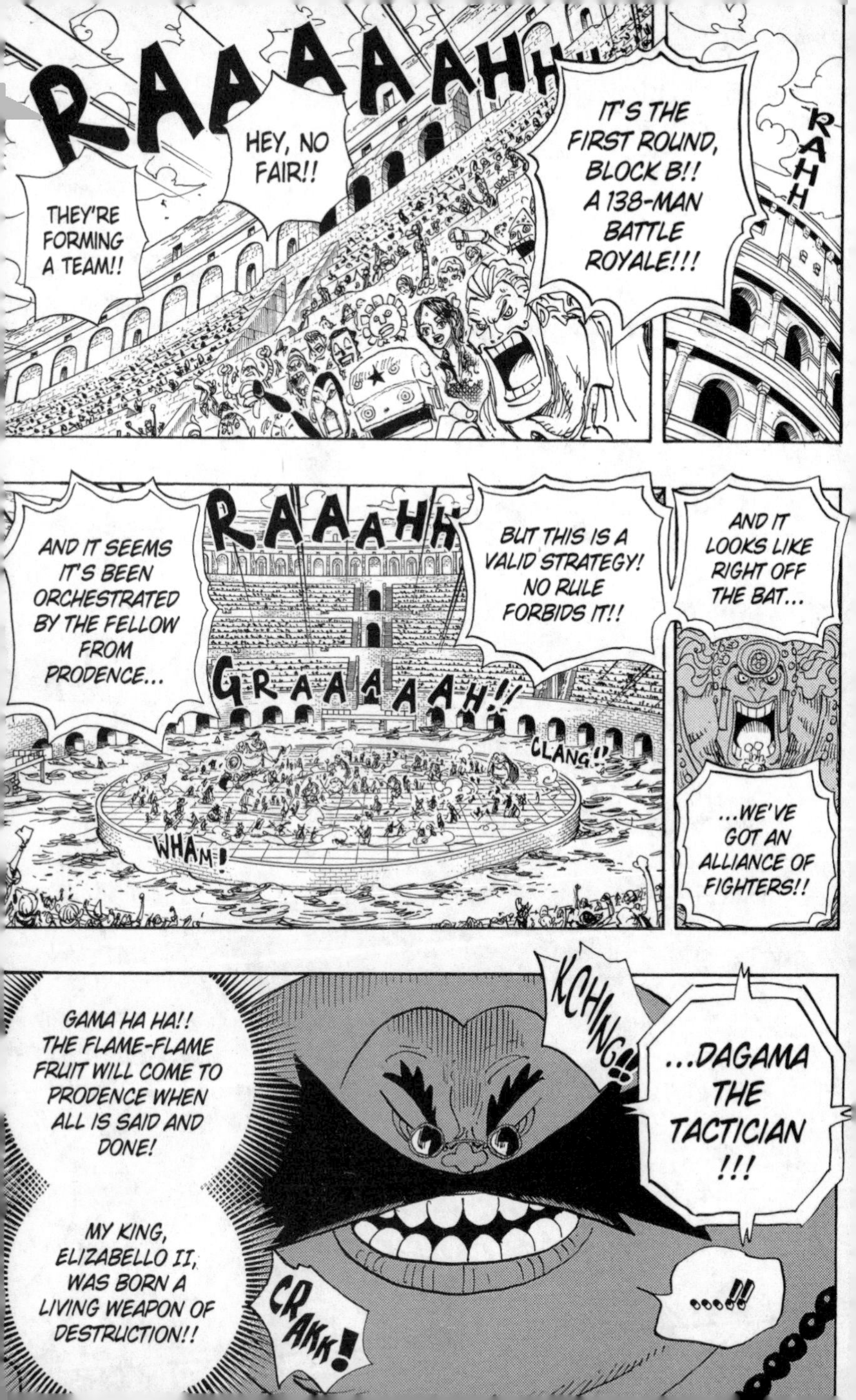
RAHH
RAAAAAHHH
IT'S THE FIRST ROUND, BLOCK B!! A 138-MAN BATTLE ROYALE!!!
HEY, NO FAIR!!
THEY'RE FORMING A TEAM!!
AND IT LOOKS LIKE RIGHT OFF THE BAT...
...WE'VE GOT AN ALLIANCE OF FIGHTERS!!
BUT THIS IS A VALID STRATEGY! NO RULE FORBIDS IT!!
RAAAHH
AND IT SEEMS IT'S BEEN ORCHESTRATED BY THE FELLOW FROM PRODENCE...
GRAAAAAH!!
CLANG!!
WHAM!
KCHING!!
...DAGAMA THE TACTICIAN!!!
GAMA HA HA!! THE FLAME-FLAME FRUIT WILL COME TO PRODENCE WHEN ALL IS SAID AND DONE!
MY KING, ELIZABELLO II, WAS BORN A LIVING WEAPON OF DESTRUCTION!!
CRAKK!
....!!

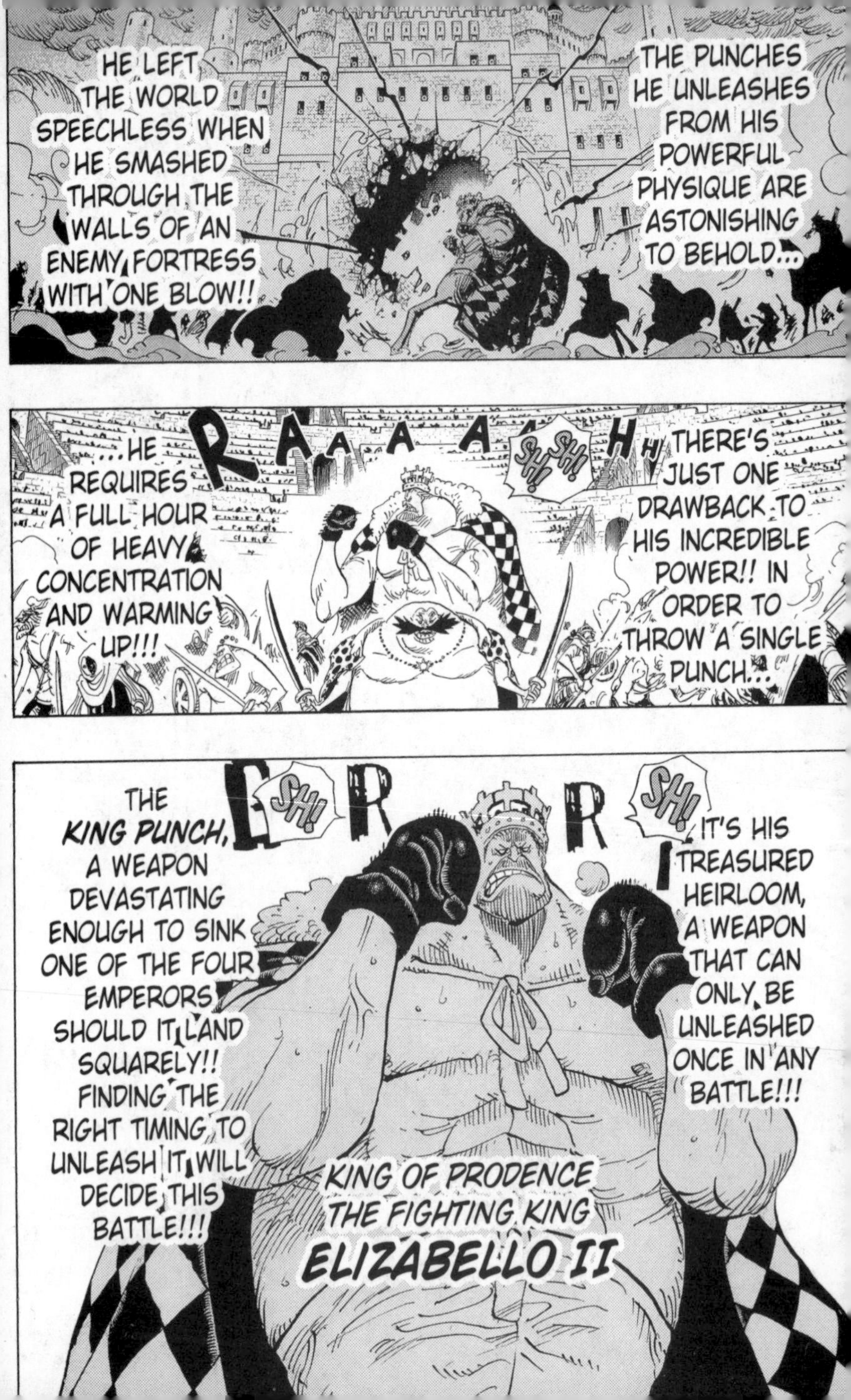

THE PUNCHES HE UNLEASHES FROM HIS POWERFUL PHYSIQUE ARE ASTONISHING TO BEHOLD...
HE LEFT THE WORLD SPEECHLESS WHEN HE SMASHED THROUGH THE WALLS OF AN ENEMY FORTRESS WITH ONE BLOW!!
RAAAAHH
SHSH!
THERE'S JUST ONE DRAWBACK TO HIS INCREDIBLE POWER!! IN ORDER TO THROW A SINGLE PUNCH...
...HE REQUIRES A FULL HOUR OF HEAVY CONCENTRATION AND WARMING UP!!!
SH!
SH!
IT'S HIS TREASURED HEIRLOOM, A WEAPON THAT CAN ONLY BE UNLEASHED ONCE IN ANY BATTLE!!!
THE *KING PUNCH*, A WEAPON DEVASTATING ENOUGH TO SINK ONE OF THE FOUR EMPERORS SHOULD IT LAND SQUARELY!! FINDING THE RIGHT TIMING TO UNLEASH IT WILL DECIDE THIS BATTLE!!!
KING OF PRODENCE THE FIGHTING KING
ELIZABELLO II

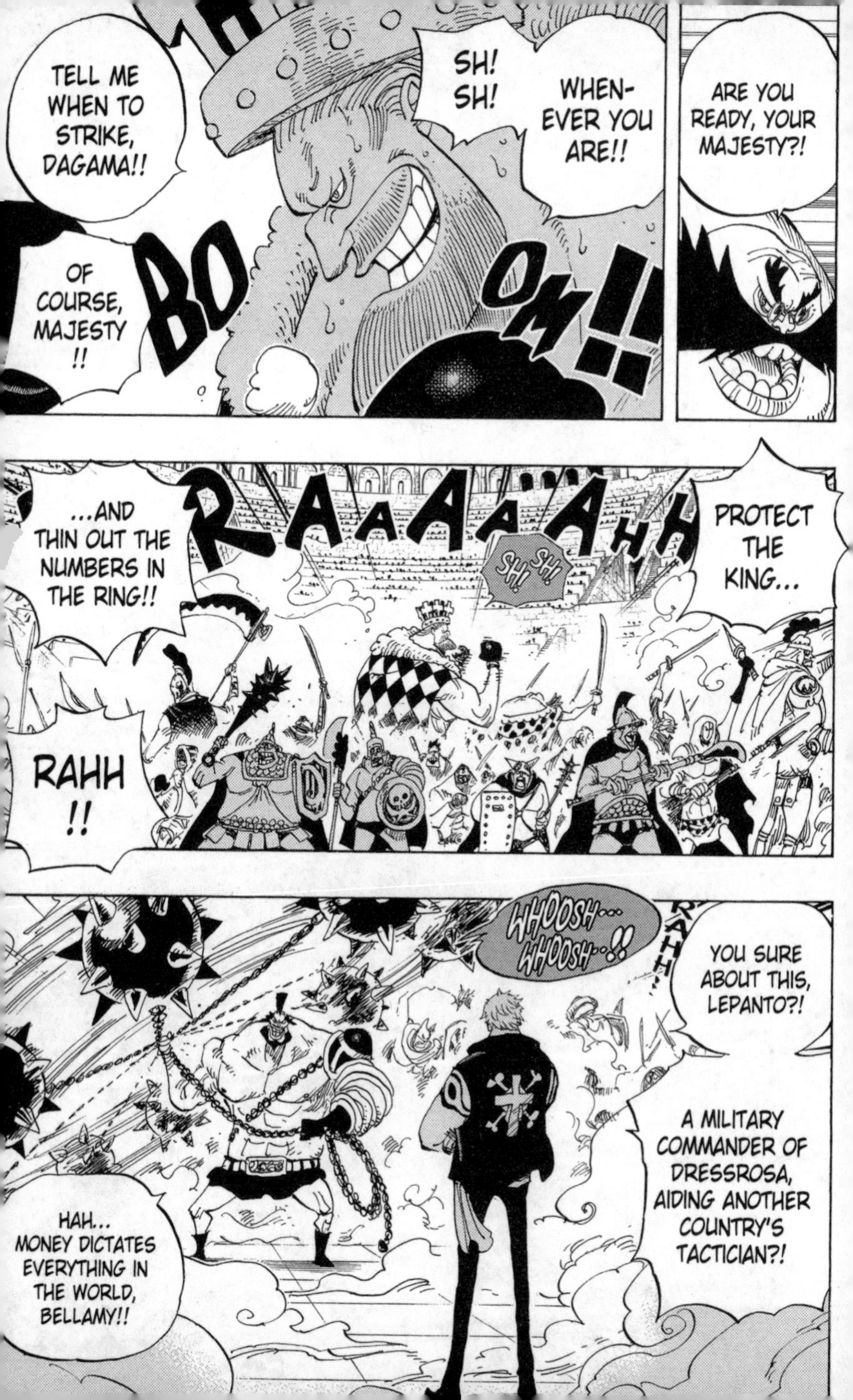
ARE YOU READY, YOUR MAJESTY?!
SH! SH!
WHEN-EVER YOU ARE!!
TELL ME WHEN TO STRIKE, DAGAMA!!
BOOM!!
OF COURSE, MAJESTY!!
PROTECT THE KING...
RAAAAAHH
SH! SH!
...AND THIN OUT THE NUMBERS IN THE RING!!
RAHH!!
RAHH!!
YOU SURE ABOUT THIS, LEPANTO?!
WHOOSH... WHOOSH...!!
A MILITARY COMMANDER OF DRESSROSA, AIDING ANOTHER COUNTRY'S TACTICIAN?!
HAH... MONEY DICTATES EVERYTHING IN THE WORLD, BELLAMY!!

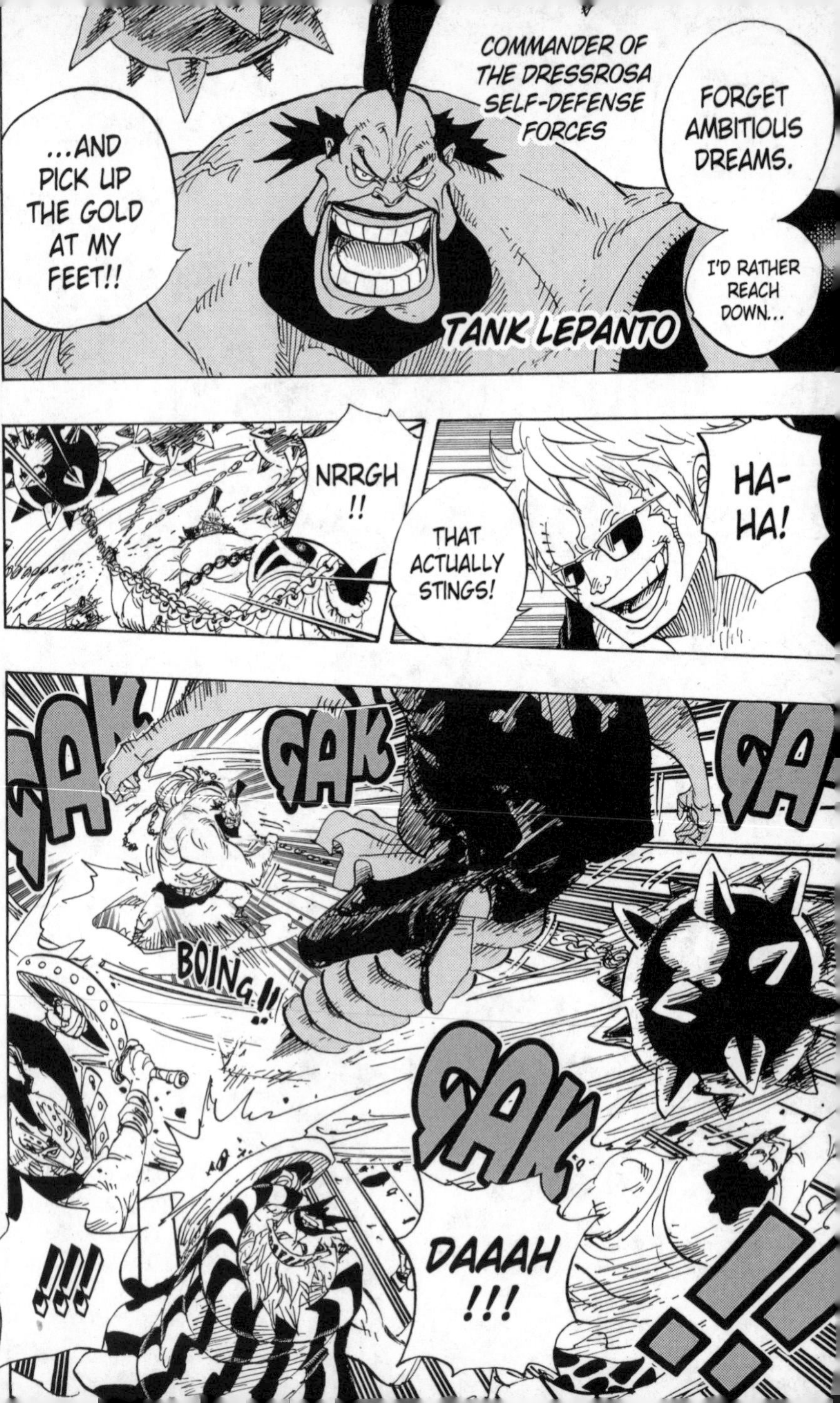
FORGET AMBITIOUS DREAMS.
I'D RATHER REACH DOWN...
COMMANDER OF THE DRESSROSA SELF-DEFENSE FORCES
TANK LEPANTO
...AND PICK UP THE GOLD AT MY FEET!!
HA-HA!
THAT ACTUALLY STINGS!
NRRGH !!
GA-
GAK
GAK
BOING!!
GAK
DAAAH !!!

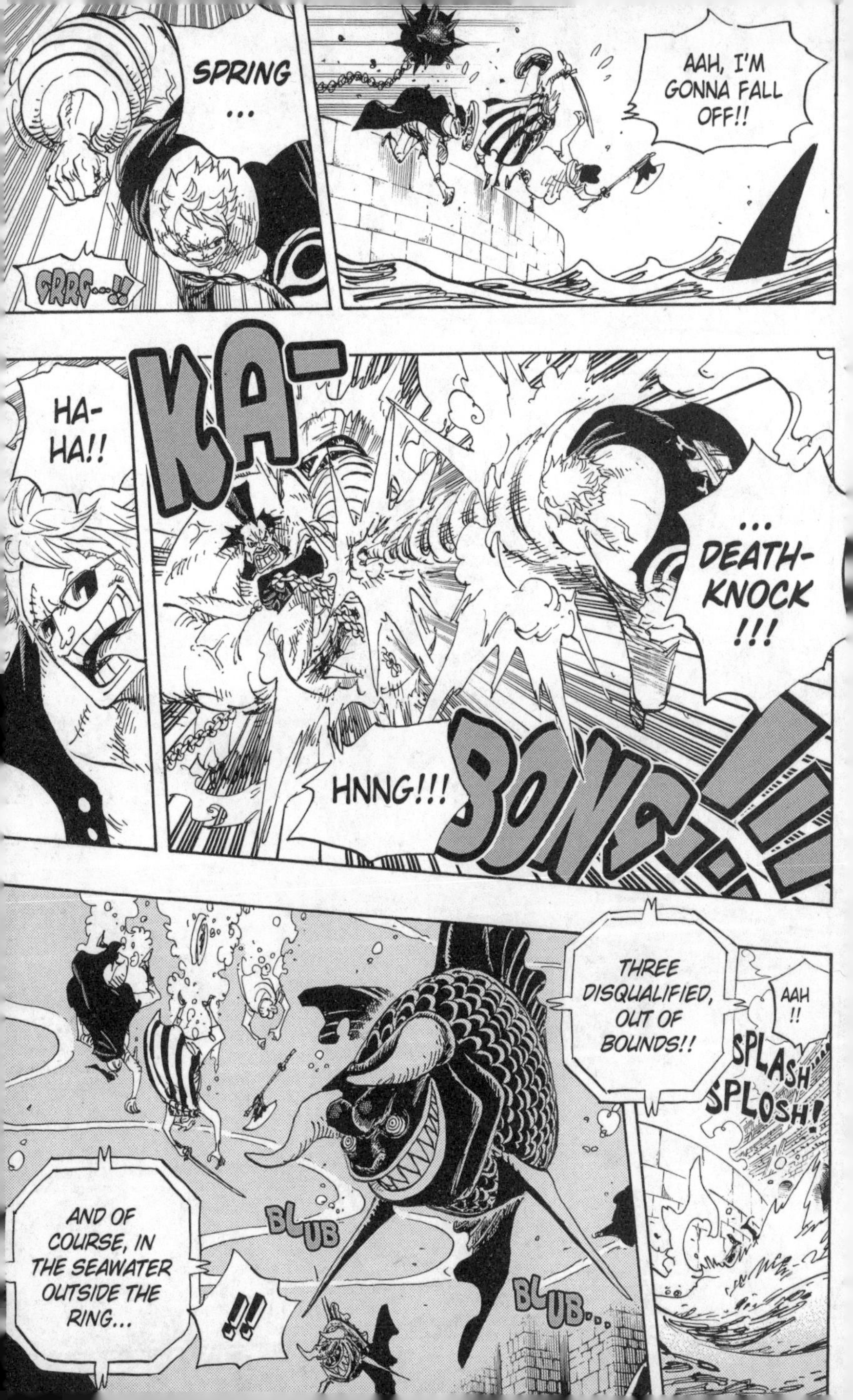
AAH, I'M GONNA FALL OFF!!
SPRING ...
GRRG...!!
... DEATH-KNOCK !!!
KA-
HA-HA!!
BONG...!!
HNNG!!!
AAH !!
SPLASH SPLOSH!
THREE DISQUALIFIED, OUT OF BOUNDS!!
BLUB
AND OF COURSE, IN THE SEAWATER OUTSIDE THE RING...
!!
BLUB...

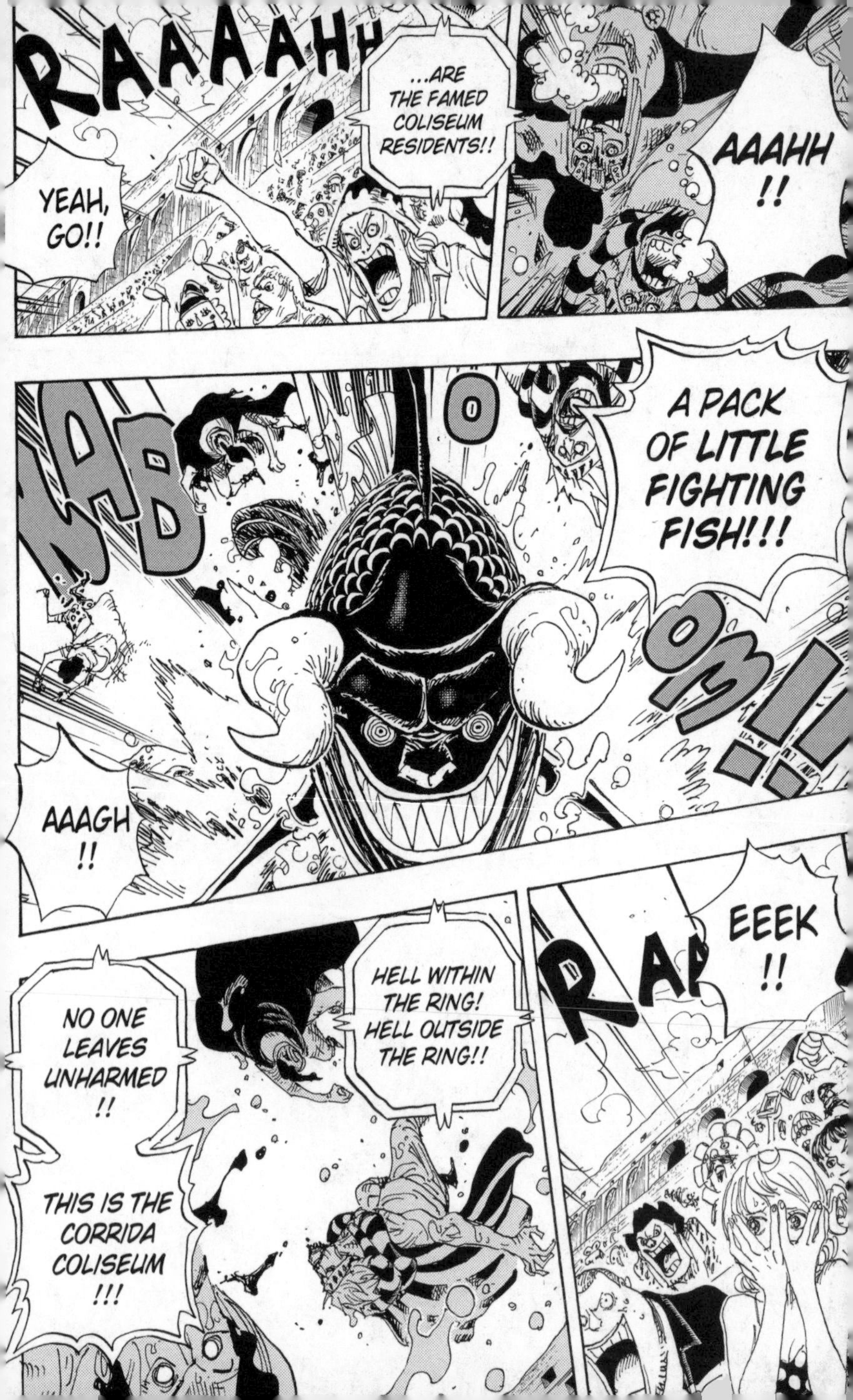
AAAHH !!
...ARE THE FAMED COLISEUM RESIDENTS!!
RAAAAHH
YEAH, GO!!
A PACK OF LITTLE FIGHTING FISH!!!
OM!!
AAAGH !!
EEEK !!
HELL WITHIN THE RING! HELL OUTSIDE THE RING!!
NO ONE LEAVES UNHARMED !!
THIS IS THE CORRIDA COLISEUM !!!

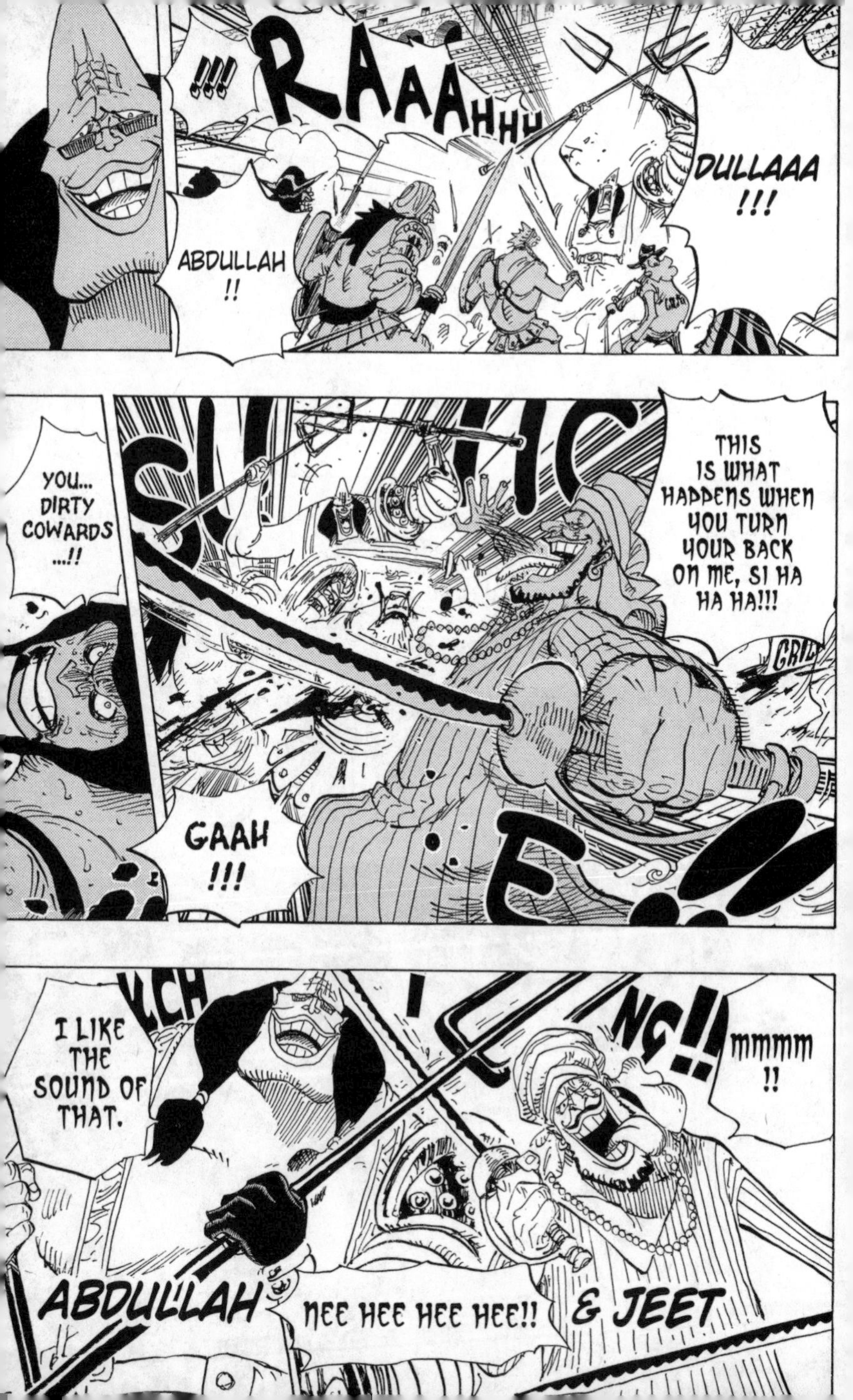

DULLAAA !!!
RAAAHHH
!!!
ABDULLAH !!
THIS IS WHAT HAPPENS WHEN YOU TURN YOUR BACK ON ME, SI HA HA HA!!!
YOU... DIRTY COWARDS ...!!
GAAH !!!
mmmm !!
NG!!
I LIKE THE SOUND OF THAT.
NEE HEE HEE HEE!!
ABDULLAH & JEET

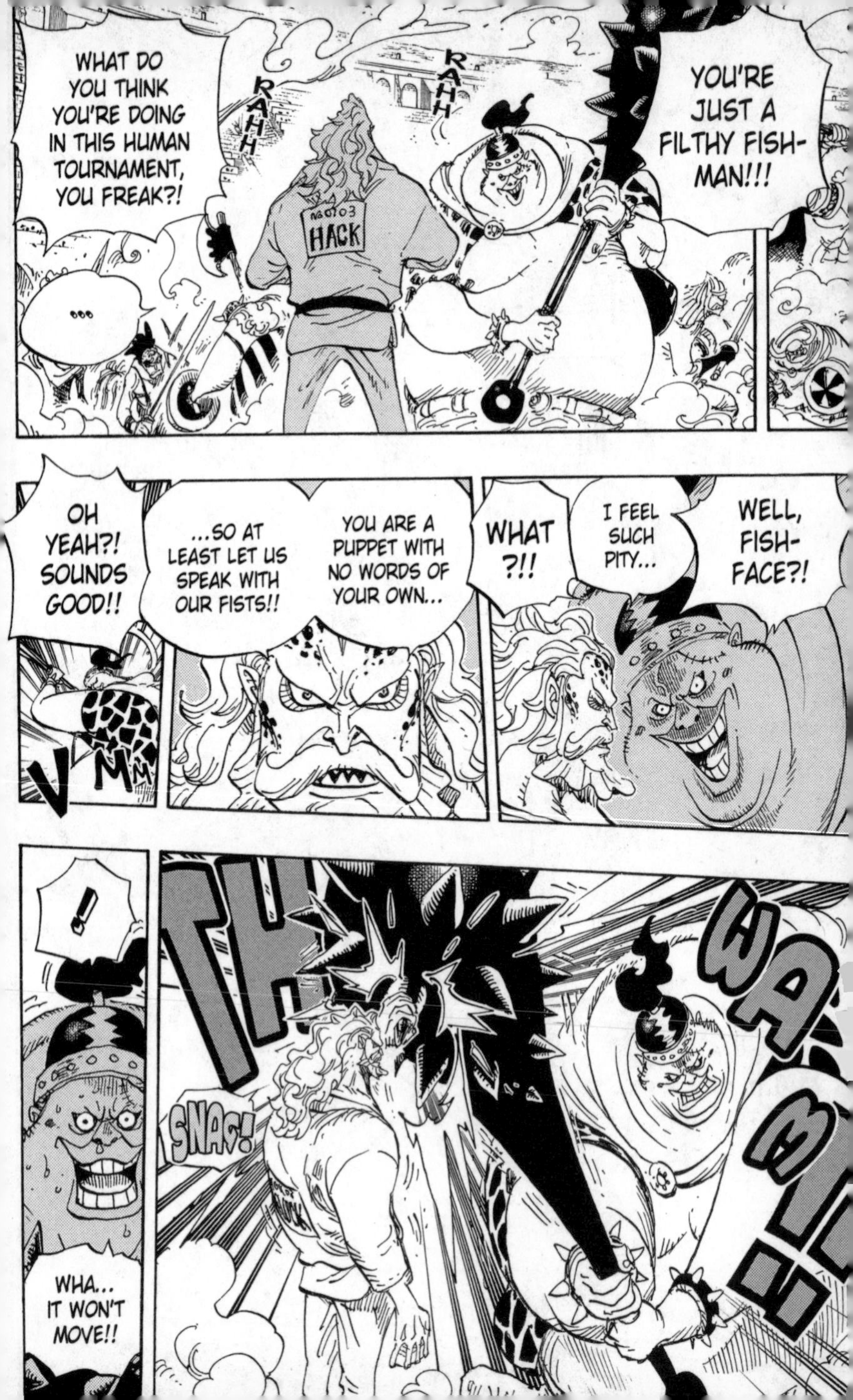
YOU'RE JUST A FILTHY FISH-MAN!!!
RAHH
RAHH
WHAT DO YOU THINK YOU'RE DOING IN THIS HUMAN TOURNAMENT, YOU FREAK?!
HACK
...
WELL, FISH-FACE?!
I FEEL SUCH PITY...
WHAT ?!!
YOU ARE A PUPPET WITH NO WORDS OF YOUR OWN...
...SO AT LEAST LET US SPEAK WITH OUR FISTS!!
OH YEAH?! SOUNDS GOOD!!
VMM
WAM!!
SNAG!
!
WHA... IT WON'T MOVE!!

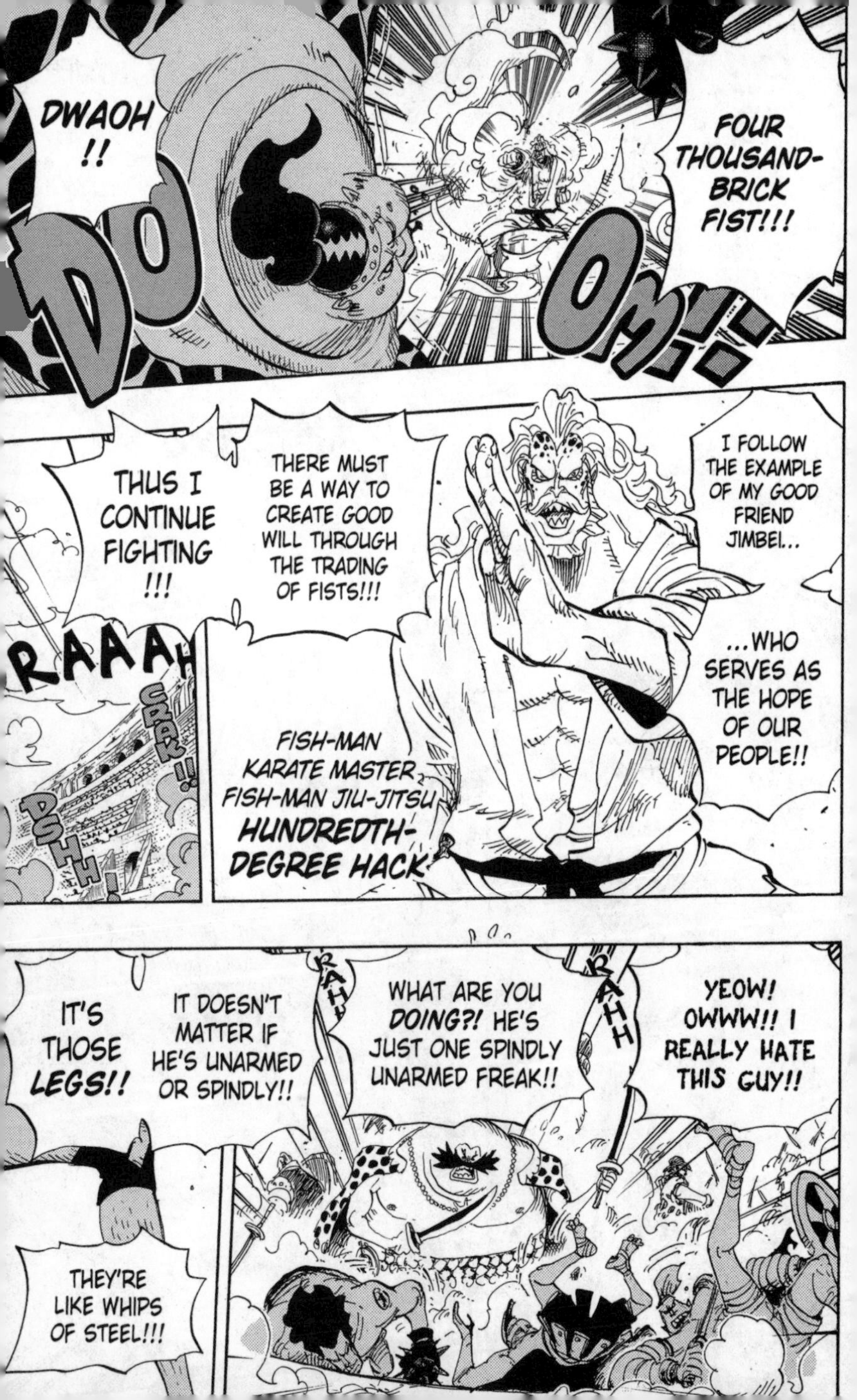
FOUR THOUSAND-BRICK FIST!!!
DWAOH !!
DOOM!!
I FOLLOW THE EXAMPLE OF MY GOOD FRIEND JIMBEI...
...WHO SERVES AS THE HOPE OF OUR PEOPLE!!
THERE MUST BE A WAY TO CREATE GOOD WILL THROUGH THE TRADING OF FISTS!!!
FISH-MAN KARATE MASTER, FISH-MAN JIU-JITSU HUNDREDTH-DEGREE HACK
THUS I CONTINUE FIGHTING !!!
RAAAH
CRAK!!
PSHH!!
YEOW! OWWW!! I REALLY HATE THIS GUY!!
RAHH
WHAT ARE YOU DOING?! HE'S JUST ONE SPINDLY UNARMED FREAK!!
RAHH
IT DOESN'T MATTER IF HE'S UNARMED OR SPINDLY!!
IT'S THOSE LEGS!!
THEY'RE LIKE WHIPS OF STEEL!!!

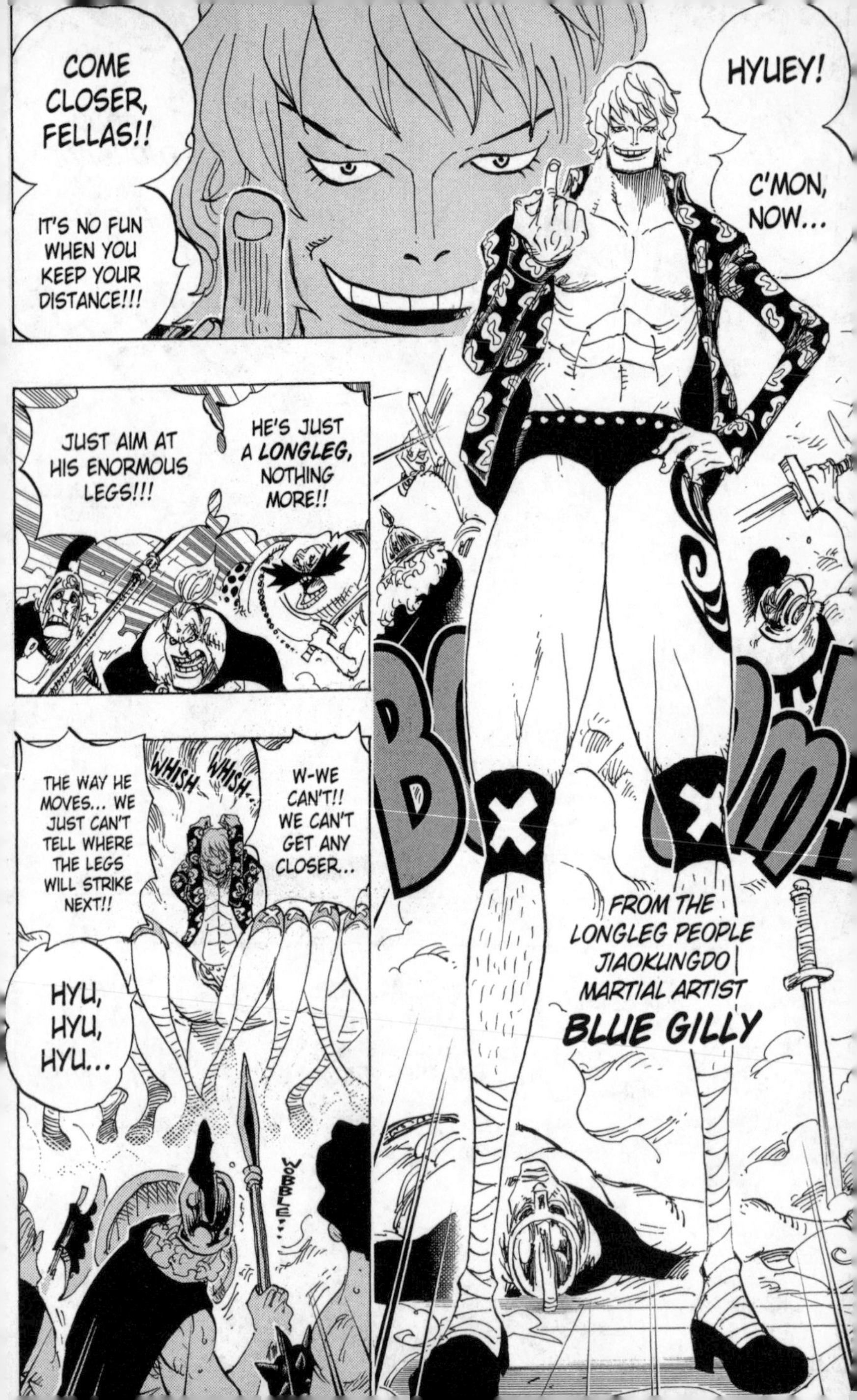
HYUEY!
C'MON, NOW...
FROM THE LONGLEG PEOPLE JIAOKUNGDO MARTIAL ARTIST
BLUE GILLY
COME CLOSER, FELLAS!!
IT'S NO FUN WHEN YOU KEEP YOUR DISTANCE!!!
HE'S JUST A LONGLEG, NOTHING MORE!!
JUST AIM AT HIS ENORMOUS LEGS!!!
W-WE CAN'T!! WE CAN'T GET ANY CLOSER...
WHISH
WHISH...
THE WAY HE MOVES... WE JUST CAN'T TELL WHERE THE LEGS WILL STRIKE NEXT!!
HYU, HYU, HYU...
WOBBLE...

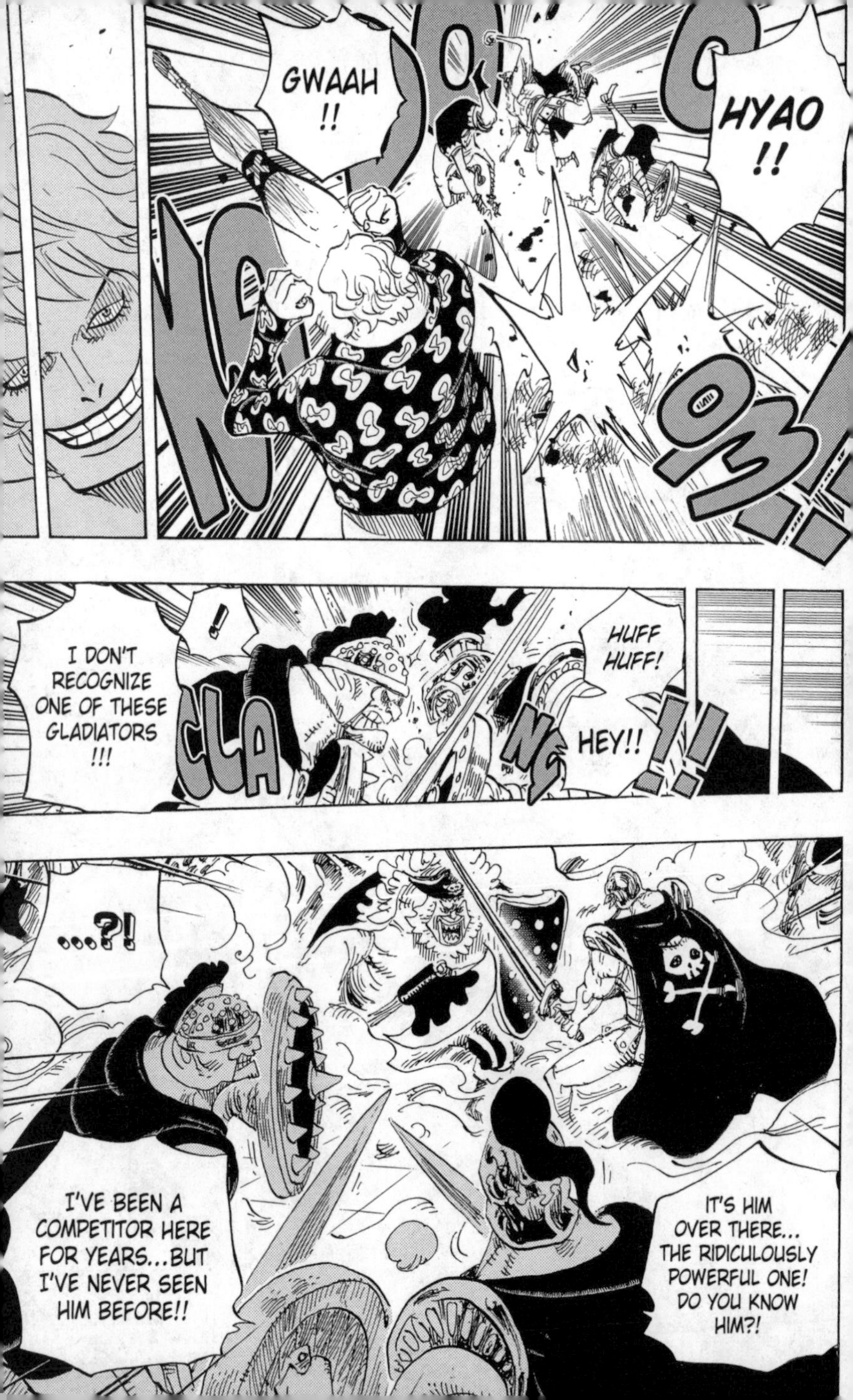
HYAO !!
GWAAH !!
HUFF HUFF!
HEY!!
CLANG!!
!
I DON'T RECOGNIZE ONE OF THESE GLADIATORS !!!
...?!
IT'S HIM OVER THERE... THE RIDICULOUSLY POWERFUL ONE! DO YOU KNOW HIM?!
I'VE BEEN A COMPETITOR HERE FOR YEARS...BUT I'VE NEVER SEEN HIM BEFORE!!

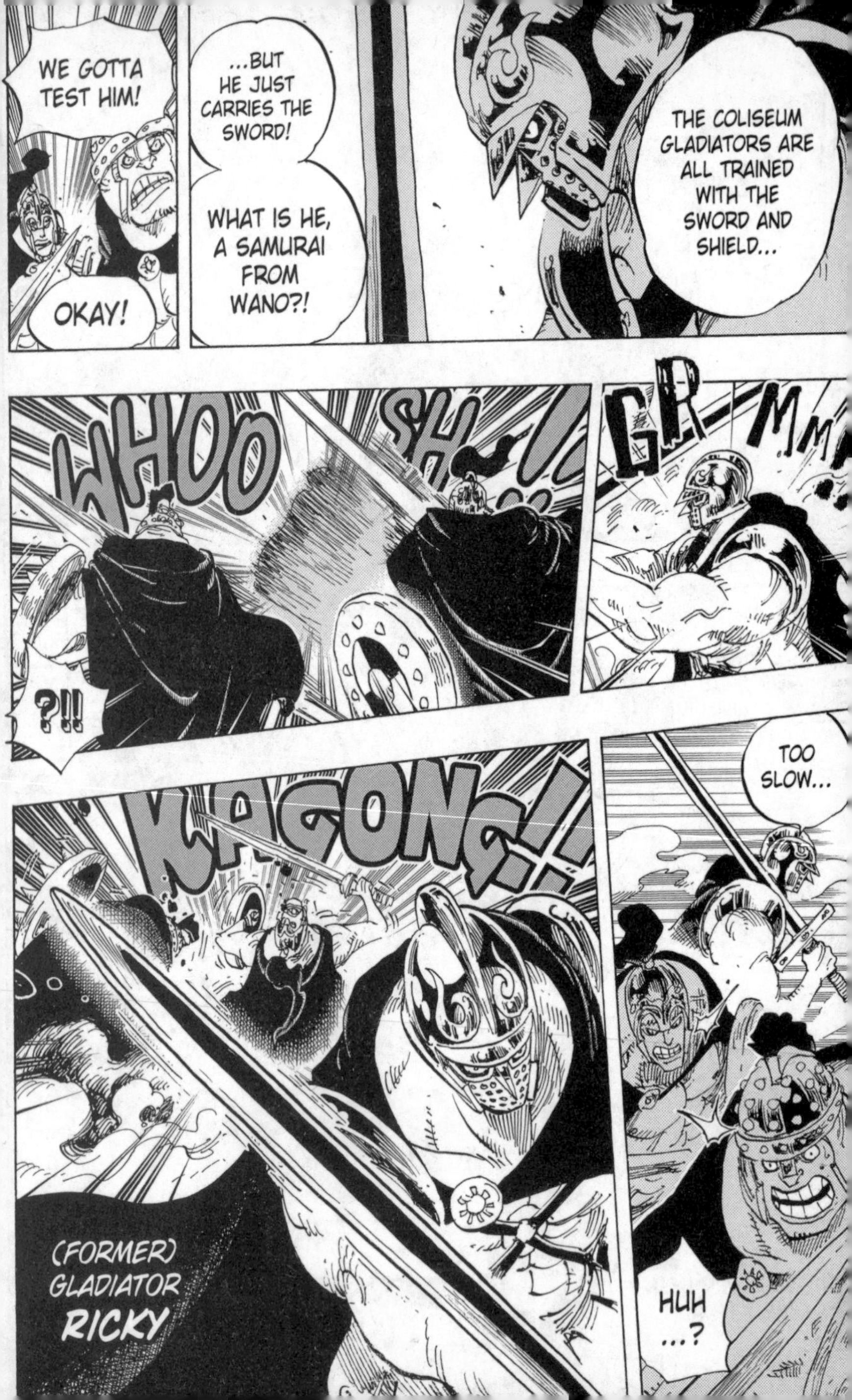
THE COLISEUM GLADIATORS ARE ALL TRAINED WITH THE SWORD AND SHIELD...
...BUT HE JUST CARRIES THE SWORD!
WHAT IS HE, A SAMURAI FROM WANO?!
WE GOTTA TEST HIM!
OKAY!
GR-MM
WHOOSH!!
?!!
TOO SLOW...
HUH ...?
KAGONG!!
(FORMER) GLADIATOR RICKY

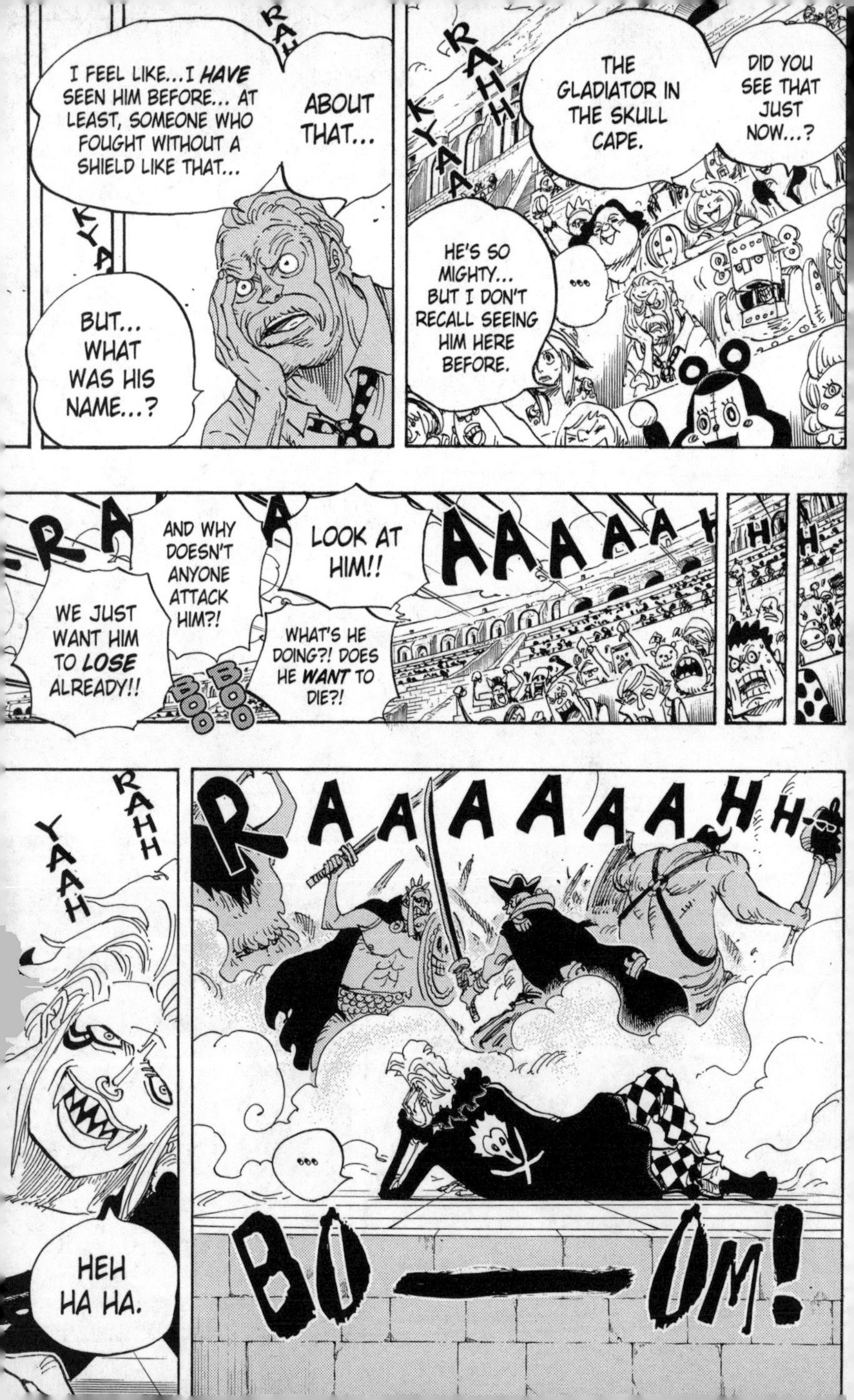
DID YOU SEE THAT JUST NOW...?
THE GLADIATOR IN THE SKULL CAPE.
KYAA
RAHH
HE'S SO MIGHTY... BUT I DON'T RECALL SEEING HIM HERE BEFORE.
...
RAH
ABOUT THAT...
I FEEL LIKE...I HAVE SEEN HIM BEFORE... AT LEAST, SOMEONE WHO FOUGHT WITHOUT A SHIELD LIKE THAT...
KYA
BUT... WHAT WAS HIS NAME...?
RAAAAAAAH
LOOK AT HIM!!
WHAT'S HE DOING?! DOES HE WANT TO DIE?!
AND WHY DOESN'T ANYONE ATTACK HIM?!
WE JUST WANT HIM TO LOSE ALREADY!!
BOO BOO
RAAAAAAHH
...
BO—OM!
RAHH
YAAH
HEH HA HA.

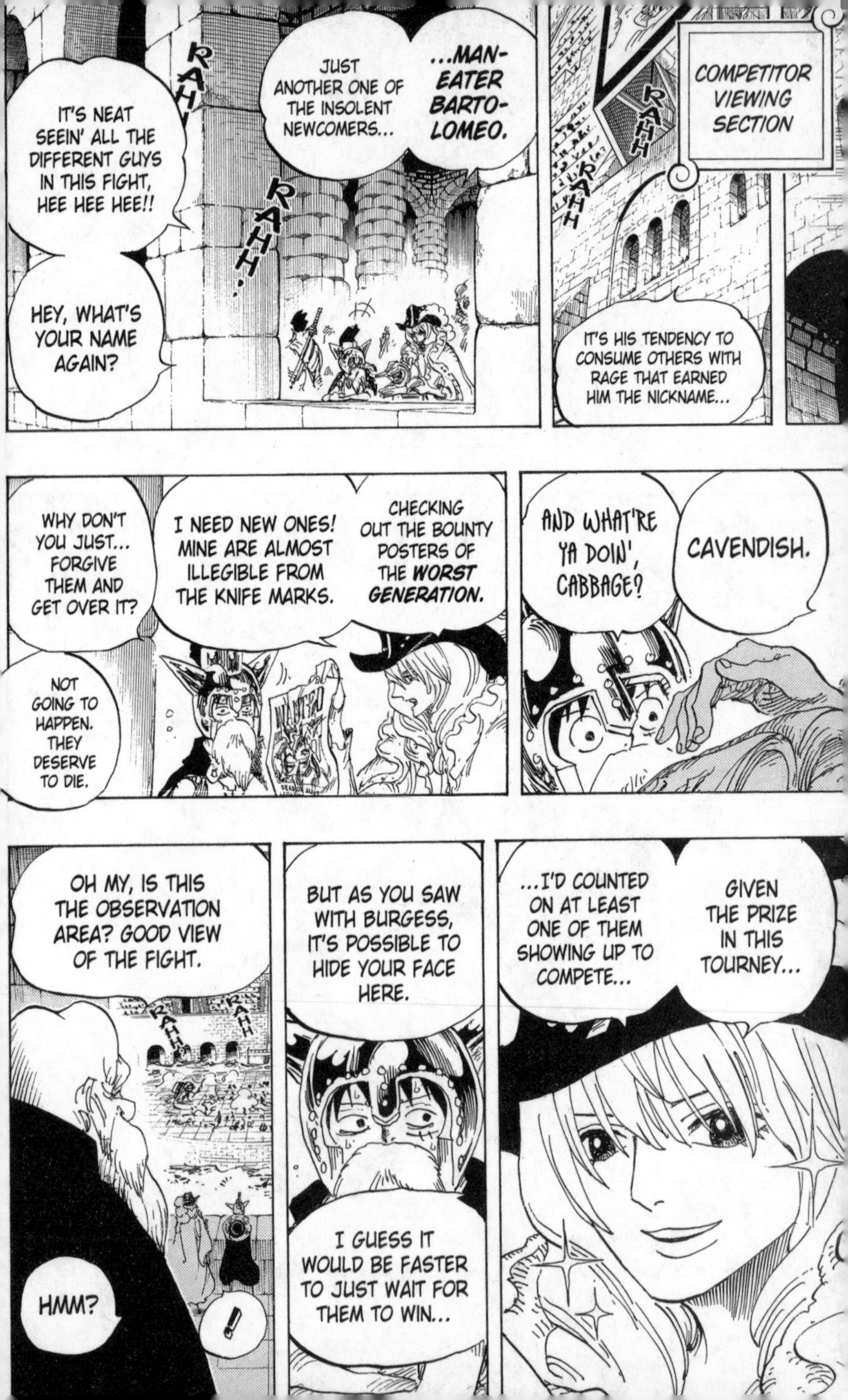
COMPETITOR VIEWING SECTION
RAHH
RAHH
RAHH
IT'S HIS TENDENCY TO CONSUME OTHERS WITH RAGE THAT EARNED HIM THE NICKNAME...
...MAN-EATER BARTO-LOMEO.
JUST ANOTHER ONE OF THE INSOLENT NEWCOMERS...
RAHH!
RAHH!
IT'S NEAT SEEIN' ALL THE DIFFERENT GUYS IN THIS FIGHT, HEE HEE HEE!!
HEY, WHAT'S YOUR NAME AGAIN?
CAVENDISH.
AND WHAT'RE YA DOIN', CABBAGE?
CHECKING OUT THE BOUNTY POSTERS OF THE ***WORST GENERATION.***
I NEED NEW ONES! MINE ARE ALMOST ILLEGIBLE FROM THE KNIFE MARKS.
WHY DON'T YOU JUST... FORGIVE THEM AND GET OVER IT?
NOT GOING TO HAPPEN. THEY DESERVE TO DIE.
GIVEN THE PRIZE IN THIS TOURNEY...
...I'D COUNTED ON AT LEAST ONE OF THEM SHOWING UP TO COMPETE...
BUT AS YOU SAW WITH BURGESS, IT'S POSSIBLE TO HIDE YOUR FACE HERE.
I GUESS IT WOULD BE FASTER TO JUST WAIT FOR THEM TO WIN...
OH MY, IS THIS THE OBSERVATION AREA? GOOD VIEW OF THE FIGHT.
RAHH
RAHH
HMM?
!

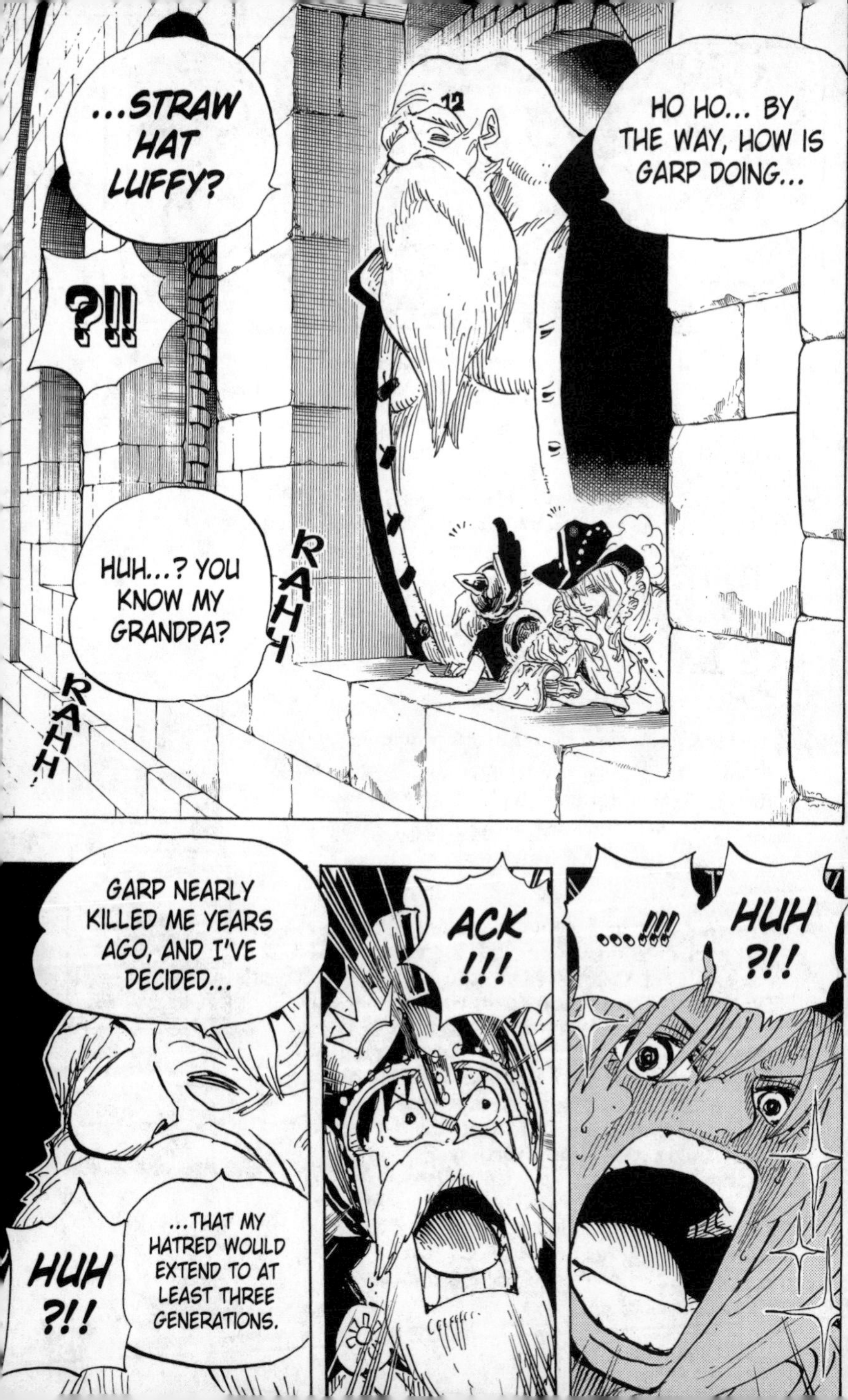
HO HO... BY THE WAY, HOW IS GARP DOING...
...STRAW HAT LUFFY?
?!!
HUH...? YOU KNOW MY GRANDPA?
RAHH
RAHH
HUH ?!!
...!!!
ACK !!!
GARP NEARLY KILLED ME YEARS AGO, AND I'VE DECIDED...
...THAT MY HATRED WOULD EXTEND TO AT LEAST THREE GENERATIONS.
HUH ?!!

質問コーナー

(Haru, Nagano)

Q: Odacchi, did you eat some toilet paper this morning?

--Haribo Monet

A: Ack!⁉ There's leftover toilet paper stuck on the side of my mouth!⁉ Excuse me.

Q: I've thought of some birthdays for Caesar and Monet!

Caesar: April 9th

Monet: August 27th

How's that? Is that okay?

--Nakamurider

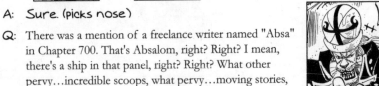

A: Sure. (picks nose)

Q: There was a mention of a freelance writer named "Absa" in Chapter 700. That's Absalom, right? Right? I mean, there's a ship in that panel, right? Right? What other pervy…incredible scoops, what pervy…moving stories, what pervy articles has he written?

--Makino♡ Love

A: That's right, it's Absalom. Doesn't it bring you back? As a matter of fact, he was at the Paramount War. After the battle was over, Doflamingo mentioned something about Moria meeting a strange fate. Why was that, do you suppose? I'm worried about Perona too. Did Moria really die? All we can confirm at this time is that Absalom is using his Clear-Clear Fruit to provide the world with major scoops under the penname "Absa." I'm sure he gets all kinds of pictures. It seems the menfolk enjoy his articles quite a bit. Well, enough of this edition of the Perv-BS! See you next volume!!

HE DISAP-PEARED?
YEAH, HONEST.
I'M TALKING LITERALLY HERE. HE JUST VANISHED!
HEH HEH HEH... IT REALLY SURPRISED ME. I DIDN'T KNOW THE SHADOW-SHADOW FRUIT HAD THAT KIND OF POWER.
THIS IS NO LAUGHING MATTER!
...
I DON'T KNOW IF HE'S ALIVE NOW, BUT...
...HE WAS THE LAST TIME I SAW HIM ON THE BATTLE-FIELD.

Chapter 708:
COLISEUM OF SCOUNDRELS

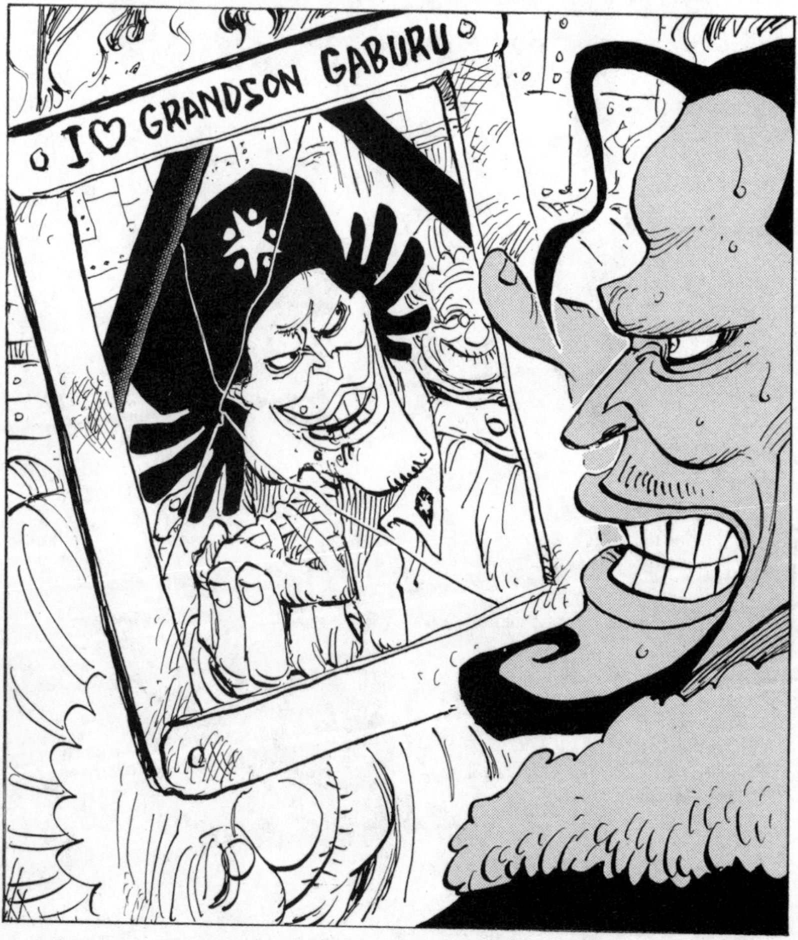
I ♡ GRANDSON GABURU

CARIBOU'S NEW WORLD KEEHEEHEE, VOL. 27 "THE HAG'S DEAD GRANDSON WAS MEAT-PIE-LOVING COMMANDER GABURU"

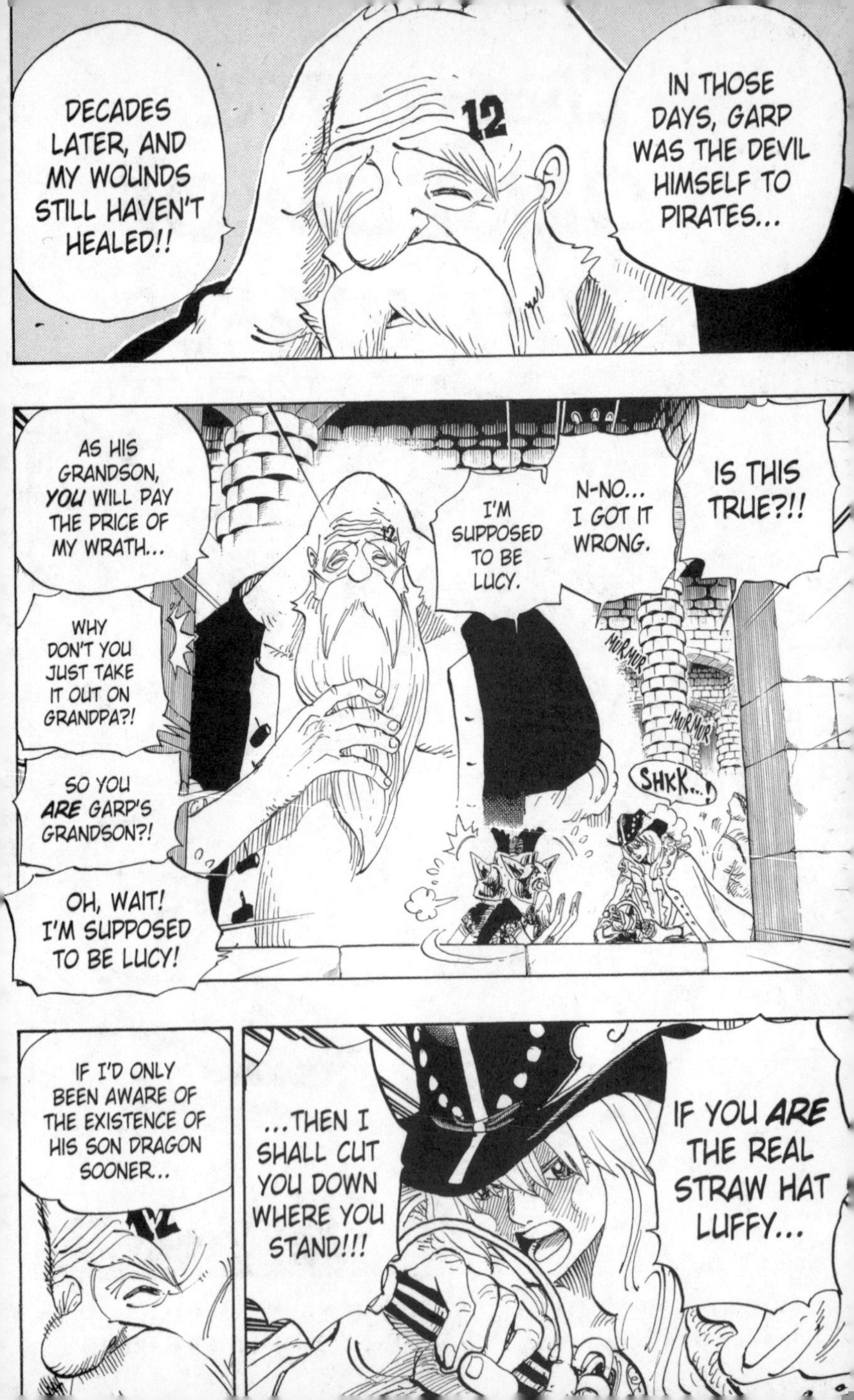
IN THOSE DAYS, GARP WAS THE DEVIL HIMSELF TO PIRATES...
DECADES LATER, AND MY WOUNDS STILL HAVEN'T HEALED!!
IS THIS TRUE?!!
N-NO... I GOT IT WRONG.
I'M SUPPOSED TO BE LUCY.
AS HIS GRANDSON, YOU WILL PAY THE PRICE OF MY WRATH...
WHY DON'T YOU JUST TAKE IT OUT ON GRANDPA?!
MURMUR
MURMUR
SHKK...
SO YOU ARE GARP'S GRANDSON?!
OH, WAIT! I'M SUPPOSED TO BE LUCY!
IF YOU ARE THE REAL STRAW HAT LUFFY...
...THEN I SHALL CUT YOU DOWN WHERE YOU STAND!!!
IF I'D ONLY BEEN AWARE OF THE EXISTENCE OF HIS SON DRAGON SOONER...

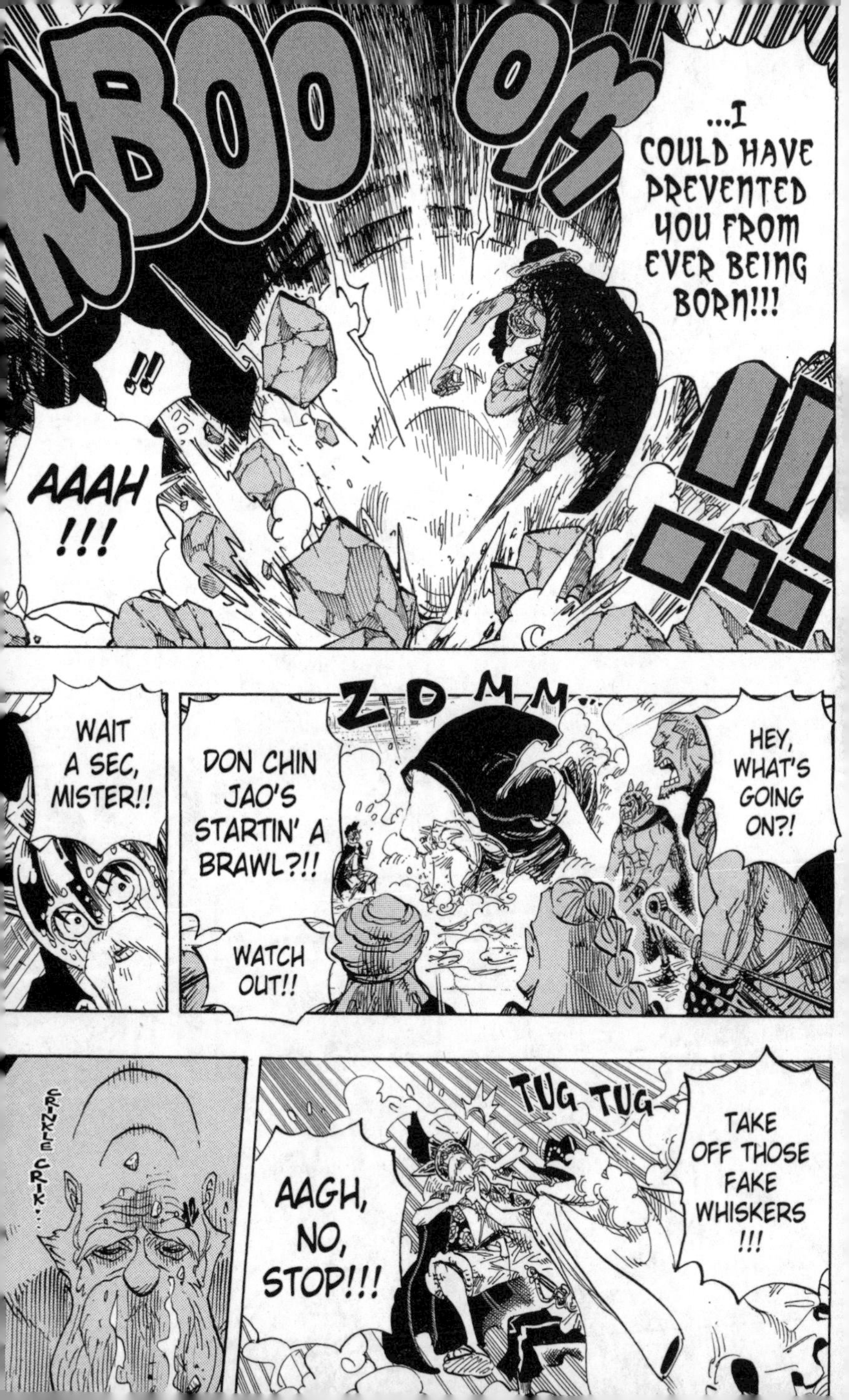
...I COULD HAVE PREVENTED YOU FROM EVER BEING BORN!!!
BOOOM
!!
AAAH!!!
HEY, WHAT'S GOING ON?!
ZDMM...
DON CHIN JAO'S STARTIN' A BRAWL?!!
WATCH OUT!!
WAIT A SEC, MISTER!!
TAKE OFF THOSE FAKE WHISKERS!!!
TUG TUG
AAGH, NO, STOP!!!
CRINKLE CRIK...

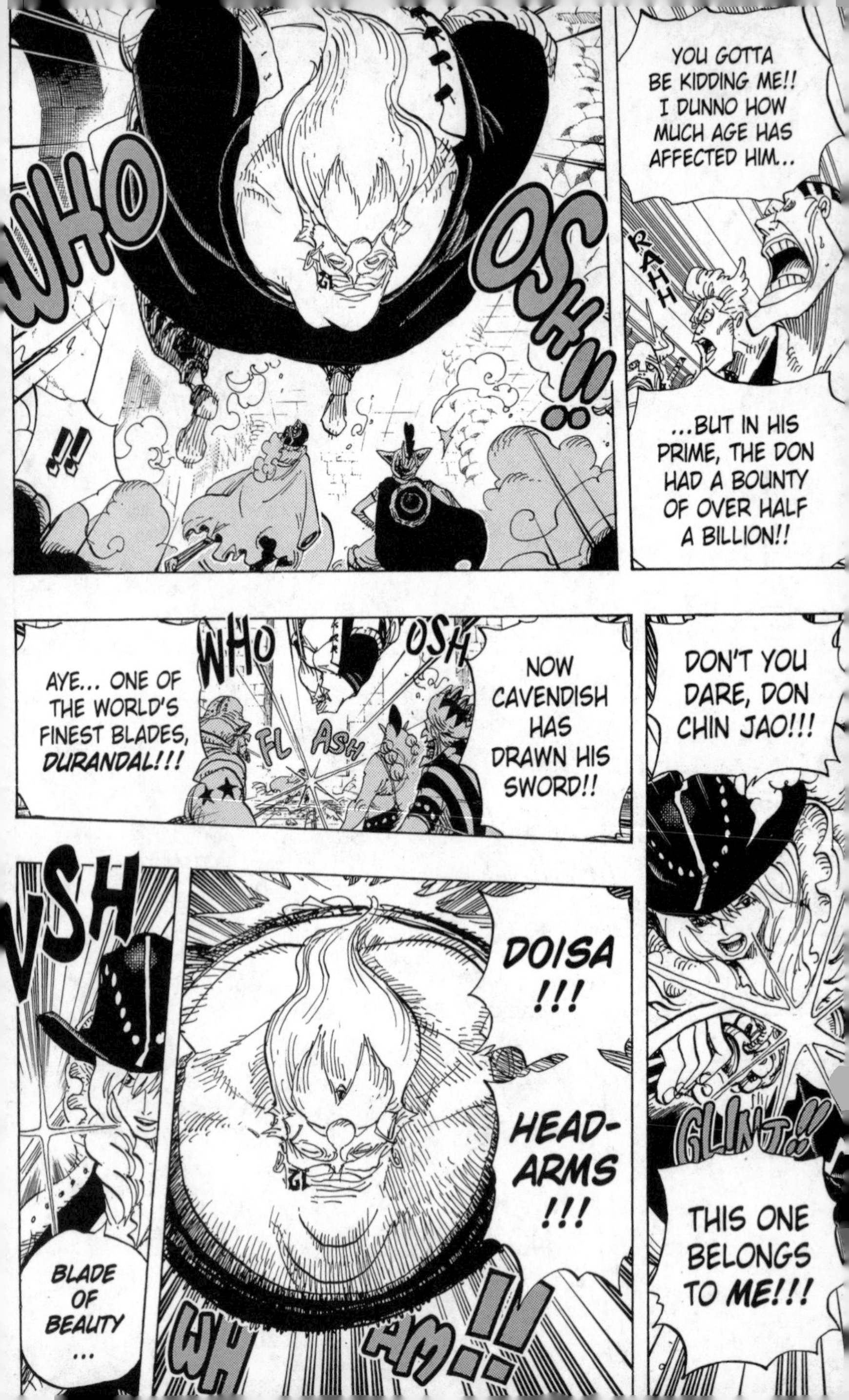
YOU GOTTA BE KIDDING ME!! I DUNNO HOW MUCH AGE HAS AFFECTED HIM...
RAHH
...BUT IN HIS PRIME, THE DON HAD A BOUNTY OF OVER HALF A BILLION!!
WHOOSH!!
!!
DON'T YOU DARE, DON CHIN JAO!!!
GLINT!!
THIS ONE BELONGS TO ME!!!
NOW CAVENDISH HAS DRAWN HIS SWORD!!
WHOOSH
FLASH
AYE... ONE OF THE WORLD'S FINEST BLADES, DURANDAL!!!
DOISA!!!
HEAD-ARMS!!!
WHAM!!
SH
BLADE OF BEAUTY...

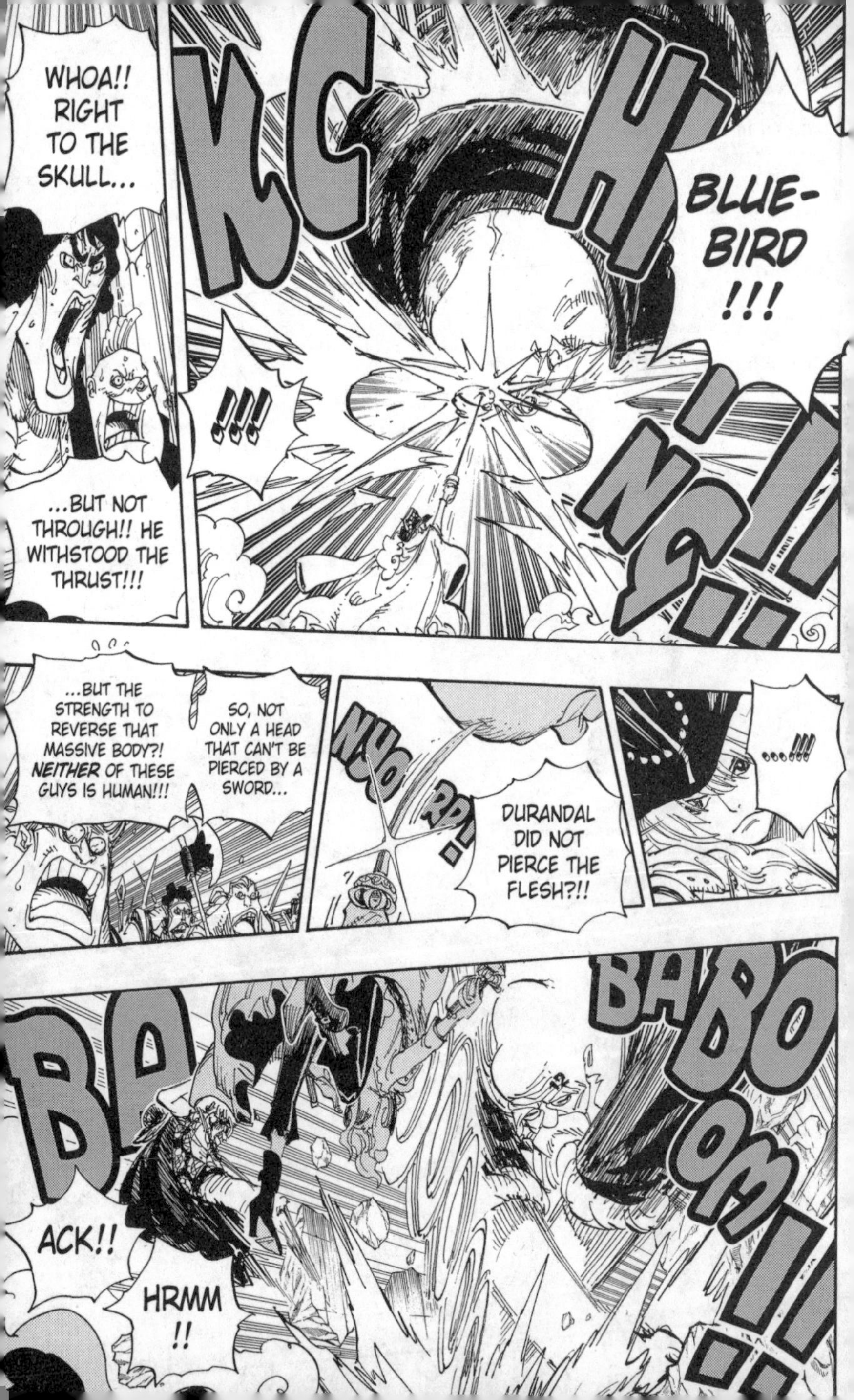

BLUE-BIRD!!!
KCH
!!!
WHOA!! RIGHT TO THE SKULL...
...BUT NOT THROUGH!! HE WITHSTOOD THE THRUST!!!
...!!!
DURANDAL DID NOT PIERCE THE FLESH?!!
SO, NOT ONLY A HEAD THAT CAN'T BE PIERCED BY A SWORD...
...BUT THE STRENGTH TO REVERSE THAT MASSIVE BODY?! *NEITHER* OF THESE GUYS IS HUMAN!!!
BABOOM!!
HRMM!!
ACK!!

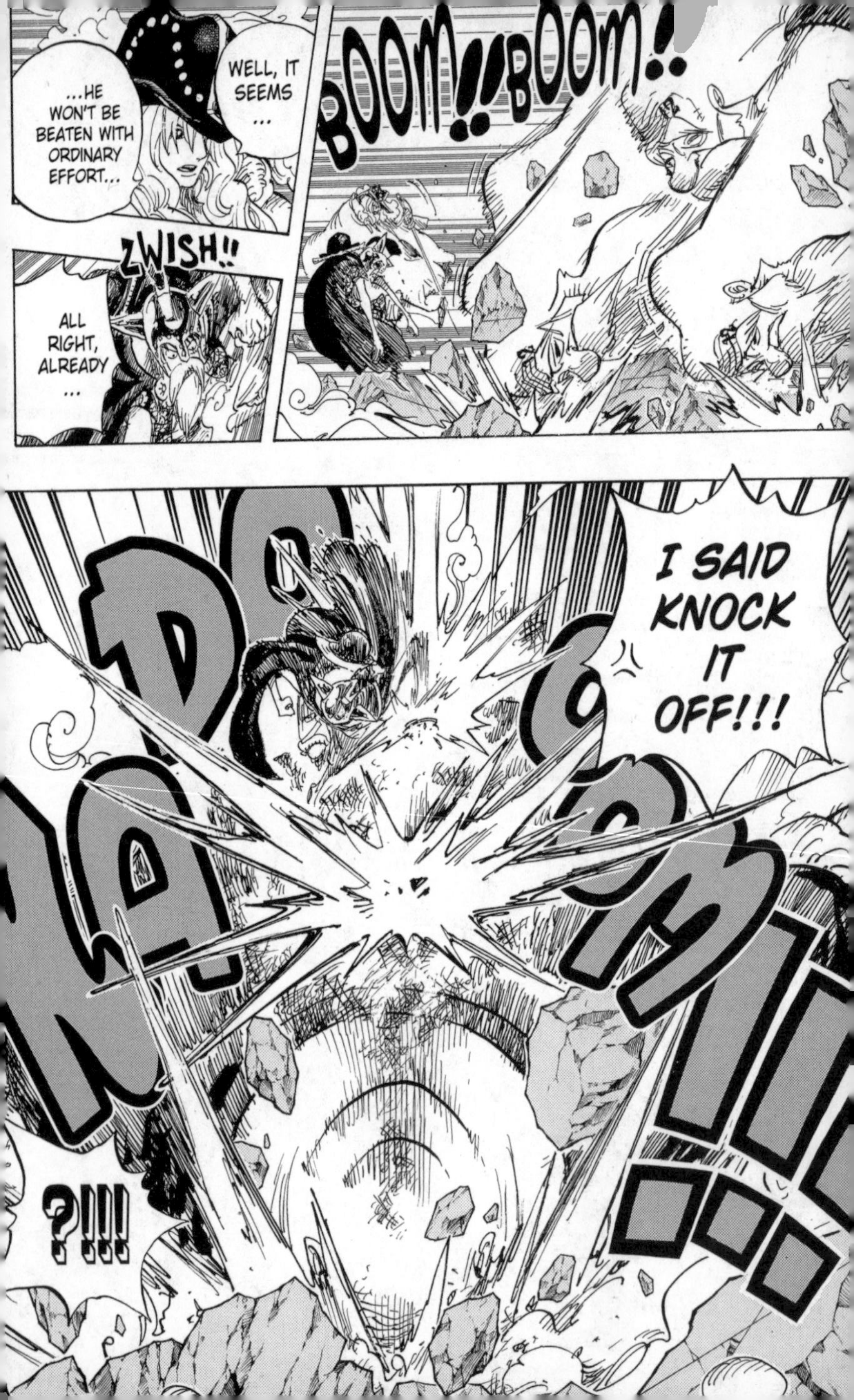
BOOM!! BOOM!!
WELL, IT SEEMS ...
...HE WON'T BE BEATEN WITH ORDINARY EFFORT...
ZWISH!!
ALL RIGHT, ALREADY ...
I SAID KNOCK IT OFF!!!
?!!!

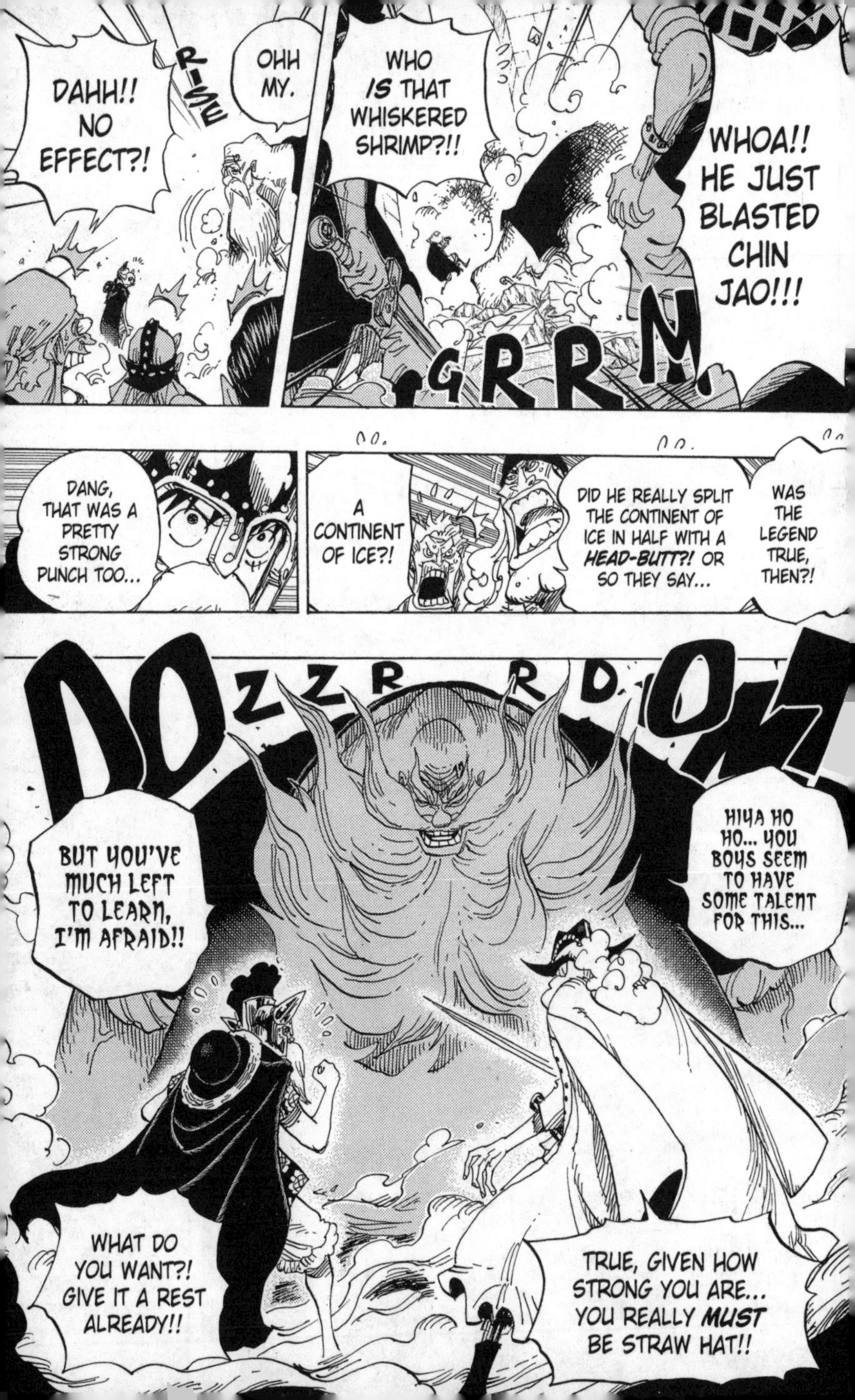

WHOA!! HE JUST BLASTED CHIN JAO!!!
WHO IS THAT WHISKERED SHRIMP?!!
GRRM
OHH MY.
RISE
DAHH!! NO EFFECT?!
WAS THE LEGEND TRUE, THEN?!
DID HE REALLY SPLIT THE CONTINENT OF ICE IN HALF WITH A HEAD-BUTT?! OR SO THEY SAY...
A CONTINENT OF ICE?!
DANG, THAT WAS A PRETTY STRONG PUNCH TOO...
DOZZRRDOM
HIYA HO HO... YOU BOYS SEEM TO HAVE SOME TALENT FOR THIS...
BUT YOU'VE MUCH LEFT TO LEARN, I'M AFRAID!!
TRUE, GIVEN HOW STRONG YOU ARE... YOU REALLY MUST BE STRAW HAT!!
WHAT DO YOU WANT?! GIVE IT A REST ALREADY!!

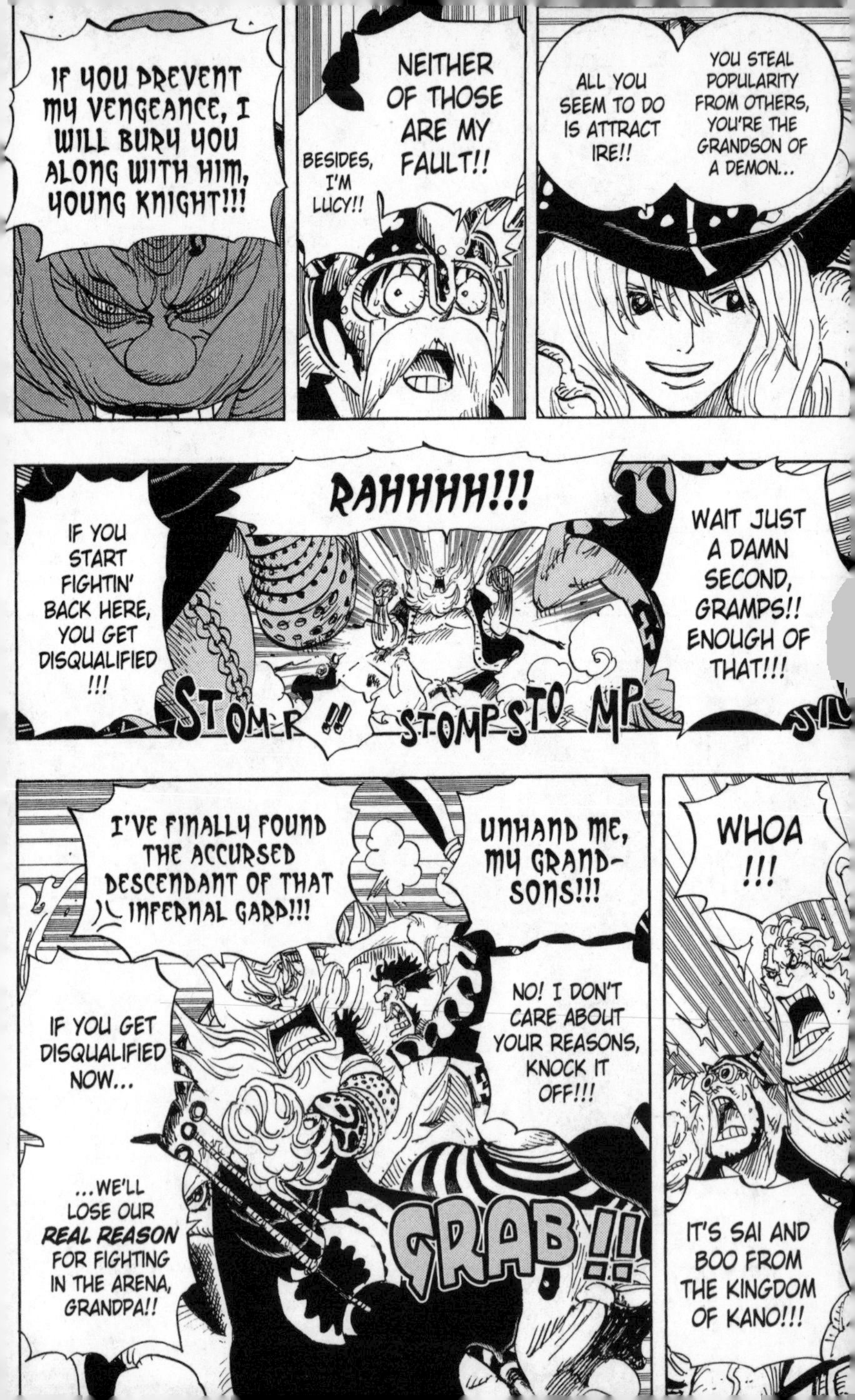
YOU STEAL POPULARITY FROM OTHERS, YOU'RE THE GRANDSON OF A DEMON...
ALL YOU SEEM TO DO IS ATTRACT IRE!!
NEITHER OF THOSE ARE MY FAULT!!
BESIDES, I'M LUCY!!
IF YOU PREVENT MY VENGEANCE, I WILL BURY YOU ALONG WITH HIM, YOUNG KNIGHT!!!
WAIT JUST A DAMN SECOND, GRAMPS!! ENOUGH OF THAT!!!
RAHHHH!!!
IF YOU START FIGHTIN' BACK HERE, YOU GET DISQUALIFIED!!!
STOMP STOMP
STOMP!!
WHOA!!!
IT'S SAI AND BOO FROM THE KINGDOM OF KANO!!!
UNHAND ME, MY GRANDSONS!!!
I'VE FINALLY FOUND THE ACCURSED DESCENDANT OF THAT INFERNAL GARP!!!
NO! I DON'T CARE ABOUT YOUR REASONS, KNOCK IT OFF!!!
IF YOU GET DISQUALIFIED NOW...
...WE'LL LOSE OUR ***REAL REASON*** FOR FIGHTING IN THE ARENA, GRANDPA!!
GRAB!!

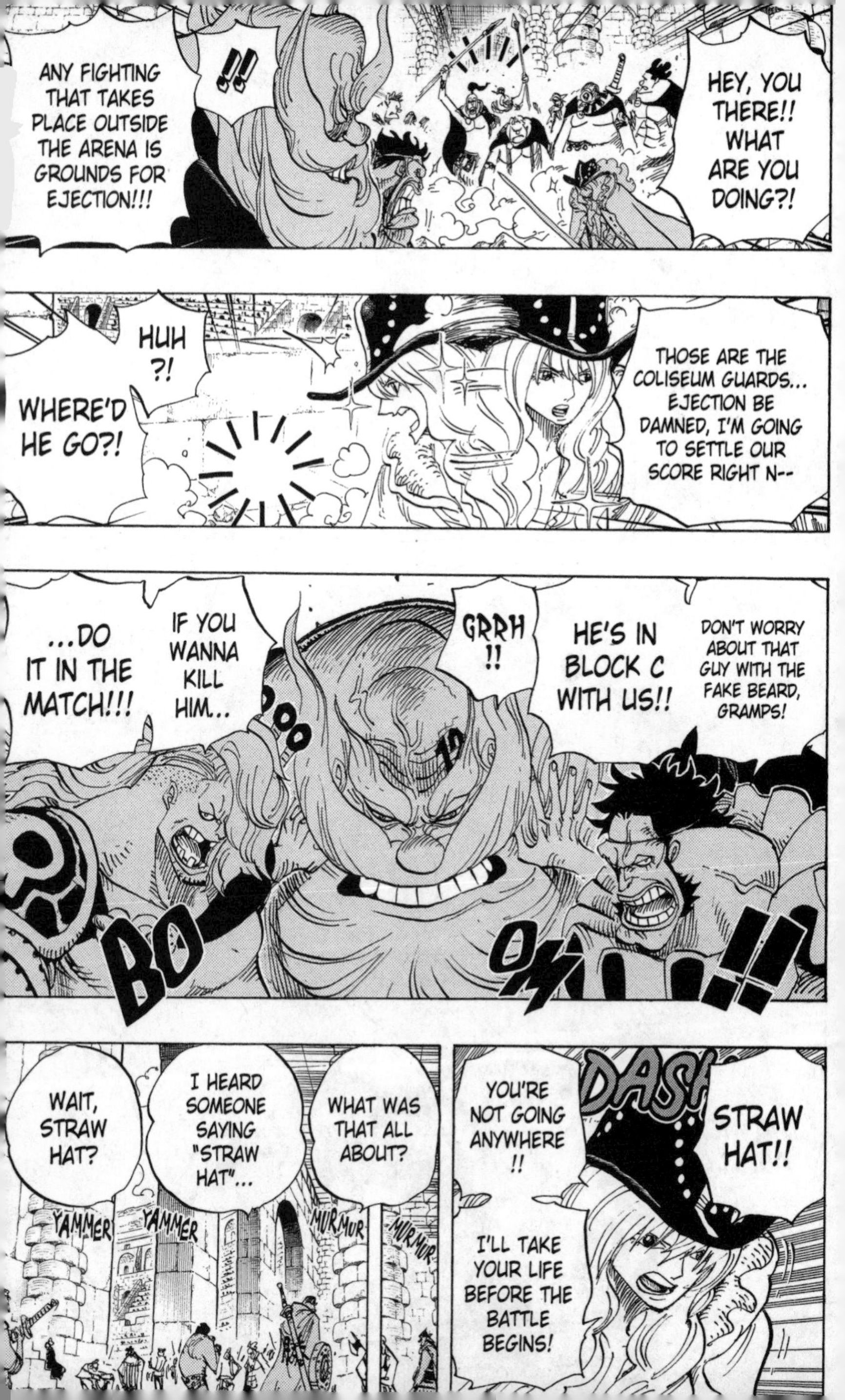
HEY, YOU THERE!! WHAT ARE YOU DOING?!
!!
ANY FIGHTING THAT TAKES PLACE OUTSIDE THE ARENA IS GROUNDS FOR EJECTION!!!
THOSE ARE THE COLISEUM GUARDS... EJECTION BE DAMNED, I'M GOING TO SETTLE OUR SCORE RIGHT N--
HUH ?!
WHERE'D HE GO?!
DON'T WORRY ABOUT THAT GUY WITH THE FAKE BEARD, GRAMPS!
HE'S IN BLOCK C WITH US!!
GRRH !!
IF YOU WANNA KILL HIM...
...DO IT IN THE MATCH!!!
BOOOM!!
DASH
STRAW HAT!!
YOU'RE NOT GOING ANYWHERE !!
I'LL TAKE YOUR LIFE BEFORE THE BATTLE BEGINS!
WHAT WAS THAT ALL ABOUT?
I HEARD SOMEONE SAYING "STRAW HAT"...
WAIT, STRAW HAT?
MURMUR
MURMUR
YAMMER
YAMMER

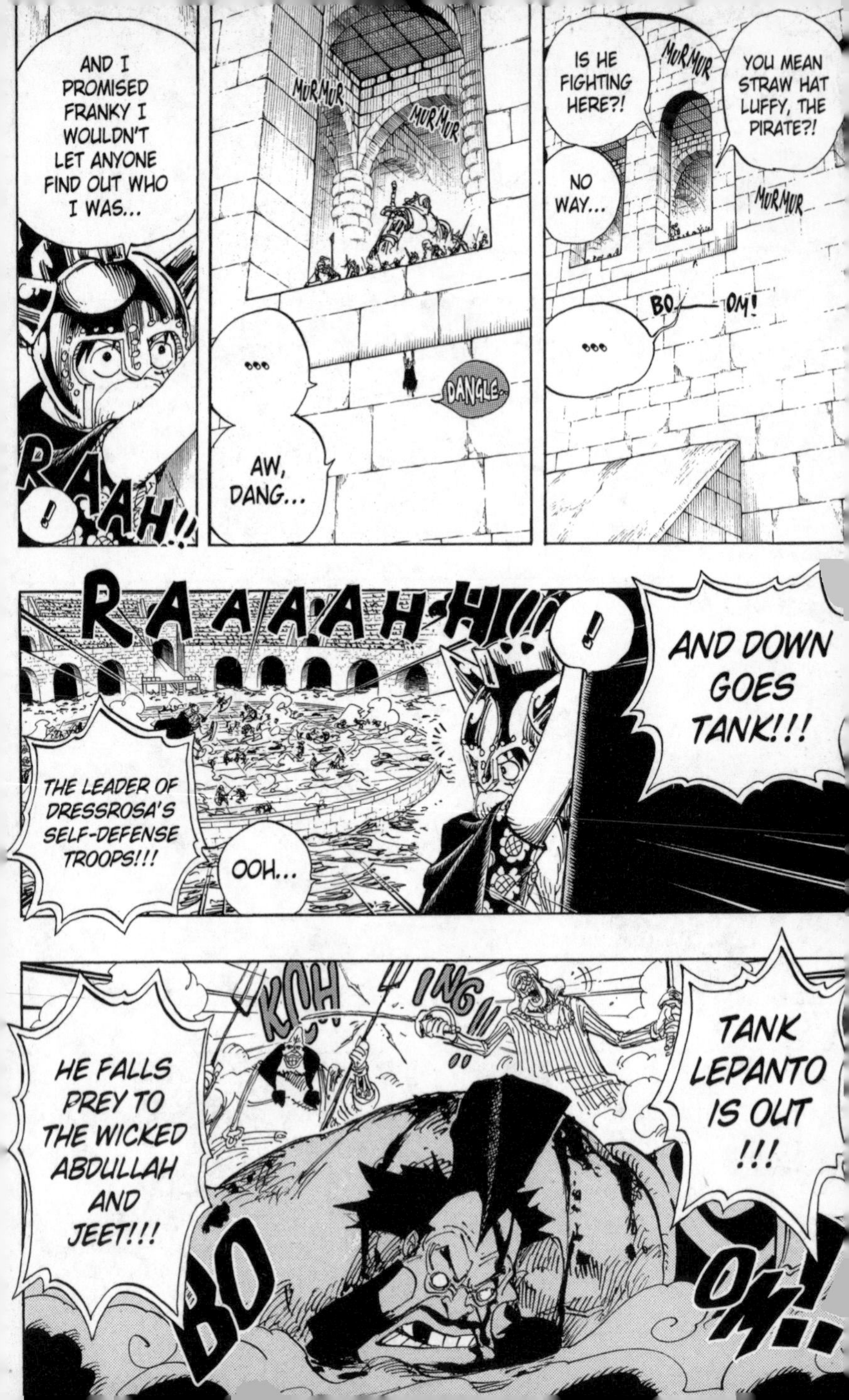

YOU MEAN STRAW HAT LUFFY, THE PIRATE?!
MURMUR
MURMUR
IS HE FIGHTING HERE?!
NO WAY...
BO—OM!
...
MURMUR
MURMUR
DANGLE..
...
AW, DANG...
AND I PROMISED FRANKY I WOULDN'T LET ANYONE FIND OUT WHO I WAS...
RAAH!!
!
AND DOWN GOES TANK!!!
!
RAAAAAH!!!
THE LEADER OF DRESSROSA'S SELF-DEFENSE TROOPS!!!
OOH...
TANK LEPANTO IS OUT!!!
KSCHING!!
HE FALLS PREY TO THE WICKED ABDULLAH AND JEET!!!
BOOM!!

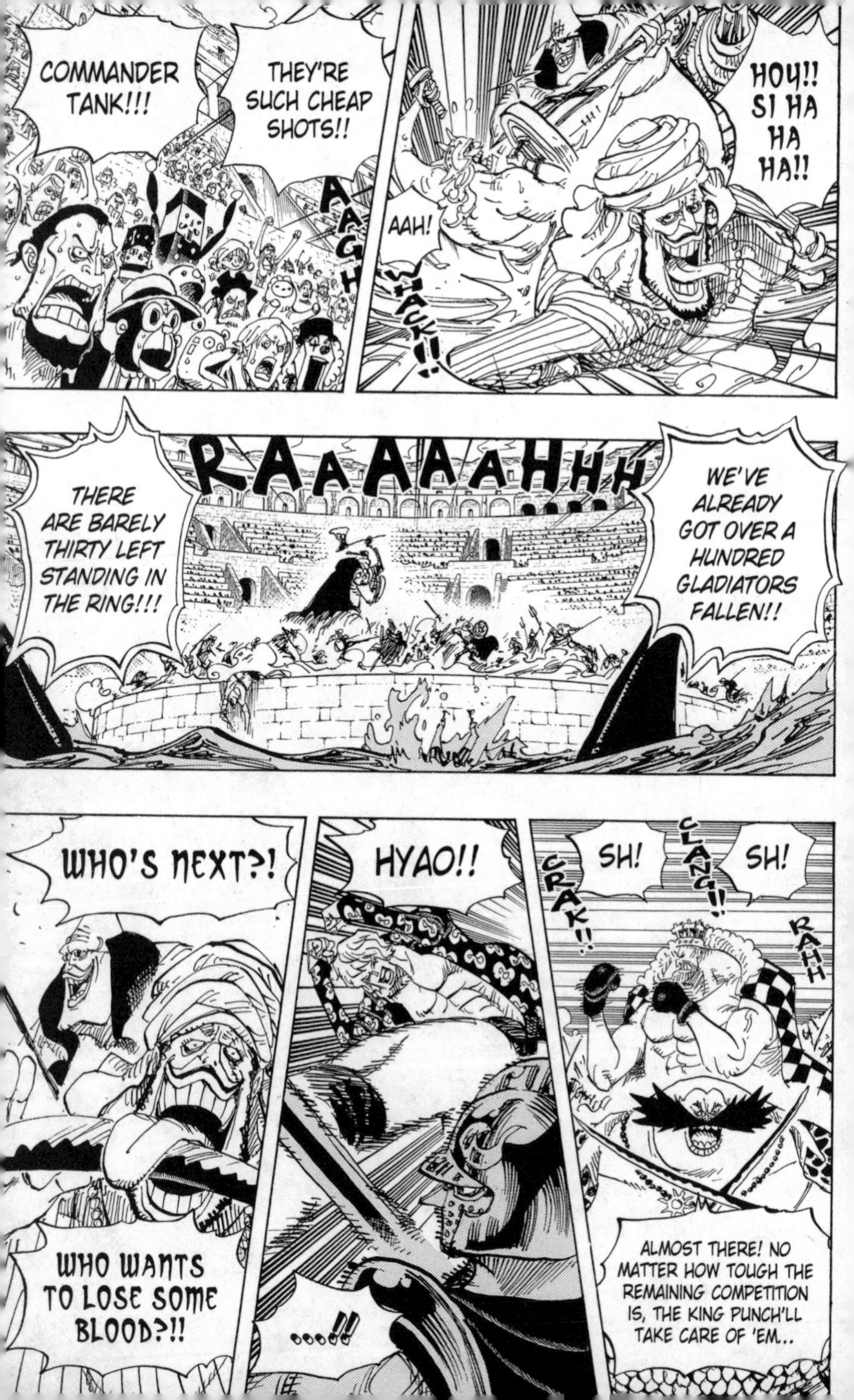
HOY!! SI HA HA HA!!
AAH!
WHACK!!
THEY'RE SUCH CHEAP SHOTS!!
COMMANDER TANK!!!
AAGH
WE'VE ALREADY GOT OVER A HUNDRED GLADIATORS FALLEN!!
RAAAAAHHH
THERE ARE BARELY THIRTY LEFT STANDING IN THE RING!!!
SH!
CLANG!!
SH!
RAHH
CRAK!!
ALMOST THERE! NO MATTER HOW TOUGH THE REMAINING COMPETITION IS, THE KING PUNCH'LL TAKE CARE OF 'EM..
HYAO!!
...!!
WHO'S NEXT?!
WHO WANTS TO LOSE SOME BLOOD?!!

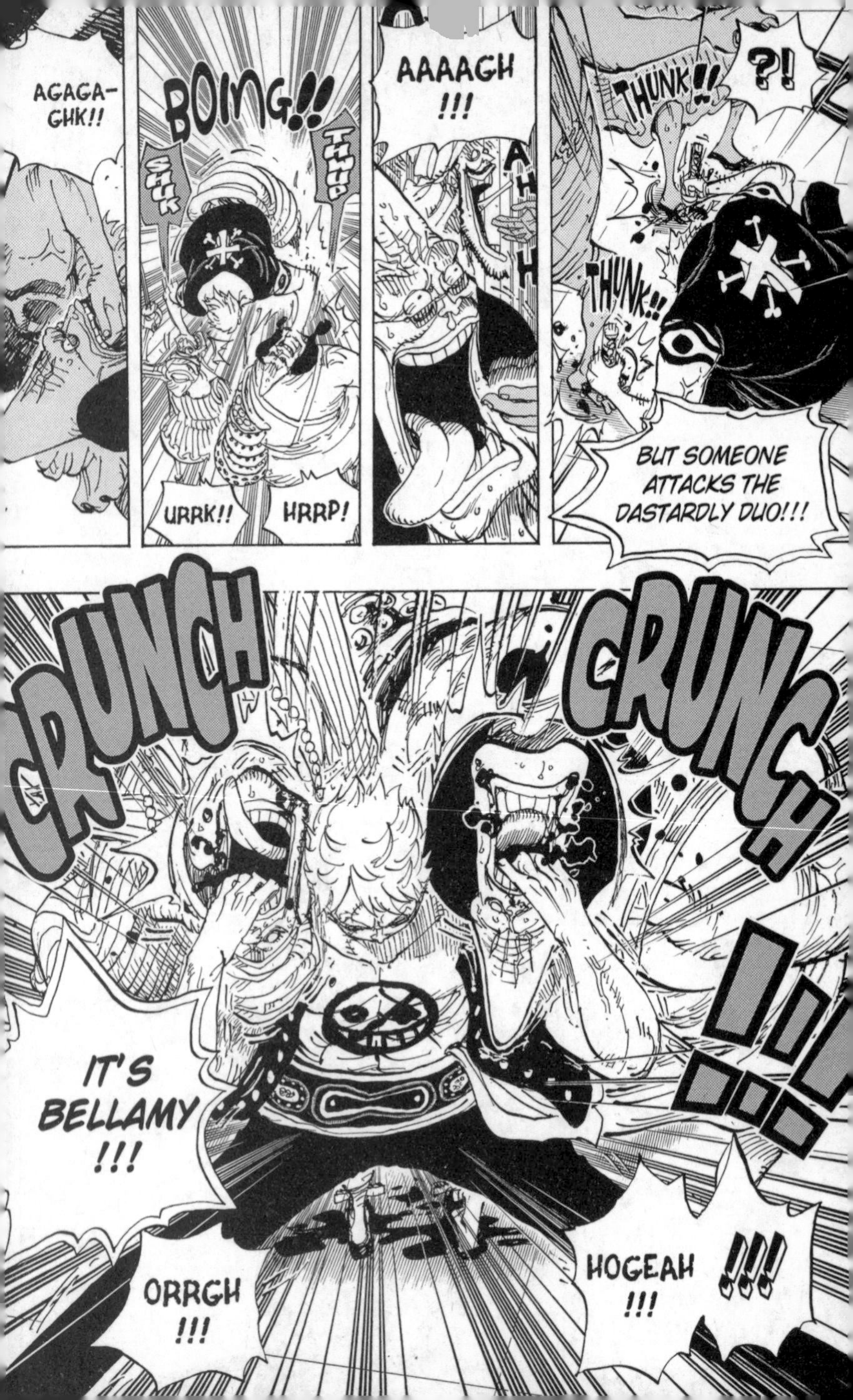
THUNK!!
?!
THUNK!!
BUT SOMEONE ATTACKS THE DASTARDLY DUO!!!
AAAAGH !!!
BOING!!
THWUP
SHUK
URRK!!
HRRP!
AGAGA-GHK!!
CRUNCH
CRUNCH
!!!
IT'S BELLAMY !!!
HOGEAH !!!
!!!
ORRGH !!!

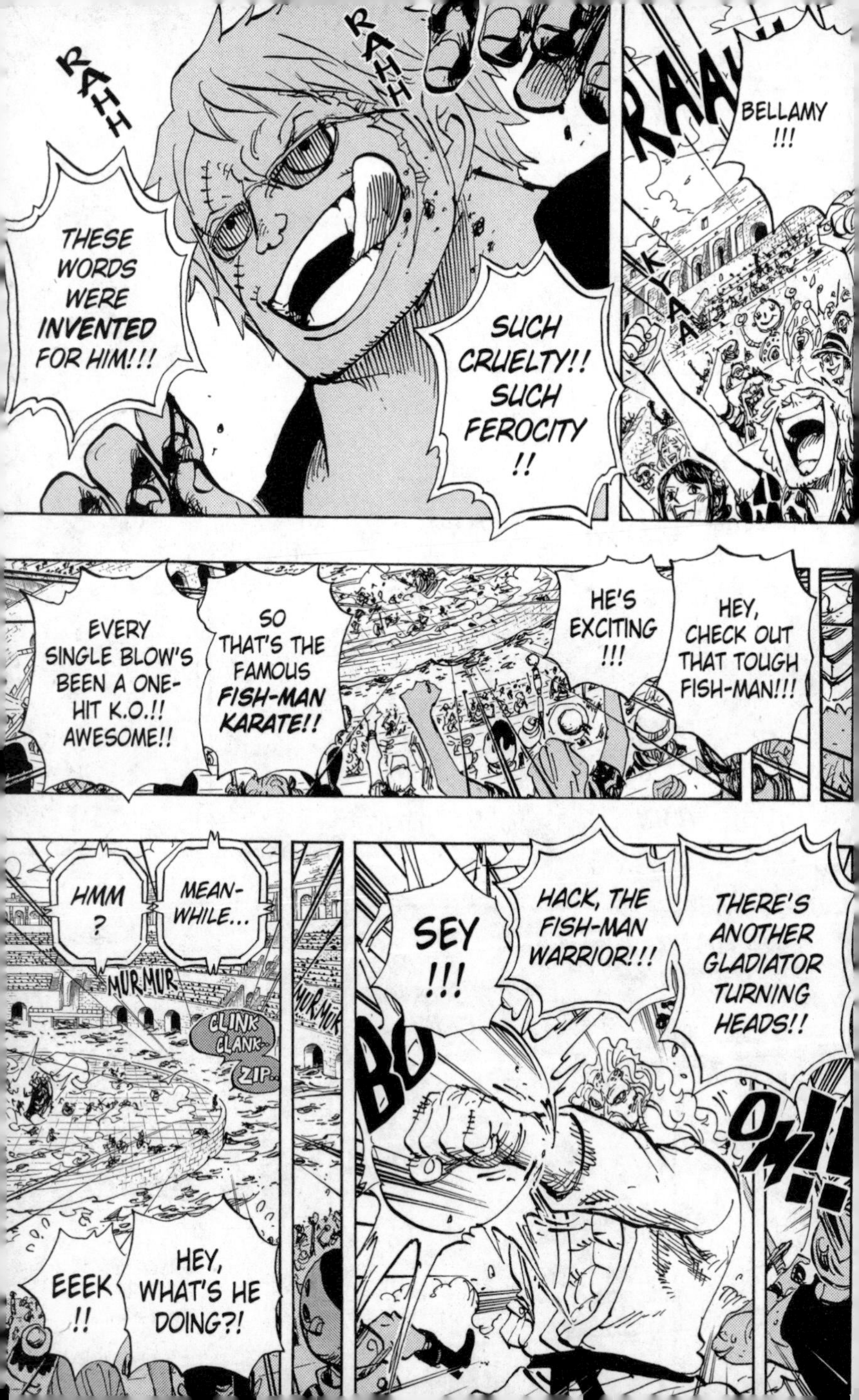
RAAAH
BELLAMY !!!
KYAA
RAHH
RAHH
SUCH CRUELTY!! SUCH FEROCITY !!
THESE WORDS WERE INVENTED FOR HIM!!!
HEY, CHECK OUT THAT TOUGH FISH-MAN!!!
HE'S EXCITING !!!
SO THAT'S THE FAMOUS FISH-MAN KARATE!!
EVERY SINGLE BLOW'S BEEN A ONE-HIT K.O.!! AWESOME!!
THERE'S ANOTHER GLADIATOR TURNING HEADS!!
HACK, THE FISH-MAN WARRIOR!!!
SEY !!!
BO
OM!!
MEAN-WHILE...
HMM ?
MURMUR
MURMUR
CLINK CLANK
ZIP
HEY, WHAT'S HE DOING?!
EEEK !!

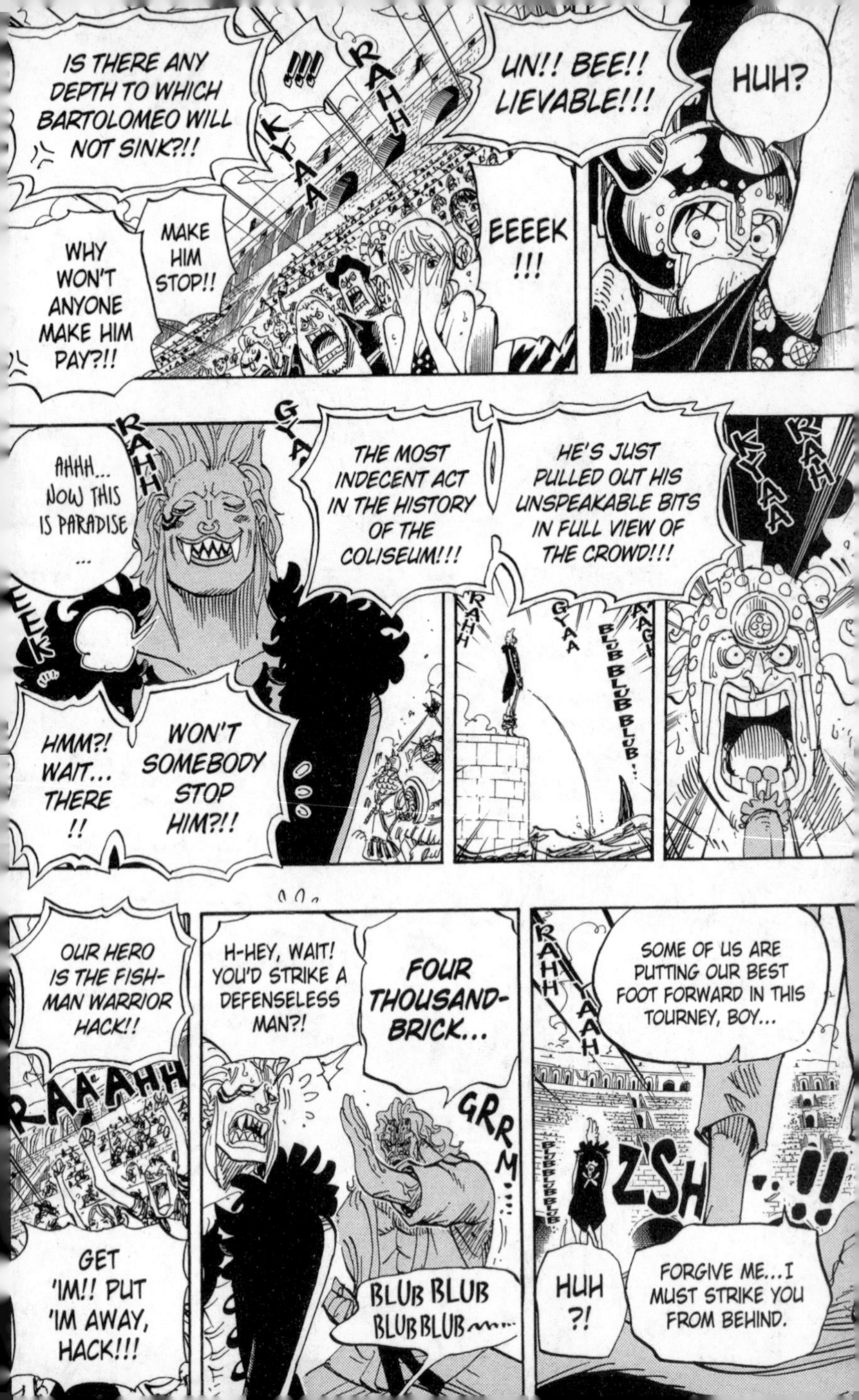
HUH?
UN!! BEE!! LIEVABLE!!!
RAHH
KYAA
!!!
IS THERE ANY DEPTH TO WHICH BARTOLOMEO WILL NOT SINK?!!
EEEEK !!!
MAKE HIM STOP!!
WHY WON'T ANYONE MAKE HIM PAY?!!
RAHH
KYAA
HE'S JUST PULLED OUT HIS UNSPEAKABLE BITS IN FULL VIEW OF THE CROWD!!!
THE MOST INDECENT ACT IN THE HISTORY OF THE COLISEUM!!!
AAGH
BLUB BLUB BLUB...
GYAA
RAHH
GYAA
RAHH
AHHH... NOW THIS IS PARADISE ...
EEEK
WON'T SOMEBODY STOP HIM?!!
HMM?! WAIT... THERE !!
SOME OF US ARE PUTTING OUR BEST FOOT FORWARD IN THIS TOURNEY, BOY...
RAHH
YAAAH
BLUB BLUB BLUB BLUB
ZSH
!!
HUH ?!
FORGIVE ME...I MUST STRIKE YOU FROM BEHIND.
FOUR THOUSAND-BRICK...
H-HEY, WAIT! YOU'D STRIKE A DEFENSELESS MAN?!
GRRRM...
BLUB BLUB BLUB BLUB...
OUR HERO IS THE FISH-MAN WARRIOR HACK!!
RAAAHH
GET 'IM!! PUT 'IM AWAY, HACK!!!

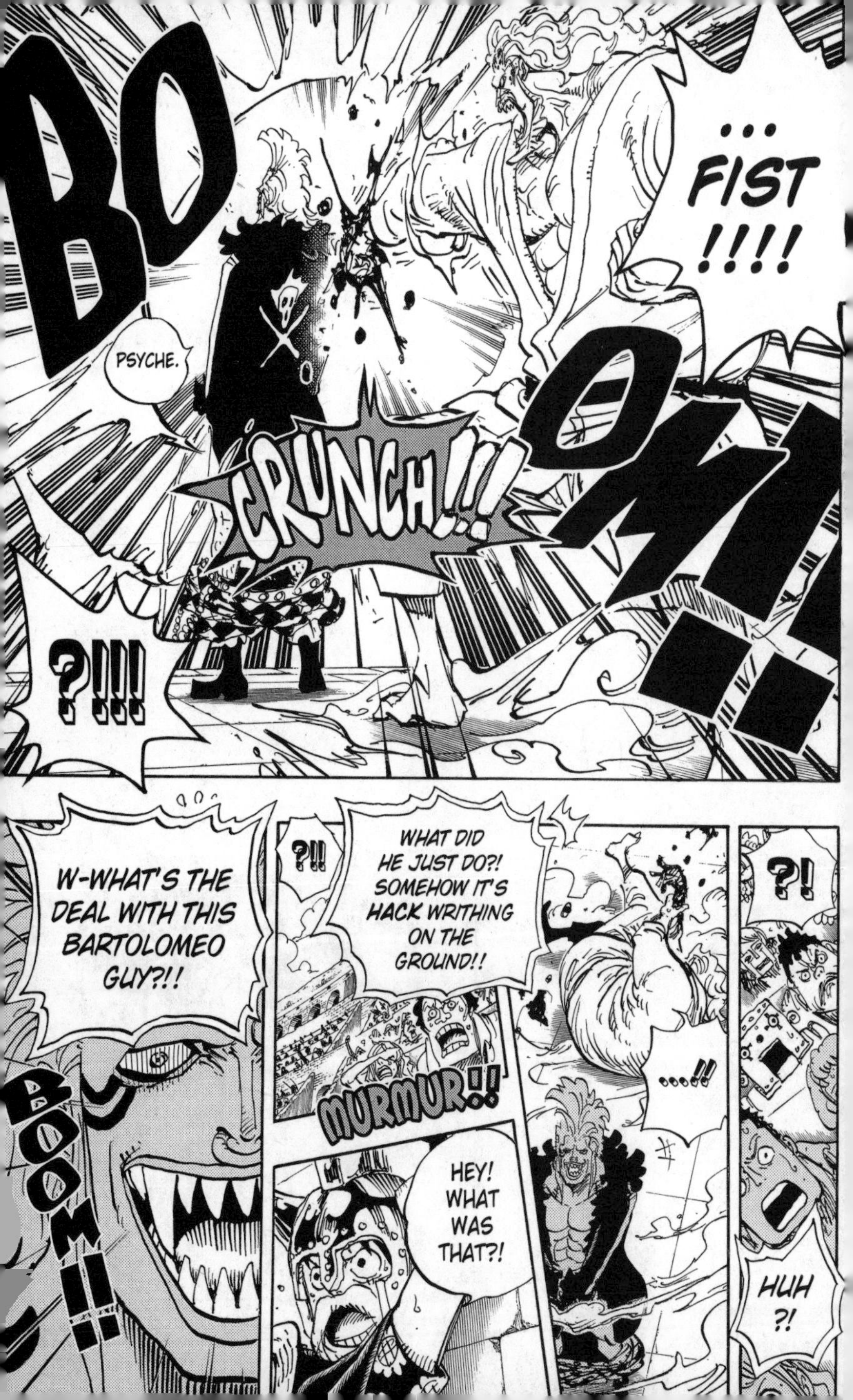
... FIST !!!!
BO
PSYCHE.
OM!!
CRUNCH!!!
?!!!
?!
HUH ?!
...!!
?!!
WHAT DID HE JUST DO?! SOMEHOW IT'S HACK WRITHING ON THE GROUND!!
MURMUR!!
HEY! WHAT WAS THAT?!
W-WHAT'S THE DEAL WITH THIS BARTOLOMEO GUY?!!
BOOM!!

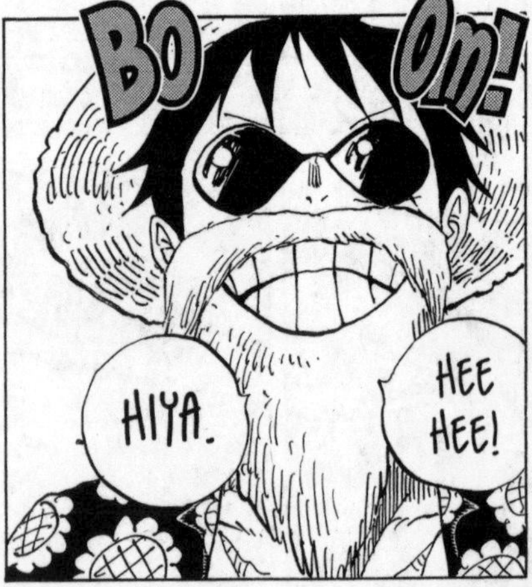
BOOM!
HIYA.
HEE HEE!

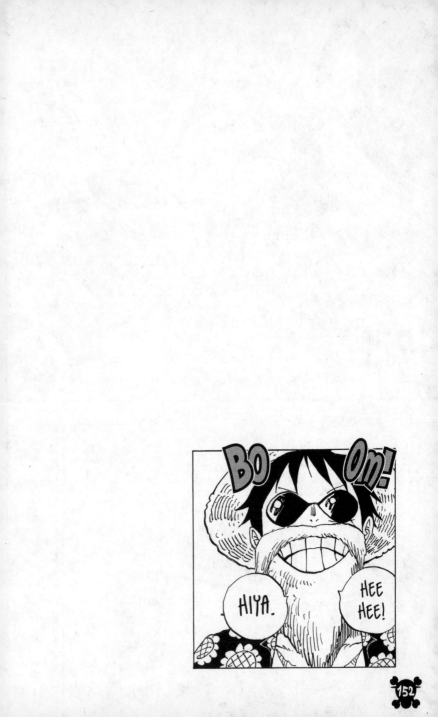

Chapter 709:
KING PUNCH!!

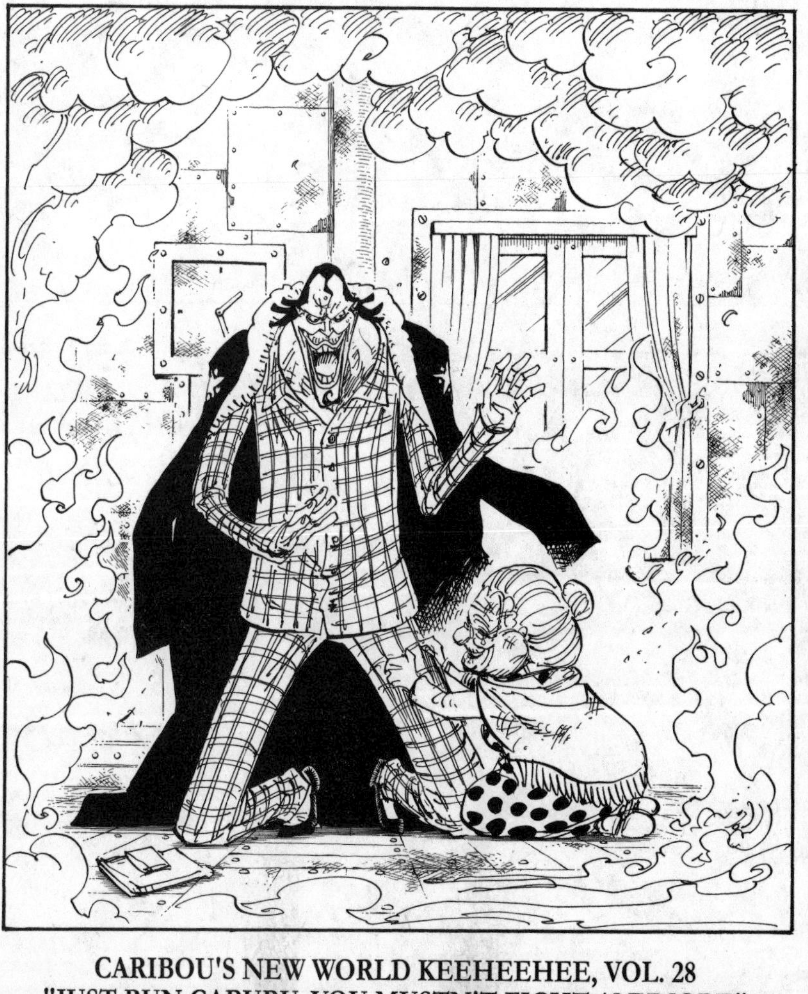

CARIBOU'S NEW WORLD KEEHEEHEE, VOL. 28
"JUST RUN GABURU, YOU MUSTN'T FIGHT ANYMORE"

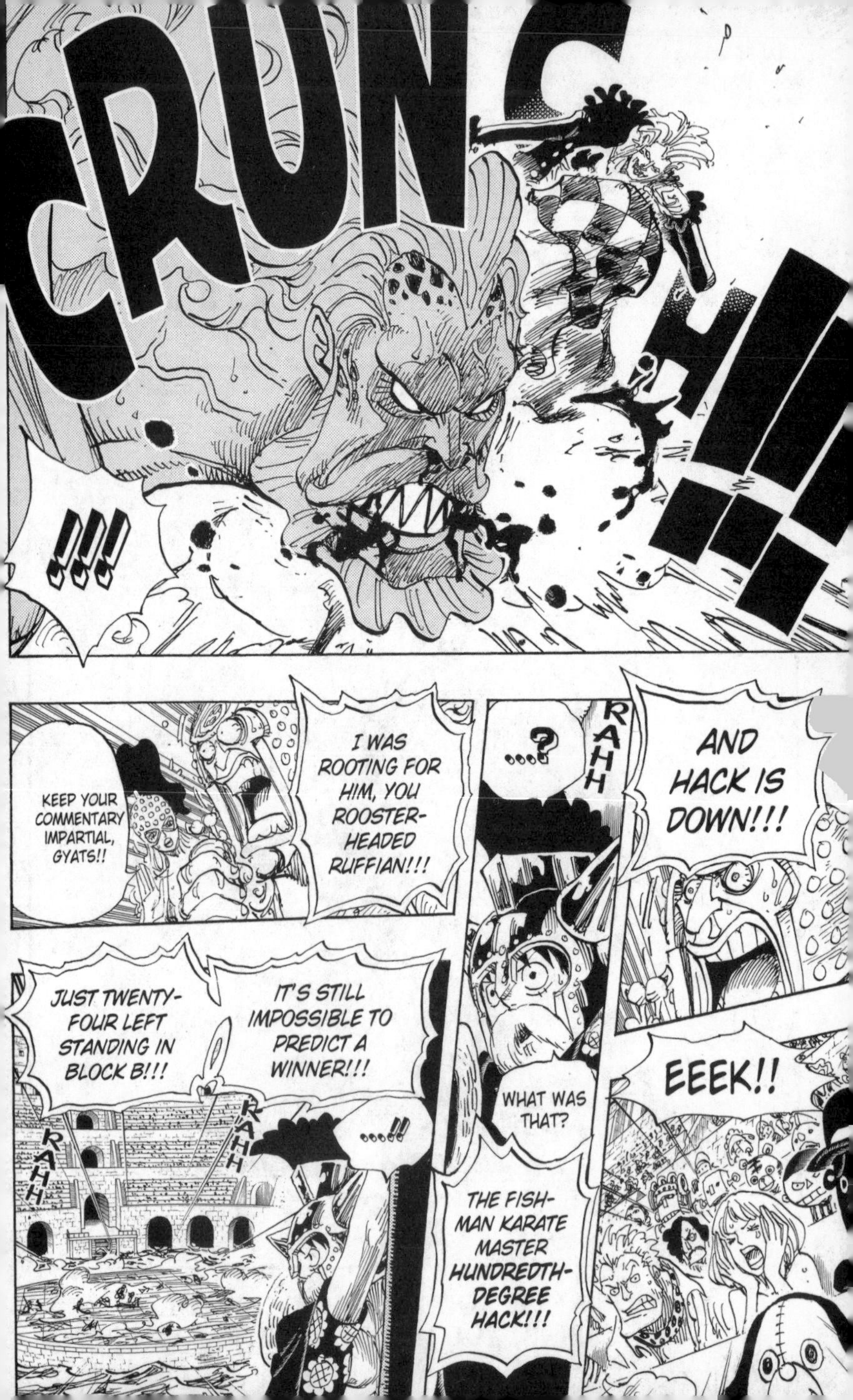
CRUNCH!!!!
!!!
AND HACK IS DOWN!!!
EEEK!!
RAHH
...?
WHAT WAS THAT?
I WAS ROOTING FOR HIM, YOU ROOSTER-HEADED RUFFIAN!!!
KEEP YOUR COMMENTARY IMPARTIAL, GYATS!!
THE FISH-MAN KARATE MASTER HUNDREDTH-DEGREE HACK!!!
....!!
IT'S STILL IMPOSSIBLE TO PREDICT A WINNER!!!
JUST TWENTY-FOUR LEFT STANDING IN BLOCK B!!!
RAHH
RAHH

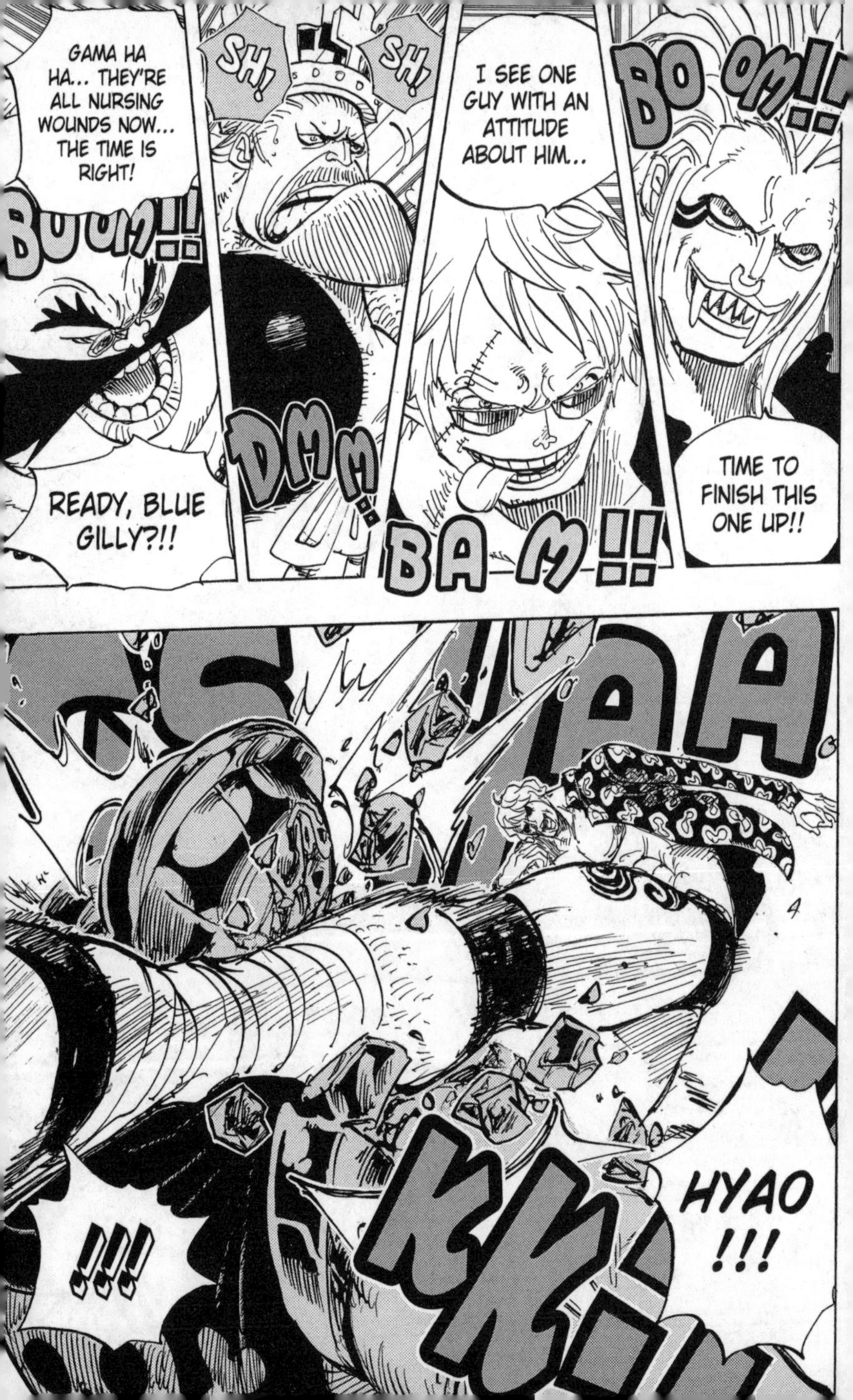
BOOM!!
TIME TO FINISH THIS ONE UP!!
I SEE ONE GUY WITH AN ATTITUDE ABOUT HIM...
BAM!!
SH! SH!
DMM!!
GAMA HA HA... THEY'RE ALL NURSING WOUNDS NOW... THE TIME IS RIGHT!
BOOM!!
READY, BLUE GILLY?!!
HYAO !!!
!!!

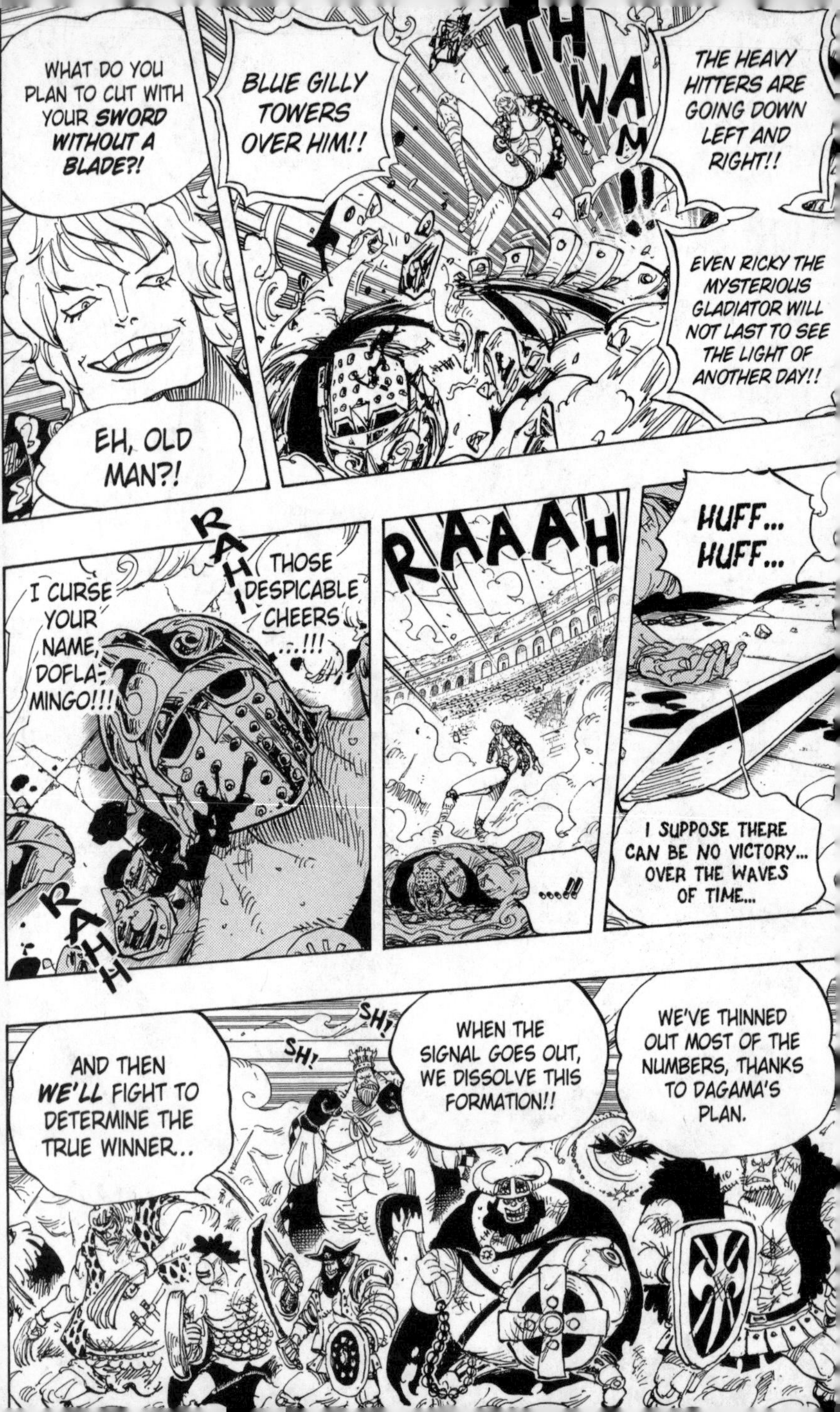
THE HEAVY HITTERS ARE GOING DOWN LEFT AND RIGHT!!
EVEN RICKY THE MYSTERIOUS GLADIATOR WILL NOT LAST TO SEE THE LIGHT OF ANOTHER DAY!!
THWAM!!
BLUE GILLY TOWERS OVER HIM!!
WHAT DO YOU PLAN TO CUT WITH YOUR SWORD WITHOUT A BLADE?!
EH, OLD MAN?!
HUFF... HUFF...
I SUPPOSE THERE CAN BE NO VICTORY... OVER THE WAVES OF TIME...
RAAAH
...!!
THOSE DESPICABLE CHEERS ...!!!
RAHH
I CURSE YOUR NAME, DOFLA-MINGO!!!
RAHH
WE'VE THINNED OUT MOST OF THE NUMBERS, THANKS TO DAGAMA'S PLAN.
WHEN THE SIGNAL GOES OUT, WE DISSOLVE THIS FORMATION!!
SH!
SH!
AND THEN WE'LL FIGHT TO DETERMINE THE TRUE WINNER...

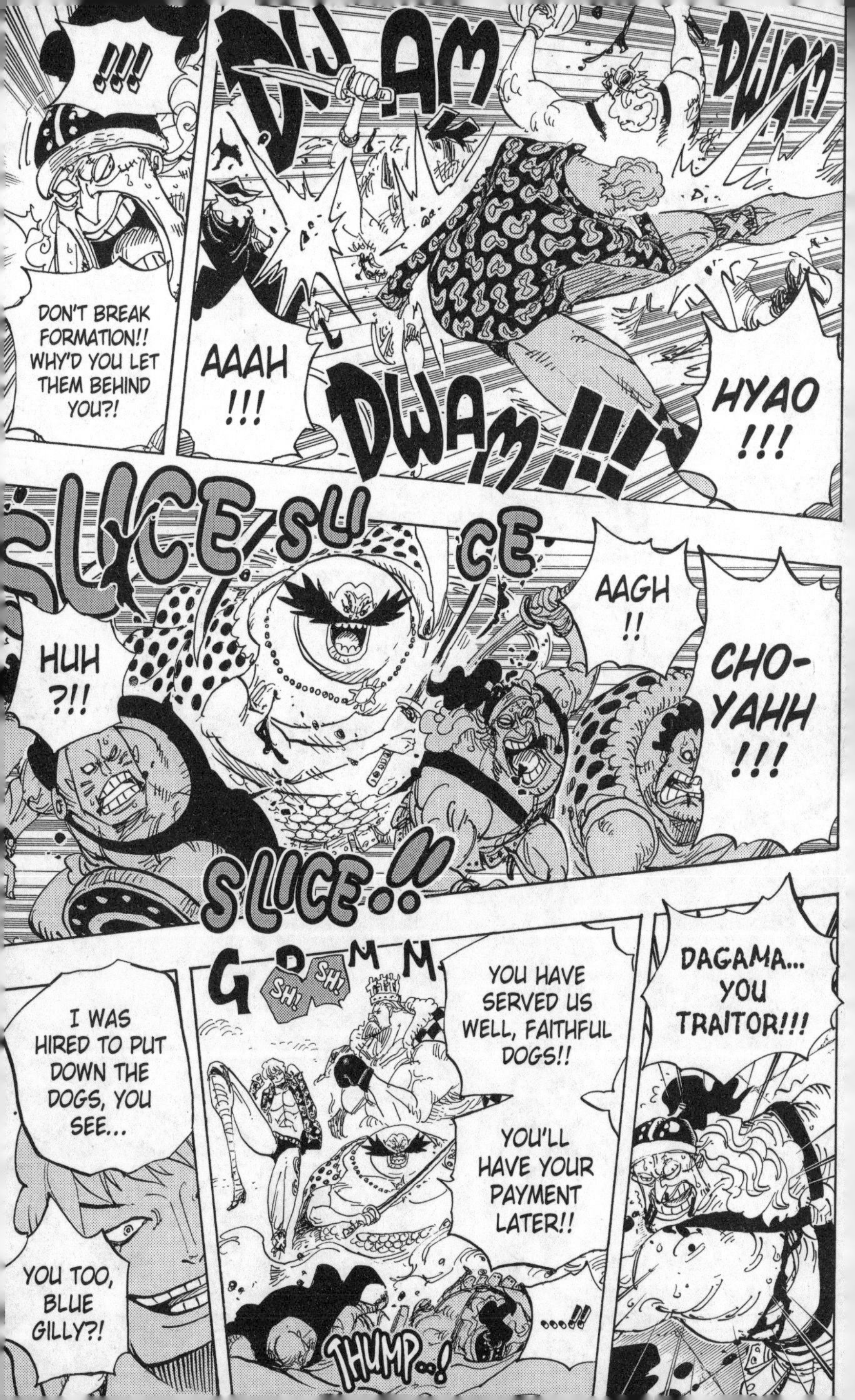
HYAO!!!
AAAH!!!
DWAM!!!
!!!
DON'T BREAK FORMATION!! WHY'D YOU LET THEM BEHIND YOU?!
SLICE
SLICE
CHO-YAHH!!!
AAGH!!
HUH?!!
SLICE..!!
DAGAMA... YOU TRAITOR!!!
YOU HAVE SERVED US WELL, FAITHFUL DOGS!!
YOU'LL HAVE YOUR PAYMENT LATER!!
SH! SH!
....!!
THUMP..!
I WAS HIRED TO PUT DOWN THE DOGS, YOU SEE...
YOU TOO, BLUE GILLY?!

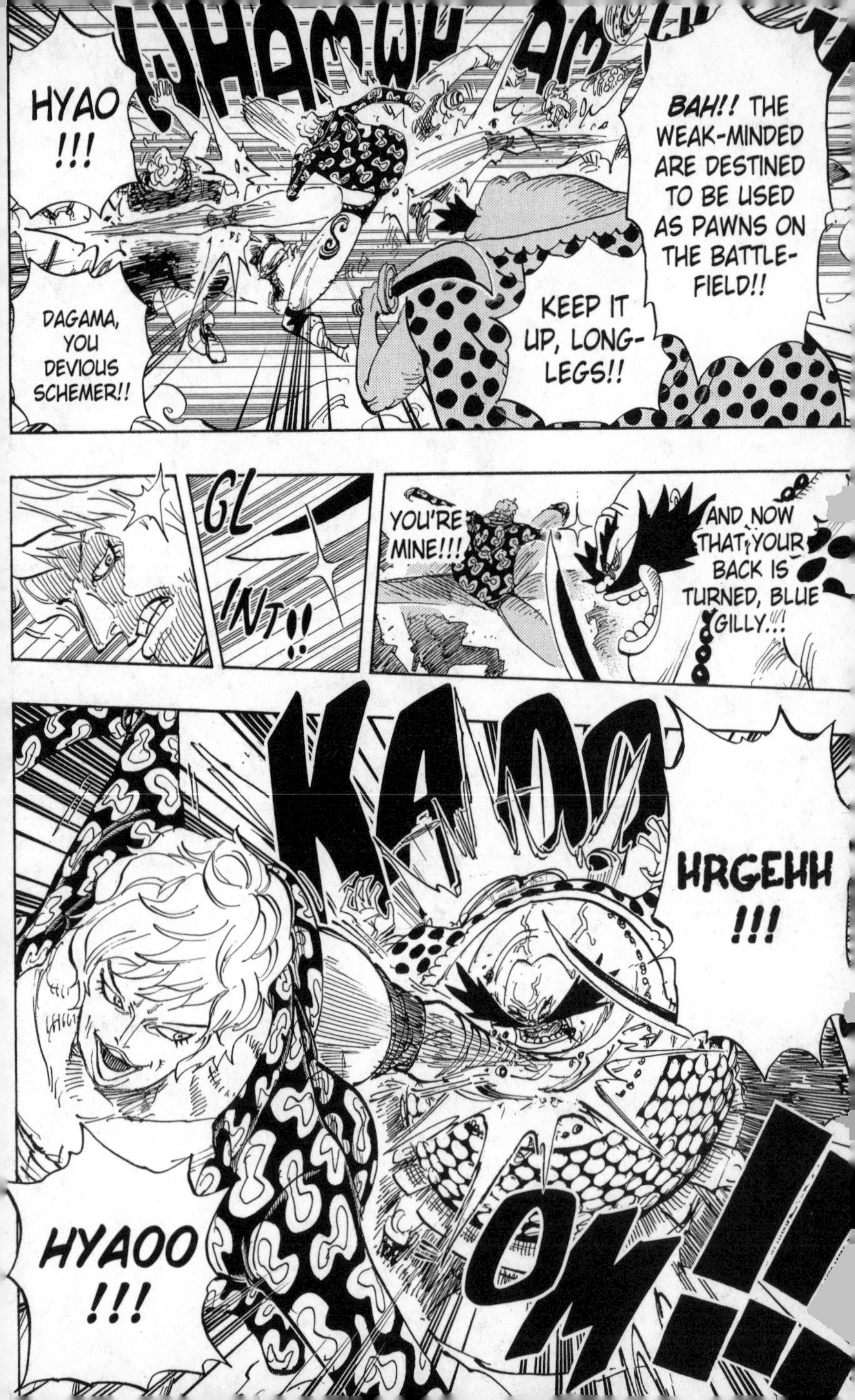
BAH!! THE WEAK-MINDED ARE DESTINED TO BE USED AS PAWNS ON THE BATTLE-FIELD!!
KEEP IT UP, LONG-LEGS!!
WHAMWHAM
HYAO!!!
DAGAMA, YOU DEVIOUS SCHEMER!!
AND NOW THAT YOUR BACK IS TURNED, BLUE GILLY...!!
YOU'RE MINE!!!
GLINT!!
HRGEHH!!!
KAOOOM!!
HYAOO!!!

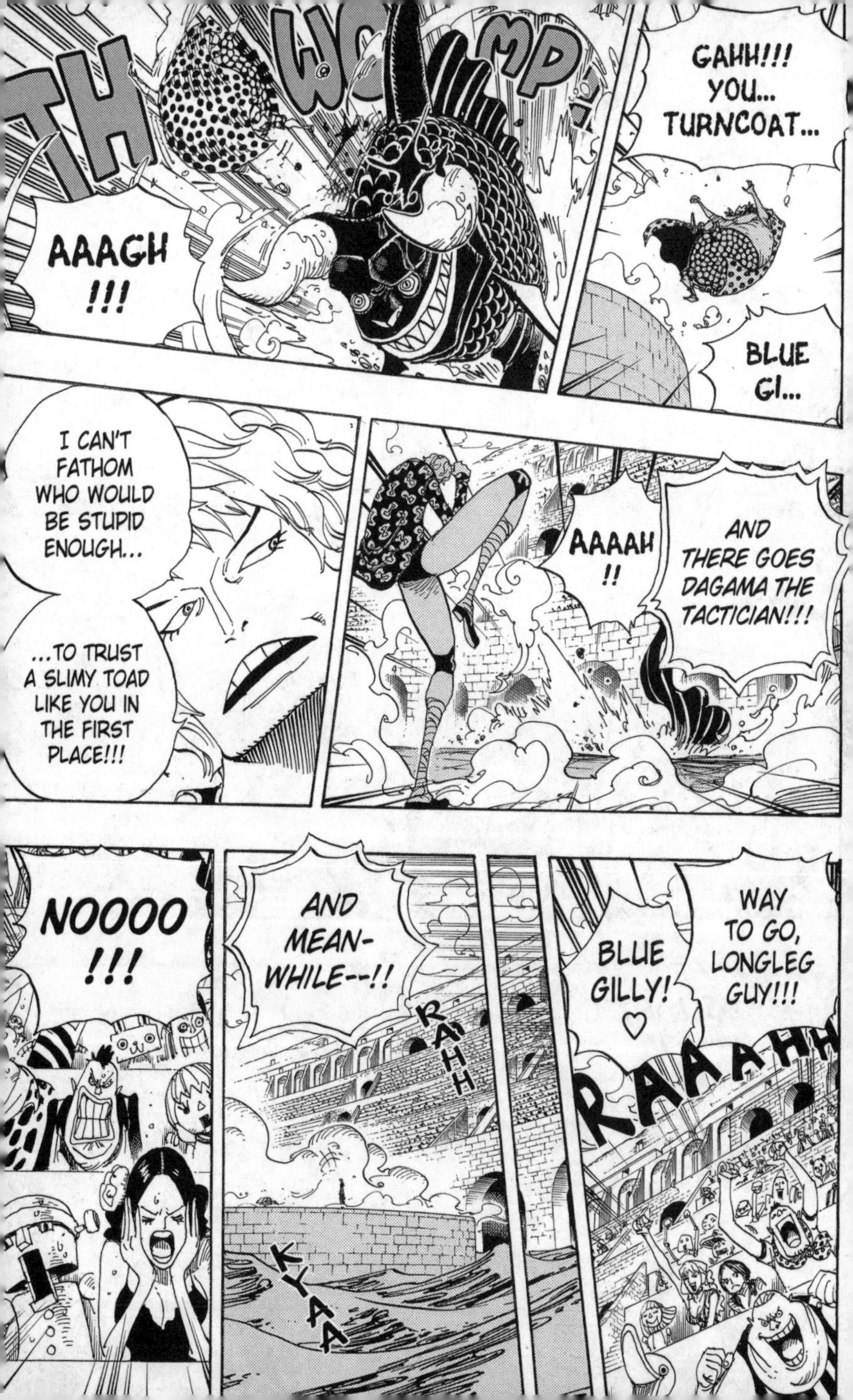
GAHH!!! YOU... TURNCOAT...
BLUE GI...
THWOMP!
AAAGH !!!
AND THERE GOES DAGAMA THE TACTICIAN!!!
AAAAH !!
I CAN'T FATHOM WHO WOULD BE STUPID ENOUGH...
...TO TRUST A SLIMY TOAD LIKE YOU IN THE FIRST PLACE!!!
WAY TO GO, LONGLEG GUY!!!
BLUE GILLY! ♡
RAAAAHH
AND MEAN-WHILE--!!
RAHH
KYAA
NOOOO !!!

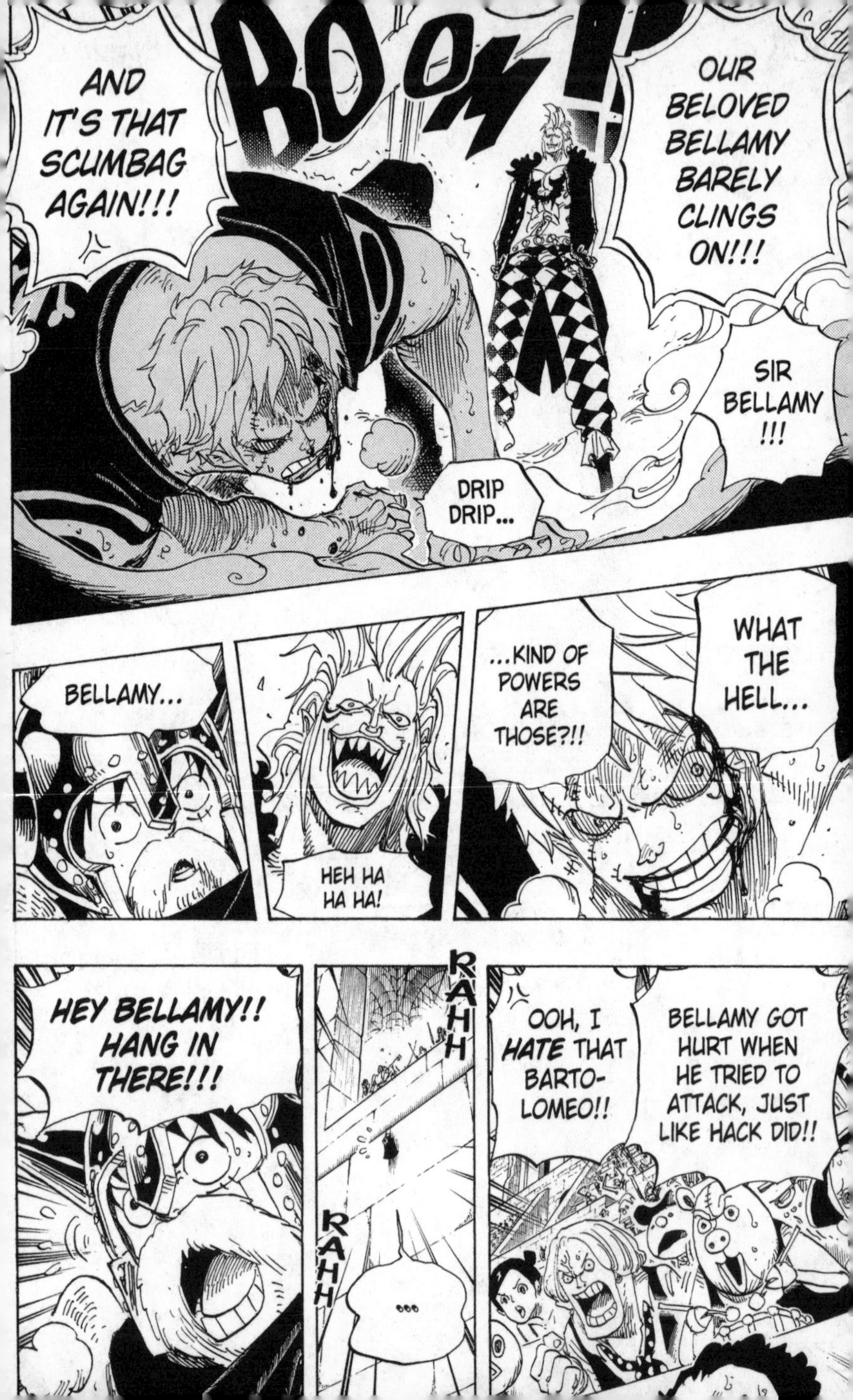
OUR BELOVED BELLAMY BARELY CLINGS ON!!!
BOOM!!
AND IT'S THAT SCUMBAG AGAIN!!!
SIR BELLAMY!!!
DRIP DRIP...
WHAT THE HELL...
...KIND OF POWERS ARE THOSE?!!
HEH HA HA HA!
BELLAMY...
BELLAMY GOT HURT WHEN HE TRIED TO ATTACK, JUST LIKE HACK DID!!
OOH, I *HATE* THAT BARTO-LOMEO!!
RAHH
RAHH
...
HEY BELLAMY!! HANG IN THERE!!!

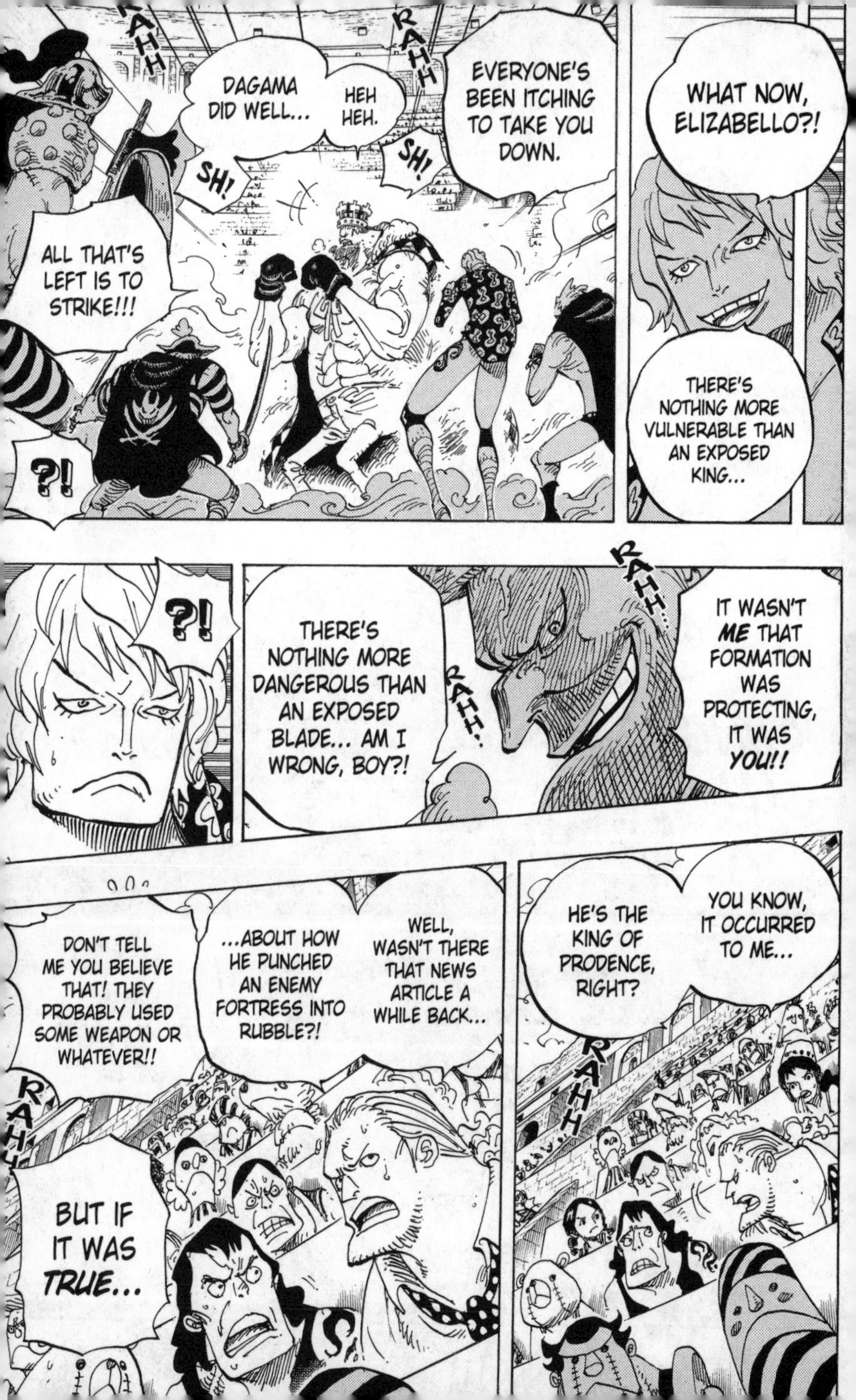

WHAT NOW, ELIZABELLO?!
THERE'S NOTHING MORE VULNERABLE THAN AN EXPOSED KING...
RAHH
EVERYONE'S BEEN ITCHING TO TAKE YOU DOWN.
SH!
HEH HEH.
DAGAMA DID WELL...
RAHH
SH!
ALL THAT'S LEFT IS TO STRIKE!!!
?!
RAHH...
IT WASN'T *ME* THAT FORMATION WAS PROTECTING, IT WAS *YOU!!*
RAHH...
THERE'S NOTHING MORE DANGEROUS THAN AN EXPOSED BLADE... AM I WRONG, BOY?!
?!
YOU KNOW, IT OCCURRED TO ME...
HE'S THE KING OF PRODENCE, RIGHT?
RAHH
WELL, WASN'T THERE THAT NEWS ARTICLE A WHILE BACK...
...ABOUT HOW HE PUNCHED AN ENEMY FORTRESS INTO RUBBLE?!
DON'T TELL ME YOU BELIEVE THAT! THEY PROBABLY USED SOME WEAPON OR WHATEVER!!
RAHH
BUT IF IT WAS *TRUE...*

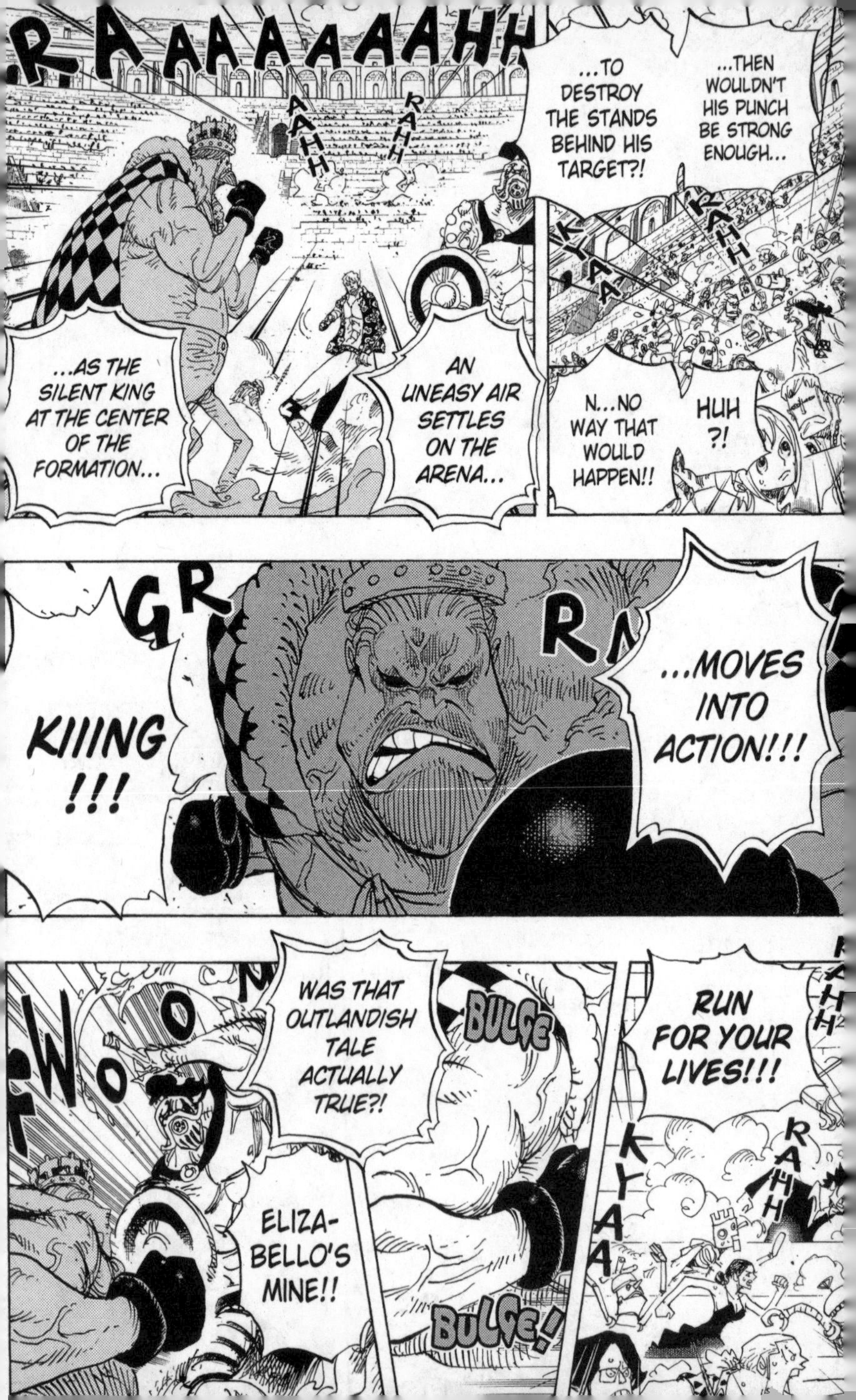
...THEN WOULDN'T HIS PUNCH BE STRONG ENOUGH...
...TO DESTROY THE STANDS BEHIND HIS TARGET?!
RAHH
KYAA
HUH ?!
N...NO WAY THAT WOULD HAPPEN!!
RAAAAAAAHH
RAHH
AAHH
AN UNEASY AIR SETTLES ON THE ARENA...
...AS THE SILENT KING AT THE CENTER OF THE FORMATION...
...MOVES INTO ACTION!!!
GR
KIIING !!!
RAHH
RUN FOR YOUR LIVES!!!
RAHH
KYAA
BULGE
WAS THAT OUTLANDISH TALE ACTUALLY TRUE?!
WOO
ELIZA-BELLO'S MINE!!
BULGE!

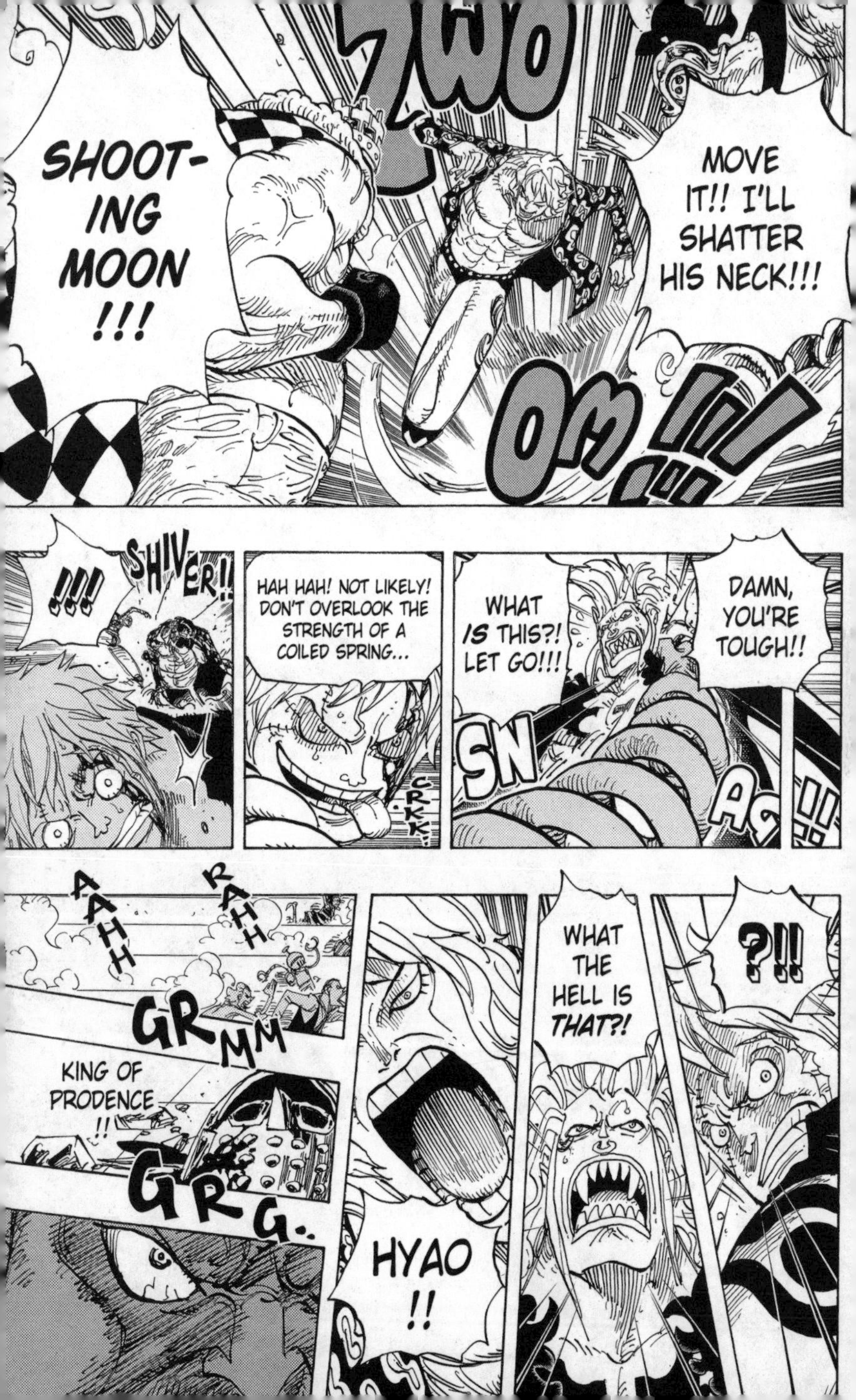
MOVE IT!! I'LL SHATTER HIS NECK!!!
ZWO
OM!!
SHOOT-ING MOON!!!
DAMN, YOU'RE TOUGH!!
WHAT *IS* THIS?! LET GO!!!
SN
AG!!
HAH HAH! NOT LIKELY! DON'T OVERLOOK THE STRENGTH OF A COILED SPRING...
CRKK
!!!
SHIVER!!
?!!
WHAT THE HELL IS *THAT?!*
HYAO!!
AAHH
RAHH
GRMM
KING OF PRODENCE!!
GRRG..

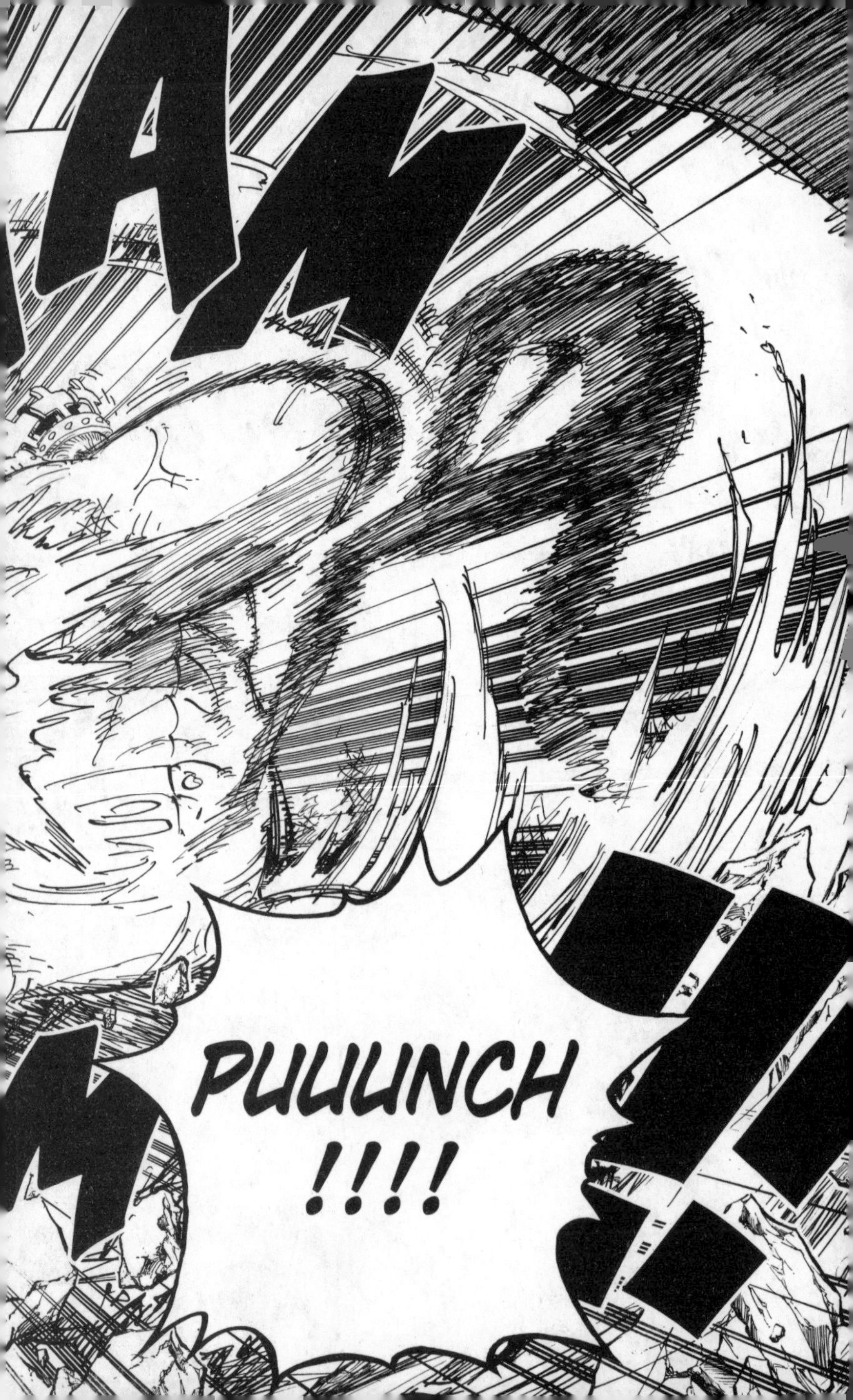
PUUUNCH
!!!!

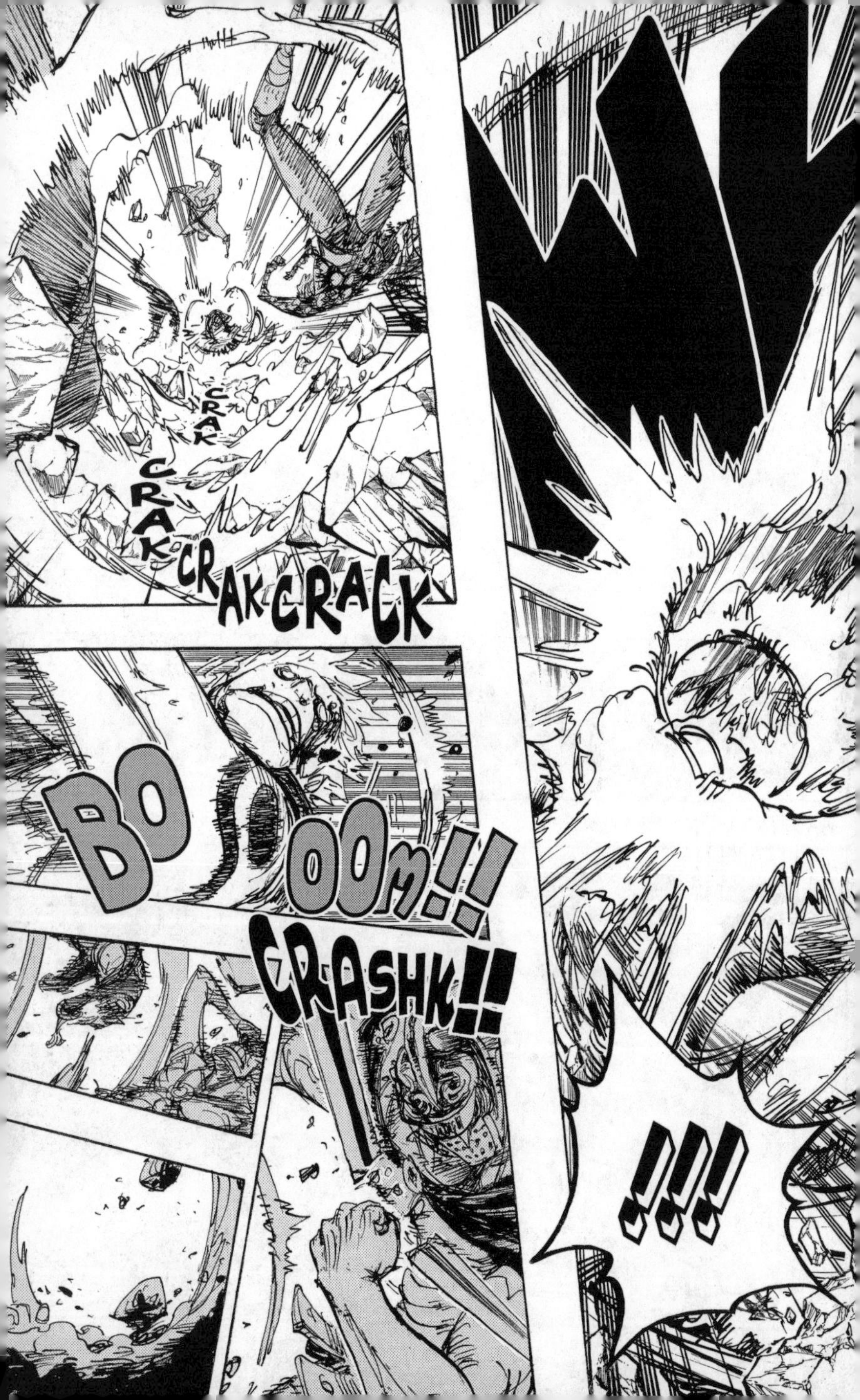
!!!
CRAK
CRAK
CRAK
CRACK
BOOOM!!
CRASHK!!

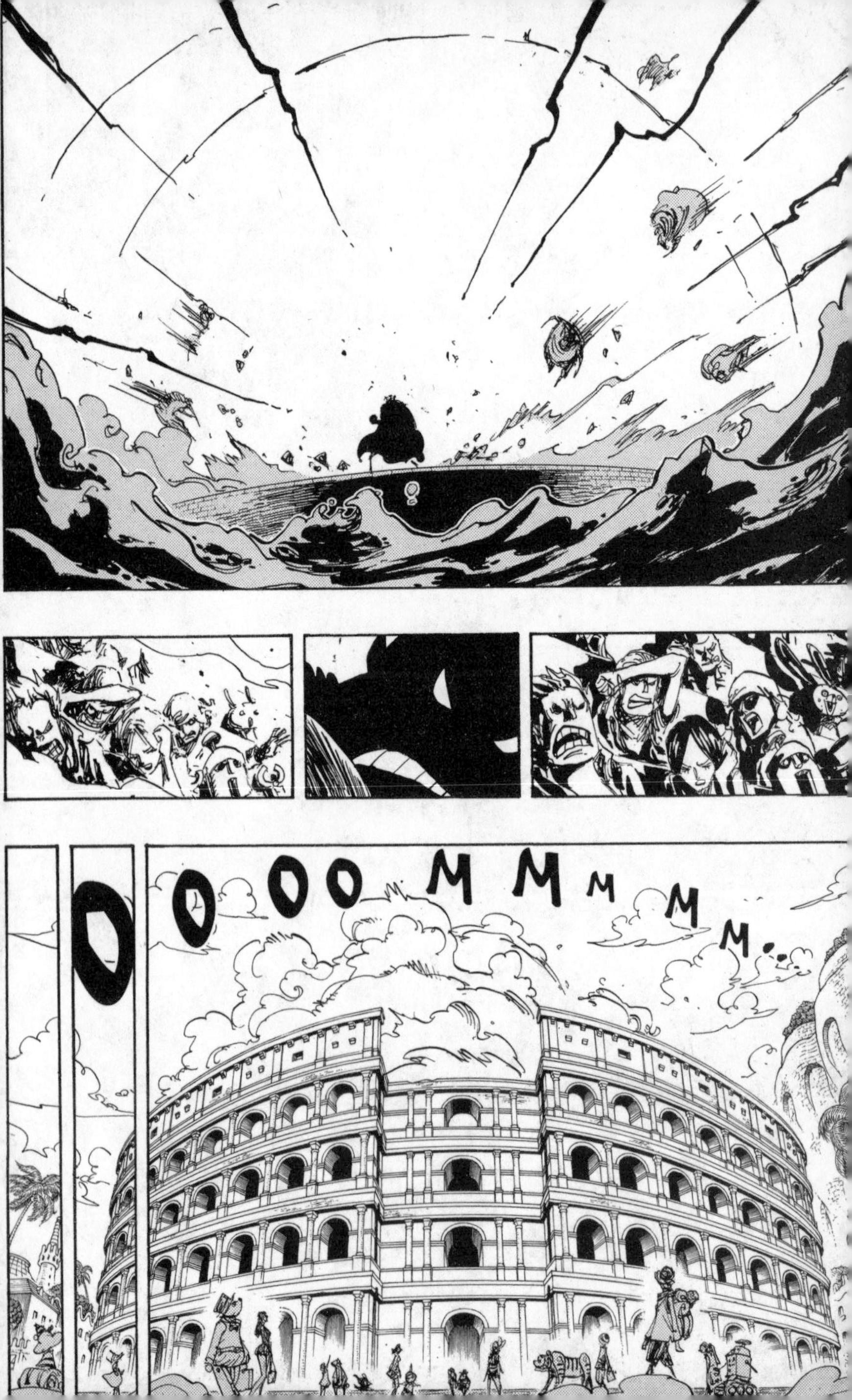
OOOOMMMMM..

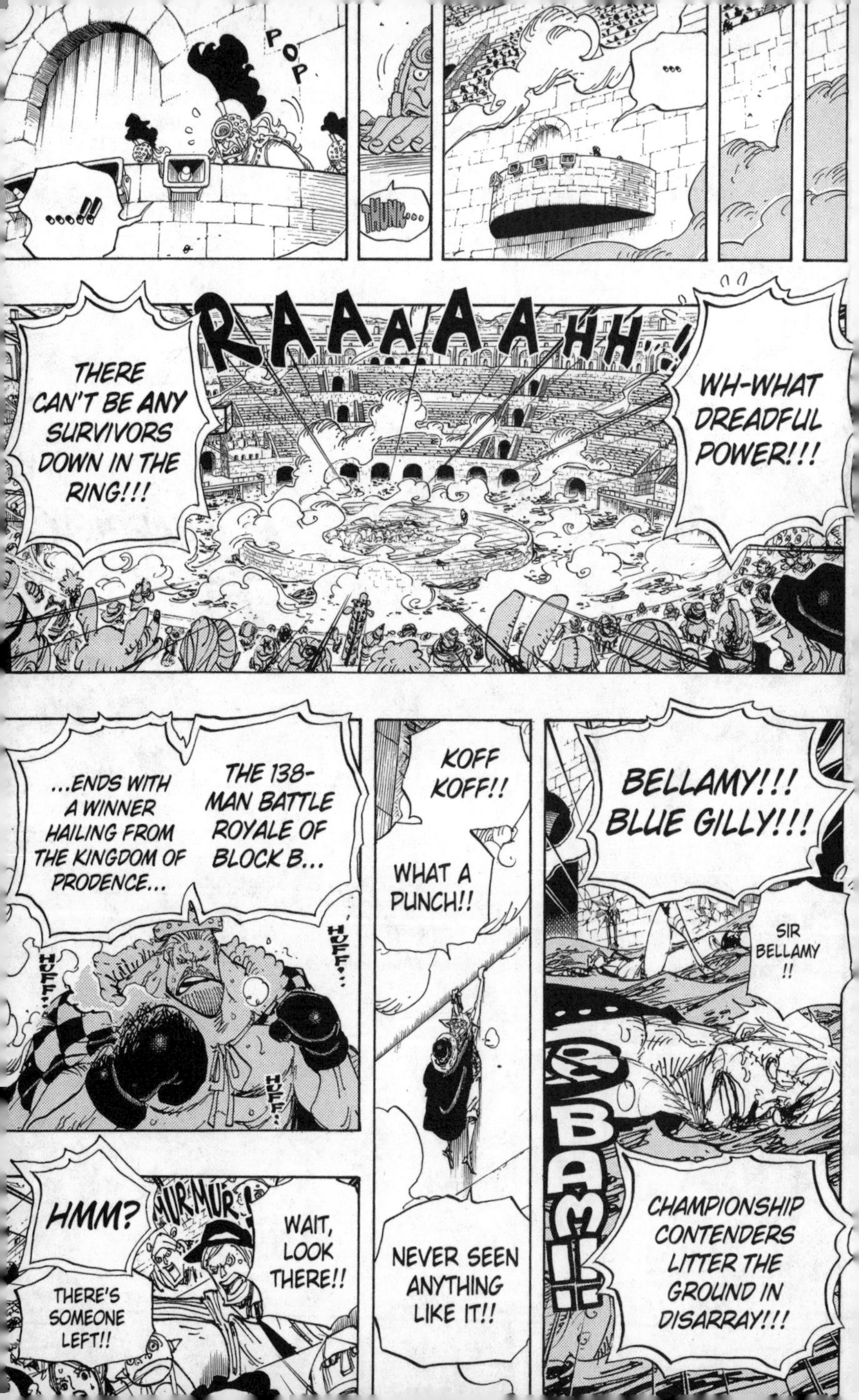
...
THUNK...
POP
....!!
WH-WHAT DREADFUL POWER!!!
RAAAAAHH..!!
THERE CAN'T BE ANY SURVIVORS DOWN IN THE RING!!!
BELLAMY!!! BLUE GILLY!!!
SIR BELLAMY !!
BAM!!
CHAMPIONSHIP CONTENDERS LITTER THE GROUND IN DISARRAY!!!
KOFF KOFF!!
WHAT A PUNCH!!
NEVER SEEN ANYTHING LIKE IT!!
THE 138-MAN BATTLE ROYALE OF BLOCK B...
...ENDS WITH A WINNER HAILING FROM THE KINGDOM OF PRODENCE...
HUFF..
HUFF..
HUFF..
MURMUR
WAIT, LOOK THERE!!
HMM?
THERE'S SOMEONE LEFT!!

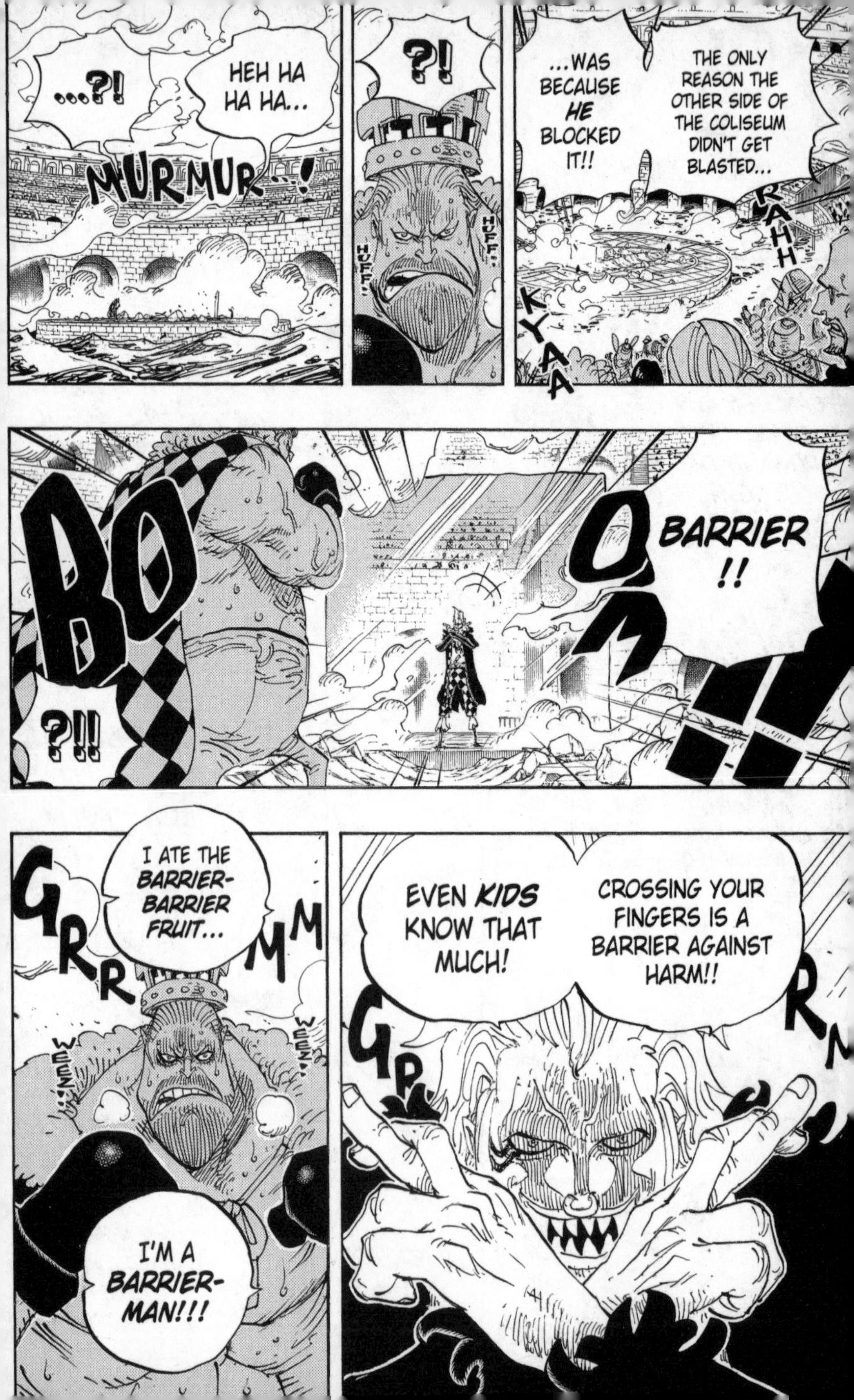
THE ONLY REASON THE OTHER SIDE OF THE COLISEUM DIDN'T GET BLASTED...
...WAS BECAUSE *HE* BLOCKED IT!!
RAHH
KYAA
?!
HUFF
HUFF
HEH HA HA HA...
...?!
MURMUR...!
BARRIER!!
BO
OM!!
?!!
CROSSING YOUR FINGERS IS A BARRIER AGAINST HARM!!
EVEN *KIDS* KNOW THAT MUCH!
I ATE THE *BARRIER-BARRIER FRUIT*...
GRRRMM
WEEZ
WEEZ
I'M A *BARRIER-MAN!!!*

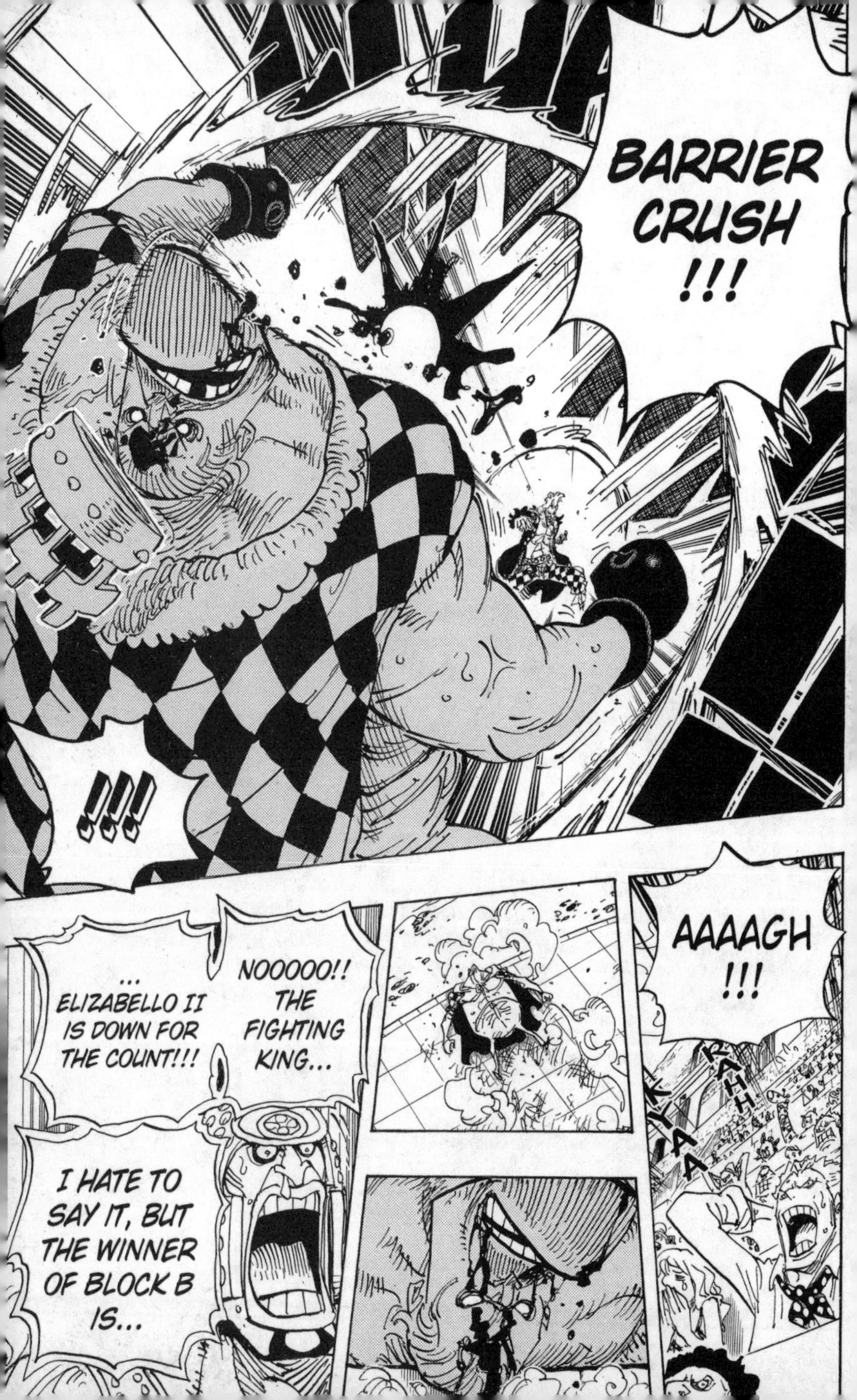
BARRIER CRUSH !!!
!!!!
AAAAGH !!!
KYAA
RAHH
NOOOOO!! THE FIGHTING KING...
... ELIZABELLO II IS DOWN FOR THE COUNT!!!
I HATE TO SAY IT, BUT THE WINNER OF BLOCK B IS...

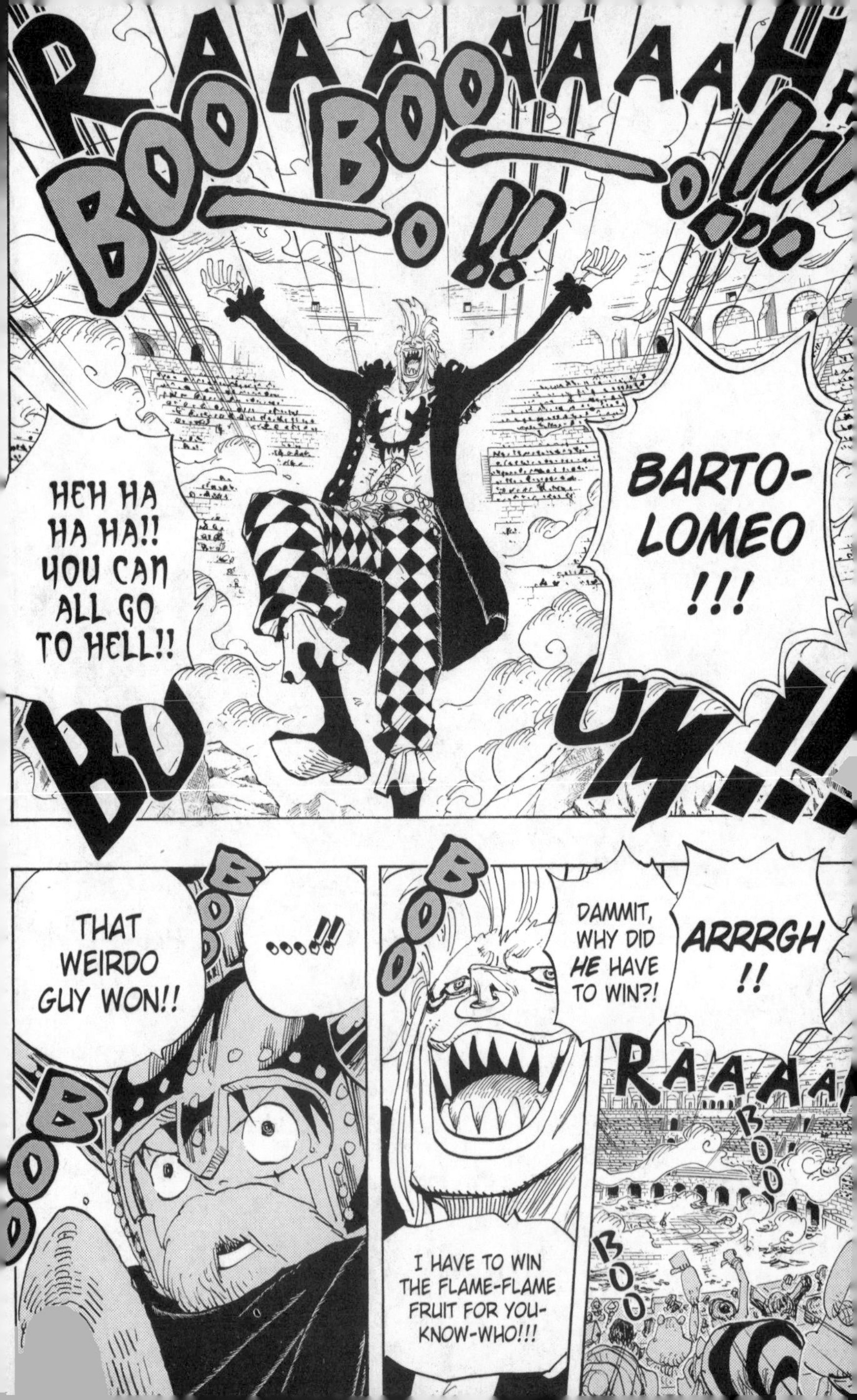
RAAAAAAAH!!
BOO—BOO—OOOO!!
BARTO-LOMEO!!!
HEH HA HA HA!! YOU CAN ALL GO TO HELL!!
BUUN!!!
ARRRGH!!
DAMMIT, WHY DID HE HAVE TO WIN?!
RAAAA
BOOO
BOOO
BOO
I HAVE TO WIN THE FLAME-FLAME FRUIT FOR YOU-KNOW-WHO!!!
BOO
...!!
THAT WEIRDO GUY WON!!
BOOO

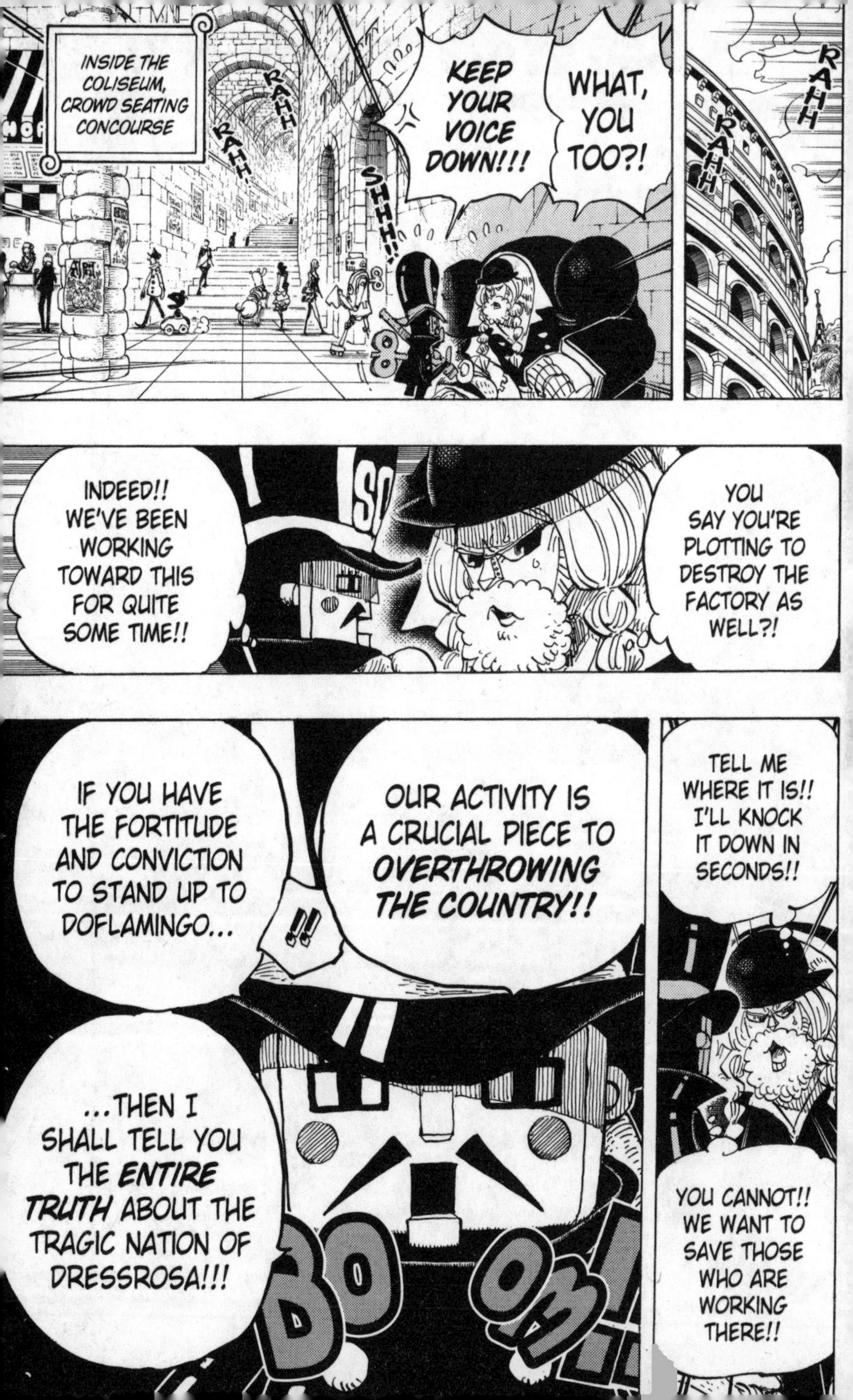
RAHH
RAHH
WHAT, YOU TOO?!
KEEP YOUR VOICE DOWN!!!
SHHHH!!
INSIDE THE COLISEUM, CROWD SEATING CONCOURSE
RAHH
RAHH
YOU SAY YOU'RE PLOTTING TO DESTROY THE FACTORY AS WELL?!
INDEED!! WE'VE BEEN WORKING TOWARD THIS FOR QUITE SOME TIME!!
TELL ME WHERE IT IS!! I'LL KNOCK IT DOWN IN SECONDS!!
YOU CANNOT!! WE WANT TO SAVE THOSE WHO ARE WORKING THERE!!
OUR ACTIVITY IS A CRUCIAL PIECE TO ***OVERTHROWING THE COUNTRY!!***
!!
IF YOU HAVE THE FORTITUDE AND CONVICTION TO STAND UP TO DOFLAMINGO...
...THEN I SHALL TELL YOU THE ***ENTIRE TRUTH*** ABOUT THE TRAGIC NATION OF DRESSROSA!!!
BOOM!!

Chapter 710: TO GREENBIT

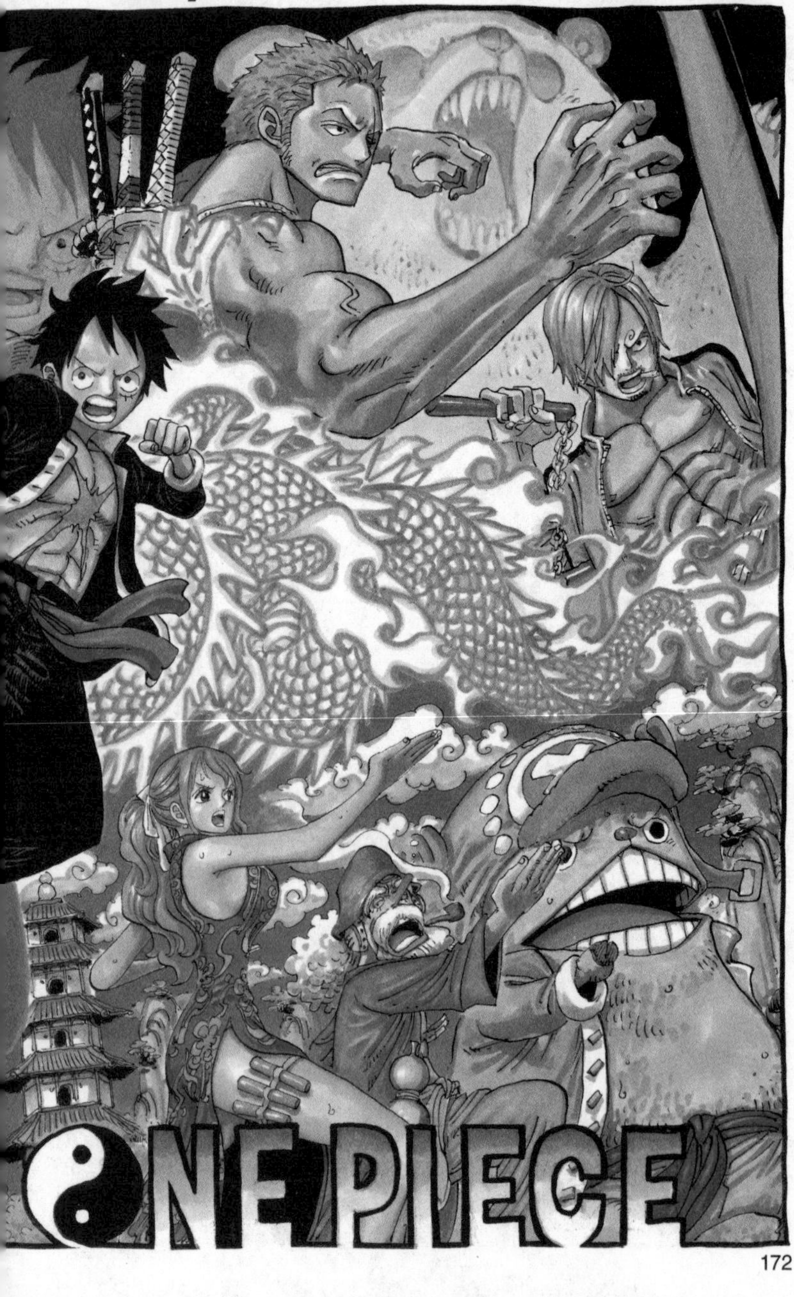
ONE PIECE

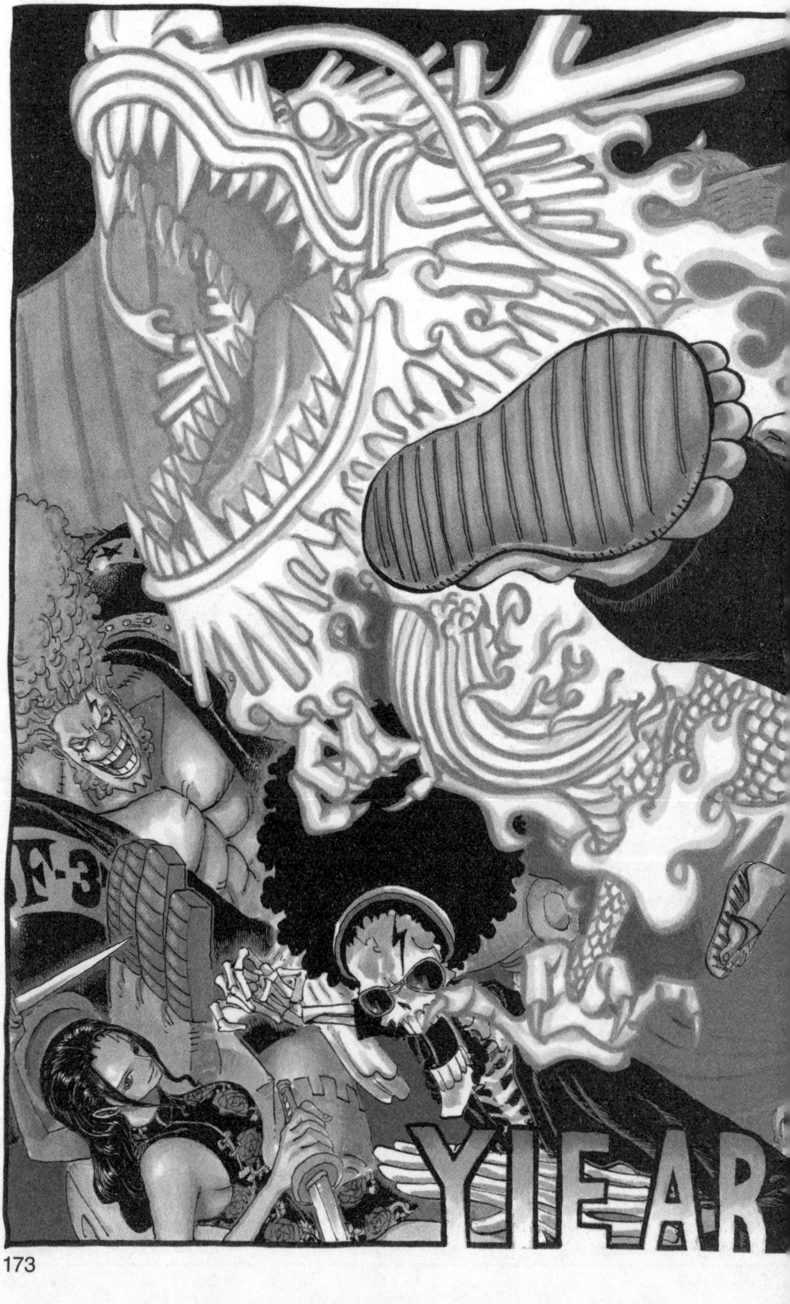

vol.71

ONE PIECE

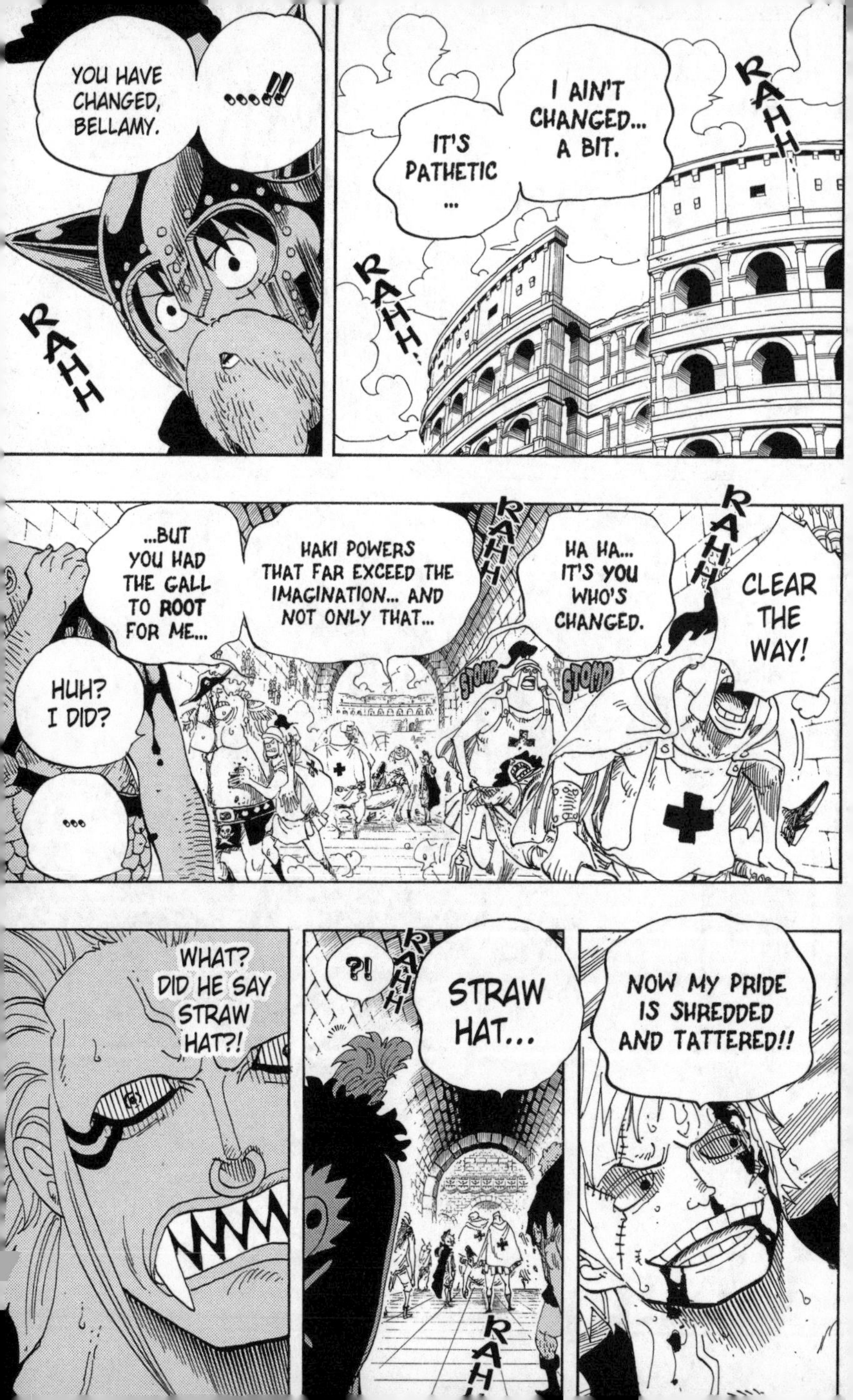
RAHH
I AIN'T CHANGED... A BIT.
IT'S PATHETIC ...
RAHH
....!!
YOU HAVE CHANGED, BELLAMY.
RAHH
RAHH
CLEAR THE WAY!
RAHH
HA HA... IT'S YOU WHO'S CHANGED.
STOMP
STOMP
HAKI POWERS THAT FAR EXCEED THE IMAGINATION... AND NOT ONLY THAT...
...BUT YOU HAD THE GALL TO ROOT FOR ME...
HUH? I DID?
...
NOW MY PRIDE IS SHREDDED AND TATTERED!!
STRAW HAT...
RAHH
?!
RAHH
WHAT? DID HE SAY STRAW HAT?!

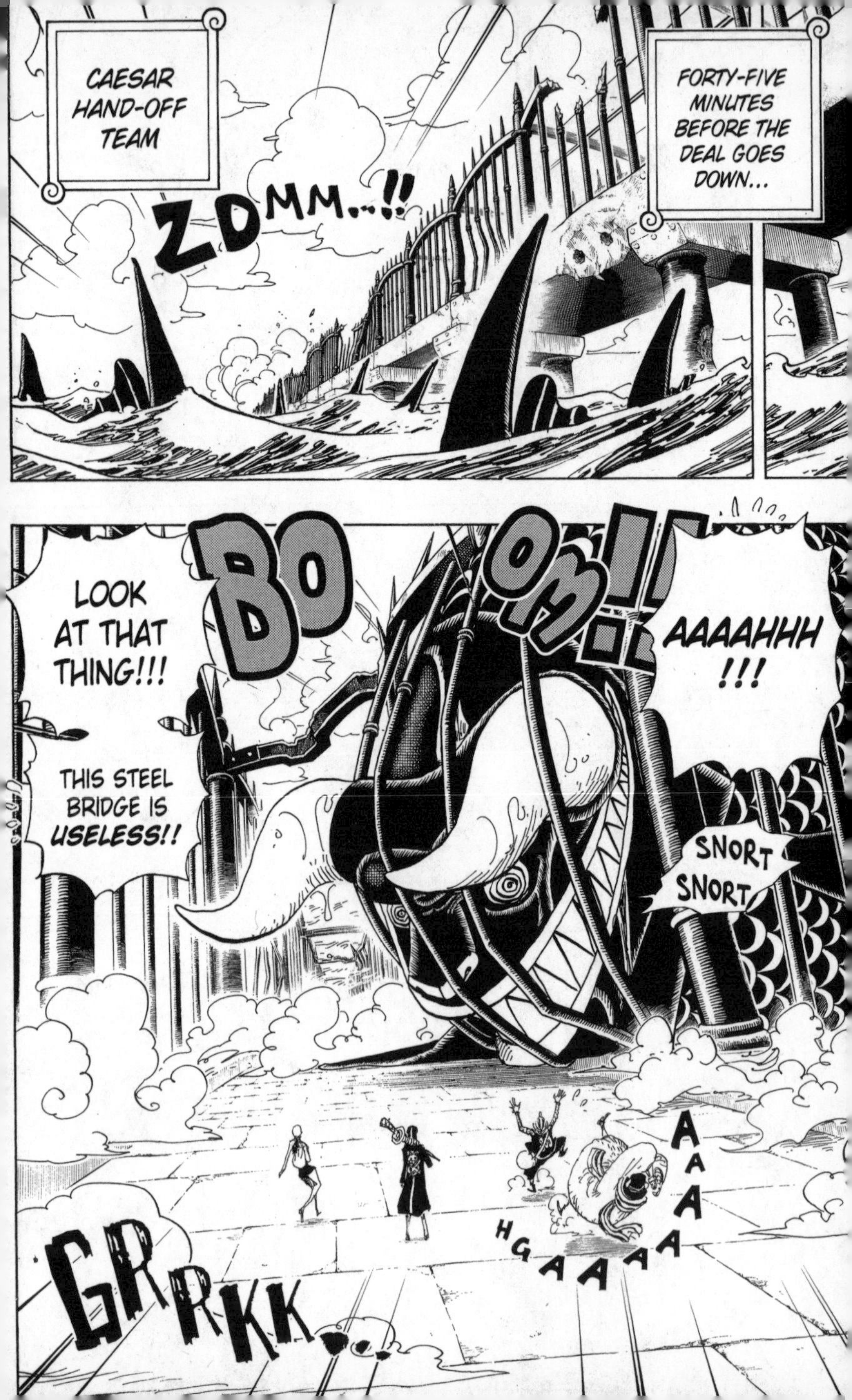
FORTY-FIVE MINUTES BEFORE THE DEAL GOES DOWN...
CAESAR HAND-OFF TEAM
ZDMM...!!
BOOM!!
AAAAHHH!!!
LOOK AT THAT THING!!!
SNORT SNORT
THIS STEEL BRIDGE IS *USELESS!!*
HGAAAAAAAA
GRRKK...

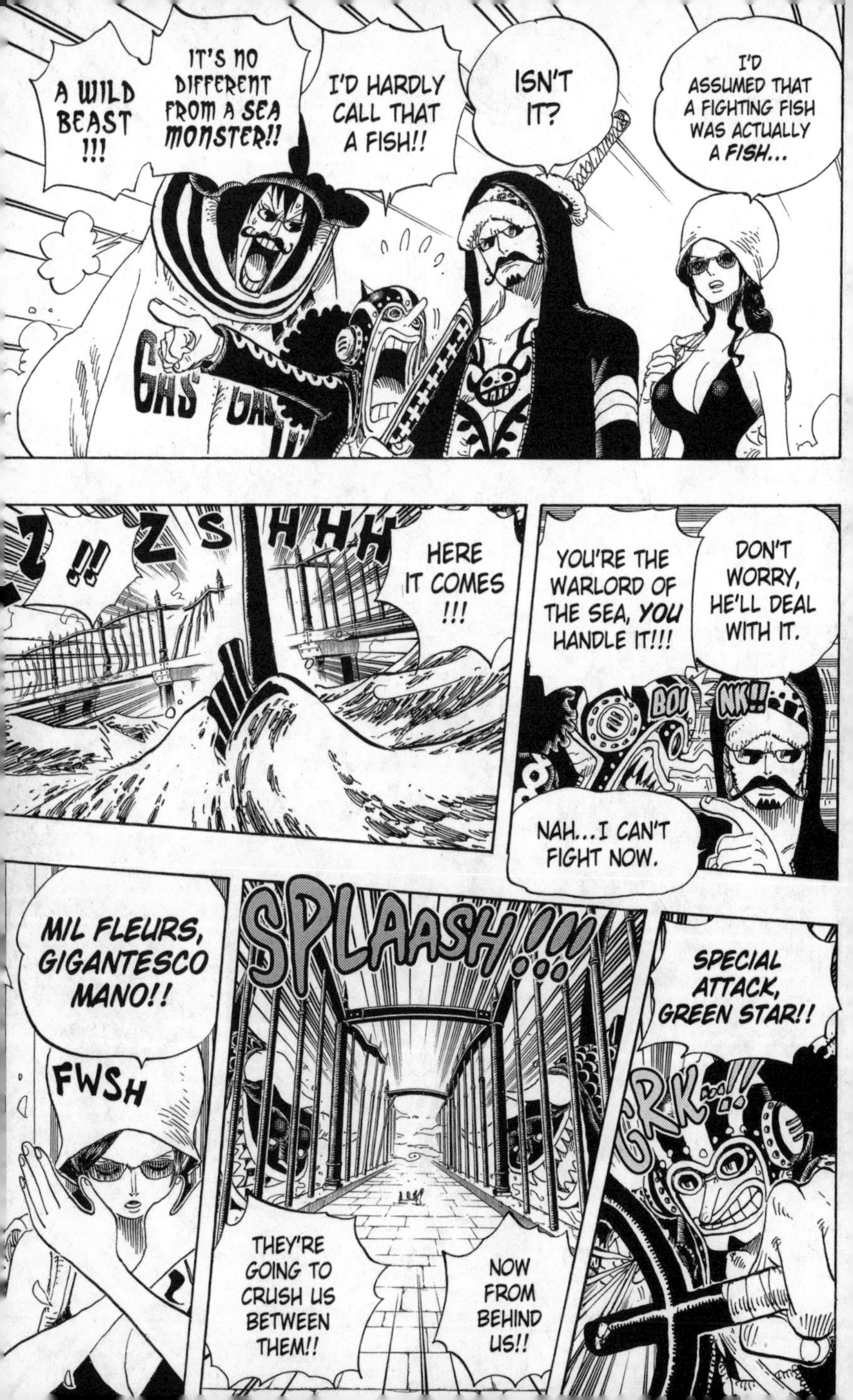
I'D ASSUMED THAT A FIGHTING FISH WAS ACTUALLY A FISH...
ISN'T IT?
I'D HARDLY CALL THAT A FISH!!
IT'S NO DIFFERENT FROM A SEA MONSTER!!
A WILD BEAST!!!
DON'T WORRY, HE'LL DEAL WITH IT.
YOU'RE THE WARLORD OF THE SEA, YOU HANDLE IT!!!
BOINK!!
NAH...I CAN'T FIGHT NOW.
HERE IT COMES!!!
ZSHHH
SPECIAL ATTACK, GREEN STAR!!
GRK...!!
SPLAASH!!!
NOW FROM BEHIND US!!
THEY'RE GOING TO CRUSH US BETWEEN THEM!!
MIL FLEURS, GIGANTESCO MANO!!
FWSH

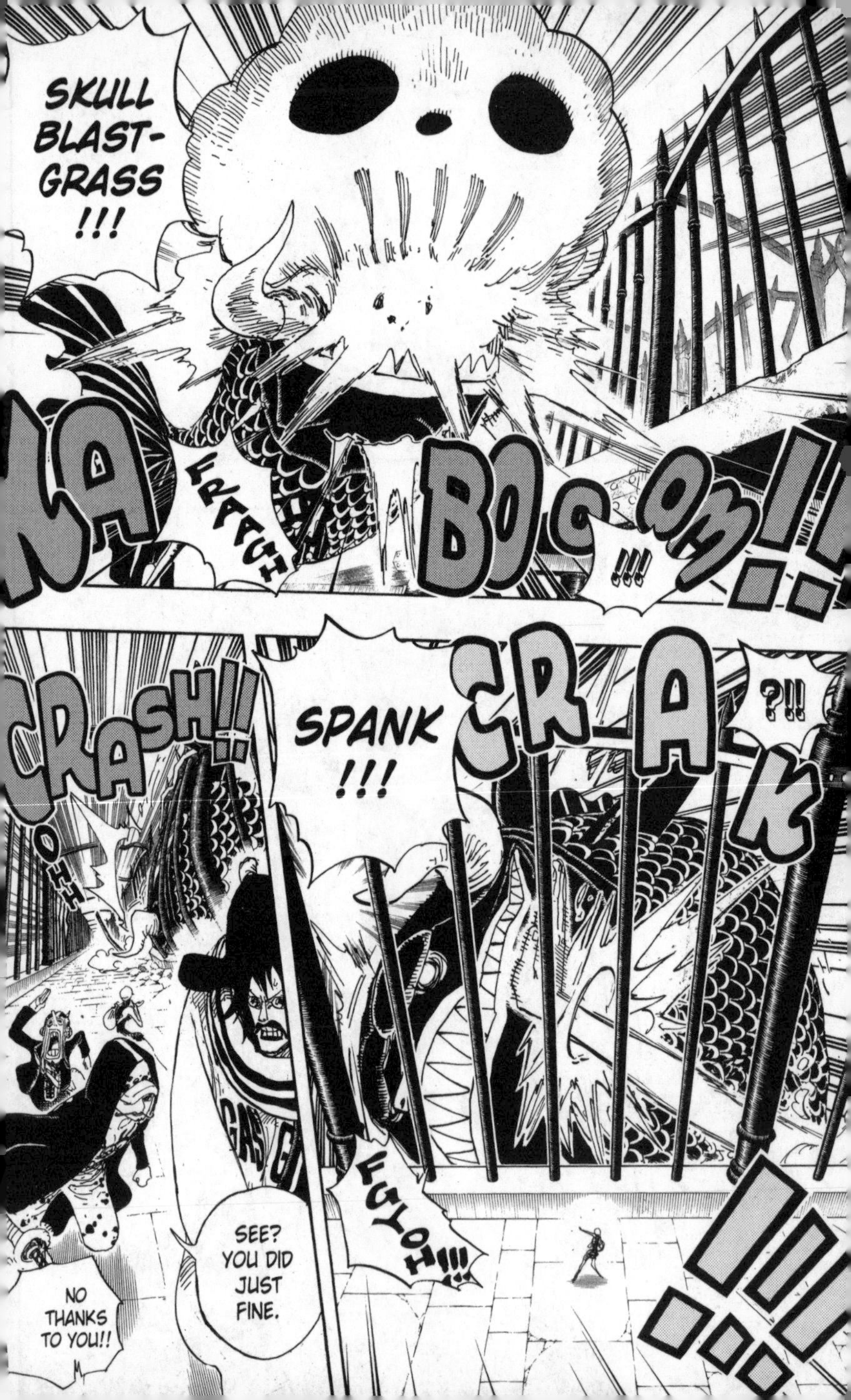
SKULL BLAST-GRASS!!!
BOOOM!!!!
FRATCH
?!!
CRAK
SPANK!!!
CRASH!!
FUYOH!!!
SEE? YOU DID JUST FINE.
NO THANKS TO YOU!!

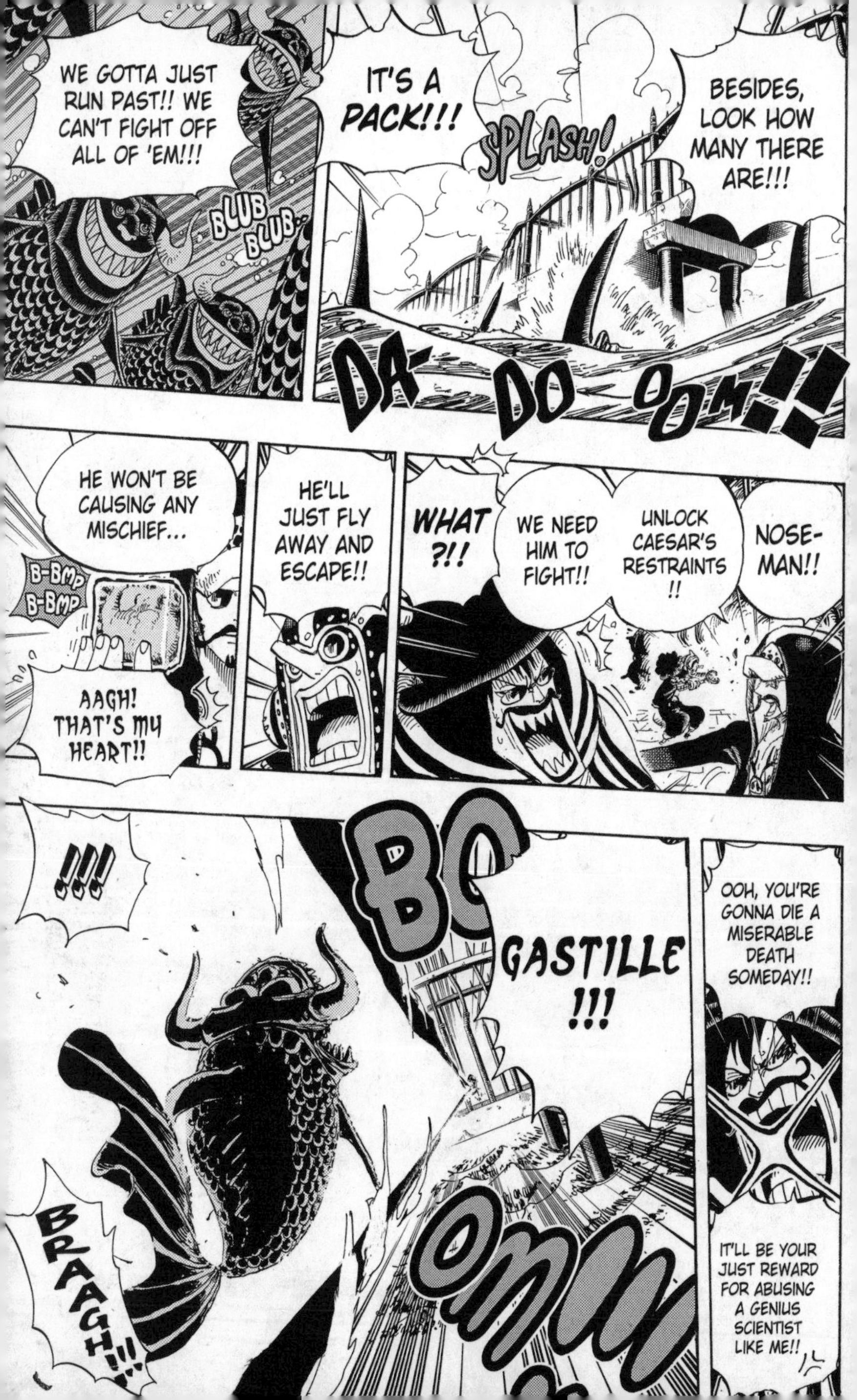
BESIDES, LOOK HOW MANY THERE ARE!!!
SPLASH!
IT'S A PACK!!!
DA-DOOOM!!
WE GOTTA JUST RUN PAST!! WE CAN'T FIGHT OFF ALL OF 'EM!!!
BLUB BLUB
NOSE-MAN!!
UNLOCK CAESAR'S RESTRAINTS!!
WE NEED HIM TO FIGHT!!
WHAT?!!
HE'LL JUST FLY AWAY AND ESCAPE!!
HE WON'T BE CAUSING ANY MISCHIEF...
B-BMP B-BMP
AAGH! THAT'S MY HEART!!
OOH, YOU'RE GONNA DIE A MISERABLE DEATH SOMEDAY!!
IT'LL BE YOUR JUST REWARD FOR ABUSING A GENIUS SCIENTIST LIKE ME!!
BO
GASTILLE!!!
OM
!!!
BRAAGH!!!

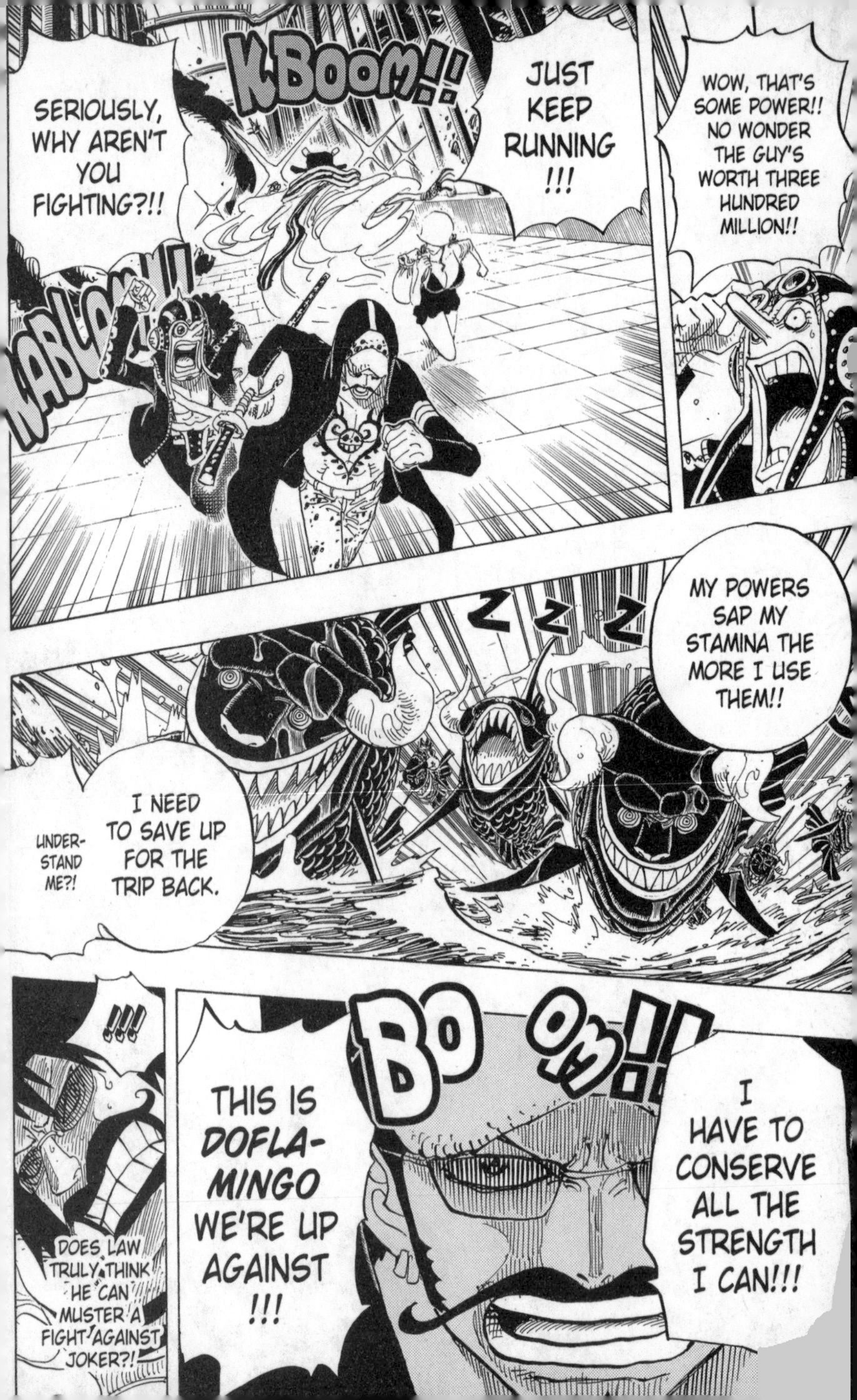
WOW, THAT'S SOME POWER!! NO WONDER THE GUY'S WORTH THREE HUNDRED MILLION!!
KBOOM!!
JUST KEEP RUNNING!!!
SERIOUSLY, WHY AREN'T YOU FIGHTING?!!
MY POWERS SAP MY STAMINA THE MORE I USE THEM!!
Z Z Z
I NEED TO SAVE UP FOR THE TRIP BACK.
UNDER-STAND ME?!
BOOM!!
I HAVE TO CONSERVE ALL THE STRENGTH I CAN!!!
THIS IS *DOFLA-MINGO* WE'RE UP AGAINST!!!
!!!
DOES LAW TRULY THINK HE CAN MUSTER A FIGHT AGAINST JOKER?!

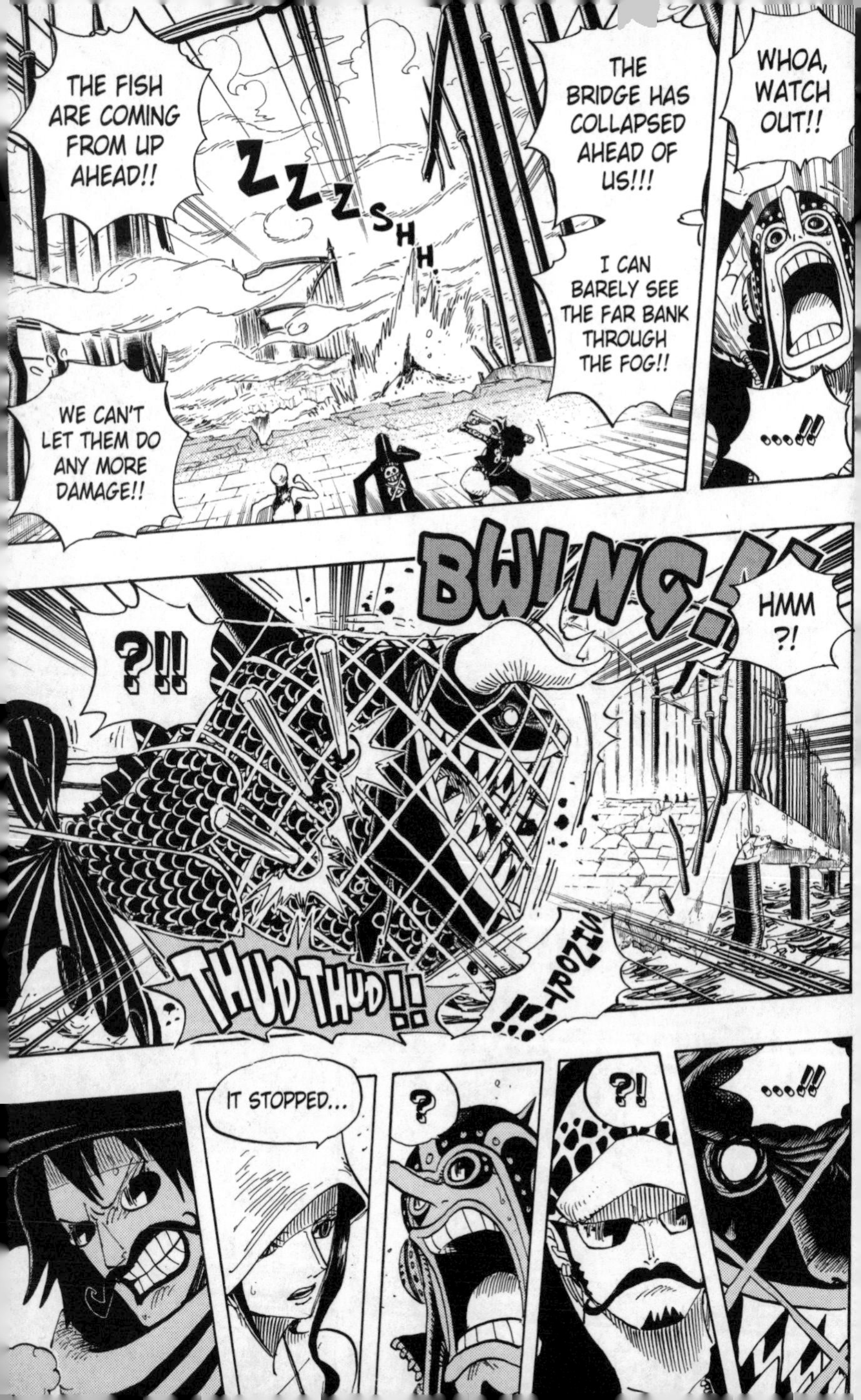
WHOA, WATCH OUT!!
...!!
THE BRIDGE HAS COLLAPSED AHEAD OF US!!!
I CAN BARELY SEE THE FAR BANK THROUGH THE FOG!!
ZZZSHHH
THE FISH ARE COMING FROM UP AHEAD!!
WE CAN'T LET THEM DO ANY MORE DAMAGE!!
BWING!!
HMM ?!
?!!
THUD THUD!!
...!!
?!
?
IT STOPPED...

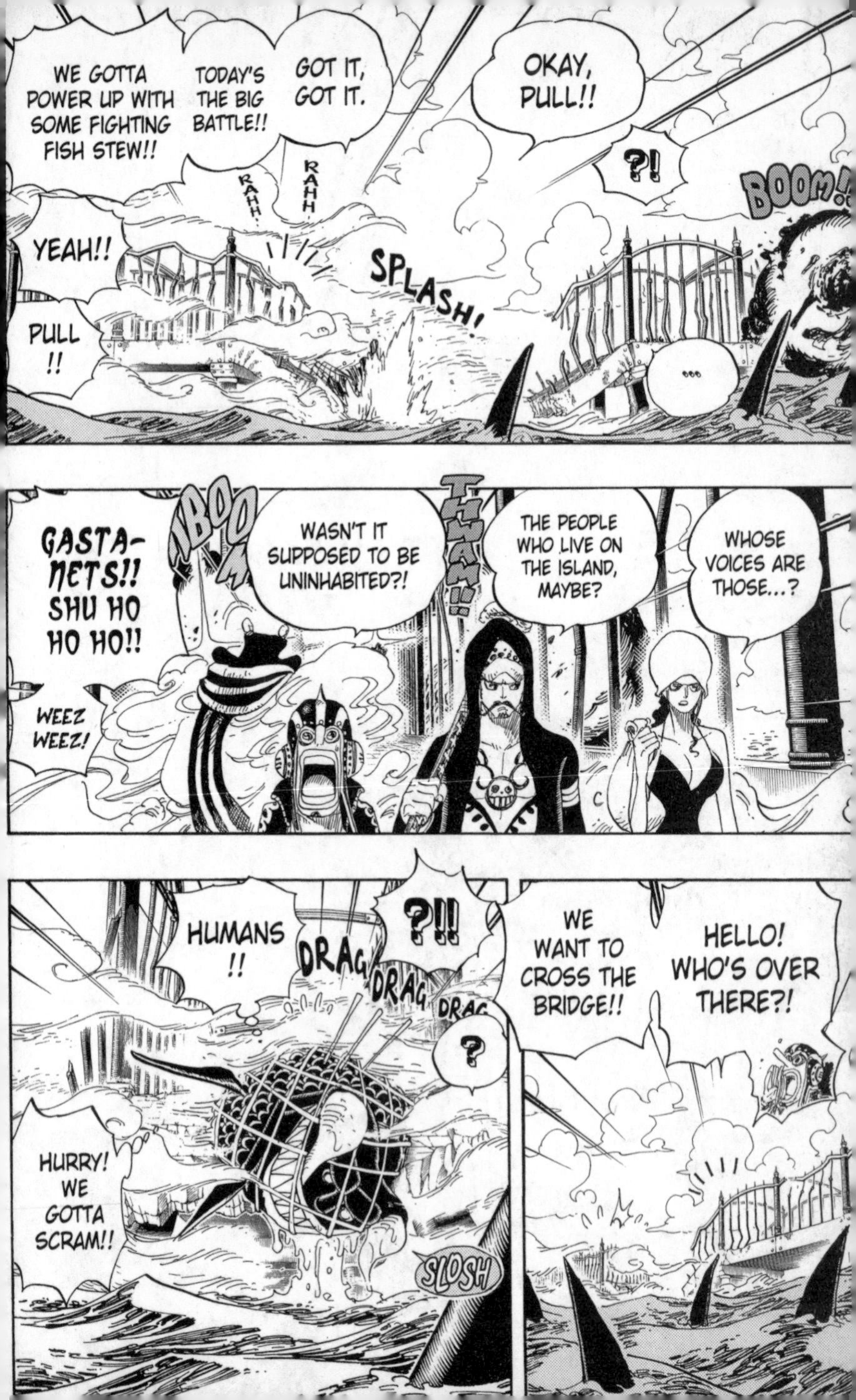
BOOM!!
?!
OKAY, PULL!!
GOT IT, GOT IT.
TODAY'S THE BIG BATTLE!!
WE GOTTA POWER UP WITH SOME FIGHTING FISH STEW!!
RAHH
RAHH
SPLASH!
...
YEAH!!
PULL !!
WHOSE VOICES ARE THOSE...?
THE PEOPLE WHO LIVE ON THE ISLAND, MAYBE?
THWAM!!
WASN'T IT SUPPOSED TO BE UNINHABITED?!
BOOM
GASTA-NETS!! SHU HO HO HO!!
WEEZ WEEZ!
HELLO! WHO'S OVER THERE?!
WE WANT TO CROSS THE BRIDGE!!
?!!
HUMANS !!
DRAG
DRAG
DRAG
?
HURRY! WE GOTTA SCRAM!!
SLOSH

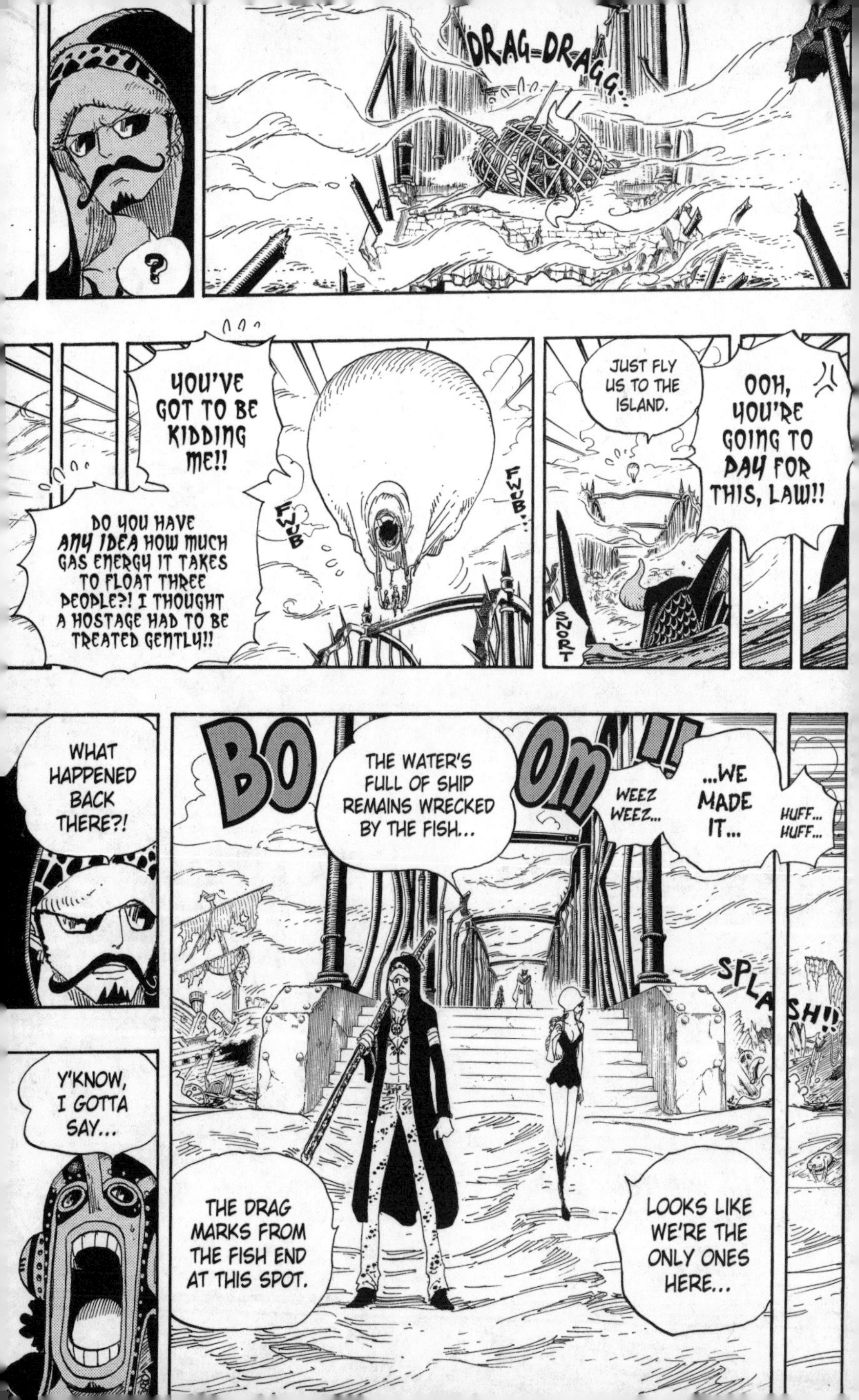
DRAG-DRAGG...
?
OOH, YOU'RE GOING TO PAY FOR THIS, LAW!!
JUST FLY US TO THE ISLAND.
SNORT
FWUB...
YOU'VE GOT TO BE KIDDING ME!!
FWUB
DO YOU HAVE ANY IDEA HOW MUCH GAS ENERGY IT TAKES TO FLOAT THREE PEOPLE?! I THOUGHT A HOSTAGE HAD TO BE TREATED GENTLY!!
HUFF... HUFF...
...WE MADE IT...
WEEZ WEEZ...
BOOM!!
THE WATER'S FULL OF SHIP REMAINS WRECKED BY THE FISH...
SPLASH!!
LOOKS LIKE WE'RE THE ONLY ONES HERE...
THE DRAG MARKS FROM THE FISH END AT THIS SPOT.
WHAT HAPPENED BACK THERE?!
Y'KNOW, I GOTTA SAY...

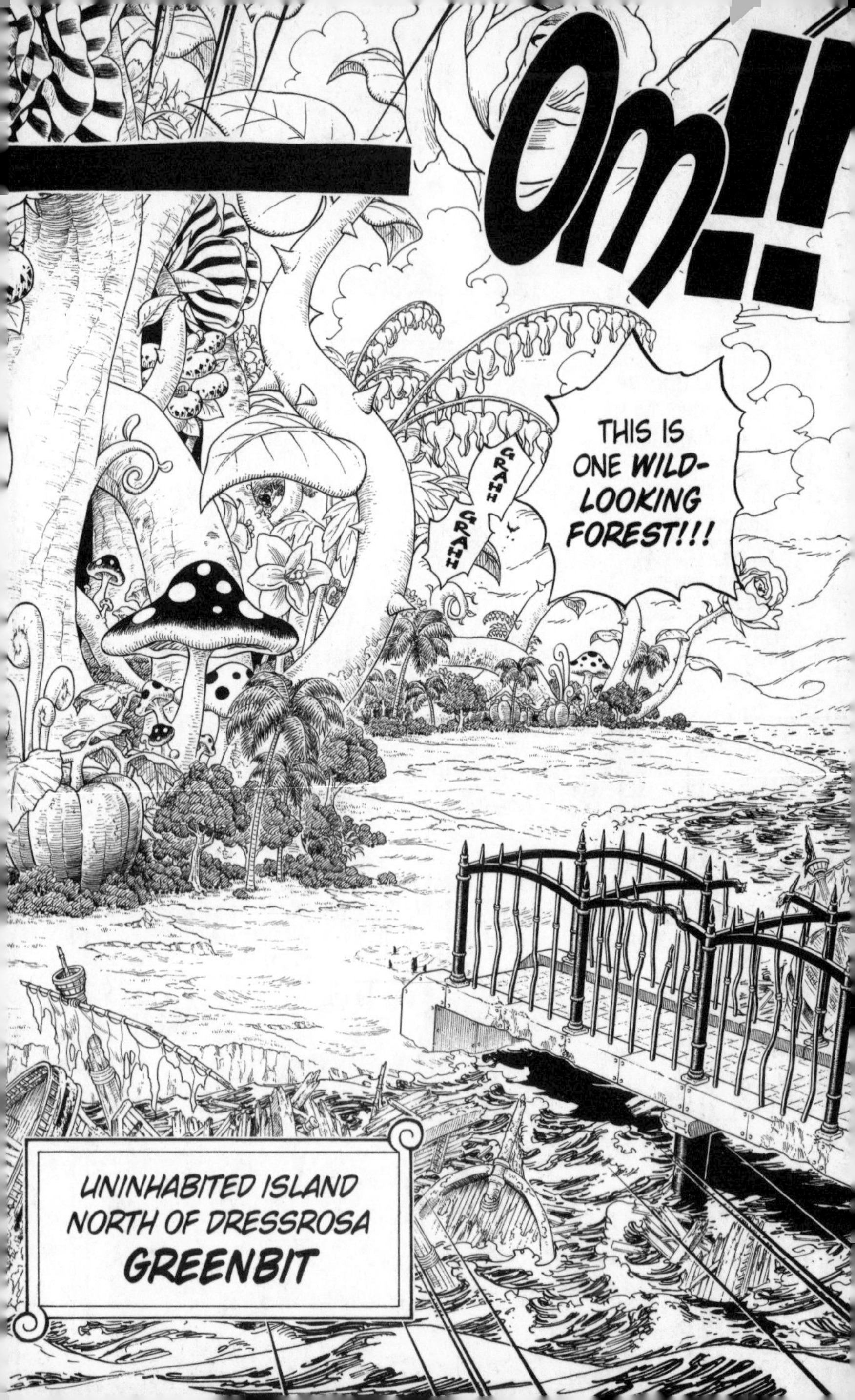
OM!!
THIS IS ONE WILD-LOOKING FOREST!!!
GRAHH GRAHH
UNINHABITED ISLAND NORTH OF DRESSROSA
GREENBIT

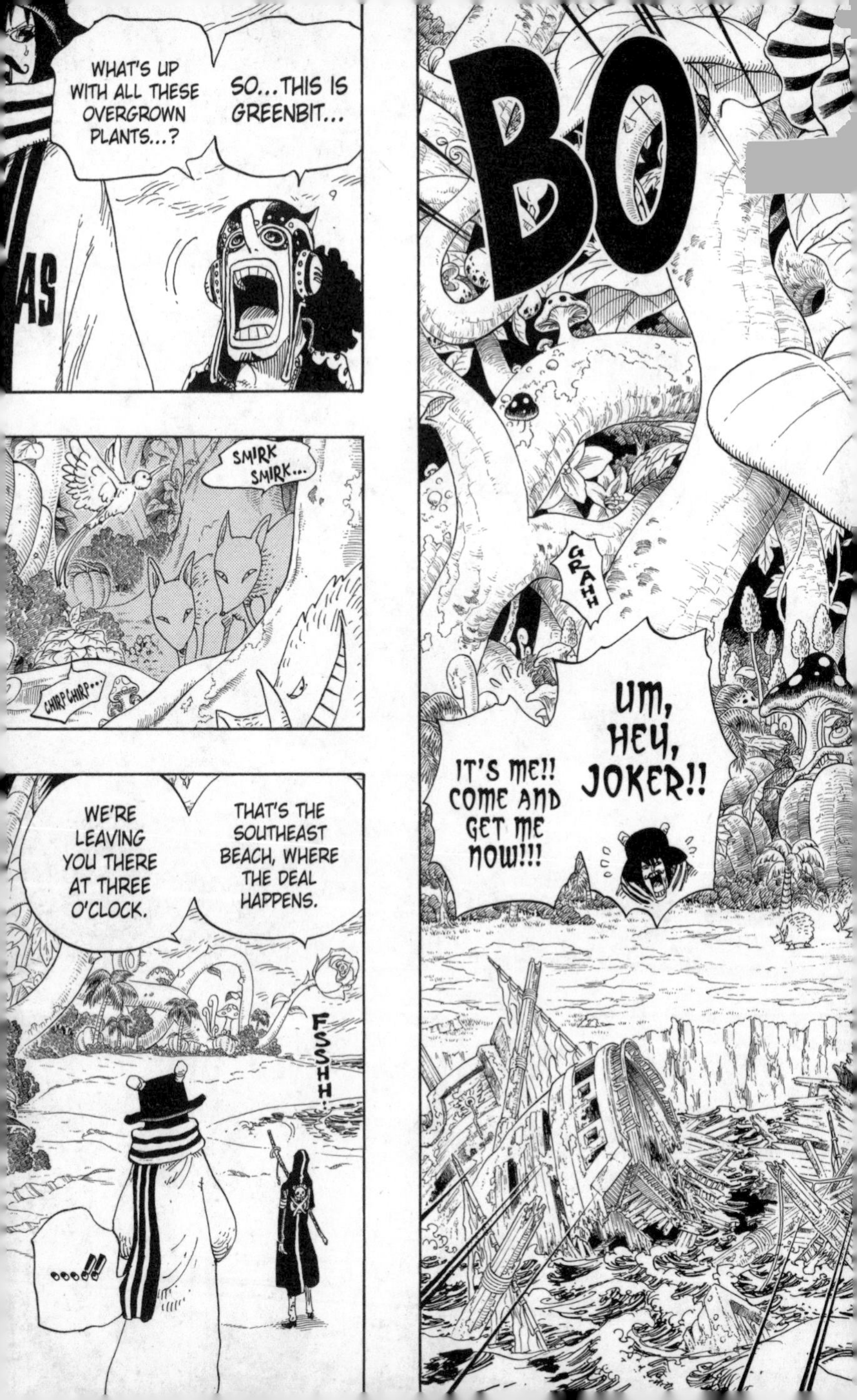
BO
GRAHH
UM, HEY, JOKER!!
IT'S ME!! COME AND GET ME NOW!!!
SO...THIS IS GREENBIT...
WHAT'S UP WITH ALL THESE OVERGROWN PLANTS...?
SMIRK SMIRK...
CHIRP CHIRP...
THAT'S THE SOUTHEAST BEACH, WHERE THE DEAL HAPPENS.
WE'RE LEAVING YOU THERE AT THREE O'CLOCK.
FSSHH!
....!!

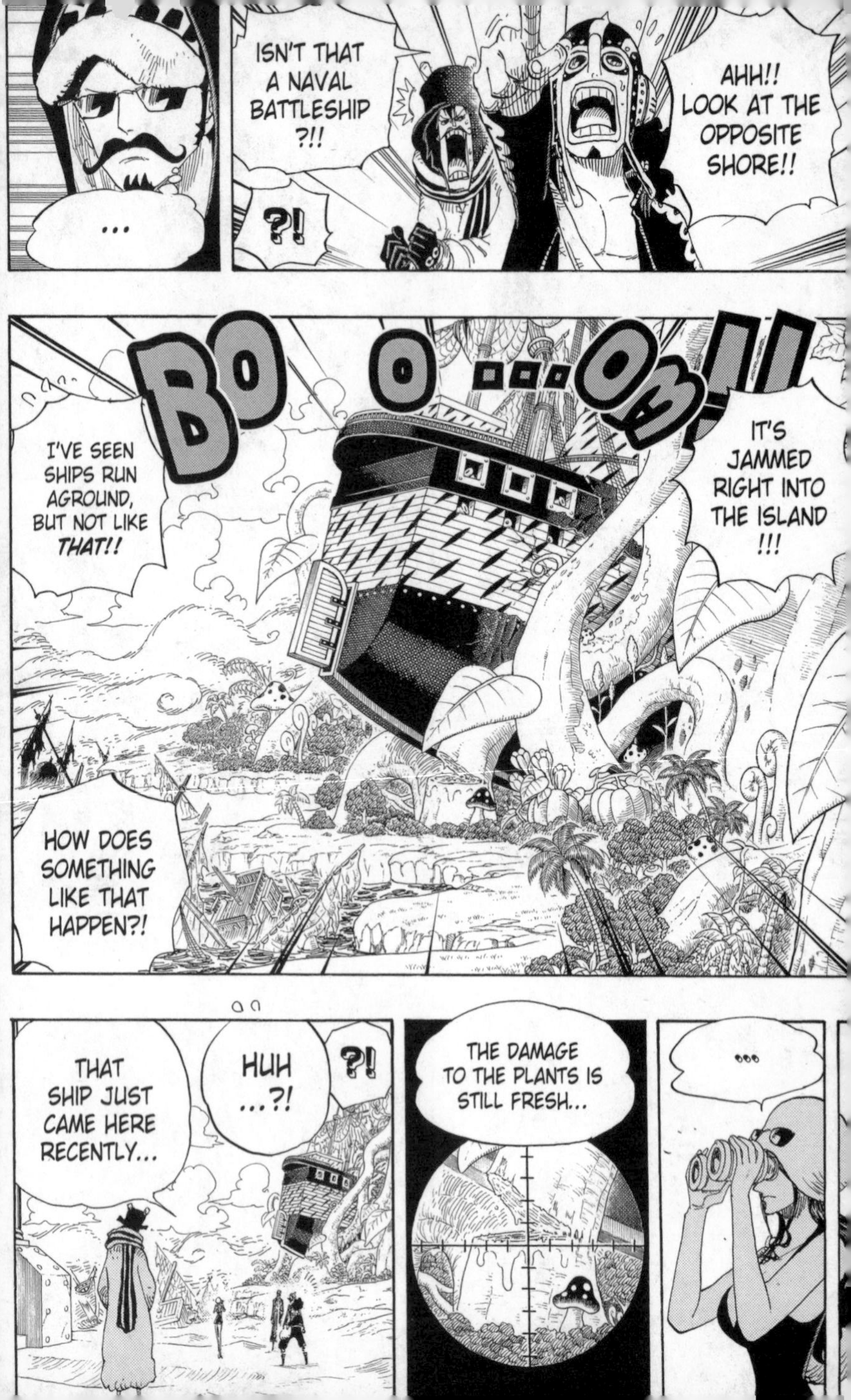
AHH!! LOOK AT THE OPPOSITE SHORE!!
ISN'T THAT A NAVAL BATTLESHIP ?!!
?!
...
BO O...OM!!
IT'S JAMMED RIGHT INTO THE ISLAND !!!
I'VE SEEN SHIPS RUN AGROUND, BUT NOT LIKE *THAT!!*
HOW DOES SOMETHING LIKE THAT HAPPEN?!
...
THE DAMAGE TO THE PLANTS IS STILL FRESH...
?!
HUH ...?!
THAT SHIP JUST CAME HERE RECENTLY...

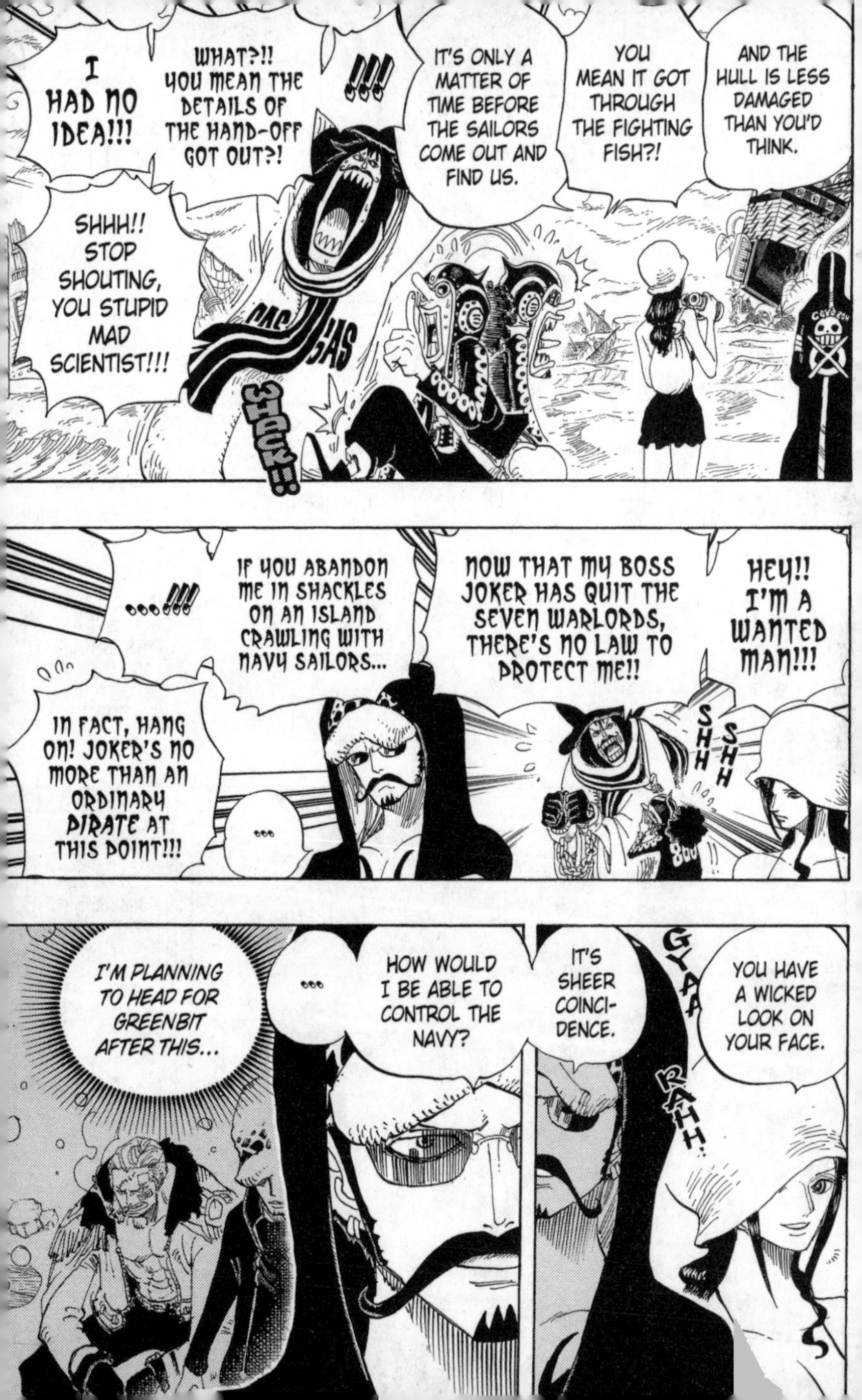
AND THE HULL IS LESS DAMAGED THAN YOU'D THINK.
YOU MEAN IT GOT THROUGH THE FIGHTING FISH?!
IT'S ONLY A MATTER OF TIME BEFORE THE SAILORS COME OUT AND FIND US.
!!!
WHAT?!! YOU MEAN THE DETAILS OF THE HAND-OFF GOT OUT?!
I HAD NO IDEA!!!
SHHH!! STOP SHOUTING, YOU STUPID MAD SCIENTIST!!!
WHACK!!
HEY!! I'M A WANTED MAN!!!
NOW THAT MY BOSS JOKER HAS QUIT THE SEVEN WARLORDS, THERE'S NO LAW TO PROTECT ME!!
SHH SHH
IF YOU ABANDON ME IN SHACKLES ON AN ISLAND CRAWLING WITH NAVY SAILORS...
...!!!
IN FACT, HANG ON! JOKER'S NO MORE THAN AN ORDINARY PIRATE AT THIS POINT!!!
...
YOU HAVE A WICKED LOOK ON YOUR FACE.
GYAA RAHH
IT'S SHEER COINCIDENCE.
HOW WOULD I BE ABLE TO CONTROL THE NAVY?
...
I'M PLANNING TO HEAD FOR GREENBIT AFTER THIS...

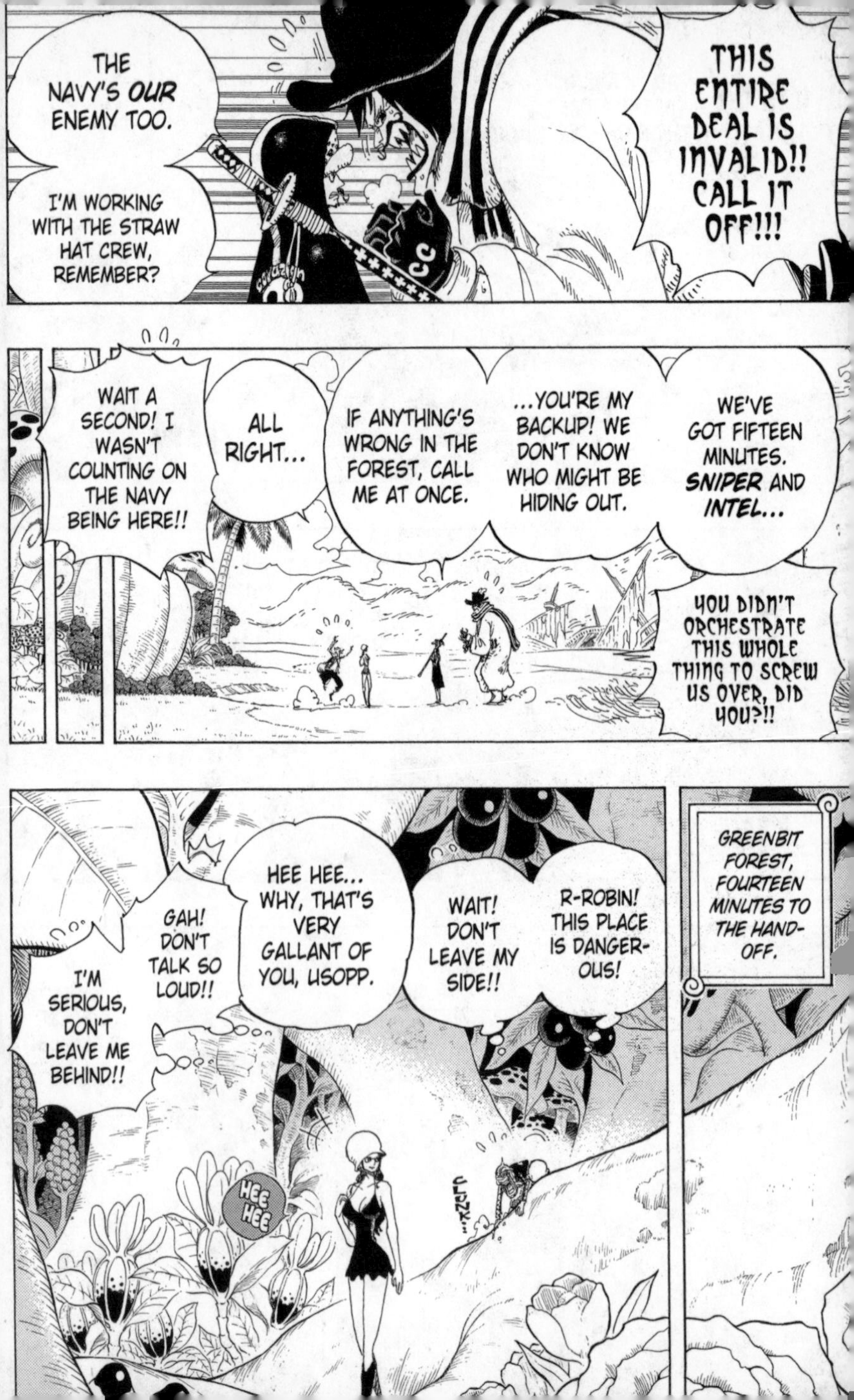
THIS ENTIRE DEAL IS INVALID!! CALL IT OFF!!!
THE NAVY'S *OUR* ENEMY TOO.
I'M WORKING WITH THE STRAW HAT CREW, REMEMBER?
WE'VE GOT FIFTEEN MINUTES. *SNIPER* AND *INTEL*...
...YOU'RE MY BACKUP! WE DON'T KNOW WHO MIGHT BE HIDING OUT.
IF ANYTHING'S WRONG IN THE FOREST, CALL ME AT ONCE.
YOU DIDN'T ORCHESTRATE THIS WHOLE THING TO SCREW US OVER, DID YOU?!!
ALL RIGHT...
WAIT A SECOND! I WASN'T COUNTING ON THE NAVY BEING HERE!!
GREENBIT FOREST, FOURTEEN MINUTES TO THE HAND-OFF.
R-ROBIN! THIS PLACE IS DANGEROUS!
WAIT! DON'T LEAVE MY SIDE!!
HEE HEE... WHY, THAT'S VERY GALLANT OF YOU, USOPP.
GAH! DON'T TALK SO LOUD!!
I'M SERIOUS, DON'T LEAVE ME BEHIND!!
HEE HEE
CLUNK...

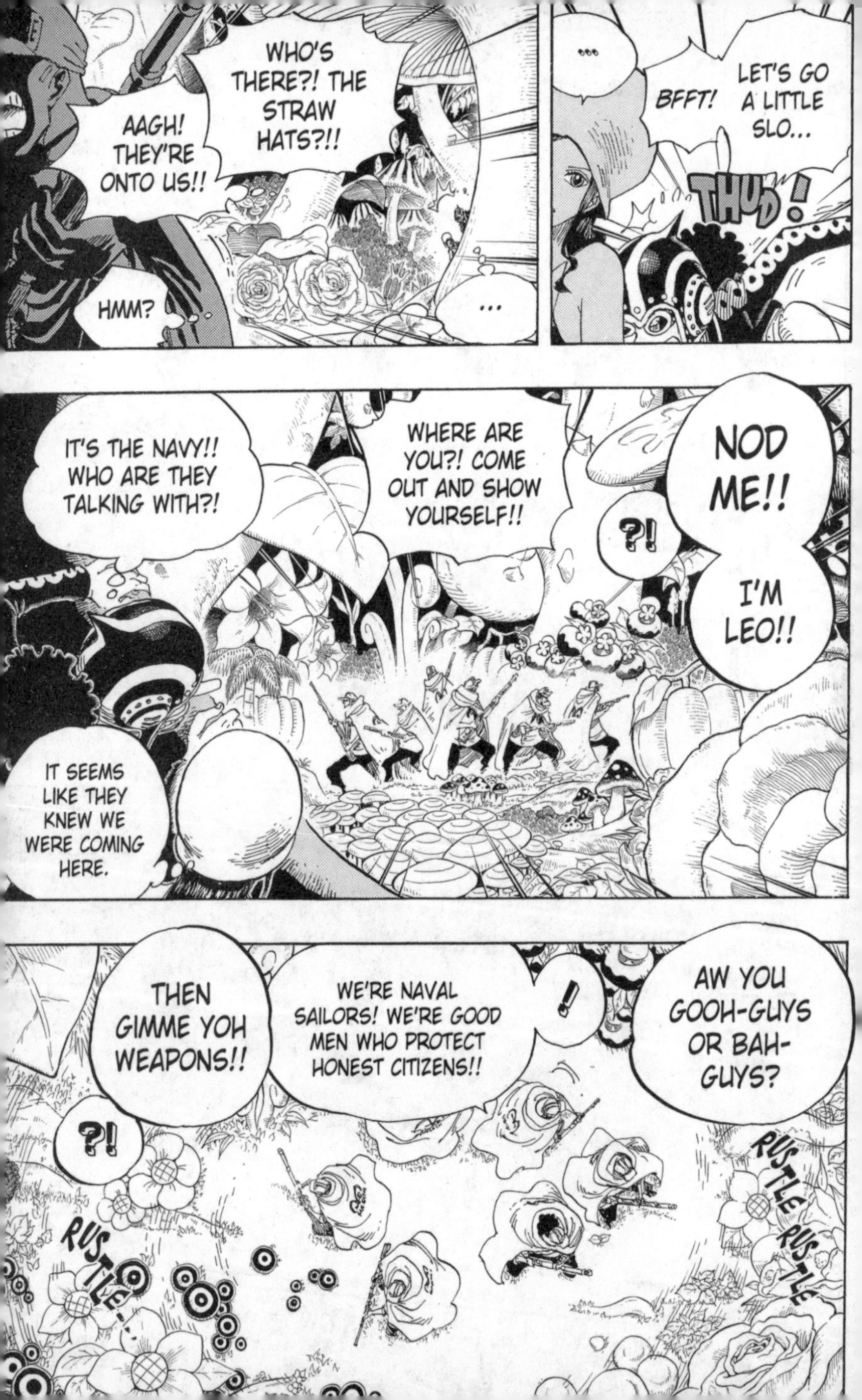
...
LET'S GO A LITTLE SLO...
BFFT!
THUD!
WHO'S THERE?! THE STRAW HATS?!!
AAGH! THEY'RE ONTO US!!
...
HMM?
NOD ME!!
I'M LEO!!
?!
WHERE ARE YOU?! COME OUT AND SHOW YOURSELF!!
IT'S THE NAVY!! WHO ARE THEY TALKING WITH?!
IT SEEMS LIKE THEY KNEW WE WERE COMING HERE.
AW YOU GOOH-GUYS OR BAH-GUYS?
!
WE'RE NAVAL SAILORS! WE'RE GOOD MEN WHO PROTECT HONEST CITIZENS!!
THEN GIMME YOH WEAPONS!!
?!
RUSTLE
RUSTLE
RUSTLE

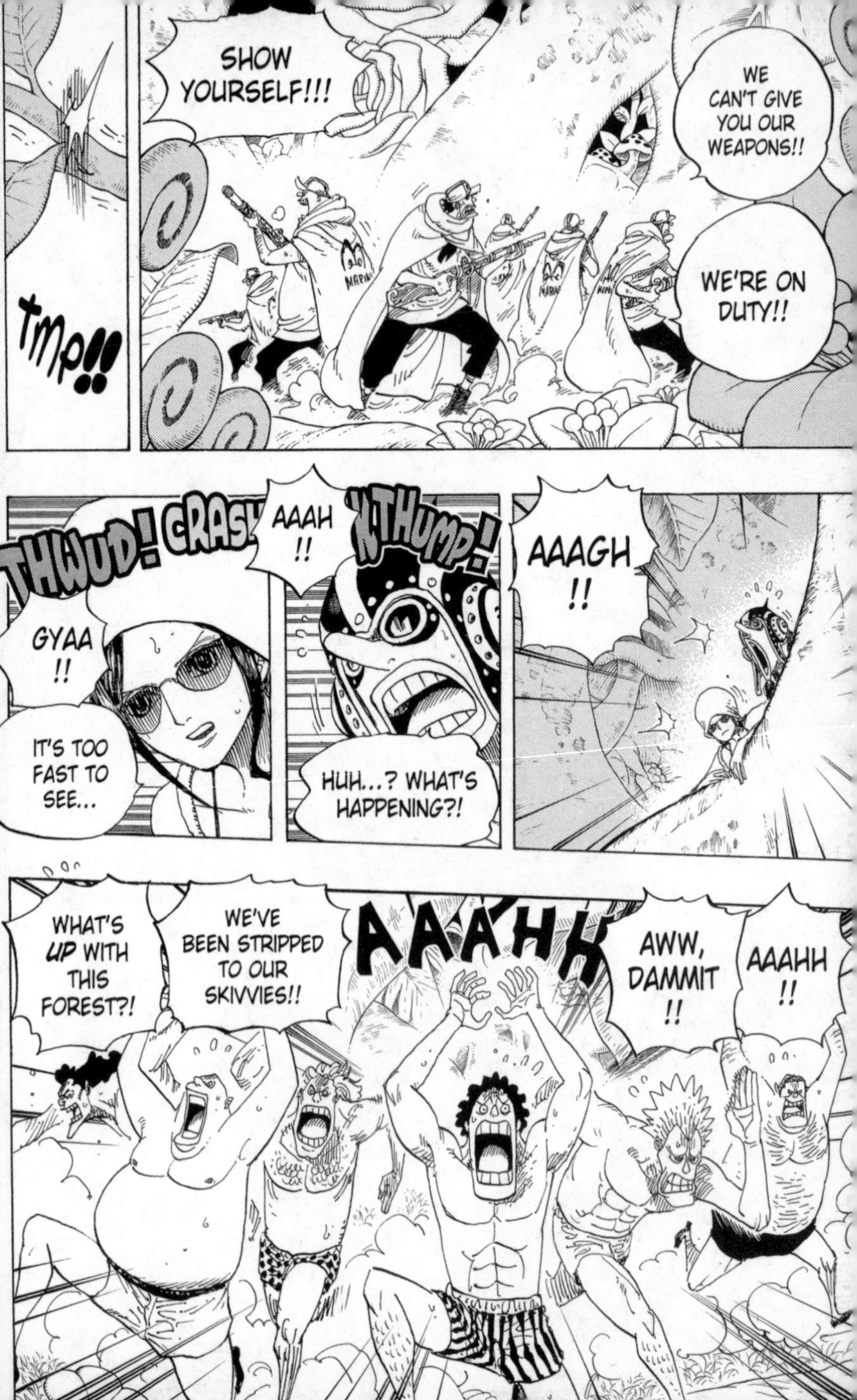
WE CAN'T GIVE YOU OUR WEAPONS!!
WE'RE ON DUTY!!
SHOW YOURSELF!!!
tmp!!
AAAGH !!
K'THUMP!
AAAH !!
HUH...? WHAT'S HAPPENING?!
THWUD! CRASH
GYAA !!
IT'S TOO FAST TO SEE...
AAAHH !!
AWW, DAMMIT !!
AAAHK
WE'VE BEEN STRIPPED TO OUR SKIVVIES!!
WHAT'S UP WITH THIS FOREST?!

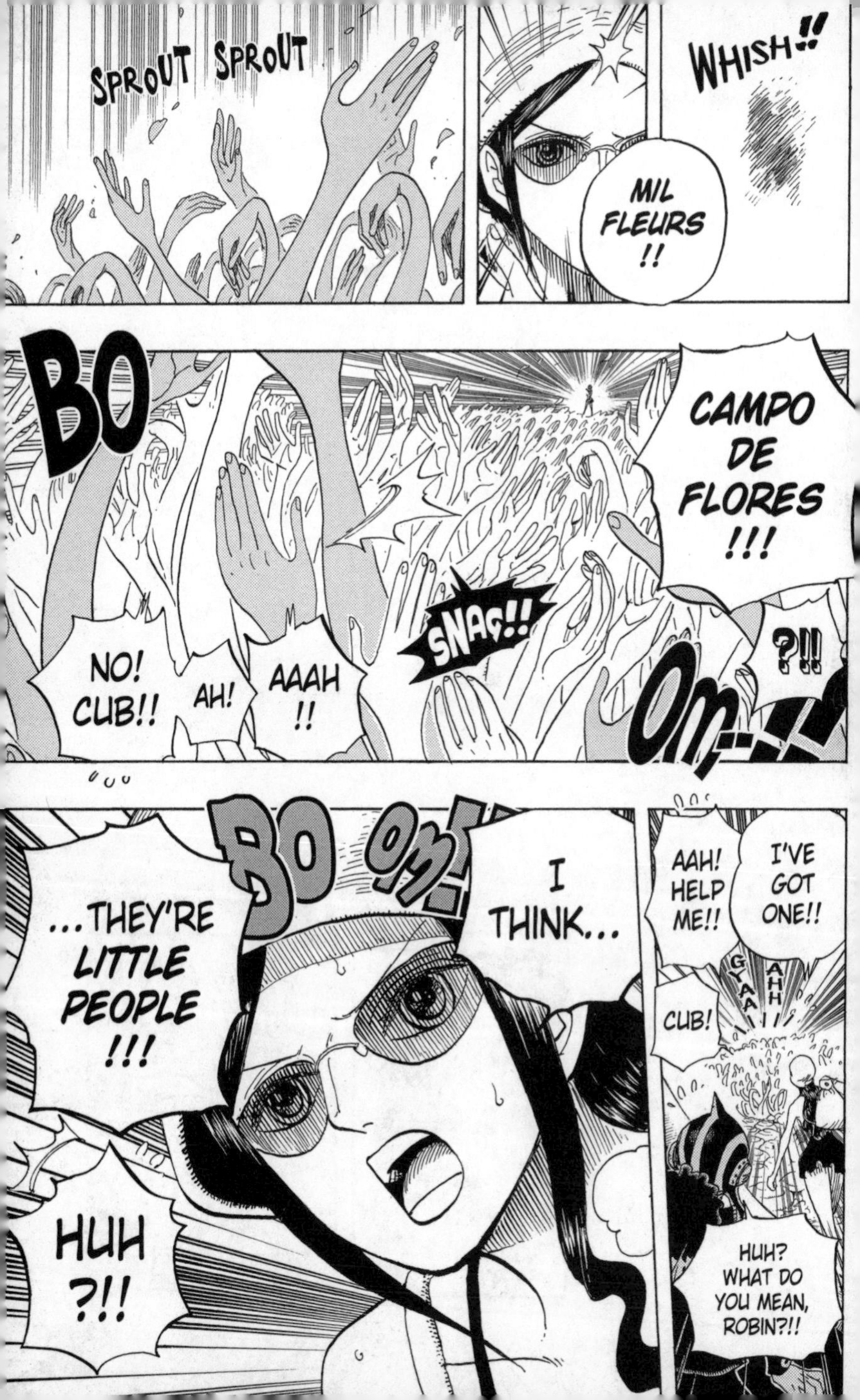
WHISH!!
MIL FLEURS !!
SPROUT SPROUT
CAMPO DE FLORES !!!
?!!
OM!!
SNAG!!
AAAH !!
AH!
NO! CUB!!
BO
I'VE GOT ONE!!
AAH! HELP ME!!
AHH
GYAA
CUB!
HUH? WHAT DO YOU MEAN, ROBIN?!!
BO OM!
I THINK...
...THEY'RE *LITTLE PEOPLE* !!!
HUH ?!!

Chapter 711:
ADVENTURE IN THE LAND OF THE LITTLE PEOPLE

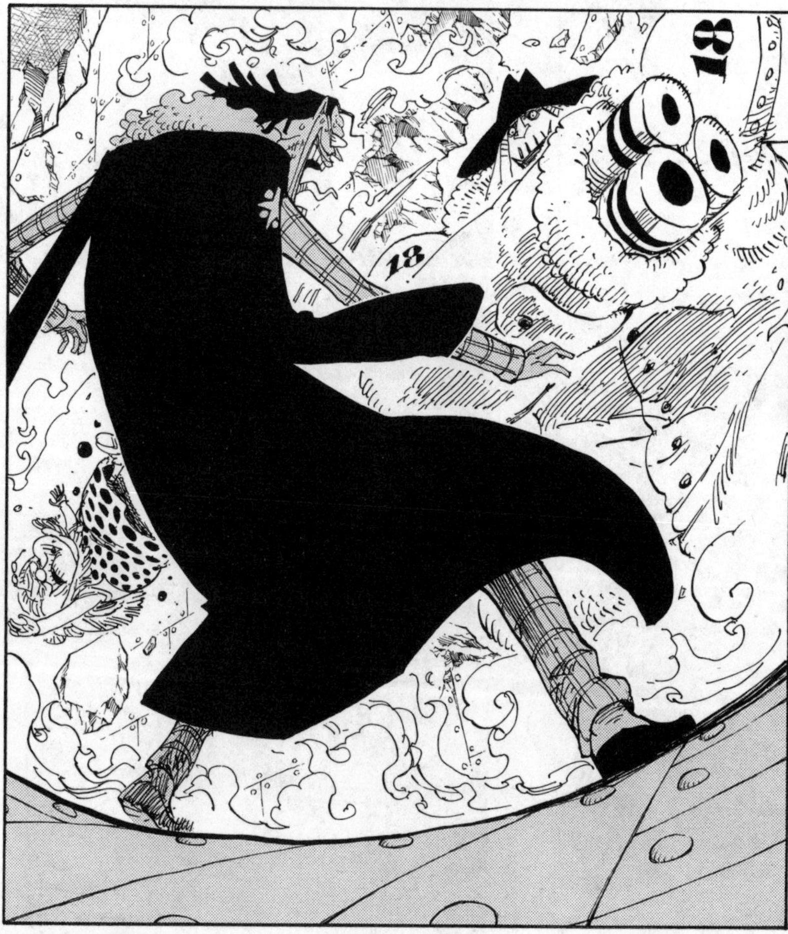
18
18

CARIBOU'S NEW WORLD KEE HEE HEE, VOL. 29:
"THE OLD HAG GETS BLASTED OFF HER FEET"

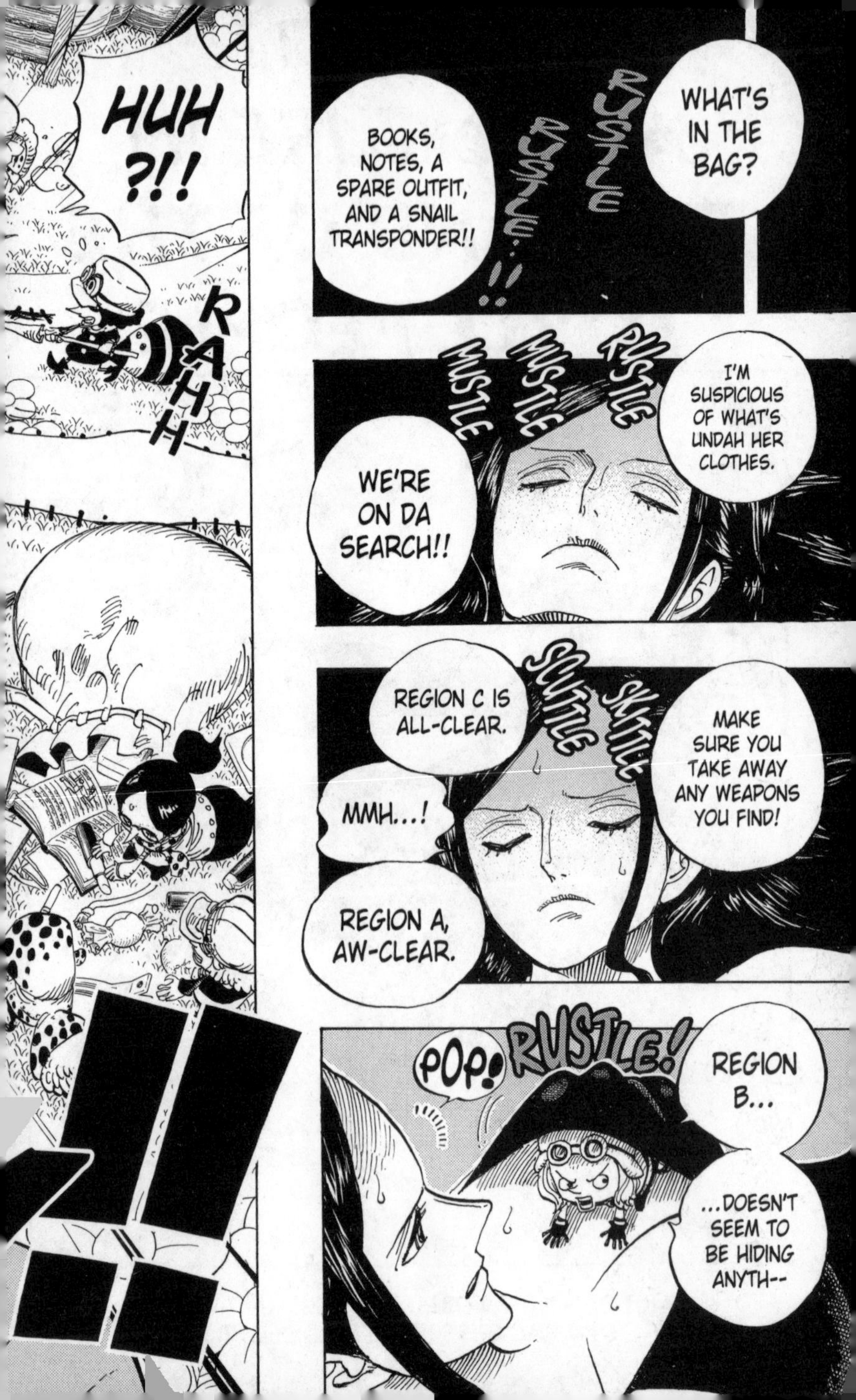
WHAT'S IN THE BAG?
RUSTLE RUSTLE..!!
BOOKS, NOTES, A SPARE OUTFIT, AND A SNAIL TRANSPONDER!!
I'M SUSPICIOUS OF WHAT'S UNDAH HER CLOTHES.
RUSTLE MUSTLE MUSTLE
WE'RE ON DA SEARCH!!
MAKE SURE YOU TAKE AWAY ANY WEAPONS YOU FIND!
SKITTLE SCUTTLE
REGION C IS ALL-CLEAR.
MMH...!
REGION A, AW-CLEAR.
REGION B...
RUSTLE!
POP!
...DOESN'T SEEM TO BE HIDING ANYTH--
HUH ?!!
RAHHH
!!

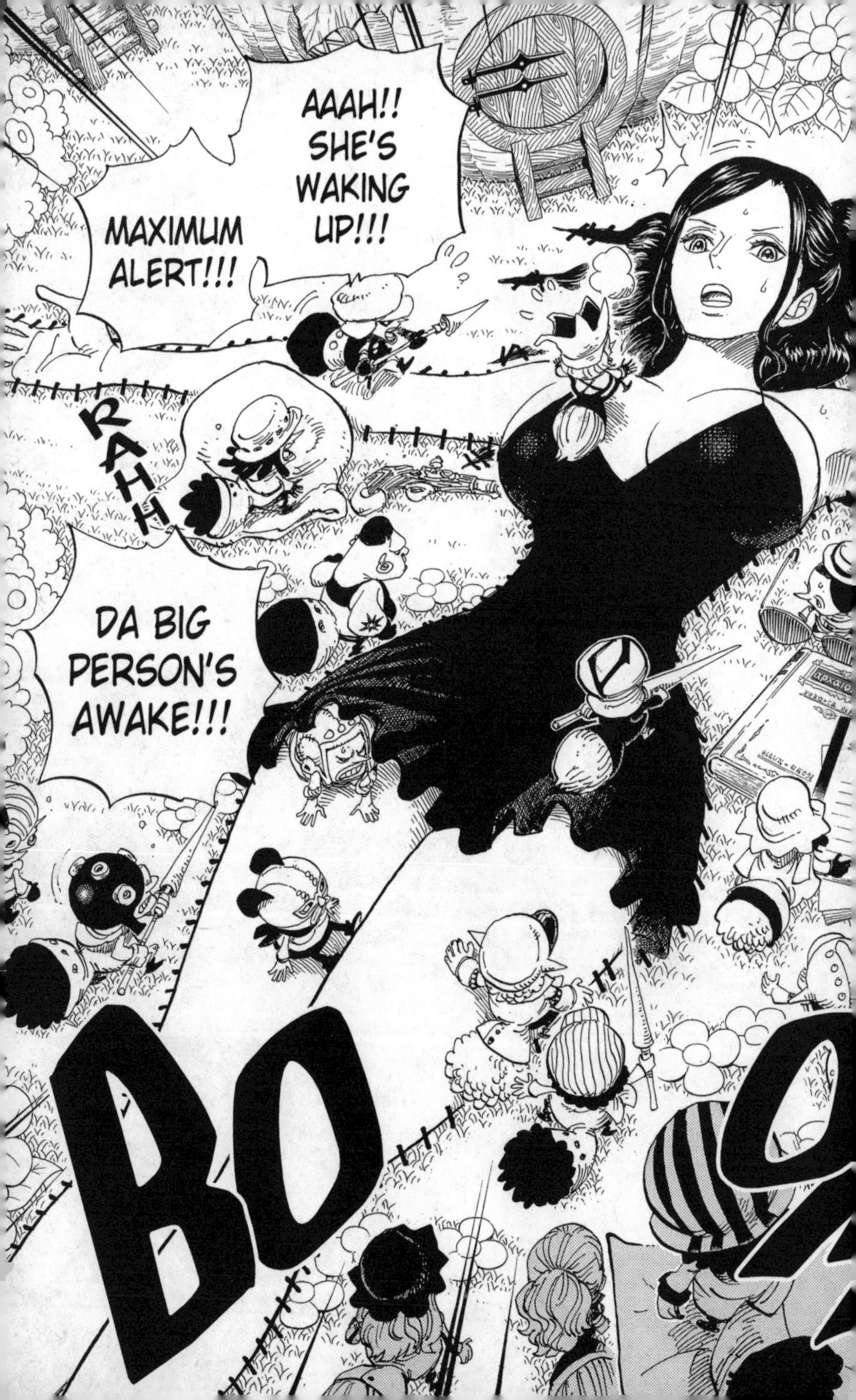
AAAH!! SHE'S WAKING UP!!!
MAXIMUM ALERT!!!
RAHH
DA BIG PERSON'S AWAKE!!!
BO

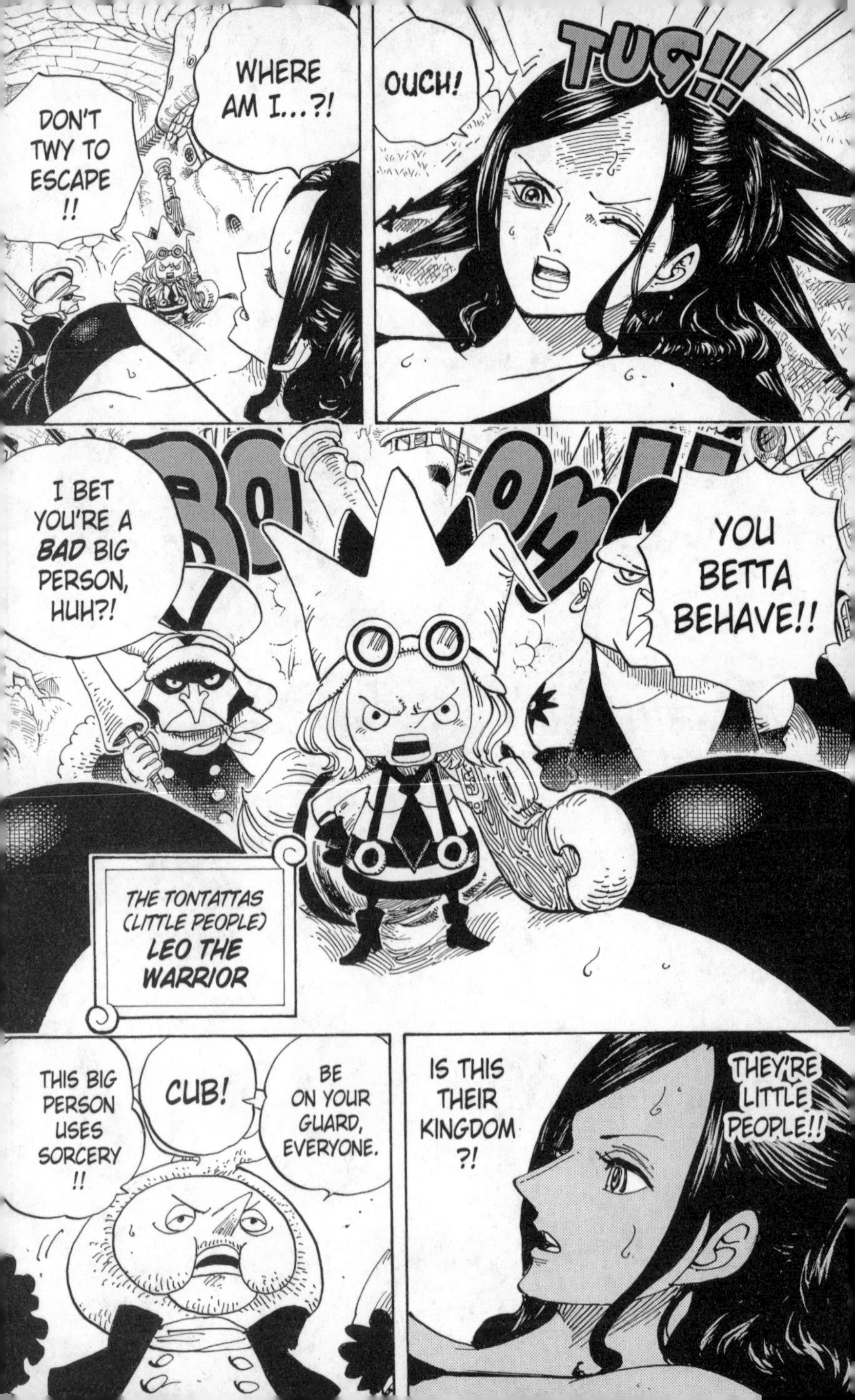
TUG!!
OUCH!
WHERE AM I...?!
DON'T TWY TO ESCAPE!!
YOU BETTA BEHAVE!!
BOOM!!
I BET YOU'RE A BAD BIG PERSON, HUH?!
THE TONTATTAS (LITTLE PEOPLE) LEO THE WARRIOR
THEY'RE LITTLE PEOPLE!!
IS THIS THEIR KINGDOM?!
BE ON YOUR GUARD, EVERYONE.
CUB!
THIS BIG PERSON USES SORCERY!!

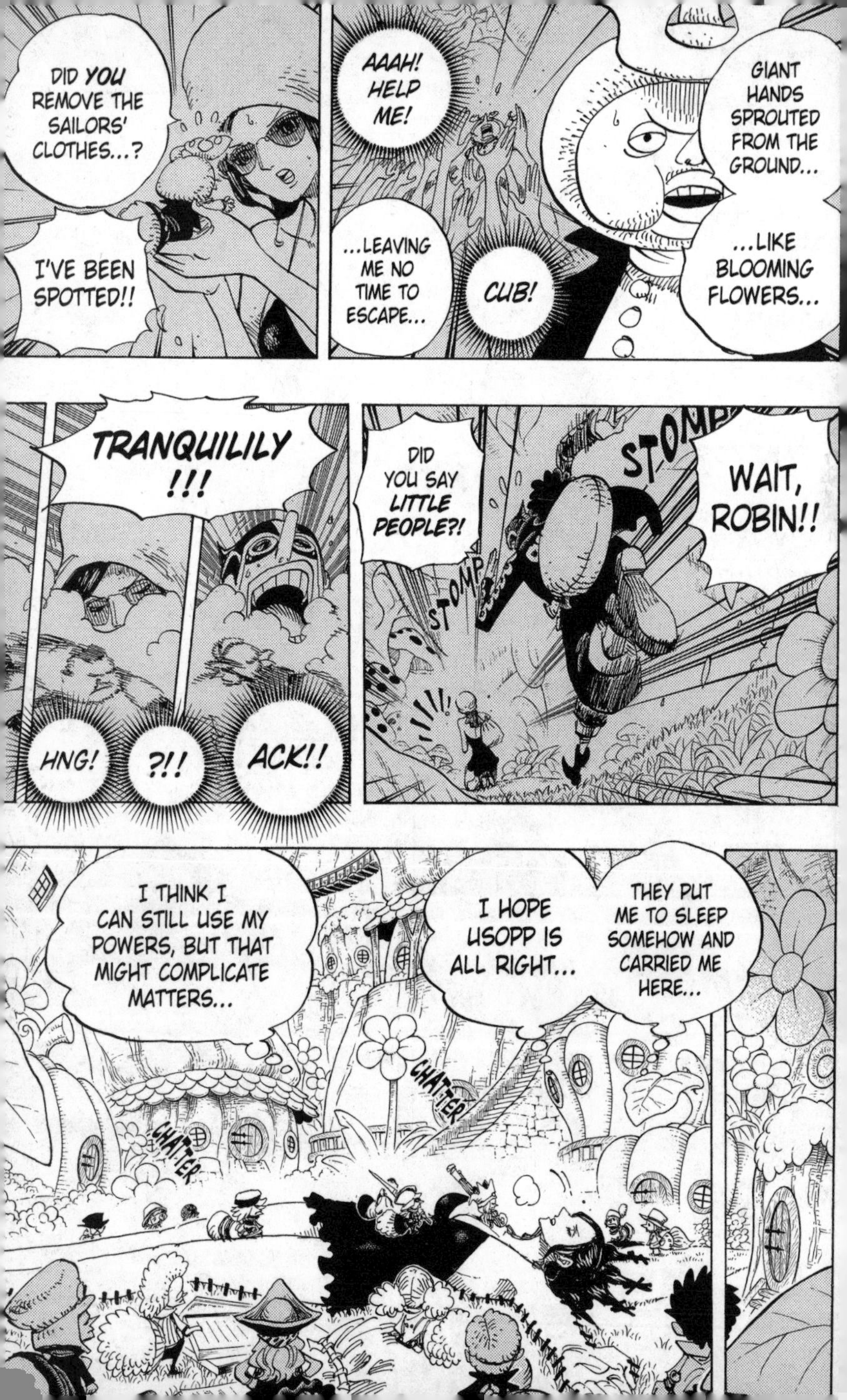
GIANT HANDS SPROUTED FROM THE GROUND...
...LIKE BLOOMING FLOWERS...
AAAH! HELP ME!
CUB!
...LEAVING ME NO TIME TO ESCAPE...
DID YOU REMOVE THE SAILORS' CLOTHES...?
I'VE BEEN SPOTTED!!
WAIT, ROBIN!!
STOMP
DID YOU SAY LITTLE PEOPLE?!
STOMP
STOMP
TRANQUILILY !!!
ACK!!
?!!
HNG!
THEY PUT ME TO SLEEP SOMEHOW AND CARRIED ME HERE...
I HOPE USOPP IS ALL RIGHT...
I THINK I CAN STILL USE MY POWERS, BUT THAT MIGHT COMPLICATE MATTERS...
CHATTER
CHATTER

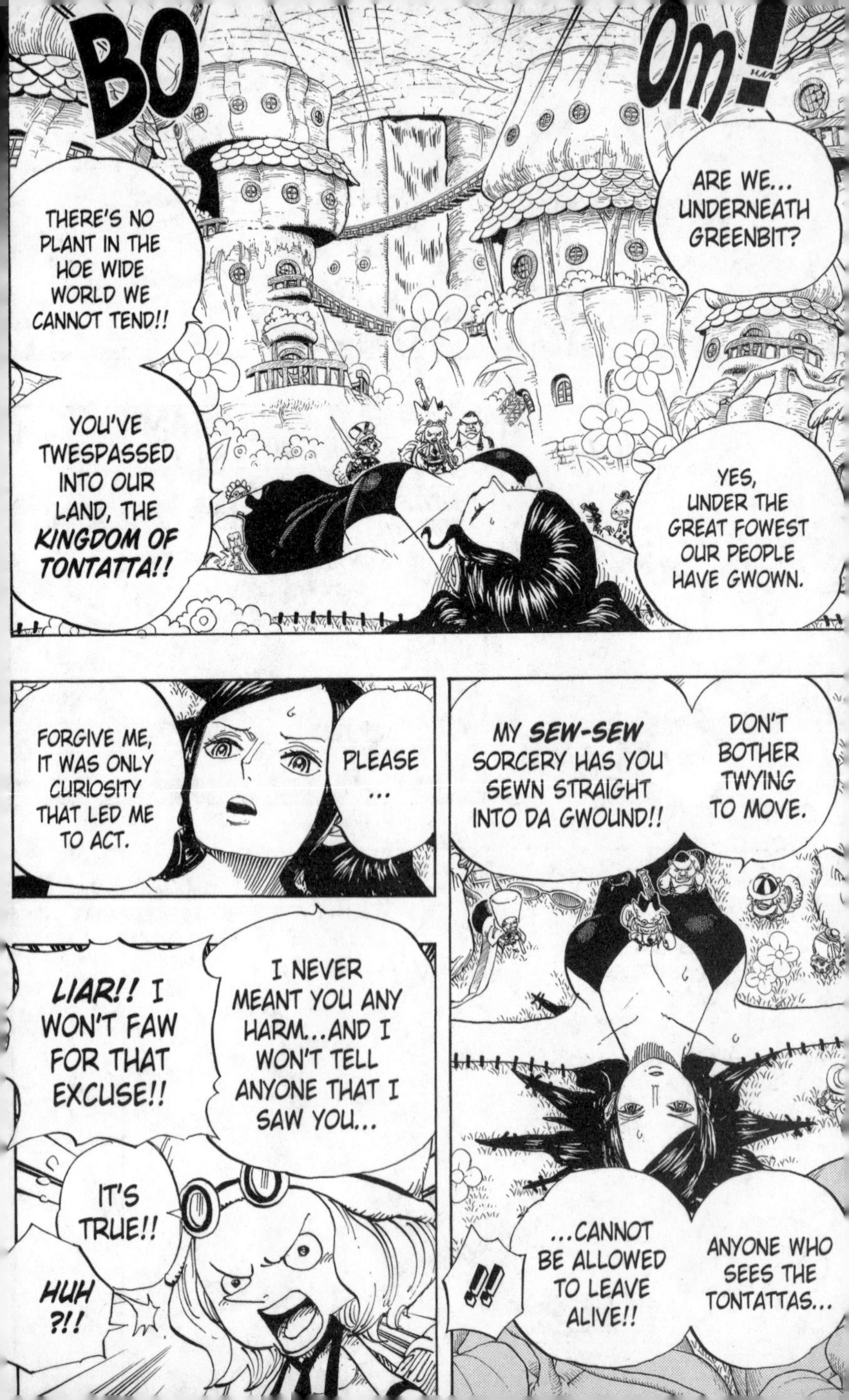
BOOM!
ARE WE... UNDERNEATH GREENBIT?
YES, UNDER THE GREAT FOWEST OUR PEOPLE HAVE GWOWN.
THERE'S NO PLANT IN THE HOE WIDE WORLD WE CANNOT TEND!!
YOU'VE TWESPASSED INTO OUR LAND, THE KINGDOM OF TONTATTA!!
DON'T BOTHER TWYING TO MOVE.
MY SEW-SEW SORCERY HAS YOU SEWN STRAIGHT INTO DA GWOUND!!
ANYONE WHO SEES THE TONTATTAS...
...CANNOT BE ALLOWED TO LEAVE ALIVE!!
!!
PLEASE...
FORGIVE ME, IT WAS ONLY CURIOSITY THAT LED ME TO ACT.
I NEVER MEANT YOU ANY HARM...AND I WON'T TELL ANYONE THAT I SAW YOU...
LIAR!! I WON'T FAW FOR THAT EXCUSE!!
IT'S TRUE!!
HUH?!!

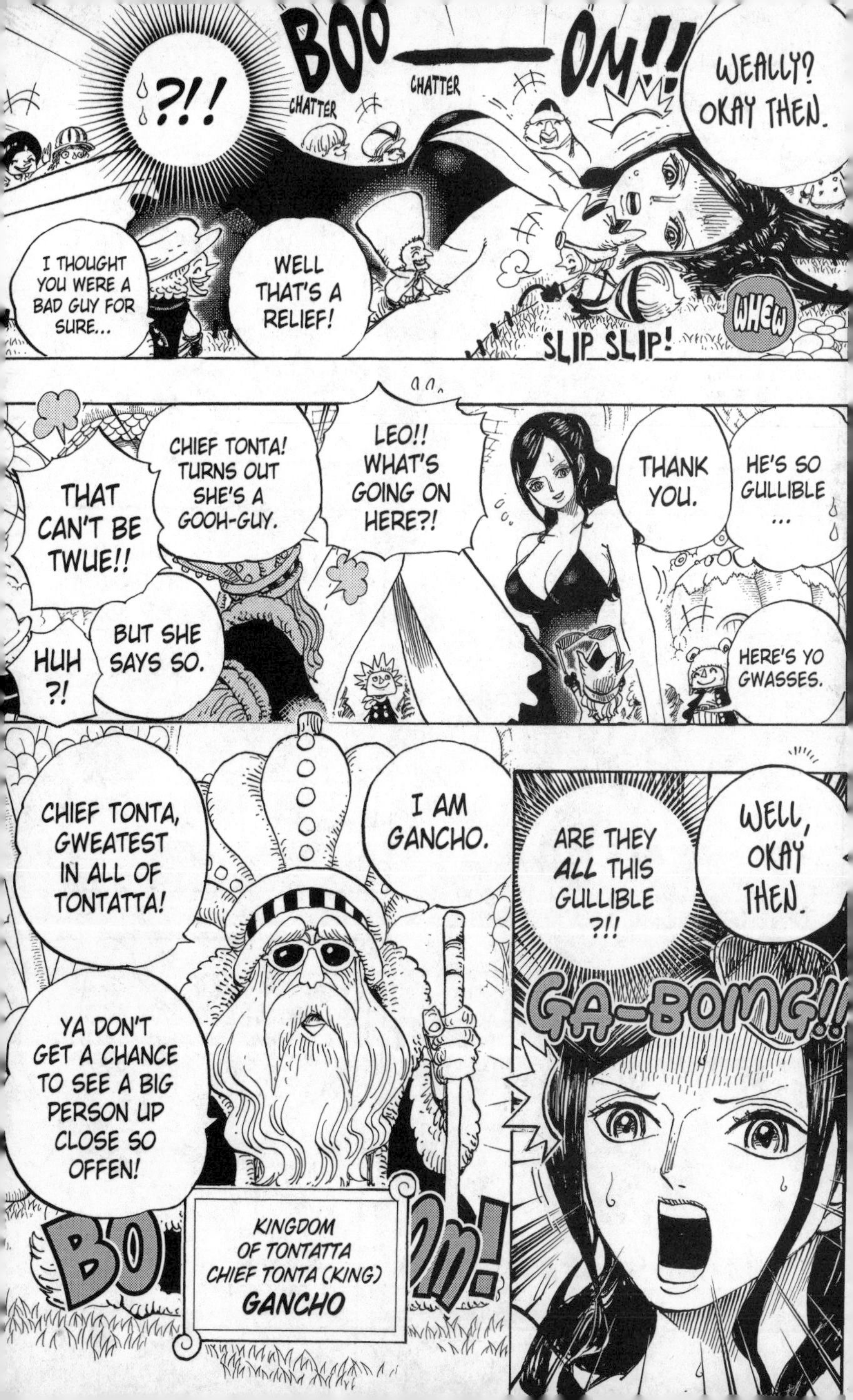
WEALLY? OKAY THEN.
BOO——OM!!
CHATTER
CHATTER
?!!
WHEW
SLIP SLIP!
WELL THAT'S A RELIEF!
I THOUGHT YOU WERE A BAD GUY FOR SURE...
HE'S SO GULLIBLE ...
THANK YOU.
HERE'S YO GWASSES.
LEO!! WHAT'S GOING ON HERE?!
CHIEF TONTA! TURNS OUT SHE'S A GOOH-GUY.
THAT CAN'T BE TWUE!!
BUT SHE SAYS SO.
HUH ?!
WELL, OKAY THEN.
ARE THEY ALL THIS GULLIBLE ?!!
GA-BOING!!
I AM GANCHO.
CHIEF TONTA, GWEATEST IN ALL OF TONTATTA!
YA DON'T GET A CHANCE TO SEE A BIG PERSON UP CLOSE SO OFFEN!
BO
OM!
KINGDOM OF TONTATTA CHIEF TONTA (KING) GANCHO

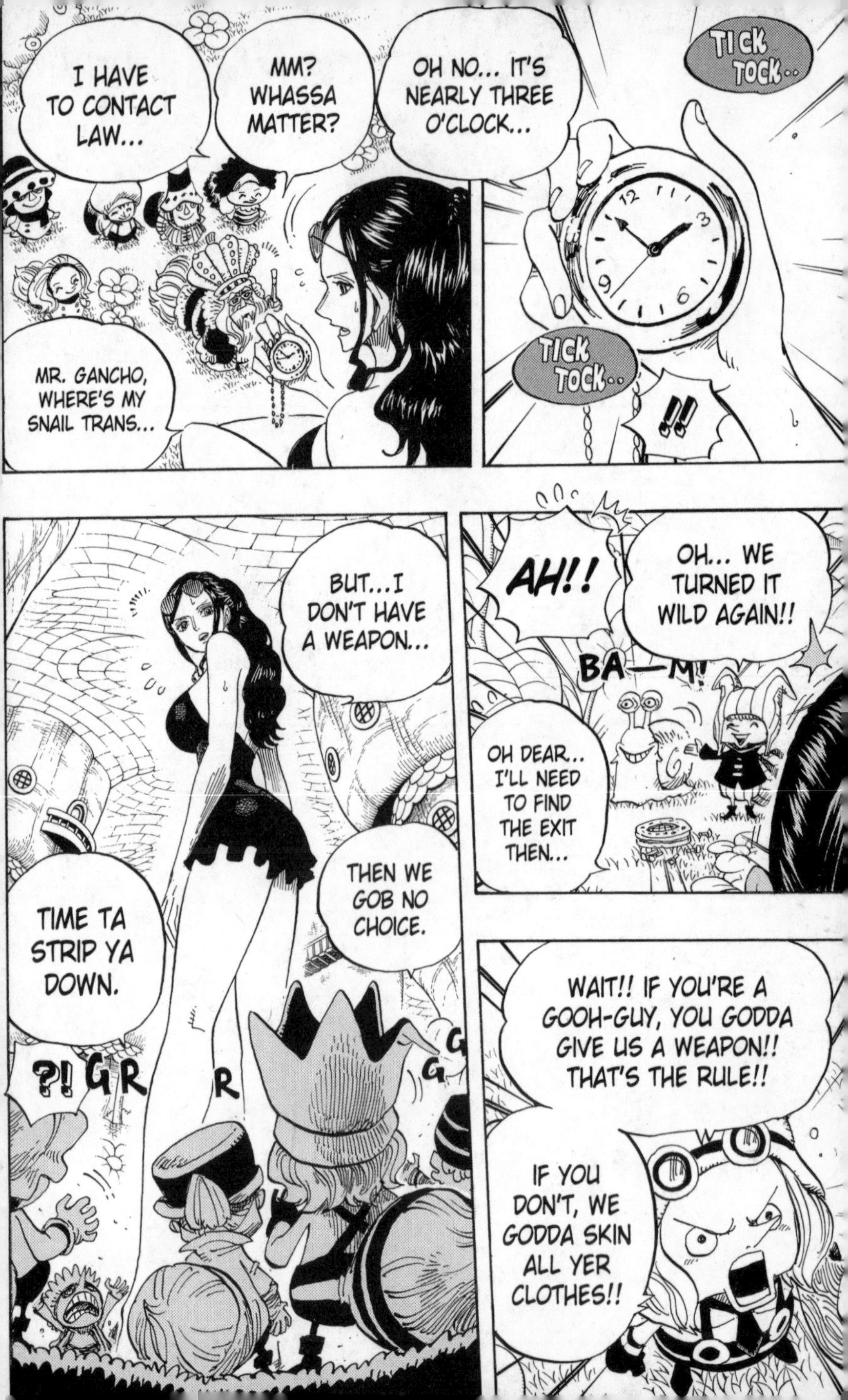
TICK TOCK..
TICK TOCK..
!!
OH NO... IT'S NEARLY THREE O'CLOCK...
MM? WHASSA MATTER?
I HAVE TO CONTACT LAW...
MR. GANCHO, WHERE'S MY SNAIL TRANS...
OH... WE TURNED IT WILD AGAIN!!
AH!!
BA—M!
OH DEAR.. I'LL NEED TO FIND THE EXIT THEN...
WAIT!! IF YOU'RE A GOOH-GUY, YOU GODDA GIVE US A WEAPON!! THAT'S THE RULE!!
IF YOU DON'T, WE GODDA SKIN ALL YER CLOTHES!!
BUT...I DON'T HAVE A WEAPON...
THEN WE GOB NO CHOICE.
TIME TA STRIP YA DOWN.
GG
?! GR R

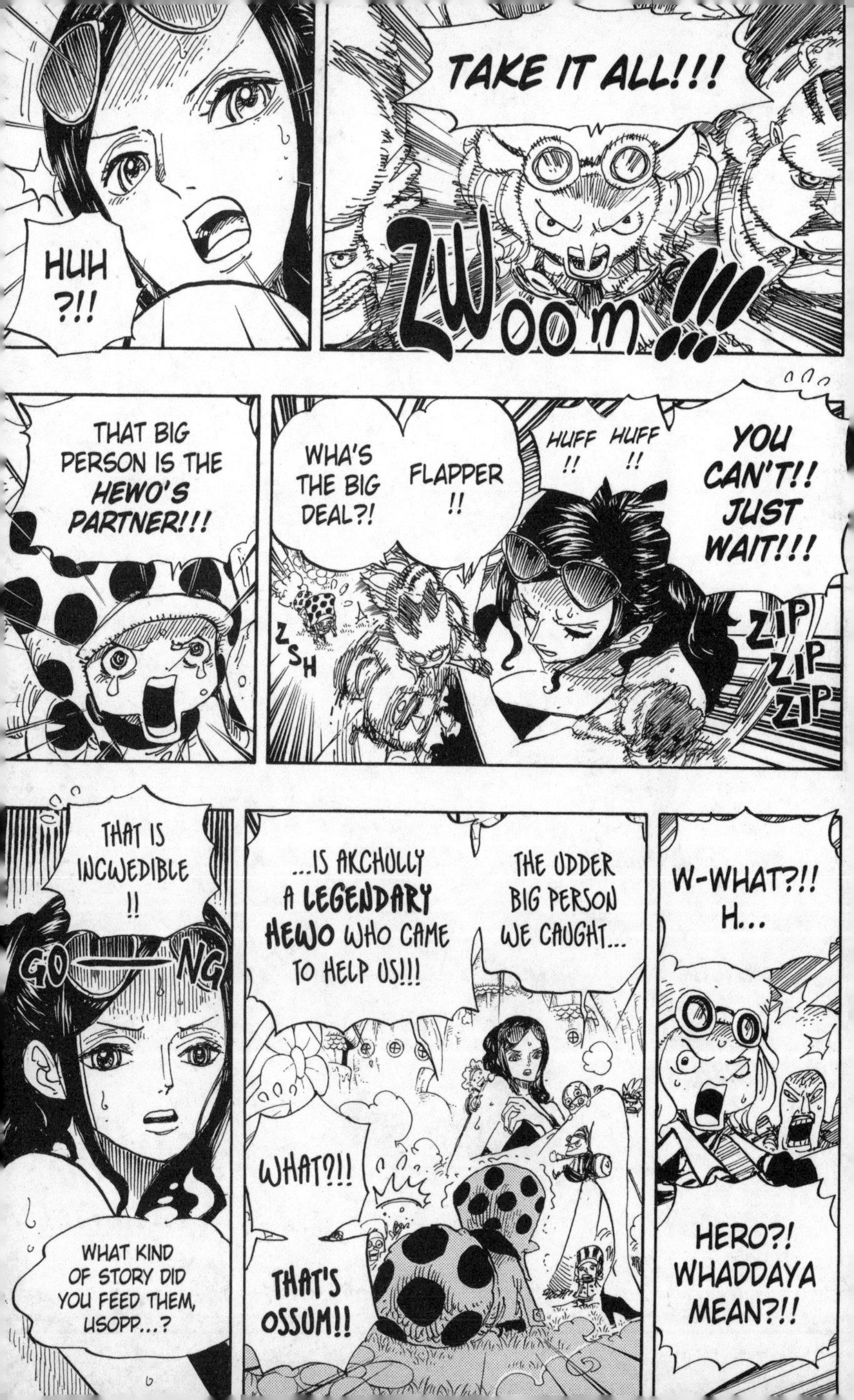
TAKE IT ALL!!!
ZWOOM!!!
HUH ?!!
YOU CAN'T!! JUST WAIT!!!
HUFF !! HUFF !!
FLAPPER !!
WHA'S THE BIG DEAL?!
ZIP ZIP ZIP
ZSH
THAT BIG PERSON IS THE HEWO'S PARTNER!!!
W-WHAT?!! H...
HERO?! WHADDAYA MEAN?!!
THE UDDER BIG PERSON WE CAUGHT...
...IS AKCHULLY A LEGENDARY HEWO WHO CAME TO HELP US!!!
WHAT?!!
THAT'S OSSUM!!
THAT IS INCWEDIBLE !!
GO—NG
WHAT KIND OF STORY DID YOU FEED THEM, USOPP...?

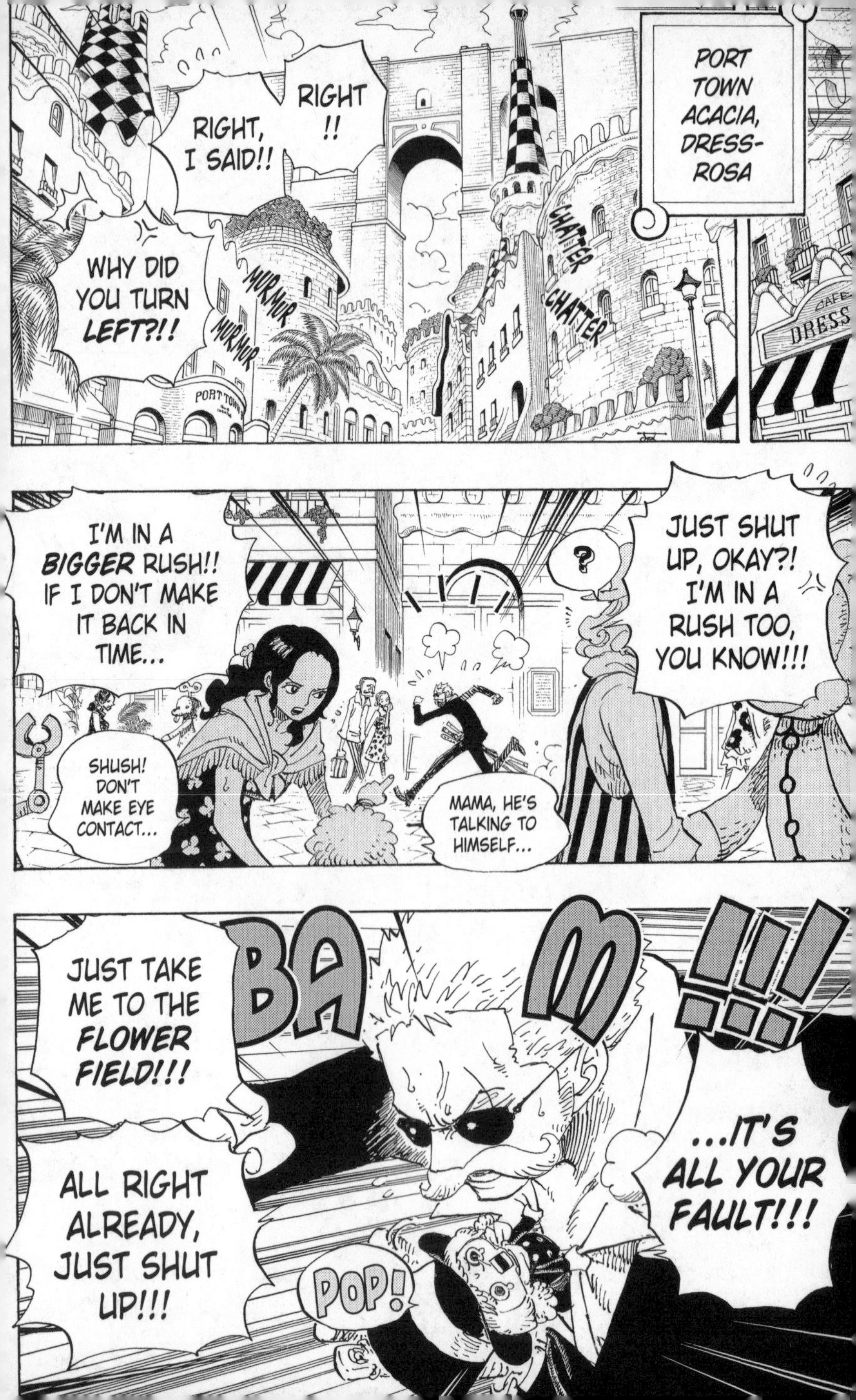
PORT TOWN ACACIA, DRESS-ROSA
CHATTER
CHATTER
RIGHT !!
RIGHT, I SAID!!
WHY DID YOU TURN LEFT?!!
MURMUR
MURMUR
CAFE
DRESS
PORT TOWN
JUST SHUT UP, OKAY?! I'M IN A RUSH TOO, YOU KNOW!!!
?
I'M IN A BIGGER RUSH!! IF I DON'T MAKE IT BACK IN TIME...
MAMA, HE'S TALKING TO HIMSELF...
SHUSH! DON'T MAKE EYE CONTACT...
BAM!!!
...IT'S ALL YOUR FAULT!!!
JUST TAKE ME TO THE FLOWER FIELD!!!
ALL RIGHT ALREADY, JUST SHUT UP!!!
POP!

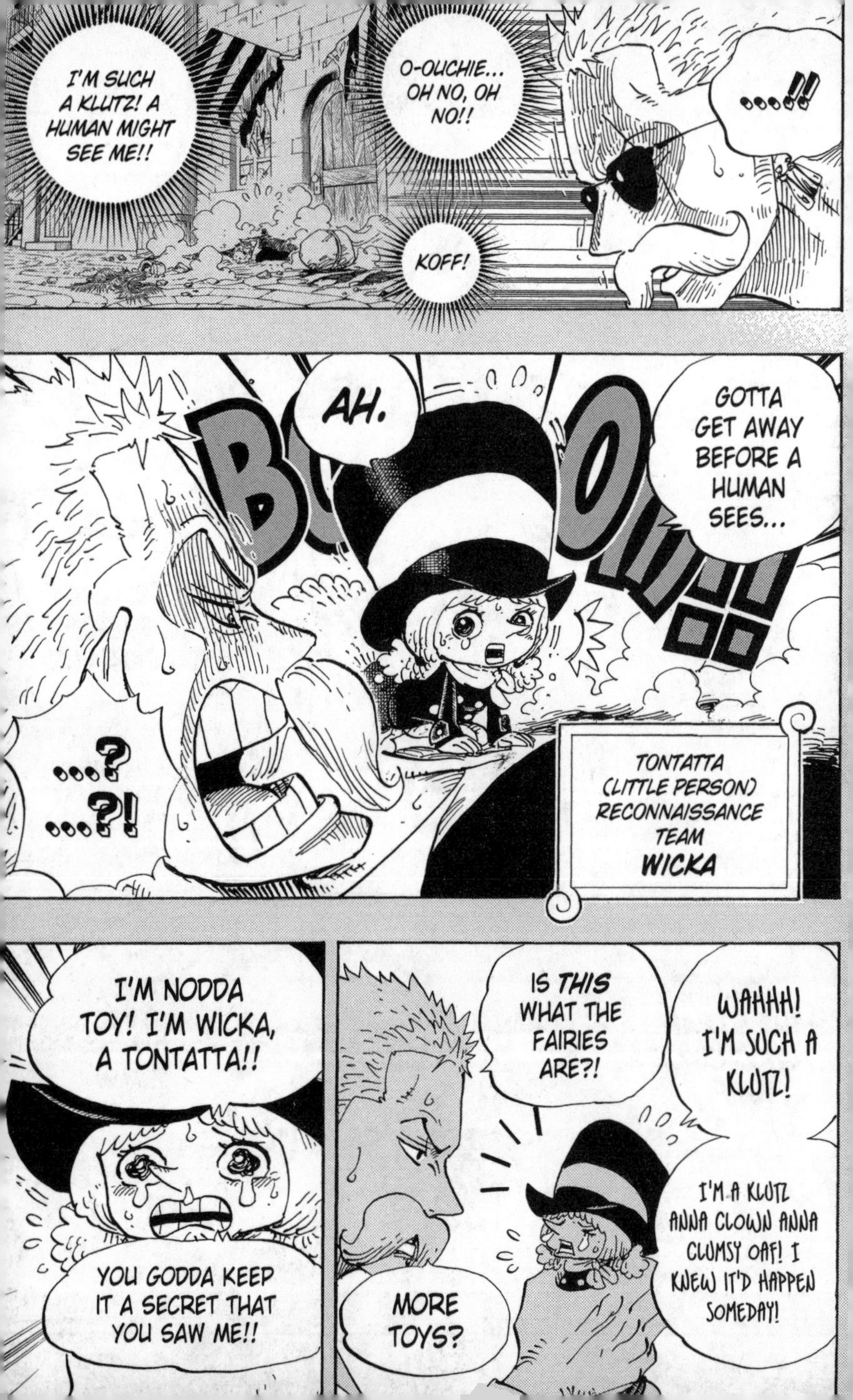
....!!
O-OUCHIE... OH NO, OH NO!!
I'M SUCH A KLUTZ! A HUMAN MIGHT SEE ME!!
KOFF!
GOTTA GET AWAY BEFORE A HUMAN SEES...
AH.
TONTATTA (LITTLE PERSON) RECONNAISSANCE TEAM WICKA
....?
....?!
WAHHH! I'M SUCH A KLUTZ!
IS THIS WHAT THE FAIRIES ARE?!
I'M A KLUTZ ANNA CLOWN ANNA CLUMSY OAF! I KNEW IT'D HAPPEN SOMEDAY!
MORE TOYS?
I'M NODDA TOY! I'M WICKA, A TONTATTA!!
YOU GODDA KEEP IT A SECRET THAT YOU SAW ME!!

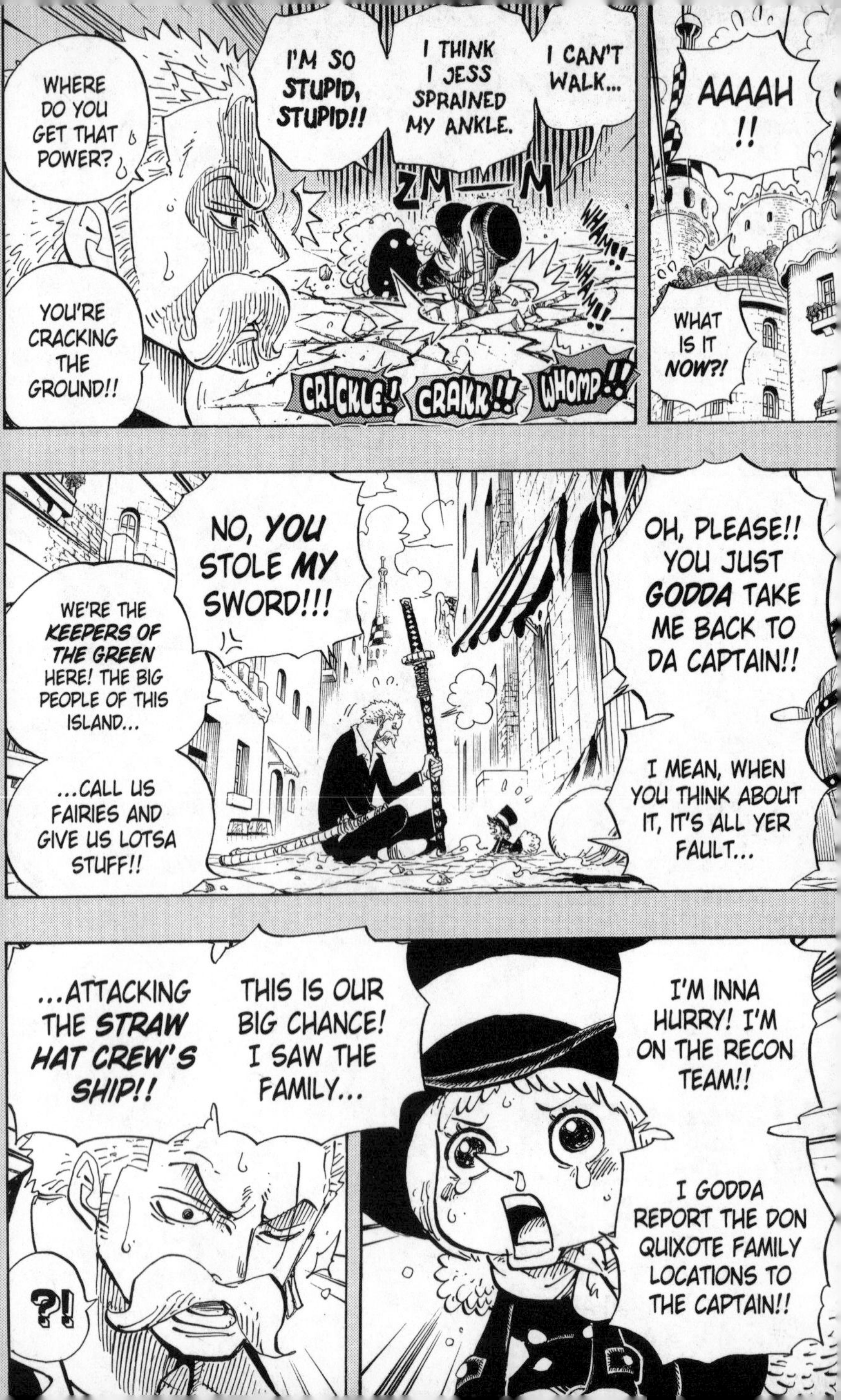
AAAAH !!
WHAT IS IT NOW?!
I CAN'T WALK...
I THINK I JESS SPRAINED MY ANKLE.
I'M SO STUPID, STUPID!!
ZM—M
WHAM!!
WHAM!!
CRICKLE!
CRAKK!!
WHOMP!!
WHERE DO YOU GET THAT POWER?
YOU'RE CRACKING THE GROUND!!
OH, PLEASE!! YOU JUST GODDA TAKE ME BACK TO DA CAPTAIN!!
NO, YOU STOLE MY SWORD!!!
I MEAN, WHEN YOU THINK ABOUT IT, IT'S ALL YER FAULT...
WE'RE THE KEEPERS OF THE GREEN HERE! THE BIG PEOPLE OF THIS ISLAND...
...CALL US FAIRIES AND GIVE US LOTSA STUFF!!
I'M INNA HURRY! I'M ON THE RECON TEAM!!
I GODDA REPORT THE DON QUIXOTE FAMILY LOCATIONS TO THE CAPTAIN!!
THIS IS OUR BIG CHANCE! I SAW THE FAMILY...
...ATTACKING THE STRAW HAT CREW'S SHIP!!
?!

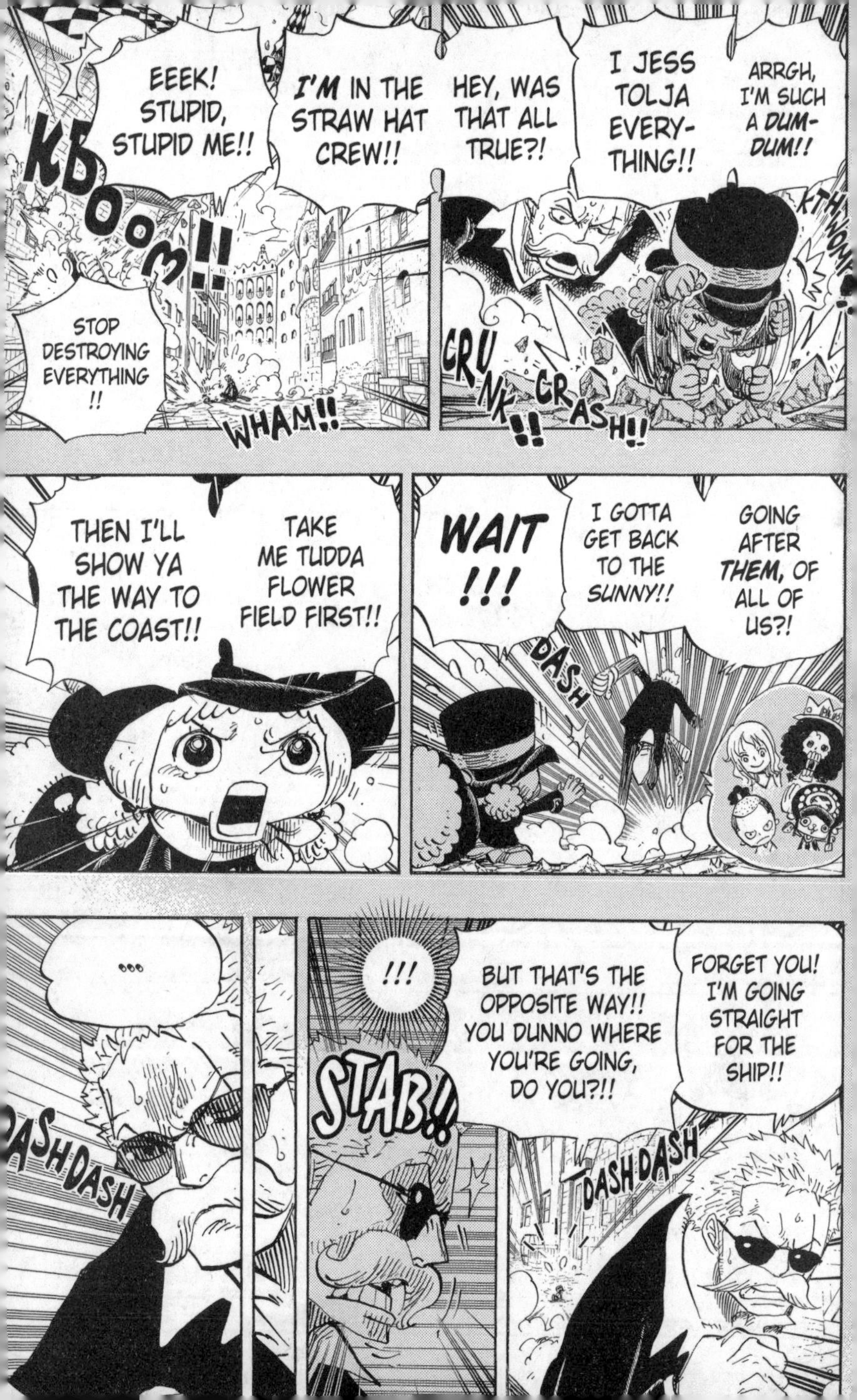
ARRGH, I'M SUCH A DUM-DUM!!
I JESS TOLJA EVERY-THING!!
HEY, WAS THAT ALL TRUE?!
KTHWOMP
CRUNK!!
CRASH!!
I'M IN THE STRAW HAT CREW!!
EEEK! STUPID, STUPID ME!!
KBOOM!!
STOP DESTROYING EVERYTHING !!
WHAM!!
GOING AFTER THEM, OF ALL OF US?!
I GOTTA GET BACK TO THE SUNNY!!
WAIT !!!
DASH
TAKE ME TUDDA FLOWER FIELD FIRST!!
THEN I'LL SHOW YA THE WAY TO THE COAST!!
FORGET YOU! I'M GOING STRAIGHT FOR THE SHIP!!
DASH DASH
BUT THAT'S THE OPPOSITE WAY!! YOU DUNNO WHERE YOU'RE GOING, DO YOU?!!
!!!
STAB!!
...
DASH DASH

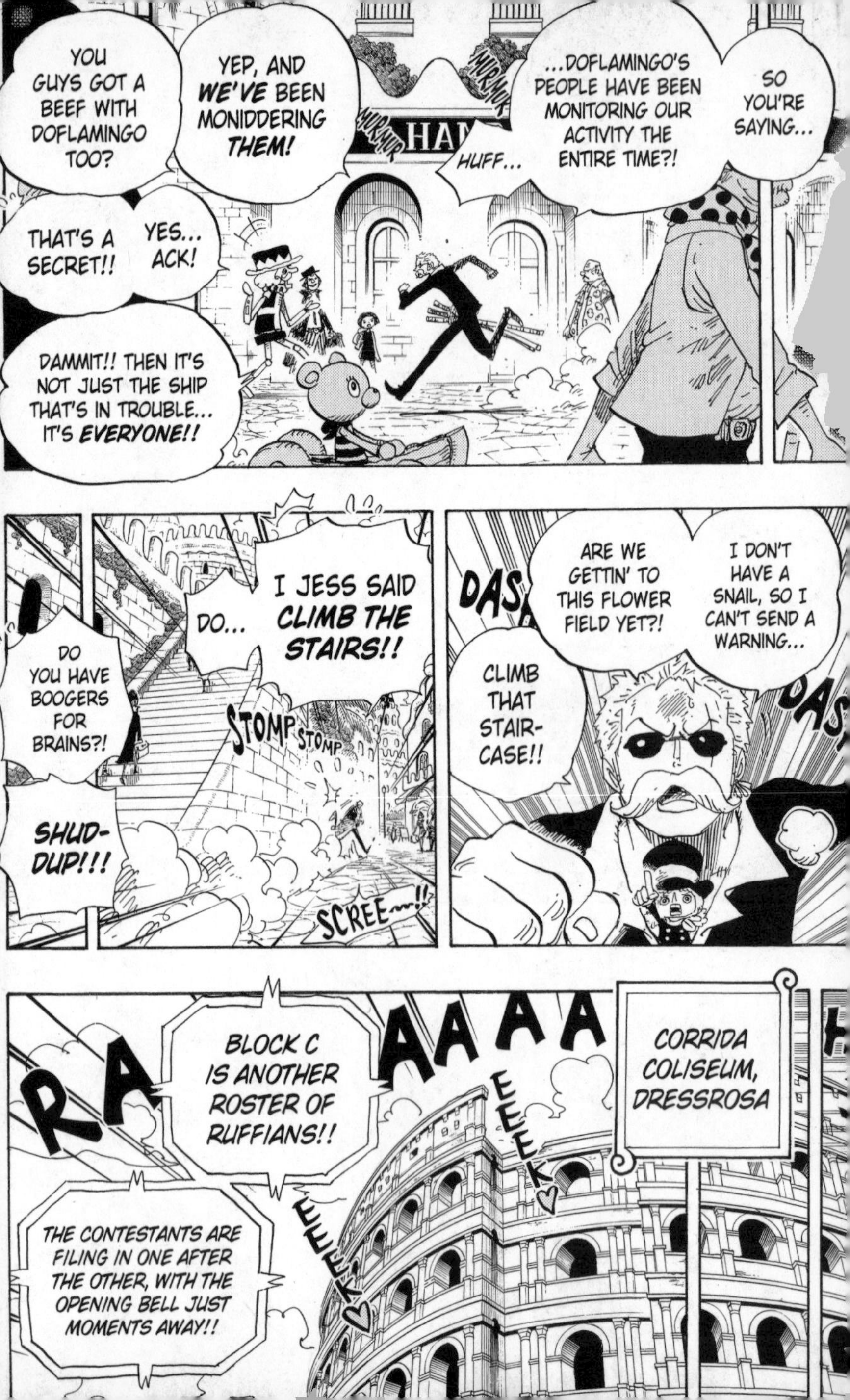
SO YOU'RE SAYING...
...DOFLAMINGO'S PEOPLE HAVE BEEN MONITORING OUR ACTIVITY THE ENTIRE TIME?!
HUFF...
MURMUR MURMUR
HAM
YEP, AND WE'VE BEEN MONIDDERING THEM!
YOU GUYS GOT A BEEF WITH DOFLAMINGO TOO?
YES... ACK!
THAT'S A SECRET!!
DAMMIT!! THEN IT'S NOT JUST THE SHIP THAT'S IN TROUBLE... IT'S EVERYONE!!
I DON'T HAVE A SNAIL, SO I CAN'T SEND A WARNING...
ARE WE GETTIN' TO THIS FLOWER FIELD YET?!
DAS
DAS
CLIMB THAT STAIR-CASE!!
I JESS SAID CLIMB THE STAIRS!!
DO...
DO YOU HAVE BOOGERS FOR BRAINS?!
STOMP STOMP
SHUD-DUP!!!
SCREE~!!
CORRIDA COLISEUM, DRESSROSA
RAAAAA
BLOCK C IS ANOTHER ROSTER OF RUFFIANS!!
EEEEK♡
EEEEK♡
THE CONTESTANTS ARE FILING IN ONE AFTER THE OTHER, WITH THE OPENING BELL JUST MOMENTS AWAY!!

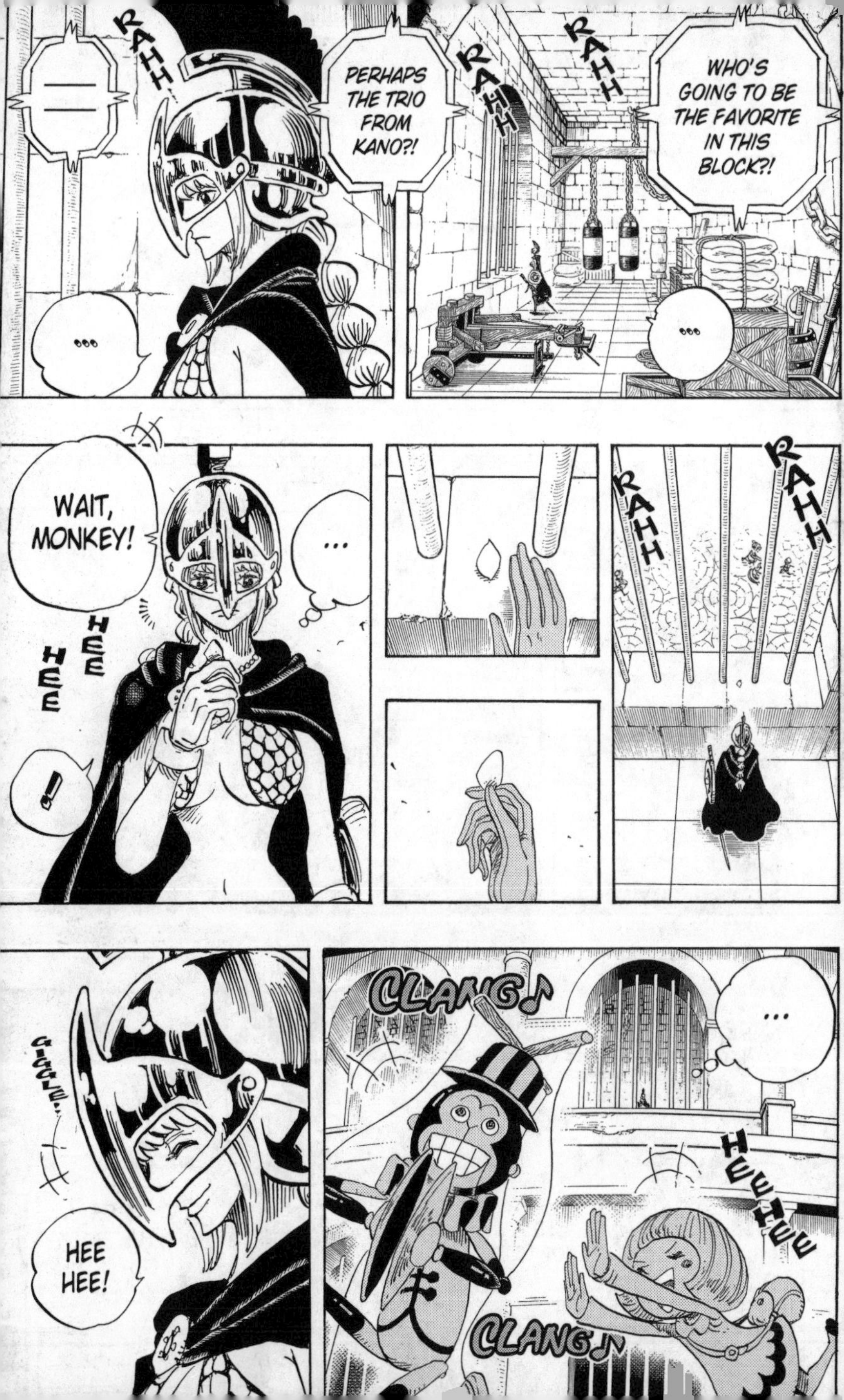

WHO'S GOING TO BE THE FAVORITE IN THIS BLOCK?!
RAHH
RAHH
PERHAPS THE TRIO FROM KANO?!
...
RAHH
——
...
RAHH
RAHH
WAIT, MONKEY!
...
HEE HEE
!
CLANG♪
...
HEHEHE
CLANG♪
GIGGLE...
HEE HEE!

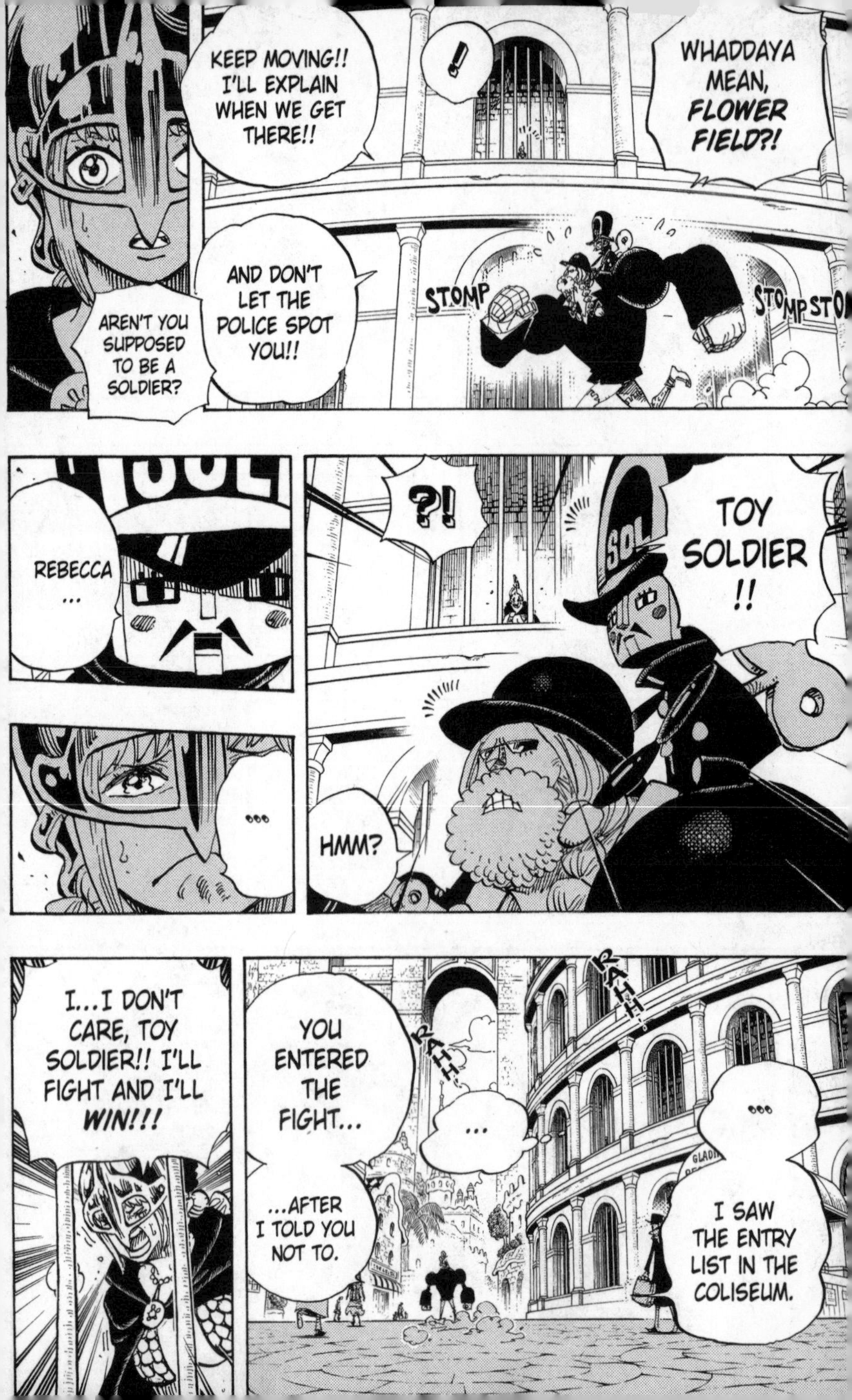
WHADDAYA MEAN, FLOWER FIELD?!
!
KEEP MOVING!! I'LL EXPLAIN WHEN WE GET THERE!!
AND DON'T LET THE POLICE SPOT YOU!!
STOMP
STOMP
AREN'T YOU SUPPOSED TO BE A SOLDIER?
?!
TOY SOLDIER !!
HMM?
REBECCA ...
...
I SAW THE ENTRY LIST IN THE COLISEUM.
...
RAHH
YOU ENTERED THE FIGHT...
...AFTER I TOLD YOU NOT TO.
...
RAHH
I...I DON'T CARE, TOY SOLDIER!! I'LL FIGHT AND I'LL WIN!!!

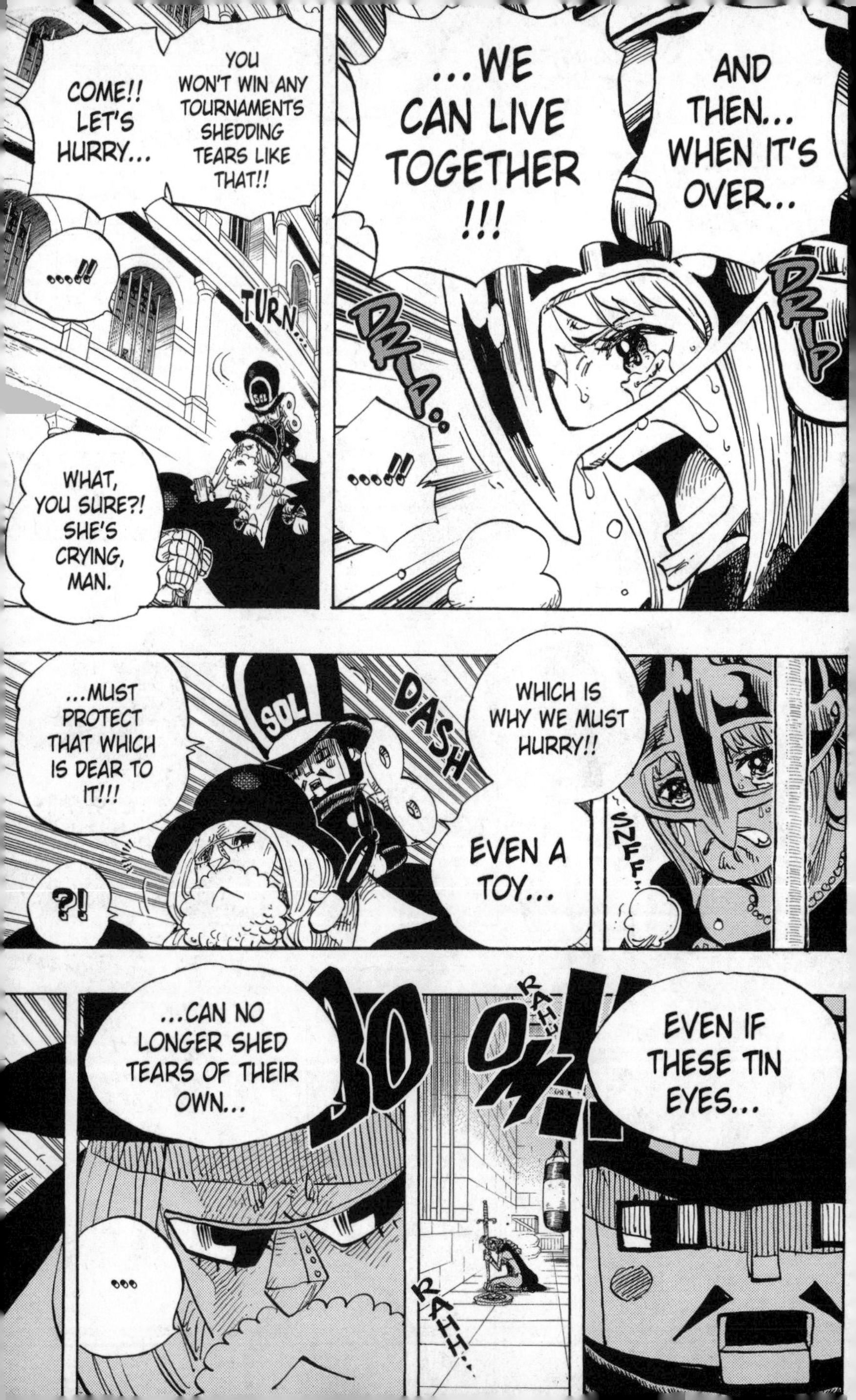
AND THEN... WHEN IT'S OVER...
...WE CAN LIVE TOGETHER!!!
DRIP
DRIP..
....!!
YOU WON'T WIN ANY TOURNAMENTS SHEDDING TEARS LIKE THAT!!
COME!! LET'S HURRY...
....!!
TURN...
WHAT, YOU SURE?! SHE'S CRYING, MAN.
SNFF
WHICH IS WHY WE MUST HURRY!!
EVEN A TOY...
DASH
...MUST PROTECT THAT WHICH IS DEAR TO IT!!!
?!
EVEN IF THESE TIN EYES...
RAHH
...CAN NO LONGER SHED TEARS OF THEIR OWN...
...
RAHH..

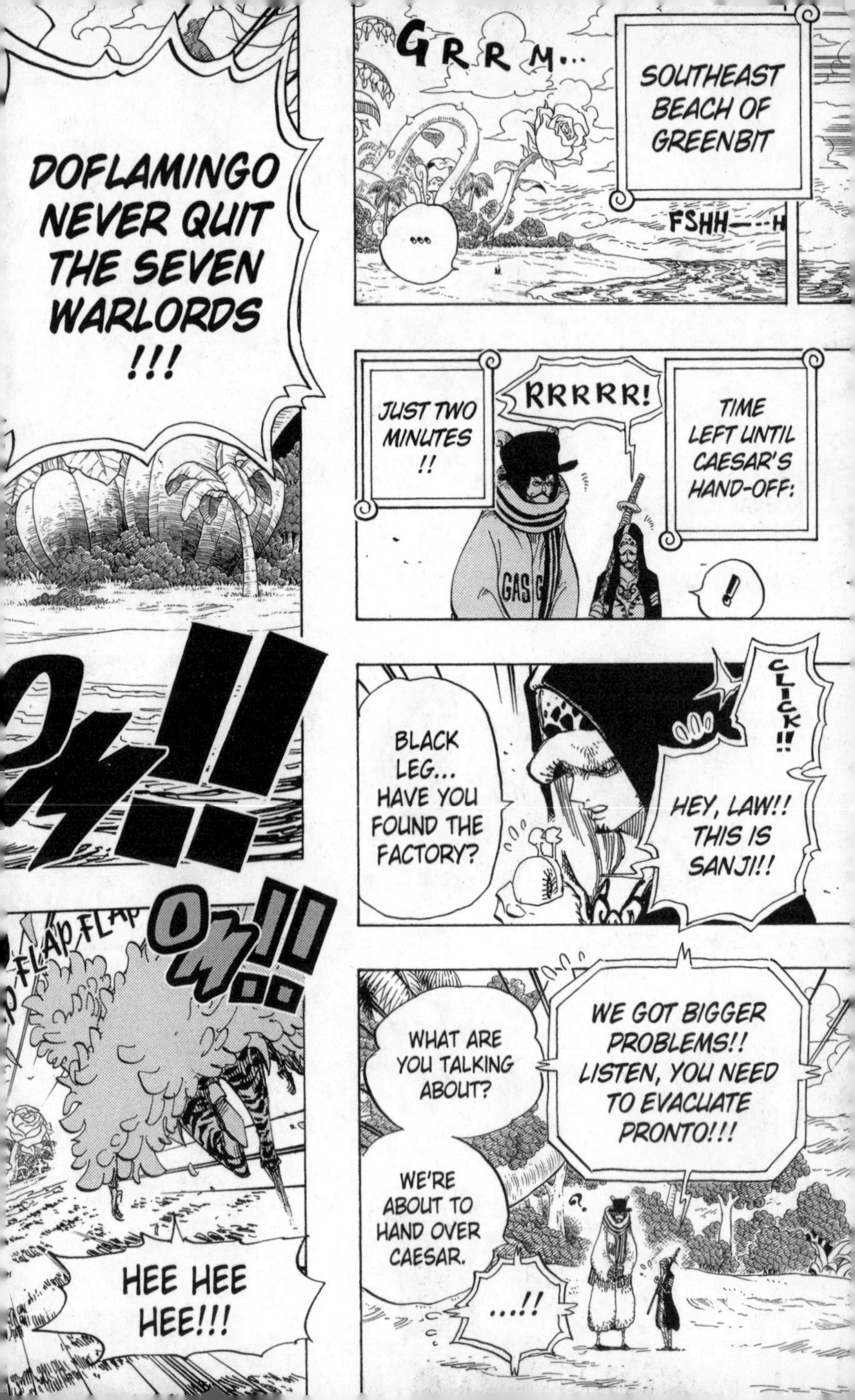

SOUTHEAST BEACH OF GREENBIT
GRRRM...
FSHH—--H
TIME LEFT UNTIL CAESAR'S HAND-OFF:
JUST TWO MINUTES!!
RRRRR!
!
CLICK!!
HEY, LAW!! THIS IS SANJI!!
BLACK LEG... HAVE YOU FOUND THE FACTORY?
WE GOT BIGGER PROBLEMS!! LISTEN, YOU NEED TO EVACUATE PRONTO!!!
WHAT ARE YOU TALKING ABOUT?
WE'RE ABOUT TO HAND OVER CAESAR.
...!!
DOFLAMINGO NEVER QUIT THE SEVEN WARLORDS!!!
FLAP FLAP
HEE HEE HEE!!!

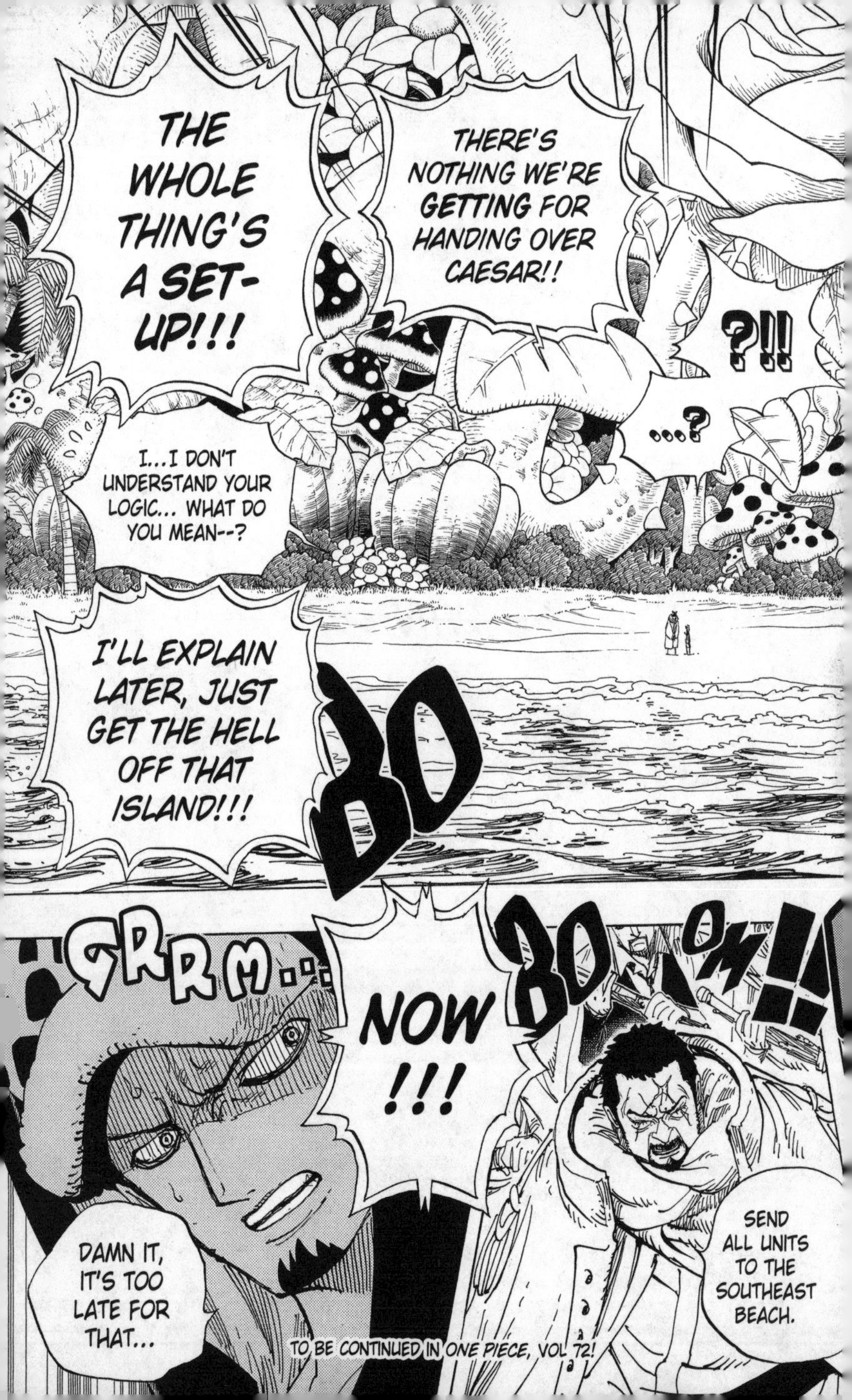

THERE'S NOTHING WE'RE GETTING FOR HANDING OVER CAESAR!!
THE WHOLE THING'S A SET-UP!!!
?!!
...?
I...I DON'T UNDERSTAND YOUR LOGIC... WHAT DO YOU MEAN--?
I'LL EXPLAIN LATER, JUST GET THE HELL OFF THAT ISLAND!!!
BO
BOOM!!
SEND ALL UNITS TO THE SOUTHEAST BEACH.
NOW!!!
GRRM...
DAMN IT, IT'S TOO LATE FOR THAT...

TO BE CONTINUED IN ONE PIECE, VOL 72!

COMING NEXT VOLUME:

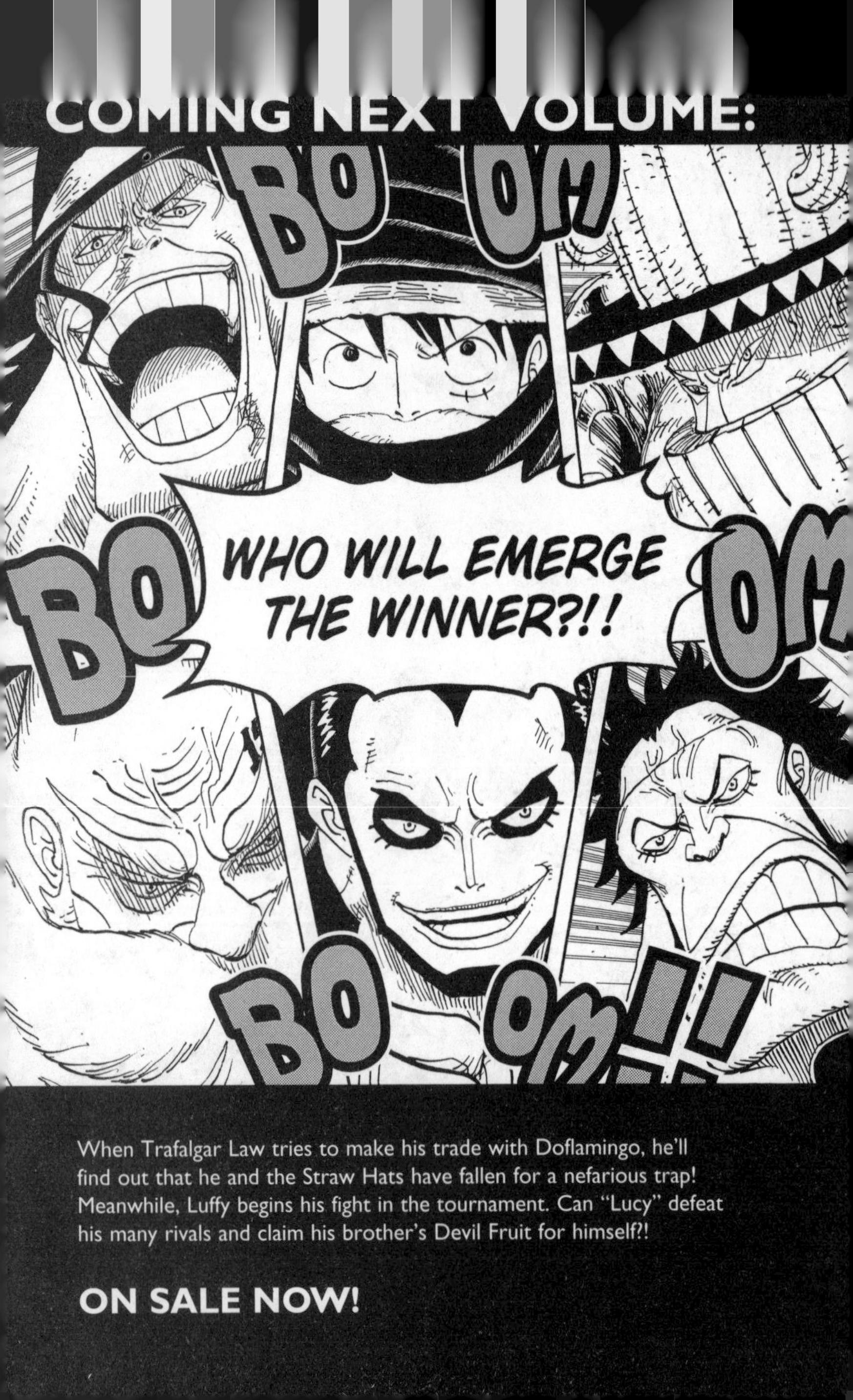
BOOM
BOOM
WHO WILL EMERGE THE WINNER?!!
BOOM!!

When Trafalgar Law tries to make his trade with Doflamingo, he'll find out that he and the Straw Hats have fallen for a nefarious trap! Meanwhile, Luffy begins his fight in the tournament. Can "Lucy" defeat his many rivals and claim his brother's Devil Fruit for himself?!

ON SALE NOW!

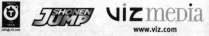

Black ✤ Clover

STORY & ART BY YŪKI TABATA

Asta is a young boy who dreams of becoming the greatest mage in the kingdom. Only one problem—he can't use any magic! Luckily for Asta, he receives the incredibly rare five-leaf clover grimoire that gives him the power of anti-magic. Can someone who can't use magic really become the Wizard King? One thing's for sure—Asta will never give up!

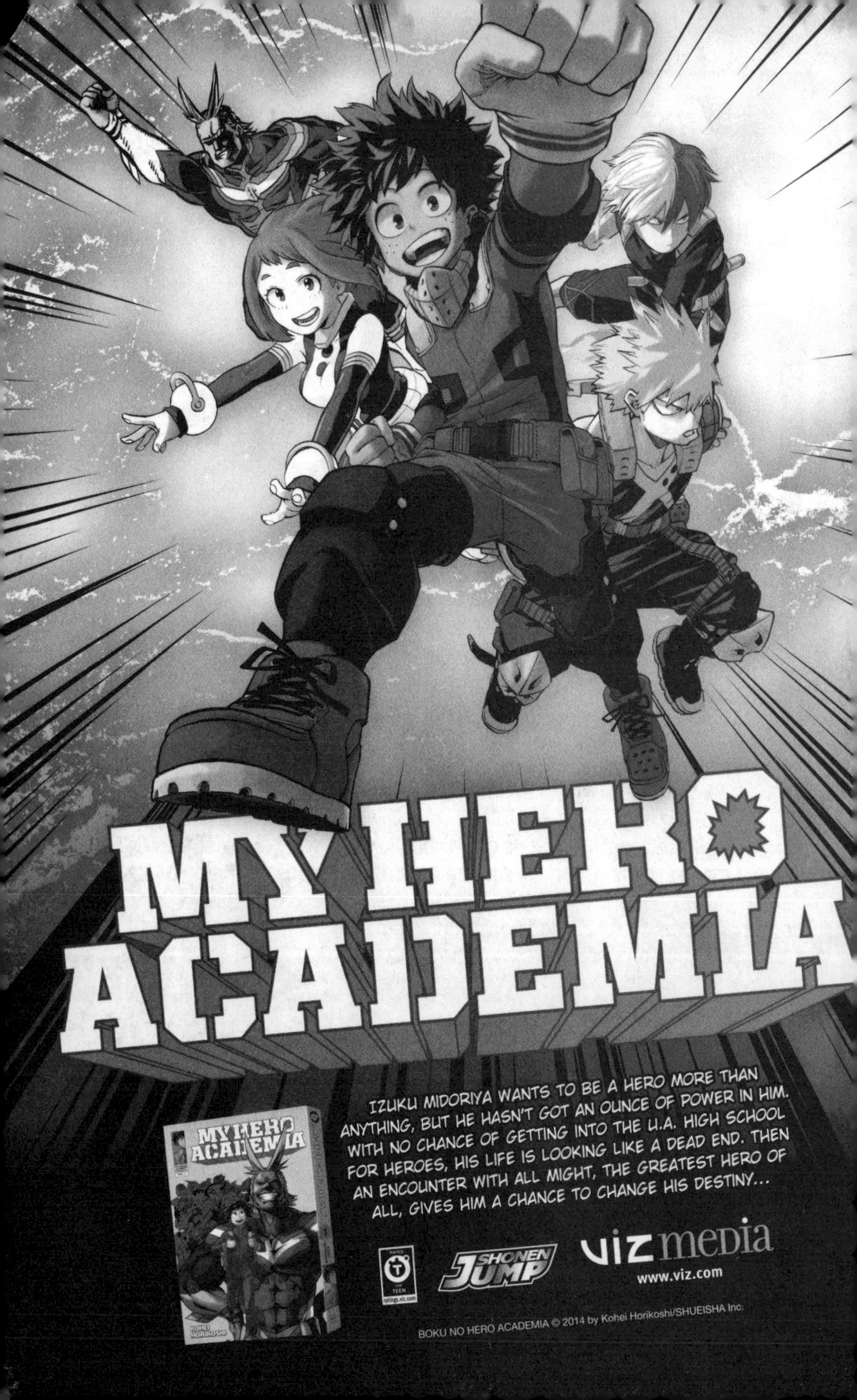

MY HERO ACADEMIA

IZUKU MIDORIYA WANTS TO BE A HERO MORE THAN ANYTHING, BUT HE HASN'T GOT AN OUNCE OF POWER IN HIM. WITH NO CHANCE OF GETTING INTO THE U.A. HIGH SCHOOL FOR HEROES, HIS LIFE IS LOOKING LIKE A DEAD END. THEN AN ENCOUNTER WITH ALL MIGHT, THE GREATEST HERO OF ALL, GIVES HIM A CHANCE TO CHANGE HIS DESTINY...

www.viz.com

You're Reading in the Wrong Direction!!

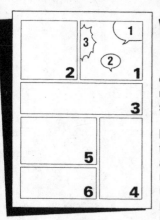

Whoops! Guess what? You're starting at the wrong end of the comic!

...It's true! In keeping with the original Japanese format, **One Piece** is meant to be read from right to left, starting in the upper-right corner.

Unlike English, which is read from left to right, Japanese is read from right to left, meaning that action, sound effects and word-balloon order are completely reversed...something which can make readers unfamiliar with Japanese feel pretty backwards themselves. For this reason, manga or Japanese comics published in the U.S. in English have sometimes been published "flopped"—that is, printed in exact reverse order, as though seen from the other side of a mirror.

By flopping pages, U.S. publishers can avoid confusing readers, but the compromise is not without its downside. For one thing, a character in a flopped manga series who once wore in the original Japanese version a T-shirt emblazoned with "M A Y" (as in "the merry month of") now wears one which reads "Y A M"! Additionally, many manga creators in Japan are themselves unhappy with the process, as some feel the mirror-imaging of their art skews their original intentions.

We are proud to bring you Eiichiro Oda's **One Piece** in the original unflopped format. For now, though, turn to the other side of the book and let the journey begin...!

—Editor

◀ • • •